Politics
in Europe

Comparative Studies of Political Life
SERIES EDITOR: MARTIN O. HEISLER

Politics
in Europe

STRUCTURES AND PROCESSES IN SOME POSTINDUSTRIAL DEMOCRACIES

Edited by Martin O. Heisler
UNIVERSITY OF MARYLAND

DAVID McKAY COMPANY, INC.   *New York*

POLITICS IN EUROPE

Structures and Processes in Some Postindustrial Democracies

Copyright © 1974 by David McKay Company, Inc.

All rights reserved, including the right to
reproduce this book, or parts thereof, in any
form, except for the inclusion of brief
quotations in a review.

Designed by Angela Foote

International Standard Book Number: 0-679-30169-0 (cloth)
0-679-30168-2 (paper)
Library of Congress catalog card number: 72-96709
Manufactured in the United States of America

For my father

Preface

Although much progress has been made in the comparative study of politics during the last twenty years, little genuinely comparative theory has been accumulated. The field, like its parent discipline, has advanced most in the realms of general conceptual frameworks and the technology of data manipulation; only rarely have these been linked, to produce empirically founded, logically structured, and conceptually coherent explanations of politics in a substantial number of societies. Two major factors impede the development of such theories: (1) a dearth of relevant and comparable data, and (2) a multitude of problems revolving around contextual control, i.e., the identification and systematic handling of actual or potential intervening factors that may affect interrelationships between the variables under investigation. Put another way, we know very little about politics in most places. But even if we had more descriptive material at our disposal we would encounter serious difficulties when trying to explain the meanings and causal relationships of particular political phenomena in different sociocultural settings. The currently preeminent conceptual frameworks are too broad to permit the analytic control needed for cross-cultural comparisons; and they are not especially helpful for plotting specific research strategies. Yet, given the multitude of problems likely to be encountered in comparative political analysis, it would be foolhardy to strike out on a purely empirical path, unaided by conceptual guidelines.

   In an attempt to overcome some of these difficulties, this book adapts a prominent, existing conceptual framework for the comparative analysis of politics in some postindustrial democracies. Our focus on highly developed systems mitigates the shortage of data, since aggregate and survey data are available for most of these countries. Historians, sociologists, and economists have studied these systems intensively for several generations, so a relatively ample base of secondary materials is also available.

On the basis of impressions derived from secondary materials and a modicum of primary data, we have constructed a model of the type of system we think characterizes most Western and Central European polities—particularly those of the numerous smaller countries. The model is, in fact, a pretheoretic statement. With it as a foundation, operational hypotheses can be formulated and tested, and can lead to genuine comparative theory. As this book goes to press, the formulation of such hypotheses, the assembly and analysis of data, and the identification of the components of such theory have been begun by a number of scholars on both sides of the Atlantic. We have emphasized structural considerations in the model, since these seem most appropriate—substantively and analytically—for this class of systems.

Two characteristics distinguish this book from most multicountry studies. First, it was self-consciously unoriginal in its beginnings. We took our departure from current theoretical work, with the hope that we could build theory in a cumulative fashion rather than return once more to point zero, with a sui generis model. Second, the bulk of the volume is devoted to substantive studies of politics in Europe. Most other pretheoretic statements in comparative politics remain somewhat abstract, and readers are asked to wait patiently until—hopefully—someone undertakes research to bring them to life. Given such a pattern, it should hardly be surprising that readers who turn to a book to *learn about politics* in particular settings become frustrated upon finding that they must make do with a statement *about how politics can be studied* there. For this reason, a degree of coherence in theoretical terms is sacrificed here in order to flesh out the framework at this early juncture in the overall venture.

One of the perquisites of editorship is the opportunity to place acknowledgments of assistance in one's own work at the front of the volume. The students in my classes at the University of Maryland were the primary audiences before which the ideas that led to this book in general and chapters 1, 2, and 5 in particular were unfolded. I am grateful for the intelligent and. mercifully, not at all timid discussions that often took place in those settings. Several colleagues made helpful comments and criticisms on earlier drafts of my contribution to chapter 2. In particular, B. Guy Peters, Eldon Lanning, James Oliver, and Paul Solano helped me avoid numerous mistakes and improved the substance and expression of my ideas. I have received similar assistance in my work on the Low Countries—some of which found its way into chapter 5—especially from European scholars. Their help will be acknowledged more fully in a forthcoming book. I expect to be blamed for all the errors that remain, which is as it should be.

Two others have provided help that, while instrumental in the shape and completion of this book, is of a more lasting sort. One of my teachers, Richard N. Rosecrance, taught me that traditional and modern paths to knowledge should converge rather than diverge; and he showed me the appropriateness of structural analysis for making the initial contacts between theory and the empirical universe. My wife, Trudie, has by now become inured to life with a very temperamental writer. During the preparation of this book, we moved our family across an ocean on two occasions. By her constancy, she made it possible for us to feel at home regardless of our address. She also proofread drafts and helped with galleys and index. Best of all, although they started from already impressive plateaus, her sense of humor, perspective, and recipe file have continued to improve. But her book is different.

M.O.H.

Brussels, Belgium
March, 1973

About the Authors

Martin O. Heisler, the editor of this volume, is the overall editor of the series, *Comparative Studies of Political Life*. An assistant professor of government and politics and chairman of the Committee on Comparative Urban Administration at the University of Maryland, he was born in Hungary and received some of his precollegiate education in Central and Western Europe. His undergraduate and graduate degrees (Ph.D. 1969) are from the University of California at Los Angeles. He has served as a visiting professor at the University of Kentucky, and taught at the University of Illinois prior to joining the Maryland faculty. He is the author of a forth-coming book on the Low Countries, where he conducted field research in 1963–64, 1971, and 1972–73. His current work is devoted to guiding the operational phase of the European polity model developed in chapter 2, stressing especially political system performance at the national and subna-tional levels in postindustrial societies; he is also engaged in studies of the cleavage-institutionalizing potentials of the output side of political systems in Western Europe.

William G. Andrews is dean of the faculty of social sciences and a professor of political science at the State University of New York, College at Brockport. He has formerly taught at Tufts University, Dartmouth College, and Cornell University, where he received his Ph.D. in 1959. He is the author and editor of numerous books including: *French Politics in Algeria, European Political Institutions,* and *Constitutions and Constitutionalism.* Dr. Andrews has also contributed articles to many professional journals. He received an NEH fellowship during 1973–74 while he is completing a book-length study on the development of presidentialism in contemporary France.

Stephen Blank is an assistant professor of political science at the University of Pittsburgh and since 1970 has served as the executive director of the Council for European Studies. His undergraduate education was received at Dartmouth College, and he did graduate work at Trinity College of Cambridge University and at Harvard University. He received his Ph.D. in government from Harvard in 1968. Professor Blank recently published *Industry and Government in Britain; the Federation of British Industries in Politics, 1945–1965* (1973).

Guy de Carmoy holds professorships at the Institut d'Etudes Politiques of the University of Paris and the European Institute of Business Administration. Prior to undertaking a full-time academic career, he served in high posts in the French Treasury and the International Bank for Reconstruction and Development. From 1948 to 1952 he was director of the Organisation for European Economic Development (OEEC). Among his books are *Fortune de l'Europe* (1953), *The Foreign Policies of France, 1944–1968* (1970), and *Le Dossier Européen de l'Energie* (1971). Professor Carmoy is also the author of numerous scholarly and policy-oriented papers. His work on European energy problems is continuing. In February 1973 he was elected chairman of the European section of the Committee on Atlantic Studies of NATO.

Robert B. Kvavik is an assistant professor of political science at the University of Minnesota, where he is also associated with the Center for Northwest European Language and Area Studies. He received his undergraduate education at Brooklyn College and his Master's and Ph.D. degrees from Stanford University. He was at the Institutt for Samfunnsforskning in Oslo in 1966–67, and was a George Marshall Fellow at the Institut for Ledelsesforskning in Copenhagen in 1972. His field of work is comparative politics, with a special emphasis on interest group structures and activity and on Scandinavian politics. He is presently engaged in a study of the development of the Danish interest group system during the period 1850–1970.

Leon N. Lindberg is a professor of political science at the University of Wisconsin, a faculty he joined in 1961, after receiving his undergraduate and graduate degrees from the University of California, Berkeley. He held research fellowships at the Center for International Affairs of Harvard University in 1964–65 and 1967, and he is spending the current year at the European center of the Carnegie Endowment for International Peace in Geneva. Among his publications are *The Political Dynamics of European Economic Integration* (1963), *Europe's Would-Be Polity* (with Stuart A. Scheingold, 1970—from which his contribution to this book was adapted), and *Regional Integration: Theory and Research* (coauthor and coeditor, 1971), as well as articles in several scholarly journals and books. Professor Lindberg was chairman of the Council for European Studies in 1971–72. He is a member of the Board of Editors of *International Organization* and

Comparative Political Studies, and is director of the Center for Comparative Studies of Post-Industrial Society at the University of Wisconsin. His current work focuses on changing cleavage patterns in advanced industrial societies, the future planning activities of elites in public and private institutions, and the development of new modes of societal analysis and planning at the national and international levels—together with their policy implications.

Richard L. Merritt is professor of political science and research professor in communications at the University of Illinois (Urbana-Champaign). He received his undergraduate education at the University of Southern California and his graduate work was done at the University of Virginia, the Free University of Berlin, and Yale—where he received his doctorate in 1962. He taught at Yale prior to joining the Illinois faculty. His scholarly work in Germany has been supported by, among other sources, a Fulbright fellowship and a Fulbright research professorship. Mr. Merritt has served on the executive councils of the American Political Science Association and the International Studies Association; and he has been a member of the editorial boards of the *American Political Science Review, Midwest Journal of Political Science, Comparative Political Studies,* and *Policy Studies Journal.* He is the author, coauthor, or editor of *Symbols of American Community, 1735–1775* (1966), *Comparing Nations* (1966), *France, Germany and the Western Alliance* (1967), *Western European Perspectives on International Affairs* (1968), *Public Opinion in Occupied Germany* (1970), *Systematic Approaches to Comparative Politics* (1970), *West Germany Enters the Seventies* (1971), *Communication in International Politics* (1972), and numerous other works. He has contributed more than fifty articles to scholarly journals and books. His interests, in addition to German politics, include international communication, international political integration, and testing political theories with the aid of quantitative data.

B. Guy Peters, an assistant professor of political science at Emory University, received his Ph.D. from Michigan State University in 1970. He has recently completed a book-length study on the subject of his contribution to this book, and has contributed articles to, among other publications, the *Midwest Journal of Political Science, Polity, Acta Sociologica,* and *Urban Affairs Quarterly.* Currently, Professor Peters is one of the principal investigators of a Ford Foundation project on "Urban Change and the Quality of Life in Industrialized Societies," and he is also engaged in the operational phase of the European polity model. In addition, he is working as coauthor on a book on comparative administration.

Rodney P. Stiefbold teaches politics and public affairs at the University of Miami, Coral Gables, Florida, is a member of the research faculty of the Center for Urban and Regional Studies at Miami, and a faculty associate of the Program for European Studies at the State University of New York at Stony Brook. Dr. Stiefbold did his undergraduate work at Cornell University and his graduate work at Columbia University and the University of Vienna. He has taught previously at the University of Wisconsin, Madison, the Institute for Advanced Studies, Vienna, the University of California at Berkeley, and the State University of New York at Stony Brook. He is the author, coauthor, or editor of several books including *Wahlen und Parteien in Oesterreich* (1966); *Nationalratswahl 1966* (1968); *Elites and Elections in a Fragmented Political System* (1973); *Politics in Advanced Nations* (1973); *Quantitative Ecological Analysis in the Social Sciences* (1969); and *Cross National Micro-Analysis* (1972). Dr. Stiefbold has also authored or co-authored several briefer monographs and research reports including *Conflict and Elites in Western Industrial Societies* (1969) and *Social Structure and Political Conflict in Austrian Community Systems* (1970). He has contributed to journals in political science, comparative politics, and sociology. Stiefbold's current research is focused on questions of conflict and accommodation in ethnically and racially diverse political systems in Europe, the Carribbean, and metropolitan Dade County, Florida.

James H. Wolfe is associate professor and director of graduate studies in the department of government and politics at the University of Maryland. He received his undergraduate education at Harvard University, and his Ph.D. from Maryland. Prior to joining the faculty at the University of Maryland, he taught at the University of South Carolina. Among his publications are *Indivisible Germany: Illusion or Reality?* (1963) and articles in *Orbis, East European Quarterly, World Affairs,* and volumes 8 and 9 of *Bohemia: Jahrbuch des Collegium Carolinum.* Professor Wolfe has also served as a senior faculty fellow in the U.S. Department of State, and he is currently conducting research in Germany on his second Alexander von Humboldt Foundation grant in eight years. His work focuses on historical and contemporary modes of corporate representation in the German Federal and Democratic Republics and in Austria.

Contents

Part I

THE STUDY OF EUROPEAN POLITICS: Conceptual and Theoretical Foundations

1

Comparative and European Politics

Introduction

This book is about politics in Europe. It attempts to shed light on the major patterns of political life in contemporary European societies, and it also suggests a strategy for studying politics in the smaller "postindustrial" systems that predominate in Western and Central Europe. Before attention is focused on European phenomena, however, a brief look at the conceptual, theoretical, and empirical positions of European political studies in the broader universe of the rapidly changing field of comparative politics is especially important, because both the origin and the future of modern comparative political analysis are intricately intertwined with European studies.

The principal aim of this chapter is to provide such a perspective. The chapter is organized into four parts. The first three follow the conceptual and theoretical course of European studies along the tracks of comparative—and general empirical—political analysis in the post-World War II period, while the fourth strives to relate the book's diverse essays to its general purposes.

The Revolt Against Traditional Comparative Government and Its European Focus

The origins of the field of comparative government can be traced back to Plato and Aristotle, nearly twenty-five hundred years ago. The seventeenth, eighteenth, and nineteenth centuries witnessed the growth of a voluminous literature devoted to the classification of governmental forms

3

and political cultures, as well as to speculations regarding the causes of differences among polities.[1] But the extant classics and the early modern works are not linked to the current literature of the field, either as the underpinnings of the bodies of knowledge that are presently being assembled and refined or as the points of departure for inquiry. Instead, to the extent that such works are "alive," their uses are restricted to explorations in the history of political thought and to the contemplation of the normative positions they embodied. Thus, while no specific work or date serves as a commonly recognized marker in time, the advent of the field of comparative governmental studies in the modern era can be said—without fear of disrupting the pattern of the field's evolution—to have occurred during the last years of the preceding century or the first years of the present century.

From that time until the early 1950s, the literature of the field evolved with relative consistency; and it was characterized by analytic formalism and cultural and intellectual parochialism. A focus on Europe and Western cultural perspectives (conceptually and normatively rooted in European antecedents) and the preeminence of specialists born and/or educated in Europe also characterized this phase, which was dubbed the "traditional period" twenty years ago. The modern field of comparative *politics* began its career in the early 1950s with a massive rejection of traditional comparative *government* studies; simultaneously, European political studies were dislodged from the central place they had occupied in the field.[2] This section notes some of the major reasons for the reorientation of the field.

The Traditional Study of Comparative Government

The books that comprised the traditional literature of comparative government were symptomatic of the ailments of the field. Generally, they could be classified into two groups: (1) they represented efforts to describe the most important countries as comprehensively as space and the scope of the writers' knowledge allowed; or (2) they were narrow-gauged, often esoteric research reports limited to a single aspect of politics or an institution in one country. They were not only not comparative per se but were frequently difficult to relate to works on other countries or on other political phenomena in the same country.

The comprehensive descriptions often performed double duty as compendia of existing "knowledge" and as textbooks in undergraduate courses. They tended to restrict their coverage to a few "important" coun-

---

1. I have not attempted to provide a historical summary of the field. For good historical treatments, see Harry Eckstein, "A Perspective on Comparative Politics, Past and Present," in *Comparative Politics*, ed. Harry Eckstein and David Apter (New York: Free Press, 1963), pp. 3–32; and Roy C. Macridis, *The Study of Comparative Government* (New York: Random House, 1955).

2. Ibid.; and Gunnar Heckscher, *The Study of Comparative Government and Politics* (London: Allen & Unwin, 1957).

tries, where importance was determined by one or more of three criteria: such countries (1) were large and populous; or (2) were very powerful in the arena of world politics; or (3) embodied the institutional and/or constitutional norms that provided the strongest reinforcements of the culturally induced biases of the writers. The same texts could be—and generally were—used in general comparative government courses and in courses in European government and politics. *In fact, more often than not, the general comparative government survey was a course in European institutions!*

The countries treated in these books were, almost without variation, the United Kingdom, France, Germany, and the Soviet Union.[3] If other countries entered the consciousness of scholars in the field, they tended to be cultural and sometimes historical or institutional extensions of the European core: e.g., the English-speaking dominions (Canada, Australia, and New Zealand), the United States, and infrequently, Italy or Switzerland.

These features of the literature need not have led to a sense of dissatisfaction, especially if they had been restricted wholly or mostly to the realm of textbooks. After all, as most present-day teachers and students of comparative politics recognize, knowledge of the basic traits of particular polities is a very important and often hard-to-attain stage in the development of a more sophisticated understanding of political life. But, in many if not most cases, the traits noted characterized the levels of achievement, awareness, and underlying goals and values of the professionals in comparative governmental and political studies in the period in question.

The development and entrenchment of such an orientation is readily explained and, in retrospect, does not appear to have been especially unreasonable. For, the field (as, indeed, the mainstream of the parent discipline of political science) had evolved from formal, legalistic concerns with the institutions and historical relationships of countries in the European cultural mold. Its conceptual apparatus consisted of such components as *state, citizenship, constitutional checks and balances, federal vs. unitary apportionment of authority,* and *executive vs. legislative prerogatives.* The work of the most important scholars in the field reflected their formalistic and legalistic training. They concerned themselves with such topics as the Weberian distinction between office and officeholder.

---

3. See, e.g., Samuel H. Beer and Adam B. Ulam, eds., *Patterns of Government: The Major Political Systems of Europe* (2nd ed., revised and enlarged; New York: Random House, 1962); Gwendolen M. Carter and John H. Herz, *Major Foreign Powers: The Governments of Great Britain, France, Germany, Soviet Union* (6th ed.; New York: Harcourt Brace Jovanovich, 1972); Alex N. Dragnich, *Major European Governments* (3rd ed.; Homewood, Ill.: Dorsey Press, 1970); Roy C. Macridis and Robert E. Ward, eds., *Modern Political Systems: Europe* (3rd ed.; Englewood Cliffs, N.J.: Prentice-Hall, 1972); and Robert G. Neumann, *European Government* (4th ed.; New York: McGraw-Hill, 1968). The three previous editions of the Neumann book carried the title *European and Comparative Government,* but dealt with the same four countries treated in the most recent edition: France, the United Kingdom, West Germany, and the Soviet Union.

These books are still among the most widely used college texts in European politics—but probably are no longer used that extensively in general courses in comparative politics.

They engaged in seemingly endless debates regarding the feasibility and/or advisability of separating politics and administration. They argued about the analytic importance of the relationship between the legally defined aspects of electoral mechanisms (e.g., the single-member district with plurality vs. the multimember or list constituency with proportional representation) on the one hand and the shape of the party structure (e.g., the two-party system vs. the multiparty system) on the other; and they frequently expended great efforts to describe in detail "how bills become laws." For them, political theory generally signified the study (customarily through textual exegesis) of the political aspects of the writings of ancient philosophers.

Further, the European forms of governmental institutions seemed much more modern and, thus, more relevant and appropriate as standards for reference than the forms found in other parts of the world. For that matter, most of the world outside Europe and North America could be divided into (1) areas in which the European patterns were being emulated—as in many Latin American countries, and (2) the "primitive" areas that were under colonial rule or the tutelage of major European powers.

Comparative analysis in the traditional mold consisted largely of a comparison of the constitutional, institutional, and other formally defined features (e.g., the number of political parties, the frequency of elections, the formal checks exercised by the legislature on the executive) of particular polities with the counterparts of these components in one or a few "model" countries—such as Great Britain, the United States, or France. The latter were used as "standards," and the "comparative analysis" was designed to show similarities and dissimilarities with the standards—or, in a real sense, deviations from the norms or ideals found in the Western systems that served as referents.

While this normative orientation was regrettable and deplorable in itself, its analytic ramifications were even more devastating. For, by simply rating the political systems of various countries on what amounted to a scale of Europeanness, the analyst was not likely to learn very much about the actual nature of their political and governmental processes and institutions. Since most countries differed sharply from the European referents, little could be said about them once their "non-Europeanness" had been noted.

The Rejection of the Traditional Orientation

The inadequacies of the traditional orientation became particularly evident in the years following the Second World War. Students and practitioners alike criticized it on one (or both) of two grounds: (1) lessened political relevance, and (2) intellectual sterility. They argued that other portions of the world had become at least as important politically as Europe, and that, because of the prevailing analytic preoccupation with Europe, these areas were not accorded enough attention. They feared that the almost exclusive focus on Europe would lead to the reduction of non-Western political forms and experiences to a "primitive" or undeveloped category, rather than permitting the drawing of possibly valuable insights from their rich diversity; and they asserted that the noticeable intellectual and cultural narrowness in traditional comparative analysis would inhibit the accumulation of broadly based bodies of knowledge necessary for the construction of widely applicable theories of politics.

The increased political importance of various portions of the world outside Western Europe in the years following World War II was hardly disputable, and it led to concerted efforts to understand the basic social and political conditions in those areas. Thus, Soviet and Eastern European studies were stimulated by the advent of the cold war. A backwater in global politics prior to the Second World War, the Soviet Union and its European satellites seemed to gain prominence in academic terms in rough proportion to their importance as a source of military and political threat to the West. The Far East, North Africa, Southeast Asia, and the Middle East had remained—until the late 1940s or early 1950s—the concerns of a handful of specialists. These scholars tended to stress the unique historical and cultural roots of the governmental and political patterns manifested in these areas, and they generally eschewed cross-cultural comparison in favor of progressively more insulated specialization. (Perhaps the most persuasive argument that could be advanced against the systematic study of politics in these areas was that a large proportion of them were colonies of the major European countries and, consequently, were more appropriately studied as adjuncts of those countries than as entities interesting and important in themselves.) Again, as with the Soviet Union and Eastern Europe, general academic interest in these areas was aroused by the occurrence of internationally significant political events,[4] rather than by more directly scholarly motives.

Most dramatic—partly because of the suddenness with which it grew into a vast scholarly movement, and partly because of the appreciable resources and human commitment it mobilized in a very short period—was the growth of African (i.e., sub-Saharan) political studies during the 1950s. Foundation support, the establishment of interdisciplinary area studies programs, and the attraction of large numbers of students—particularly at the graduate level—spurred research and publication, language training, and

4. Most prominent among these events were: for the Far East, the war in the Pacific, the Chinese civil war (culminating, in 1949, in the victory of the Communists), and the Korean war; for North Africa, the Desert War (between the Axis and the Allies), and the independence movements of Tunisia and Algeria; for Southeast Asia, the anticolonial wars in Indonesia (against the Netherlands) and in Indochina (against France) were the most dramatic; and for the Middle East, the war in Palestine surrounding the establishment of Israel, and the advent of independence for such Arab countries as Syria, Lebanon, Egypt, and Jordan. In general, the sweeping force of decolonization, while not as suddenly and massively experienced in these areas as in sub-Saharan Africa (see below), and the exposure to many mobilizing stimuli during World War II were probably the dominant factors underlying change.

curriculum development in the "developing areas" at many universities; but African studies was perhaps the single greatest beneficiary of this movement.[5]

These shifts in interest hastened the rejection of the parochial, formalistic tradition in the field. For, as I have already observed, students of political life in a newly independent region, or in an area on the threshold of independence from colonial rule, or in a regime characterized by the self-acknowledged dictatorship of the only political party tolerated, did not find the traditional orientation workable. In order to avoid repeating the well-known charges made in numerous scholarly indictments of the field prior to the early 1950s,[6] I shall note only the most important among the factors that made the development of new approaches desirable.

As a consequence either of colonial rule in the Third World or of major system transformations, especially in Eastern Europe, the political processes and structures of most of these systems were new.[7] Institutional continuity, constitutional stability, and other formal relationships deemed analytically significant because of their longevity were less important for understanding politics in the non-(Western) European systems. Newly emerging, rapidly changing forms and practices had to be grasped; and, perhaps most important, *the political often had to be located* in the midst of mixtures of cultural, religious, economic, and social processes and structures. These features called for capabilities to ferret out the political aspects of often amorphous or diffuse social activity, and to develop systematic means for studying the interplay of the political system with its cultural, economic, religious, and other societal environments. The concepts, analytic tools, and data associated with the traditional orientation were not appropriate for these tasks.

The formal aspects of government and politics in the newly independent countries of Africa, Asia, and the Middle East, and in the Soviet Union and the Eastern European countries in whose politics it played a prominent role, frequently did not reflect the important day-to-day realities of political life. In the Third World the formal aspects often amounted to little more

5. See Ralph Braibanti, "Comparative Political Analytics Reconsidered," *Journal of Politics* 30, no. 1 (February 1968): 25–65 passim, esp. 29–30.

6. See esp. Macridis, *Comparative Government*, chaps. 1–3.

7. To be sure, some colonial areas could point with pride to highly developed patterns of political independence and governmental and institutional stability in their precolonial histories. But time, the movement of populations, and, above all, the intrusion of European rule, destroyed the historical continuity of those patterns. See, e.g., Robert I. Rotberg, *A Political History of Tropical Africa* (New York: Harcourt, Brace, 1965). The traditional patterns are elaborated in chaps. 1–6; their disruption is narrated in chaps. 8–10. See also Robert W. July, *A History of the African People* (New York: Charles Scribner's, 1970), in which the major political forms in precolonial Africa are distinguished, and the massive migrations and European impact are assessed. Traditional societies in Asia, the Middle East, and pre-Columbian America often had similarly elaborated, complex governmental institutions and political processes; these were often admixed with social, religious, economic, and other structures, however.

than the administrative and legal baggages left behind by colonial countries: they were vestiges of a European phase. With the advent of independence different, indigenous, processes and structures began to supplant them. Independence, in fact, was often followed by conscious assertions of cultural autonomy in the new countries; and one manifestation of such drives was the rejection of vestiges of the despised colonial period. In brief, the forms with which the new countries entered the ranks of independent states often proved to be hardly more than points of departure for the structuring of individual styles of government and politics. (Thus, most African, Asian, and Middle Eastern countries that gained independence since World War II have altered their political and governmental structures several times—frequently through military coups or revolutions.) In the Soviet Union and its Eastern European satellites, form often reflected the public image of the system that its leaders sought to project, rather than political realities. And changes in form did not serve as reliable indicators of changes in substance. These characteristics favored modes of study that were sensitive to swift and comprehensive changes and that were capable of grasping the dynamic rather than merely the static nature of politics.

Once the interests of comparativists concerned with non-European phenomena had been articulated, it became apparent to Europeanists as well that the intellectually stifling consequences of their preoccupation with the formal aspects of major powers weighed no less heavily on them than on their colleagues in African, Asian, or Soviet studies. [8] Preliminary investigations of politics in non-Western systems showed that political functions were often performed by different types of structures than those that were customarily—and often normatively—associated with them by Europe-oriented traditionalists. The central questions for students of politics in any and all settings became in the early 1950s: "What is political?" "What are the boundaries of the political system?" "How do social and economic concerns become political subject matter?"

It is interesting, in this regard, that the scholar who provided the first comprehensive and forceful statement in print about the inadequacies of the traditional orientation and the need for a conceptual, theoretical, and empirically grounded comparative politics was himself a Europeanist—Roy C. Macridis.

Macridis indicted the traditional approach for being "essentially noncomparative," "essentially descriptive," "essentially parochial," "essen-

---

8. The parochialism of the traditional approach created problems more because of the analytic blinders it put on scholarship in the field than as a direct result of its geographical narrowness. Jorgen Rasmussen, in an otherwise perceptive assessment of the field's evolution, seems to lose sight of this broader, more important consequence. See his essay, " 'Once You've Made a Revolution, Everything's the Same': Comparative Politics," in *The Post-Behavioral Era: Perspectives on Political Science*, ed. George J. Graham, Jr., and George W. Carey (New York: David McKay, 1972), pp. 71–87.

tially static," and "essentially monographic" (i.e., not cumulative).[9] But, while many of the insights into the past and a large portion of the proposals for the future were his, Macridis was, in effect, speaking for a small group of very influential scholars in the field. This group—the Committee on Comparative Politics of the Social Science Research Council—defined the issues and set the tone in comparative political inquiry for approximately one and a half decades, from the early 1950s to the late 1960s. This was the "behavioral revolution" phase of the field and of its parent discipline; and its impact upon comparative politics in general and on European studies in particular is assessed in the next section.

The Universalistic Thrust of the "Behavioral" Phase

Many influential members of the Committee on Comparative Politics focused on the developing areas,[10] and these interests helped to shift the intellectual targets of the field. Six traits marked the new direction: (1) concern for the informal as well as the formal phenomena of politics—often stressing the former and underemphasizing the latter; (2) a structural-functional approach, with a markedly functional emphasis; (3) a preoccupation with the societal setting of politics; (4) emphasis on the generation, transmission, and conversion of "inputs" from the societal environments into the political system; (5) a conceptual thrust—to be distinguished from a theoretical one—which had a tenuous link to the empirical universe; and (6) a general tendency to assume that political life in highly industrialized Western societies—with high levels of mobilization and pervasive politicization, structural differentiation, and institutional elaboration—could be studied through the same conceptual, theoretical, and methodological means that were being readied for application in the developing areas.[11]

9. Macridis, *Comparative Government*, pp. 7–12.

10. Roy C. Macridis, "Comparative Politics and the Study of Government: The Search for Focus," *Comparative Politics* 1, no. 1 (October 1968): 83, 83n. While committee membership changed during the 1950s and 1960s, during its important early years Lucian W. Pye, a specialist in Southeast Asian politics; Leonard Binder, Middle East; James S. Coleman, sub-Saharan Africa; Robert E. Ward, Japan; and Myron Weiner, India exercised great influence. Equally significant were roles played by Gabriel A. Almond and Sidney Verba, both of whom were preoccupied with "input-side" phenomena during these years. Of the long-term associates, only Joseph LaPalombara was primarily concerned with the output side.

The overall thrust of the committee's work is accurately characterized by eight books—seven of which appeared under its sponsorship—that focused on political development; their highly influential seminal precursor was Gabriel A. Almond and James S. Coleman, eds., *The Politics of the Developing Areas* (Princeton, N.J.: Princeton University Press, 1960). For an interesting personalized view of the committee, see Gabriel A. Almond, "Propensities and Opportunities," in his *Political Development: Essays in Heuristic Theory* (Boston: Little, Brown, 1970), pp. 11–23.

11. From the outset, some committee members recognized the implications of this tendency for the study of political and governmental phenomena in Western European systems. See

The short-term consequences of this new orientation were generally beneficial: an escape from the limitations associated with the traditional approaches; the possibility for studying politics in the emerging countries; and, in general, the promise of developing a more genuinely comparative, more rigorous (perhaps even scientific), and, eventually theoretically cumulative field. From the vantage point of nearly two decades, however, it is possible to see some of the less salutary affects of the behavioral phase. Two of the most important among these—in my judgment, as well as in that of a number of others in the field[12]—are (1) the tendency to underestimate the importance of political structures, and (2) the ignoring or downgrading of contextual factors—the sources of unknown or unspecifiable intervening variables. These two problem children of the behavioral revolution have been particularly troublesome for those whose principal foci of study have been the political systems of highly developed or postindustrial societies; at the same time, the directions taken of late by some of the students of such systems may lead to means for coping with these problems.

Emphasizing Functions and Downgrading Structures: Underdeveloped Comparative Politics

If formal, institutional, guides to political life were either suspect or unavailable, could basic political processes be identified, described, and explained—especially in new, protean, and relatively obscure systems—through other heuristic means? Taking his cues principally from social anthropological and sociological theory, Gabriel A. Almond proposed to identify the common properties of all political systems—in abstract terms, of course.[13] He noted that all political systems possess political structures and political functions. But, he argued, the latter tend to be more reliable analytic foci than the former, since structures are multifarious, often perform more than one function (depending largely on the cultural milieus in which they are found), and are sometimes intermittent; while, if the

Gabriel A. Almond, R. Taylor Cole, and Roy C. Macridis, "A Suggested Research Strategy in Western European Government and Politics," *American Political Science Review* 49, no. 4 (December 1955): 1042–49.

12. See Macridis, "Comparative Politics"; Joseph LaPalombara, "Macrotheories and Microapplications in Comparative Politics: A Widening Chasm," *Comparative Politics* 1, no. 1 (October 1968): 52–78 passim, esp. p. 54; Giovanni Sartori, "Concept Misformation in Comparative Politics," *American Political Science Review* 64, no. 4 (December 1970): 1033–53; Fred W. Riggs, "Structure and Function: A Dialectical Approach" (Paper presented at the 1967 Annual Meeting of the American Political Science Association, Chicago, September 1967); idem, "Systems Theory: Structural Analysis," in *Approaches to the Study of Political Science*, ed. Michael Haas and Henry S. Kariel (Scranton, Pa.: Chandler, 1970), pp. 194–235; and idem, "The Comparison of Whole Political Systems," in *The Methodology of Comparative Research*, ed. Robert T. Holt and John E. Turner (New York: Free Press, 1970), chap. 3.

13. "Introduction: A Functional Approach to Comparative Politics," in Almond and Coleman, *Politics of the Developing Areas*, pp. 10–11.

analyst succeeds in identifying the most indispensable functional requisites of the system, then he can assume their continued presence. In this vein, Almond wrote: "If the functions are there, then the structures must be, even though we may find them tucked away, so to speak, in nooks and crannies of other social systems."[14]

The seven universal functions Almond initially identified were derived from "a series of questions based on the distinctive political activities existing in complex Western systems."[15] They were comprised of four "input" or "political" functions and three "output" or "governmental" functions. From the outset, this structural-functional model, with its functional emphasis, was sharply skewed toward the input side. This reflected, in Almond's words, ". . . the political bias of this undertaking."[16] As he put it,

> It was the conviction of the collaborators [in *The Politics of the Developing Areas*] that the political functions rather than the governmental ones, the input functions rather than the output, would be most important in characterizing non-Western political systems, and in discriminating types and stages of political development among them.[17]

The practical consequence of this orientation was to reinforce the tendency to ignore structural factors. This was so because, in the developing areas, input structures were generally weakly articulated and differentiated, and they were undergoing constant and drastic changes as a concomitant of modernization.

Admittedly, the output structures—generally governmental agencies—did not usually provide good indicators of the nature of politics in a developing system. But the analytic bias in favor of the input-side functions tended to be carried over into analyses of political life in Western systems as well.[18] This should hardly have been surprising, in light of the often stated goal of Almond and other structural-functional analysts to generate an analytic framework that would be applicable in general or universal comparative analysis. The consequences of this tendency were that such phenomena as socialization, communication, electoral activity, and the like came to dominate the work of students of comparative politics in most settings, not merely in the developing areas, for nearly a decade after the appearance in print of *The Politics of the Developing Areas* and of another influential collaborative venture led by Almond, the five-country study of political culture entitled *The Civic Culture*.[19]

14. Ibid., p. 12.
15. Ibid., pp. 16–17.
16. Ibid., p. 17.
17. Ibid.
18. Macridis, "Comparative Politics," pp. 84 ff.; and LaPalombara, "Macrotheories and Microapplications," pp. 59–60.
19. Gabriel A. Almond and Sidney Verba, *The Civic Culture* (Princeton, N.J.: Princeton University Press, 1963).

In political systems in which interest groups, parties, executives, bureaucracies, judiciaries, role structures in the legal subsystems, and intricate linkages between social, economic, and other types of formal and informal political structures are highly developed and differentiated—in other words, in systems such as those found in Western Europe, the English-speaking countries, Japan, and a few other places—neither the heuristic preeminence of functions over structures nor the relative significance of the input functions over the output side of the system seems a useful a priori assumption. And, as the thrust of the argument in chapter 2 indicates, the theoretical concerns that are likely to be derived from input-side emphases and from putting structural factors into the background are probably inappropriate for the study of politics in the highly modernized, structurally elaborate systems of Western Europe. The inappropriateness of an analytic stress on the input side over the output side, for the study of politics in Western Europe at any rate, can be better illustrated through reference to the other seminal universalistic framework developed in the period under discussion—David Easton's systemic model of political life.

The structural-functional political system paradigm developed by Almond and his associates set the tone of the behavioral phase in comparative political studies; but the analytic framework proposed by David Easton was probably the most influential heuristic scheme to emerge from the period. Beginning with a profound and pervasive critique of existing political theory,[20] Easton argued for a strategy of working toward general empirical theory through comparative analysis.[21] He moved toward this goal between 1957[22] and 1965,[23] by first sketching and then progressively elaborating a highly abstract, universal conceptual framework with which he hoped to facilitate the identification of the fundamental concepts and dynamics of political flow.

Easton suggested that all political systems could be conceived as entities striving to cope or persist by processing environmental tasks ("demands") into responses ("outputs") with the aid of resources ("supports"). While he noted the existence of intrasystemic inputs ("withinputs"), and while he was aware that the authoritative policies and decisions he identified as outputs had far-ranging consequences ("outcomes"—"an output is the stone tossed into the pond and its first splash; the outcomes are the ever widening and vanishing pattern of concentric ripples"),[24] he restricted his

20. *The Political System* (New York: Alfred A. Knopf, 1953).
21. Ibid., p. 319.
22. "An Approach to the Analysis of Political Systems," *World Politics* 9, no. 3 (April 1957): 383–400. This was a skeletal outline of the framework; consequently, since it wasn't grounded by empirical referents, it was conceptually the most flexible formulation of Easton's scheme.
23. *A Framework for Political Analysis* (Englewood Cliffs, N.J.: Prentice-Hall, 1965); and *A Systems Analysis of Political Life* (New York: John Wiley, 1965). The second volume is the most extensive and authoritative but, alas, the most grounded statement.
24. *Systems Analysis of Political Life*, p. 352. In fairness to Easton, it should be noted that he extended his formulation of the concept "outputs" to performances as well as verbalizations

analysis to environmental inputs and to outputs. In many highly differentiated Western systems, however, "withinputs" seem to be as important as—or more important than—inputs; and outcomes may be more crucial than outputs in considerations of the system's capability to cope or to persist.

Chapter 2 presents an assessment of the relative utility of Easton's framework for the study of political life in the types of societies found in Western Europe. At this juncture, it should suffice to note that while the basic concepts delineated by Easton—demands, supports, conversion processes, feedback loops, outputs, outcomes, inputs, withinputs, and the like—seem to be as useful for the analysis of politics in Europe as in any other setting, the arrangement of these concepts into a flow-model must be either so abstract as to make operationalization problematic or it must be grounded in terms of empirical referents. The empirical bases Easton used in fleshing out his rudimentary framework—generally not identified in terms of specific systems or phenomena—appear to be somewhat remote from the conditions that obtain in continental Western Europe. Consequently, as scholarship in the field progresses from the conceptual through the pretheoretic to the empirical levels, it is increasingly evident that

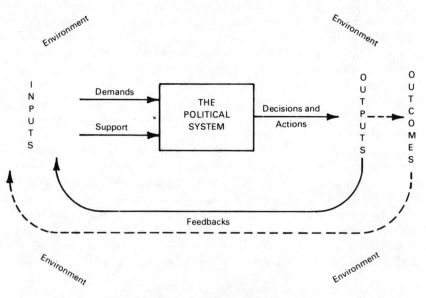

Figure 1. Diagram of Easton's Framework

Source: Adapted from David Easton, *A Framework for Political Analysis* (Englewood Cliffs, N.J.: Prentice-Hall, 1965), p. 112. ©1965. By permission.

(ibid., pp. 353–57). However, he was not concerned with *the politics of converting outputs into outcomes;* while this conversion process is one of the central dimensions of the type of system with which this book is occupied.

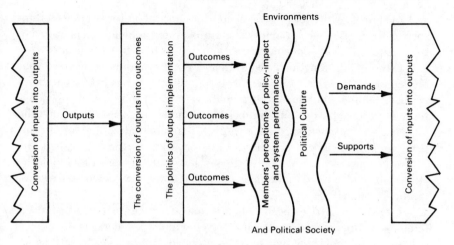

Figure 2. Diagram of Output-side Dominant Framework

referent biases inherent in the framework or flow-model make the model less than appropriate for the student of politics in certain classes of systems.

In a somewhat different manner than the structural-functional approach, Easton's system framework, then, is also inappropriate for the study of politics in systems characterized by high levels of mobilization, structural elaboration and differentiation, and other hallmarks of some "developed" societies. In sum, the conceptual thrust of the two seminal universalistic frameworks is in a direction that misses the objects of principal concern to Europeanists. They are suited for bringing into focus questions related to the boundaries and environments of political systems, and for considering the interrelationships of political functions and structures inside systems. They are inadequate for closing in on the empirical universe of actual political phenomena in some types of systems.

Correlational Analysis—Or, Downgrading Contextual Factors

In addition to universalistic conceptual frameworks, the behavioral revolution brought another analytic dimension to the forefront of comparative political analysis: the statistical treatment of quantified data. While some applications of quantitative techniques have produced impressive results and promise to become even more important, they are not without some serious pitfalls.[25] Potentially dangerous errors are especially likely when universalistic frameworks are used, since they make it virtually impossible to take contextual factors into account in a systematic fashion,

25. See, for instance, Adam Przeworski and Henry Teune, *The Logic of Comparative Social Inquiry* (New York: Wiley-Interscience, 1970); Sartori, "Concept Misformation"; and Macridis, "Comparative Politics."

and because they do not provide means for controlling for unknown or un-specifiable intervening variables. The most severe problems encountered in this regard are *functional equivalence* and various *inferential fallacies.*[26]

Establishing functional equivalence entails finding indicators that measure the same thing in different sociopolitical settings. At this juncture in the development of quantitative political research, very few, if any, quantitative indicators exhibit appreciable functional equivalence at the universal level of analysis. In this respect, the quantitative student of comparative politics is plagued by a form of what Sartori has called the "travelling problem": he is able to say less with less precision when he strives to deal with data from a large and loosely selected universe of political systems.[27]

Inferential fallacies occur when erroneous or unwarranted causal inferences are drawn from statistical analyses of quantified data. They are projections of relationships that have been tested at one level to settings at which the relationships have not been verified. Thus, the *ecological fallacy* consists of the inference that relationships between individuals in a particular setting are the same as those that have been established for collectivities. The *individualistic fallacy* is the obverse of the ecological: it assumes that generalizations about individual behavior are valid for aggregates. According to Alker "Political science generalists . . . are especially susceptible" to the *universal fallacy*, which consists of attempts "to infer statements with regional validity from imperfectly valid universal generalizations."[28] The *selective fallacy* is encountered when only supportive or "friendly" evidence is admitted into the analysis by the consciously or unconsciously biased scholar.

One other inferential fallacy among the multitude of those I have not specified above needs to be noted here, given our interest in cross-national comparison: the *contextual fallacy*. Simply stated, this error is encountered when the intervention of contextual or environmental factors in the relationship between the variables under examination is not taken into account in a systematic manner. Bivariate or multivariate analyses should be enlightened or qualified by some form of control for unknown or unspecified variables—those that might be significant intervening variables.

In brief, some knowledge of the context of the interrelationship under investigation must be available, for purposes of statistical and theoretical control. Comparative politics entails the formulation and testing of theoretical propositions across systems. Clearly, therefore, we must escape

26. My discussion follows Richard L. Merritt, *Systematic Approaches to Comparative Politics* (Chicago: Rand McNally, 1970), pp. 13–17; and Hayward R. Alker, Jr., *Mathematics and Politics* (New York: Macmillan, 1965), pp. 101–6. See also Mattei Dogan and Stein Rokkan, eds., *Quantitative Ecological Analysis in the Social Sciences* (Cambridge, Mass.: MIT Press, 1969), esp. chaps. 1–5, 12, and 21.

27. Sartori, "Concept Misformation," pp. 1036–40.

28. Alker, *Mathematics and Politics*, p. 103.

from the bonds of system-specific variables—i.e., variables with differing or indeterminate meanings in different systems; and we must search for appropriate levels at which cross-system generalization will prove meaningful. In the early stages of exploration—where interesting statistical relationships can be found, anomalies uncovered, and hypotheses formulated—the universal level of analysis may have some utility, but actual testing and theory construction demand much more contextual control and sensitivity than simple correlational analyses can provide. The universalistic frameworks are either too abstract or too amorphous to yield the kind and degree of control needed. Further, as Sartori has pointed out, it is inefficient to try to use our increasingly more sophisticated quantitative tools of study at the universal plane. They are more appropriately used for distinguishing *degrees* of difference among essentially similar phenomena than for distinguishing *kinds* of difference along universal continua.[29] Put another way, I suggest that at this juncture in comparative political research we will be better served by trying to discern similarities and differences among various types of apples than by making "comparisons" between apples and oranges by noting that they are similar in that they are both fruits. When the field was striving to overcome the narrowness inherent in the traditional orientation it was progressive to note basic similarities in substance that cut across differences in form. For heuristic purposes, it was useful to identify common denominators across wide ranges of variation. At this stage in the evolution of the field, however, substantive knowledge needs to be generated: the heuristic aims have been largely attained.

What has the behavioral revolution wrought for comparative political studies? In general, the rejection of the narrow concerns of the traditional orientation has been more beneficial than harmful. At the same time, the universalistic thrust of the behavioral phase has exacted its own price. In a real sense, this parallels the shortcomings of the traditional phase.

First, because its salient analytic constructs were erected at the universal level, and because it lacks meaningful ways for imposing contextual control, the field is still largely noncomparative. Second, most of the theoretical speculations in the field remain ungrounded, because the pursuit of knowledge has not led to systematic contact with the empirical universe. Empirical research has tended to parallel rather than intersect theoretical work; thus, explanation and description are not as closely associated as we might like. Most comparative politics research, therefore, remains descriptive. Third, the conceptual, theoretical, and research innovations emanating from the behavioral revolution have tended to move the focus of the field toward prepolitical phenomena. This tendency was embodied in the preoccupation with the input side and in the general disregard for output- and outcome-related processes and structures. While

29. Sartori, "Concept Misformation," pp. 1038 ff.

such emphases might be appropriate for the identification and study of politics in some types of systems, they are clearly less useful in others. The analytic skewness embodied in the approaches that came to the forefront of the field in the 1950s and 1960s thus appears somewhat parochial from the vantage point of European studies. Fourth, parallelling Macridis's 1955 charge that the traditional orientation was static, the theoretical and empirical work in the field has tended toward linear projections of change— assuming progression from "underdeveloped" toward "developed" political systems in terms of culture-bound and often no-longer-relevant indicators.[30] Finally, like its predecessor, the behavioral phase witnessed the development of a literature that was essentially monographic, in the sense that it did not lead to appreciable cumulative scholarship.

One possible path to utilizing the beneficial aspects of the frameworks and research techniques developed during the 1950s and 1960s is to construct models that are narrower than universal but broad enough to encourage genuine cross-systemic comparison.[31] If the models are constructed in such a fashion that they encompass essentially similar systems—i.e., systems presumed on noninductive grounds to be similar—then both analytic control and theoretical cogency may be attained. This orientation has been called the "most similar systems design,"[32] and a few successful comparative studies have already utilized it.[33] This book experiments with such an approach to the study of European politics, and a formal "most similar systems" model is presented in the next chapter. At this juncture, I shall only note why I believe European studies to be an appropriate area for the development of such models, and why such a venture is likely to benefit the field of comparative politics as a whole.

European Studies and Comparative Politics

Whether those traveling on universalistic tracks will reach worthwhile destinations in the near future or will be compelled to change directions remains to be seen. For reasons already noted, however, it has become clear that European political phenomena do not lend themselves readily to study through such means.

30. For a description and thorough criticism of this tendency, see A. E. Keir Nash, "Pollution, Population, and the Cowboy Economy: Anomalies in the Developmentalist Paradigm and Samuel Huntington," *Journal of Comparative Administration* 2, no. 1 (May 1970): 109–28.

31. Sartori, "Concept Misformation," pp. 1038–45 and passim.

32. Przeworski and Teune, *Logic of Comparative Social Inquiry*, pp. 32–34. The authors have a less favorable view of this orientation than I have, and after describing it they proceed to advocate a variant of its opposite.

33. Perhaps the most fruitful application to date can be found in Robert R. Alford's *Party and Society: The Anglo-American Democracies* (Chicago: Rand McNally, 1963). See also the items listed in note 3 of chap. 2; and those cited by Przeworski and Teune, *Logic of Comparative Social Inquiry*, p. 33n.

There was, as we have seen, an intricate relationship between the passage of the traditional orientation into the behavioral phase and the shift of analytic foci from European systems to the developing areas. There is, I believe, a new and mutually beneficial symbiotic relationship emerging between (general) comparative and European political studies. Far from constituting a return to the prebehavioral parochialism, however, this new thrust derives from the convergence of theoretically salient questions and practical considerations of empirical research in the field in general.

From a broad analytic perspective, European systems—particularly those in continental Western Europe—seem to provide promising material for a "most similar systems" design or a model that can be used for within-type comparisons. The justification of this position is presented in the next chapter. It should suffice here to note that these systems seem to exhibit similar levels of economic and political development and political mobilization; they confront similar human and physical environmental problems; and most important, many of them appear to have similar political structures. Further, most of these countries are intimately associated with each other in both intergovernmental and supranational agencies,[34] and such associations possess the potential for reinforcing existing similarities.

Similarities among systems selected for study serve two important heuristic purposes. First, they provide the comparative analyst with a degree of control over unknown or unspecified variables. Second, they can serve as a *pretheoretic core*, around which theories for the system type can be generated. Pretheoretic cores or models are developed when initial contact is made between conceptual frameworks and the empirical universe. They consist of estimates of real-world situations, and are based on existing knowledge. Once such a model has been sketched, *anomalies* can be discovered. Anomalies are phenomena that are not explicable in terms of existing knowledge. In order to understand or explain anomalous conditions, *hypotheses* are formulated; and these are cast into operational or testable form. *Operationalized* hypotheses are then *tested with empirical data*. Verified hypotheses lead to the formulation of *propositions*, or partial explanations of anomalies; and these are, in turn, integrated into *theories*, with the aid of the conceptual framework that served as the point of departure.

If analytic neutrality is reintroduced into Easton's framework, it can serve as a valuable heuristic device in the study of politics in European societies. Two steps need to be taken to achieve the goal of analytic neutrality. First, a firm and vigilantly sustained distinction between the con-

---

34. The North Atlantic Treaty Organization, the Council of Europe, and the Organization for Economic Co-operation and Development are prominent among the intergovernmental agencies; while the European Communities are moving, albeit slowly, toward supranational unification.

ceptual and pretheoretic realms (i.e., the realms of analysis and explanation) must be made, in order to avoid distortions in the former from the latter. Second, "withinputs" and "outcomes" must be accorded the same degree of importance granted the other major components of the framework. In this way, peculiarities of one type of system will not distort the general framework, and the analytic salience of one or another conceptual dimension (e.g., inputs, outcomes, feedbacks) in some settings will not be mistaken for universally applicable analytic salience. Instead, it will be possible to develop numerous models of types of polities, and then, using the general framework as the point of reference, to interrelate the models.

The European setting possesses four valuable qualities for the rapid development of cumulative, hierarchically interrelated comparative politics theory, in addition to the feasibility of constructing "most similar systems" models. It has (1) bodies of substantive knowledge that can serve as pretheoretic points of departure; (2) a politically relevant theoretical thrust—i.e., a link between academic and policy interests; (3) the least unsatisfactory data sets necessary for the testing of hypotheses for a large number of countries and across time; and (4) indigenous scholars, whose work can lead to the rapid accretion of both data and theory.[35]

Relative social and institutional continuity and the availability of loosely comparable country studies make possible the distillation of salient patterns in Western European politics. Such patterns should not be viewed as testable statements in themselves, of course, since considerable subjectivity and empirical selectivity may be involved in their identification. But they can be used to make up pretheoretic cores. Three such patterns serve as the point of departure for the model sketched in chapter 2, and they recur in the other essays that comprise this book. These patterns are essentially noncontroversial or consensus-based observations about trends in Western European politics.

A dual theoretical thrust characterizes the renaissance of European political studies. One aspect derives from a widespread value reorientation that has been termed the "postbehavioral revolution." Again, as at the time of the movement from the traditional to the behavioral orientations, actual political events exerted a reinforcing force for the nascent analytic value-hierarchy. In this instance, a growing concern with *the impact of policies and the consequences of political systems* was articulated by growing numbers of Europeans and North Americans. This was the advent of a preoccupation with outputs and outcomes in politics, and it paralleled a similar development in political science. As Easton noted, "Post-behavioralism is both a movement, that is, an aggregate of people, and an intellectual tendency."[36] Such concerns have cut across most of the Western world

---

35. Cf. Stephen Blank, "Afterword: The Future of European Studies," in this volume.

36. David Easton, "The New Revolution in Political Science," *American Political Science Review* 63, no. 4 (December 1969): 1051.

during the past three or four years. The analytic redirection they make possible seems most relevant for the comparative study of politics in systems in which the basic allocative or distributional arrangements that characterize the regime are generally acceptable to most people. This is so because it is in such systems that the postbehavioral preoccupations with outcomes and quality of life factors are likely to rise to the forefront of political concerns.

The other aspect consists of an analytic stress on structural rather than functional features of polities. Four papers mark this passage in the literature of comparative politics: the essays by LaPalombara and Macridis in the inaugural issue of *Comparative Politics* and by Sartori in the *American Political Science Review* and a paper presented by Fred W. Riggs at the 1967 meeting of the American Political Science Association—all previously cited. LaPalombara, Macridis, and Sartori expressed, albeit in different terms, the growing impatience of some comparativists with the universalistic, prepolitical, nonstructural, and correlational tendencies noted above. It is not a coincidence, I submit, that the first three scholars named specialize in the study of politics in European settings. Riggs advanced a universally applicable, trenchant argument for redressing the balance between structural and functional concerns.

From an empirical or research-oriented perspective, the European setting is more promising for such studies than any other—given the *relative* plenitude of appropriate classes of data. In particular, quantitative indicators of system performance and policy impact, electoral behavioral and attitudinal data, and detailed historical records (for longitudinal analyses) are required; and, with the possible exception of the United States and one or two other systems, such data are most likely to be found in Western Europe.[37]

From a theoretical standpoint, taking the postbehavioral concerns into the setting of Western Europe seems particularly appropriate; it is there that a substantial number of systems, with different developmental histories and varied social, cultural, and other background conditions seem, nevertheless, to share similar political structures. *Thus it may be feasible, for the first time in the career of modern comparative political studies, to test theoretically important propositions of current political concern, across several systems, with data, over time.* This appears to me to be a useful and

---

37. See Michael Aiken, "A Preliminary Inventory of Machine-readable Data on Urban and Other Sub-national Units in Western European Nations and the United States: Sources Located in the United States," mimeographed (Madison, Wisc., 1972). Janowitz and Segal observed that "Empirical research on the political sociology of the multiparty nations of western Europe has been pursued with great vigor and a sense of historical perspective in part because some of the major propositions of the leading theorists could be explored by means of a growing body of sample survey data" (Morris Janowitz and David R. Segal, "Social Cleavage and Party Affiliation: Germany, Great Britain, and the United States," *American Journal of Sociology* 72, no. 6 [May 1967]: 601). See also the essay by B. Guy Peters, chap. 7 in this volume.

interesting setting for comparative political analysis at this time. It promises
to yield theoretical outcomes that will be of general benefit for the field.

Illustrations of the Posttraditional and Postbehavioral Orientation in European Studies

Part 1 of this volume seeks to relate the study of political life in Europe
to the comparative study of politics in general. Following the general introduction of the analytic and research contexts of modern European
studies given in this chapter, an ideal-type model of the "European polity"
is presented in chapter 2. The principal purpose of the model is to indicate
the dimensions in terms of which a class of systems can be considered to be
similar, in order to utilize a "most similar systems" design.

Three basic patterns—alluded to above—are discernible in the politics
of most contemporary European systems, and these served as a springboard
for the model: (1) the decreasing importance of input-side activity as a
policy-influencing factor, (2) the growing importance of political structural
factors in shaping political activity and orientations, and (3) the increasing
political importance of administration in everyday life. While these gross
patterns may well be manifested in many or most political systems in
postindustrial societies, they seem most pronounced in some Western and
Central European settings. And, more specifically, these patterns are accompanied by a political structural form that is most noticeable in small,
markedly pluralistic or cleaved postindustrial systems—most, but not all of
which are continental European.

The model is presented as a pretheoretical statement. It can serve as a
starting point for the formulation of testable hypotheses about, for
example, interrelationships between highly developed and differentiated
political and governmental structures on the one hand and levels of satisfaction with outcomes on the other; or the efficacy of group or segmental
representation on the input side as a means for alleviating the centrifugal
tendencies often associated with cleaved systems; or the capabilities of
regimes to use the value of continuous access to the policy-making
subsystem as a stimulus for diffuse supports.

In calling our model the "European polity" type, Professor Kvavik and
I were aware of and sensitive to two criticisms. First, we outlined a system
type which may, in fact, be applicable outside Europe and which does not
readily subsume all systems in Europe. In fact, the largest and politically
most important European countries, such as France, West Germany, the
United Kingdom, and Italy, do not fit neatly into the type-cell, if the type-
defining criteria are applied rigorously. Second, there is something
theoretically primitive or "unscientific" about the use of a proper name—
European—to designate a model in comparative politics. Przeworski and
Teune have reviewed a number of injunctions in this regard. Thus, "The

bridge between historical observations and general theory is the substitution of variables for proper names of social systems in the course of comparative research"; and ". . . lawlike statements are possible in the social sciences if and only if spatiotemporal parameters are treated as residua of variables potentially contributing to the explanation."[38]

But at this juncture in the development of empirical theory, we are only slightly removed from the stage of making historical observations. As Przeworski and Teune observed, "Probably dominant within political science today [is the making of] social science statements [that] are relative to classes of nations or 'areas' that share syndromes of historical, cultural, and social characteristics."[39] We believe that our model goes one step further: in the "European polity" model, we have sought to develop a framework for comparative analysis that brings together systems that share certain political structural characteristics. Inasmuch as the political is the central concern and "historical, cultural, and social characteristics" are environmental or background features only, we feel we have taken a modest step toward genuinely political comparative politics theory. Substantive—as distinguished from merely heuristic—progress will follow from the operationalization and testing of the basic components of our model, however. The model holds out promise; it should not be confused with the achievement of that promise.

The price that had to be paid for taking the step from the identification of mere background factors for the type to the delineation of the basic political structure was the exclusion of some major countries in the area. The historically oriented reader may object that some of our reasons for drawing the type-cell's boundaries in the manner we chose were arbitrary or unjustifiable. From the traditional perspective, such an accusation might be valid. But our reasons were not historical—or, for that matter, social, or cultural. In fact, it is precisely because we eschewed the historical, social, and cultural reasoning used by writers whose narrower constructs preceded ours that we were able to project a framework that appears to be directly applicable to the study of politics in eight to ten countries and in the European Communities. Thus, while France, the United Kingdom, and perhaps other countries share some or many background conditions with the members of our type-cell, we do not discern in those larger countries some of the political characteristics (or, for that matter, some of the crucial background characteristics) shared by the systems we have tentatively included. Finally, if it becomes possible—at the operational stage—to disassociate the type's characteristics from the "spatiotemporal parameters" of postindustrial Western or European systems that we have made explicit, then we shall propose a nonproper name for the type-model, derived from its salient characteristic: the "cooptive polity."

38. *Logic of Comparative Social Inquiry*, p. 25.
39. Ibid., p. 7.

Testing the "European polity" model with data is clearly a long-term proposition, involving many years' work by several specialists. Nor is it to be taken for granted that its heuristic potential merits such a massive effort. At this preliminary stage, then, as editor of this volume, I decided to begin with an indirect "test" of the feasibility and worth of planning actual operationalization. Instead of working with my collaborators in a concerted manner to integrate their contributions through the model, I asked them to address themselves, in brief essays, to whatever *they* deemed to be the salient features of politics in the countries or problem areas in which they were specialists. Only two measures of "control" were used to enhance the prospects for a coherent volume, and they could hardly be considered rigorous. First, I approached scholars whom I believed to be principally occupied with output-related phenomena. Second, in extending my invitations, I indicated that my own theoretical prejudices consisted of a structural emphasis and a focus on output-side processes. The reader can judge the extent to which the volume does or does not cohere around the themes developed in chapter 2. My own conclusion is that the concerns of others in the field seem to be converging on those themes, at least sufficiently to warrant moving to the operational stage—and such a step is being taken as this book goes to press.

The four chapters that comprise part 2 illustrate the range of European polity type structures. Norway seems—both to Robert B. Kvavik and to myself—closest of all to the ideal-type model. While Austria and Belgium are rather removed, they are still clearly within the type-cell, since the cooptive structure is operative, and all other characteristics seem to be present.

Norway, then, serves as an archetypal case. It is also illustrative of a system in which the underlying dimensions of division are largely those of differently conceived interests. It approaches the rational or economic pluralist mold. Austria, in distinction, exhibits the primacy of political and social cleavages; while in Belgium the politicization of a profound ethnic cleavage has come to replace a rather more "traditional" set of socioeconomic and ideological divisions. The cooptive or linking mechanisms differ in the three systems, but they serve the same integrative function. (Here, then, we have an instance of structural variation in the performance of a function—and this in a structurally oriented model!)

The structure of the political system of the European Communities approximates the model somewhat. It provides an illustration of the applicability of the model to nonnation-state systems.

Part 3 consists of studies that illustrate the policy-oriented thrust of politics in the European polity type systems—and in systems resting just outside the type-cell. The major policy issues in European politics seem to me to be a concern with enhancing the "quality of life," now that basic distributional values have been attained; regionalization; and coping with environmental problems—both in international relations and vis-à-vis the natural universe.

B. Guy Peters' consummate study of the development of social policy, assessed in terms of "quality of life" indicators, provides many valuable insights not only into its formal subject but also into the type of theoretical and research orientation that will be useful in comparative political studies in developed systems for the forseeable future. It combines the policy impact-related theoretical primacy that is popularly and academically being demanded. It focuses sharply on the question: what difference do the political system and the government make? It contextualizes a sophisticated multivariate method of analysis, through historical and sociological sensitivity, and it illustrates the research techniques that promise high returns for quantitative comparative analysis.

William G. Andrews' study provides insights into the executive decision-making process that has emerged in Fifth Republic France, in addition to narrating the unfolding of an important political phenomenon. From his essay we can judge the relative distance of France from the European polity model: the processes of structured consultation and access seem to be operating, but in many important respects, France is unlike her northern neighbors. From Andrews' essay we might conclude, however, that the direction of the French system's evolution is toward rather than away from that model.

James Wolfe's paper serves many valuable purposes in this volume. Two of the most important among these are the demonstration of the relevance and theoretical legitimacy of structural analysis, and the depiction of one of the few truly corporatist regimes. Since the European polity construct is essentially structural and since one of its important dimensions can be described as quasi corporatist (in analytic rather than ideological terms, of course), the essay is a vital link in the demonstration of the heuristic possibilities of the model.

The papers by Guy de Carmoy and Richard L. Merritt are intended principally to provide insights into the environmental problems of European systems, and into the manner in which they seek to cope with such problems. Clearly, both serve other purposes as well. Thus, from Carmoy's discussion of the making of energy policy and the variety of relationships between the private and public sectors in different European countries, we can glean insights into the degree to which, in a given country, the characteristics of the European polity type are operative.

The volume concludes with a report by Stephen Blank, executive director of the Council for European Studies, on the current status and immediate prospects of the field. In light of the degression of European studies during the "behavioral phase," it is heartening to learn that the intellectual excitement manifested at this time is buttressed—for the first time in modern history—with organizational and financial support. While the latter may be of modest proportions, it is significantly greater in relation to support accorded to other areas than it has been at any time since the end of World War II. In general, the innovative and promising ventures in European studies that have been undertaken will now have the opportunity to enhance the field in additive terms—and the advantages of modern social scientific scholarship (especially exchangeability of information, sharing of data, time-saving divisions of labor, and cooperative and cumulative research) will now accrue to specialists in the developed areas on a scale that is comparable to that enjoyed by their non-Western system-oriented colleagues in the last two decades. While Professor Blank's prognoses are conservative, the overview of the present and the expectations for the future seem to justify the conclusion that comparative political studies in this field of specialization will progress steadily toward substantively significant goals.

2

Martin O. Heisler

with the collaboration of

Robert B. Kvavik

Patterns of European Politics: The "European Polity" Model

The preceding chapter noted that the field of comparative politics is moving from highly abstract, conceptual disquisitions about politics in everyplace—and, hence, in no place—toward conceptually self-conscious theory building. In recent years progress in this direction can be seen in the study of what we generically characterize as "European politics." Chapter 1 also argued that the next major phase in the comparative study of political life should focus on the development of broad but clearly mid-range theories. Such theories should be grounded in empirically testable realities and, at the same time, should be closely linked with logically coherent frameworks such as those that provided the impetus for the phenomenal growth of comparative political theory and research during the past two decades.

With the preceding discussion in mind, this chapter presents a model of a system type we call the "European polity." We delineate the salient structural and behavioral dimensions of this type of political system, the identification and linkages of which constitute an intermediate step in the building of mid-range theories of politics in Europe. Together with a discussion of what we consider the distinguishing features of the "European polity type" system, we offer a strategy for the study of political life in the smaller European democracies.

Introduction

Three distinct analytic approaches are available for the construction of mid-range theory in comparative politics: (1) we could focus on some functional or sectoral aspects of whole political systems;[1] (2) we could attempt to bridge the great chasm that separates the general framework from the empirical universe of a single, concrete political system by initially treating each system sui generis and then generalizing from the specific;[2] or (3) we could undertake the comparison of several whole systems, *provided that we restrict ourselves to a purposefully delineated class of systems.*[3]

We chose the third alternative for reasons at once simple and compelling. Representing a form of analytic compromise between the universalistic and system-specific approaches, it makes manageable the task of comparative analysis with no significant loss in the theoretical scope and salience of the problems and findings. This approach permits the formulation of readily operationalized hypotheses that can be tested through available or relatively easily generated synchronic and longitudinal data.

1. For example, the system sector of political socialization was selected for focal treatment in David Easton and Jack Dennis, *Children in the Political System* (New York: McGraw-Hill, 1969); legislative process and structure-related questions engaged the attention of the symposium contributors in Allan Kornberg, ed., *Legislatures in Comparative Perspective* (New York: David McKay, 1973). An especially forceful and cogent argument against whole-system comparison and in favor of sectoral comparative analysis is Joseph LaPalombara, "Parsimony and Empiricism in Comparative Politics: An Anti-Scholastic View," in *The Methodology of Comparative Research*, ed. Robert T. Holt and John E. Turner (New York: Free Press, 1970), chap. 4.

2. Illustrations of partially successful attempts in following such a strategy, together with justifications for the case study approach, include Harry Eckstein, *Division and Cohesion in a Democracy: A Study of Norway* (Princeton, N.J.: Princeton University Press, 1966); Arend Lijphart, *The Politics of Accommodation: Pluralism and Democracy in the Netherlands* (Berkeley and Los Angeles: University of California Press, 1968); Lucian W. Pye's study of Burma—*Politics, Personality and Nation Building* (New Haven: Yale University Press, 1962); and, to a lesser extent, some of the country studies in the Little, Brown series in comparative politics. Perhaps the only two generally successful country studies of this kind are Walter Bagehot's classic from another era, *The British Constitution* (London: Oxford University Press, 1928, originally published in 1867); and William C. Mitchell, *The American Polity* (New York: Free Press, 1962).

3. This path, selected for the present venture, has been marked by a number of writers during the past few years. See Robert R. Alford, *Party and Society* (Chicago: Rand McNally, 1963), esp. chap. 1; Stein Rokkan, "The Structuring of Mass Politics in the Smaller European Democracies: A Developmental Typology," *Comparative Studies in Society and History* 10, no. 2 (January 1968): 173–210; and Giovanni Sartori, "Concept Misformation in Comparative Politics," *American Political Science Review* 64, no. 4 (December 1970): 1033–53. The works of three writers, offering applications of this approach to differing segments of the universe with which we are concerned, served as the theoretical underpinning for our own effort: Gerhard Lehmbruch, "A Non-competitive Pattern of Conflict Management in Liberal Democracies: The Case of Switzerland, Austria and Lebanon" (Paper presented at the Seventh World Congress of the International Political Science Association, Brussels, September 1967); Arend Lijphart, "Consociational Democracy," *World Politics* 21, no. 2 (January 1969): 207–25; and Val R. Lorwin, "Segmented Pluralism: Ideological Cleavages and Political Cohesion in the Smaller European Democracies," *Comparative Politics* 3, no. 2 (January 1971): 141–75. For logical and methodological contextualizations of this approach, see Adam Przeworski and Henry Teune, *The Logic of Comparative Social Inquiry* (New York: Wiley-Interscience, 1970), pp. 7–8, 32–34, passim; and Arend Lijphart, "Comparative Politics and the Comparative Method," *American Political Science Review* 65, no. 3 (September 1971): 687 ff. It should be noted that Przeworski and Teune do not advocate this approach.

Such an undertaking will be cumulative, in relation to broader theoretical endeavors. Further, the third approach helps avoid many pitfalls and limitations usually encountered with the excessively general first approach and the overly narrow second approach.

For example, the comparison of subsystemic phenomena may lead to the erosion of meaning or to massive problems of equivalence, or both, if it is taken across a wide or undelineated range of systems. This problem in large part reflects what Giovanni Sartori has identified as the "conceptual stretching" that accompanies the "travelling problem":

> . . . the net result of conceptual straining is that our gains in extensional coverage tend to be matched by losses in connotative precision. It appears that we can cover more—in travelling terms—only by saying less, and by saying less in a far less precise manner.[4]

In cross-national comparisons of such political structures and behavior as elections, party organization, or elite recruitment, the analyst is generally compelled to hold constant vast—and sometimes unknown or incalculable—numbers of often markedly different variables. This makes it difficult to relate the fruits of systematic comparative analysis back to the contexts from which the phenomena had been abstracted, unless some of the previously frozen system-specific indicators are admitted into the analysis in ways that may weaken or destroy the scientific character of the more rigorous limited comparisons.

The problem of comparability encountered with the first approach is obviously not limited to the kind and number of explanatory variables required: it extends to the phenomena studied as well. Thus, focusing on interest groups, one might discover that not only do their relationships with one another as well as with other units in the polity change from system to system, but that their structures and functions vary also, perhaps to such a degree that they become indistinguishable from such other units in the system as political parties. Indeed, perhaps only in name are they the same, and the inclusion of vast numbers of variables to explain the differences is, in the end, theoretically meaningless.

The second alternative—the comprehensive, intensive country study— avoids many difficulties encountered in the cross-system comparisons of subsystemic phenomena by holding fewer systemic variables constant, and by stressing the importance of particular juxtapositions of variables over the system's various dimensions—including the historic. Nevertheless, this approach carries a prohibitive cost of its own from the perspective of the student of comparative politics. Even if explicit universal or comparative conceptual frameworks are used as guides, the particularistic context in

4. Sartori, "Concept Misformation," p. 1035.

which the problems were initially identified and the data generated and analyzed tends to emphasize the essentially unique features of the system. If comparison through a concentration of a few variables in a number of systems raises problems of equivalence, then single-country studies that aim at comprehensiveness are likely to sidestep major issues in comparative political theory; and the enterprise of building cumulative, hierarchical theory will suffer.

These factors militate against the development of mid-range theories; yet such theories are necessary for the understanding of European politics. Accordingly, we suggest the comparison of specific whole systems—an approach that avoids (at least in magnitude) the problems encountered above and is more efficacious, in terms of at least two criteria. First, from the perspectives of students of general comparative as well as European politics, the approach promises results in the form of building blocks for more comprehensive theoretical efforts. Second, it seems a more direct route to usable propositions that can be interrelated to comprise explanations of what is happening in European politics and why it is happening— explanations that are not likely to be obtained if each polity is treated sui generis. Tangible support for our strategy will be found only when our model is subjected to repeated and multifarious tests and only after a more thorough discussion of the contents and logic of the approach has taken place. Before presenting the dimensions of the model, let us take a closer look at some of the promises and limitations of the approach itself.

Typologies and a Type

During the past few years several writers have urged that universalistic analytic frameworks in comparative inquiry be eschewed or, minimally, that they be supplemented with taxonomic approaches.[5]

(Taxonomic preoccupations among students of comparative politics are not new, of course. Our point here is that—as noted earlier—universalistic frameworks for analysis occupied center-stage in comparative political studies during most of the post-World War II "behavioral revolution" phase of political science, and an understandable impatience with the difficulties encountered in attempts to relate such frameworks to specific political phenomena has taken, as one of its manifestations, the form of typology construction.)

5. See, e.g., Gabriel A. Almond, "Comparative Political Systems," *Journal of Politics* 18, no. 3 (August 1956): 391–409, for an early effort which, regrettably, has not been consistently sustained, even by its author; Arend Lijphart, "Typologies of Democratic Systems," *Comparative Political Studies* 1, no. 1 (April 1968): 3–44; Fred W. Riggs, "The Comparison of Whole Political Systems," in Holt and Turner, *Methodology of Comparative Research*, chap. 3; and Sartori, "Concept Misformation."

Thus Arend Lijphart asserts that the proper kind of

> typology of political systems should ideally perform two functions: (1) It should facilitate comparison among different types and aid in the discovery of significant characteristics that are logically independent of the criteria defining the types but empirically associated with the different types. (2) It should also facilitate comparisons within each type, with the attributes held in common by all of the systems within the type serving as the "control" variables, or parameters.[6]

Sartori convincingly argues the complementary point that the most sophisticated use of modern tools of research (especially quantitative ones) and analysis is likely to be *within types*. Such tools as factor and regression analyses of aggregate data, survey research, and content analysis make it possible to ascertain *degrees* or gradations of difference; and such variations are more likely to be discerned and meaningfully analyzed among similar systems than among those that are grossly different. The latter are more appropriately characterized as different in kind rather than in degree, and the task of comparing them should entail cross-type analyses.[7]

The benefits promised to students of comparative politics by the two functional attributes of typologies noted by Lijphart seem substantial indeed. While such qualities of type-constructs make them appropriate for the study of political life in systems that vary within a delimited range, they should not be considered a panacea for the concerns of comparative political analysts in general, however. Regrettably, *usable* comprehensive typologies do not seem to be much more readily attainable at this stage in the development of political studies than is a viable general theory: attempts to construct *comprehensive* typologies of political systems are as likely to encounter the "travelling problem" as are attempts to build comprehensive, testable theories through universal concepts. The reasoning is simple. The basic dimensions used to classify political systems into mutually exclusive and collectively exhaustive categories will be stretched beyond available empirical grounding—even if they retain a modicum of logical coherence.[8] To avoid the "stretching problem" in the course of typology construction and to obtain type-models that yield substantive returns in the form of test-

6. Lijphart, "Typologies of Democratic Systems," p. 7.
7. Sartori, "Concept Misformation," pp. 1044–45 and 1033–53 passim.
8. See, for instance, the use of two gross dimensions of comparison not only as characteristics in terms of which a specific class of systems ("polyarchies") can be delineated, but also for arraying most other extant polities, in Robert A. Dahl, *Polyarchy: Participation and Opposition* (New Haven and London: Yale University Press, 1971), chap. 1 and appendix A. Our criticism is restricted to Dahl's attempt to use as a universal set of indicators the specific characteristics that he used to demarcate polyarchies. The polyarchy type does not exhibit symptoms of the "travelling problem"; and, in fact, it can be cited as an illustration of a useful limited-type-construct.

able explanatory and predictive theories, restrictions have to be imposed on the analytic purposes the type construct is expected to serve, as well as on its scope (i.e., on the range of variation among systems and the comprehensiveness of system aspects treated).[9]

It is clearly outside the scope of this paper—and possibly outside the realm of feasibility, given the present theoretical and empirical wherewithal of the field—to provide specific criteria for delineating types of political systems in general. For our particular purposes, keeping in mind the aims outlined in the preceding paragraphs, we seek to put into a single type-cell systems that share certain environmental conditions and structural characteristics—i.e., where such conditions and characteristics vary within a narrow range.

We look to these similarities for two kinds of analytic control. First, if the environmental conditions under which several systems exist are markedly similar, then it is reasonable to expect that the environmental inputs with which they will have to cope will vary within a moderate, analytically manageable range. Second, shared structural characteristics militate in favor of the assumption that tasks which originate inside the system will be essentially similar in kind and degree—though not in specifics. Further, if the political structures of several systems are similar, it may be warranted to hypothesize that they will approach the performance of such tasks through readily comparable means.

In the model sketched below, we enumerate the system characteristics that constitute the "European polity" type. Parallel constructs, dealing with other system types and other regions, may not be feasible at this time. As noted in chapter 1, the major analytic prerequisites of such a model are not evenly distributed throughout the world. A series of academic, governmental, social, and economic developments must occur before such type-models can be formulated. Thus, for instance, shared processes and similar levels of economic, social, and political development, continuity in the evolution of structures, similarity of economic, demographic, world political, and other environmental conditions, and well-patterned, systematic interactions among component sectors of the systems in the type-cell (i.e., cross-system reinforcement of structural similarities) may be found in greater degree in Western Europe than in the Middle East, or sub-Saharan Africa, or the Far East, or Latin America.

The model projected here is presented as a formal (Weberian) ideal type of the European polity. Since appreciable confusion exists in the social sciences regarding the nature of ideal types—particularly as to whether

---

9. See ibid. (in the restricted sense noted—i.e., the polyarchy construct), as well as Lijphart, "Typologies of Democratic Systems," for examples of analytically delimited, workable typologies.

they are wholly, mostly, or hardly removed from empirical referents—at this point it may be useful to recall Weber's classic formulation:

> An ideal type is formed by the one-sided *accentuation* of one or more points of view and by the synthesis of a great many diffuse, discrete, more or less present and occasionally absent *concrete individual* phenomena, which are arranged according to those one-sided emphasized viewpoints into a unified *analytical* construct. In its conceptual purity, this mental construct cannot be found empirically anywhere in reality. It is a *utopia*. Historical research faces the task of determining in each individual case, the extent to which this ideal-construct approximates to or diverges from reality.[10]

While we use the notion of ideal type in the Weberian sense in this paper, we also partake of the mood of the generalized, more comprehensive form of the ideal type set by John C. McKinney. After linking his notion of the constructed type to Weber's ideal-type formulation by suggesting that the latter is a special form of the former, McKinney proceeds to

> define the constructed type as a *purposive, planned selection, abstraction, combination, and (sometimes) accentuation of a set of criteria with empirical referents that serves as a basis for comparison of empirical cases.*[11]

We have, in effect, purposely and in a planned manner, selected, abstracted, combined and (sometimes) accentuated a set of characteristics we have associated with a number of European political systems; and, thus, we have derived a constructed, ideal-type model of the European polity. Inasmuch as McKinney's formulation lends itself to operationalization more readily, in our judgment, than does Weber's, we have chosen to interpret the latter through the former. McKinney stipulated twenty characteristics of constructed types;[12] and the reader is referred to the presentation and subsequent elaboration and discussion of those as a guide to our logical position and our expectations regarding the methodological conditions that are likely to be encountered at the operational (research) phase of the European polity model.

This model should be regarded as one cell in a matrix for the classification of political systems in general; but, cognizant of the difficulties already adumbrated, we attempt neither to sketch the outlines of the whole matrix within which the European polity is located nor to make empirically

10. Max Weber, *The Methodology of the Social Sciences*, trans. and ed. Edward A. Shils and Henry A. Finch (New York: Free Press of Glencoe, 1949), p. 90. Italics in the original.
11. John C. McKinney, *Constructive Typology and Social Theory* (New York: Appleton-Century-Crofts, 1966), p. 3. Italics in the original.
12. Ibid., pp. 5–7.

grounded assertions about the relationship of the system type under discussion to other types of political systems. The scope of this venture is restricted to comparisons within the type delineated. Distinctions between the European polity and systems that diverge markedly from it can be made only in the grossest and most casual terms.[13]

Focusing upon the cell containing the European polity serves two purposes. First, we strive to identify the salient structural features of this type of system and to suggest the manner in which its characteristics interrelate, in order to give form and substance to the processes of politics in such systems. These are the political processes that, when accentuated, distinguish the European polity from other types of political systems. Second, we present some rudimentarily supported judgments regarding the relative proximity to or distance from the model of several concrete political systems; that is, we posit a highly tentative scale of "Europeanness."

From an Anomaly Toward a Model

The dimensions that shape the broader matrix in which the European polity constitutes one cell were not derived inductively. Rather, our point of departure was an implicit general theory of politics—probably currently the most important of its kind—which, when applied in its entirety, we (1) consider highly inappropriate for the explanation (indeed, for the study) of politics in most of Europe; and (2) regard as an impediment to the attainment of the stated purposes and analytic priorities of its author. The theoretical statement in question is embodied in David Easton's *model* of political life.[14]

If Easton's framework is considered solely as a heuristic device or a conceptual tool that, given the theoretical purposes at hand and the particular objects of application, identifies relevant aspects of the political process in abstracto,[15] then using it to relate mid-range theoretical proposi-

---

13. Cf. Lijphart's discussion of the functions of "natural typologies" in his "Typologies of Democratic Systems," p. 7.

14. David Easton, *A Systems Analysis of Political Life* (New York: John Wiley, 1965). See also the criticisms at pp. 13–15 in chap. 1.

15. Easton has characterized the status of concepts as heuristic rather than theoretical components of analytic schema: "Concepts are neither true nor false; they are only more or less useful" (David Easton, *A Framework for Political Analysis* [Englewood Cliffs, N.J.: Prentice-Hall, 1965], p. 33). His first sketch of the political system framework ("An Approach to the Analysis of Political Systems," *World Politics* 9, no. 3 [April 1957]: 383–400) was almost entirely free from "theoretical noise." However, in the course of elaborating the framework into a model (in *Framework for Political Analysis, Systems Analysis of Political Life*, and in portions of *Children in the Political System*), he has progressively grounded it with explicit and implicit references to the concrete universe of politics; and, thus, Easton has increased the likelihood of spurious reification by his readers and the users of his framework. (Cf. Easton's own statement regarding the relationship of empirical referents to the overall framework: "I propose in this book to stand back, quite far compared to what our distance has been in the past, but not so far as to lose all sense of detail. At times, indeed, we may wish to take a very close look but only to

tions to each other may be feasible and conducive to the systematic, cumulative construction of hierarchical theory in comparative politics. If the framework is accorded the status of theory, however—that is, if it is used as a *model of politics in a concrete universe* or if it is taken to be a set of logically interrelated statements with more or less empirical grounding—then some monumental problems are encountered. Two of these are of special importance for students of European politics.

First, a causal assumption of behavior indwells the framework qua model: it is difficult to escape the conclusion that "input-type behavior" (e.g., voting, party and interest-group activity) is the principal source of influences on outputs (i.e., on authoritative decisions, rules and laws).[16] Second, and in part as a corollary of the problem identified in the last sentence, there is a clear assumption of the preeminence of inputs over what Easton has termed "withinputs" in terms of substantive—i.e., policy-influencing, output-determining—importance and volume.[17]

We suggest that the empirical referents that *seem* to underpin Easton's *theoretical* superconstruct have skewed his model in a direction that makes it relatively inefficient for the study of politics in the highly mobilized political societies and structurally massively developed systems that can be found in most of Western and Central Europe (and perhaps, in a few instances, in extra-European settings). In particular, we contend that the behaviors and structures identified in most generalized models of political life[18] with "inputs," especially as they impinge upon outputs of the political

---

illustrate a point here and there" [*Systems Analysis of Political Life*, p. viii].) We contend that the influence of the empirical referents—consciously or otherwise—became more pervasive than Easton might have intended; and the consequences of grounding were rather more comprehensive than illustrative.

16. For a cogent statement of the existence and analytic consequences of this tendency, see Murray Edelman, *Politics as Symbolic Action* (Chicago: Markham, 1971), pp. 3 f., passim.

17. Clearly, Easton has made room for structural inputs and other classes of internal adjustments and responses—including "responses" by the authorities to *anticipated* feedback-induced inputs—a point we discuss below; see Easton, *Systems Analysis of Political Life*, parts 4 and 5, esp. chaps. 27–28. Further, it would be unfair to imply that he assumes a unisequential flow from inputs to outputs in all the concrete universe (cf. ibid., pp. 431 ff.). But, while Easton recognizes the existence of "withinputs"—his term for structurally induced and other intrasystemic inputs—he denies the importance of consistently maintaining their analytic discreteness (*Framework for Political Analysis*, pp. 114–15; *Systems Analysis of Political Life*, pp. 55–56); and generally relegates alternative sequences of flow and the possible cases in which withinputs are the predominant class of inputs to analytically as well as theoretically unimportant and uninteresting positions. This tendency, we suggest, can be attributed to the segment of the universe of real and imaginable political systems from which Easton's referents tend to come.

18. Gabriel A. Almond's general model exhibits a similar skewness toward the input side, making it also less appropriate for the study of European politics. See, in particular, his "Comparative Political Systems," in which a taxonomy of system types is derived with the aid of criteria drawn almost exclusively from the input side. See also Gabriel A. Almond "A Functional Approach to Comparative Politics," in *The Politics of the Developing Areas*, ed. Almond and James S. Coleman (Princeton, N.J.: Princeton University Press, 1960), pp. 3–64; and Gabriel A. Almond, "A Developmental Approach to Political Systems," *World Politics* 17, no. 2 (January

system, have been overemphasized. We suggest, instead, that in systems which approximate closely the European polity model, "withinputs" in general and structurally induced phenomena in particular may be more important influences in determining the contents, timing, form, and intensity of outputs (including the patterns of legitimacy through which the outputs will be presented to the political society) than are environmental inputs.

These comments and modifications should not be taken as criticisms of the Easton framework *as an analytic framework*. Rather, we argue that when that framework is treated as theory, then better or more appropriate theories of politics in a particular type of polity can be generated. This is to be expected, as a concomitant of delimitations of the empirical referents that underlie the generalizations that make up the theory. As empirical bases are narrowed, made more coherent and uniform, they lend themselves to more meaningful, testable, and accurate generalizations— but obviously generalizations of narrower scope.

The framework offered by Easton still serves the very important purposes of (1) identifying, and (2) logically (though, as noted, not causally, sequentially, or empirically) relating the salient processual and structural components of political systems; and, perhaps most important, (3) helping to organize and interrelate verified and hypothetical propositions about politics in other kinds of settings. Put simply, Easton's framework has many important uses for students of politics in general and of comparative politics in particular; but it is not an especially useful or appropriate theory or pretheory of European politics.

The empirical referents that moved us to make these critical observations also constitute the salient dimensions of the European polity model. They can be grouped into three classes of phenomena:

1. the decreasing importance of "input-side" activity in political life, especially as it influences the content and focus of public policy;
2. the growing importance of structural parameters as the major determinants of activity in and orientations toward the authorities and the regime; and
3. the increased political importance of administration in everyday life, with administration viewed broadly, as the processes and structures involved in the implementation of outputs.

1965): 183–214. As noted in chapter 1, the predominance of the input side in the theoretical work of scholars in comparative politics during the 1950s and 1960s accompanied and was probably developmentally related to the growing concern with political life in Asia, Africa, the Middle East, and, to a lesser extent, Latin America. Almond's general model (but not Easton's!) can be traced to such preoccupations.

These are, we believe, the salient patterns of politics in Europe.[19] Phenomena classed under these rubrics have been observed for some time. (We cite some of these observations and take into account their theoretical products forthwith.) It is our aim to juxtapose the phenomena in question in a particular manner, and, eventually, to use their cumulative import to explain European politics. Clearly, such explanations must await the generation or collation and analysis of data. Our immediate aim is the positing of a special pretheory of European politics, from which operationalized hypotheses can be distilled.

Relying almost entirely on existing mid-range theories as our building blocks and on general Eastonian concepts as our blueprint, we argue that these three dimensions allow the generation of a model through which a broader range of systems—and, incidentally, political life in a larger number of societies—can be studied than through such sound but unnecessarily narrow mid-range theories as those posited recently in Lijphart's "consociational democracy" model and Lorwin's "segmented pluralism" construct.

The European Polity Model

The three patterns noted above combine to characterize a particular type of political system, the European polity. The sections that follow elaborate these patterns and illustrate the manifestations of such phenomena in actual political systems. Subsequently, we note some of the linkages between each class of political behavior and structures, in order to depict the dynamic nature of the ideal-type European polity.

Each of the type's characteristics differentiates it from other kinds of political systems. As the list of attributes grows, the European polity's distance from other kinds of systems increases. Thus, for instance, while

19. As noted elsewhere, "Europe" need not refer exclusively to political milieus found on the European continent; nor must it encompass all things political that occur in Europe. Rather, the term here is intended to denote *a type of political life*, most manifestations of which will *probably* be found in European settings. For some purposes of political analysis, however, Israel, Lebanon, or even Japan, Canada, or Uruguay may be treated as "European" (cf. Lijphart, "Consociational Democracy"; Lehmbruch, "A Non-competitive Pattern of Conflict Management"; and note that Lorwin, "Segmented Pluralism," excludes Lebanon from consideration with a superficial and hardly tenable "classification": it is not a "modern democracy"). Conversely, some countries that are geographically and historically parts of Europe deviate sharply from the type in one or more important respects (e.g., Spain, Portugal, Albania) and should be excluded. Here we are mainly interested in highlighting those theoretically salient and empirically (eventually) verifiable patterns of process and structure characteristic of politics in most European countries and most nearly approached by actual European political relationships. Thus, the type serves heuristic purposes, but, we aver, it transcends the heuristic level and has genuine theoretical justification. *In order to maximize the analytic and explanatory potential of our model we have refrained from lessening its sharp outlines rather than extend its coverage to include such important European countries as France, West Germany, and the United Kingdom.*

many systems may share with the European polity one or more of the first four characteristics (A through D) elaborated below, in terms of our model only European polities exhibit *all* the traits (A through Q). Further, *it is the interplay of all the traits, rather than a mere inventory of them, that depicts the essence of the system type.*

The Decreasing Significance of the Input Side of the System in the European Polity

In comparison with other types of political systems, European polities exhibit

A. *very high levels of social and political mobilization, economic development, and political development or efficiency.*[20] *As a concomitant of the very high levels of mobilization, citizen participation—measured in terms of electoral participation, associations of citizens for political ends, and similar indicators*[21]*—tends to be quite high, but*

B. *in substantive terms and in its consequences on the generation of outputs, such participation tends to be indirect in the European polity. Inputs, in the traditional Eastonian sense, do not translate directly into the outputs of the political system. The relationship of inputs to outputs is far more complex.*

It is essential to distinguish among several distinct consequences of participation. Minimally, three can be identified in European polities, not as mutually exclusive categories, but rather as overlapping, with differing degrees of salience:[22]

20. These characteristics are demonstrable: structured social and political activity can be measured; economic development can be ascertained with the aid of data on outputs, sectoral and actual per capita distributions, levels of productivity, and the like; some indications of political efficacy (used here as a measure of political development) can be obtained through policy "impact" or system performance measures of the kind utilized by B. Guy Peters in chapter 7 in this volume. The term "efficiency" is used here to connote delivery of values, goods, and services. For a broader framework for the measurement of political efficiency in the sense in which the notion is used in this essay, see Karl de Schweinitz, Jr., "On Measuring Political Performance," *Comparative Political Studies* 2, no. 4 (January 1970): 503–11; Harry Eckstein, *The Evaluation of Political Performance* (Beverly Hills, Calif.: Sage Professional Papers in Comparative Politics, 2 [1971]), 65 f., passim; and the work of Mancur Olson, Jr., especially his *The Logic of Collective Action* (Cambridge, Mass.: Harvard University Press, 1965). See also B. Guy Peters, "The Development of Social Policy: A Longitudinal Analysis of Social Expenditures and Their Impacts in the United Kingdom, France and Sweden," (Ph.D. dissertation, Michigan State University, 1970).

21. See, for example, Stein Rokkan, *Citizens, Elections, Parties: Approaches to the Comparative Study of the Processes of Development* (New York: David McKay, 1970), esp. chap. 1.

22. This tripartition of the "motives" of political participation parallels the tripartite classification of political opinion by M. Brewster Smith, Jerome Bruner, and Robert White, *Opinions and Personality* (New York: John Wiley, 1956), p. 41. Cf. the distinctions of different types of participation made by Ulf Himmelstrand, "Depoliticization and Political Involve-

B_1.   *participation that is principally instrumental—i.e., directed toward obtaining specific outputs from the decision-making subsystem through the articulation and conveying of specific demands and/or through the manipulation of specific supports;*

B_2.   *participation that is more affective and/or existential than it is instrumental—i.e., people participate in order to express themselves and perhaps indirectly influence the authorities, but participation is not a direct component of the decision-making process; and*

B_3.   *participation that leads to adjustments—within the confines of rigid structural parameters (to be discussed below)—in the roles and/or role incumbencies constituting the decision-making subsystem.*

Participation that is principally instrumental (B_1) is far less prevalent in Western Europe today than it was several decades ago. Nor is it likely to manifest a strong resurgence, given the changing nature of mass participation, parties, and social structure. As students of European politics have pointed out, a consensus concerning goals is developing among the electorate and leadership.[23] The issues of economic equality and rights of social classes are no longer presented in contradictory ideological frameworks but are discussed in the practical terms of implementation. Parties, in turn, represent differences of degree rather than differences of kind, thereby reflecting the changing character of the electorate and at the same time minimizing the policy significance of electoral results.

Our point here is not, by any means, that "ideology is dead" as a political factor in Western Europe. As we shall have occasion to note, below, there are, in fact, signs of a reemergence of ideological divisions in these societies.[24] But certain input-generating and shaping consequences of

---

ment: A Theoretical and Empirical Approach," in *Mass Politics: Studies in Political Sociology*, ed. Erik Allardt and Stein Rokkan (New York: Free Press, 1970), chap. 3. See also the distinction made by Lester W. Milbrath, *Political Participation* (Chicago: Rand McNally, 1965), pp. 12–14, passim. The tripartite analysis of participation was first presented in M. O. Heisler, "Toward a Comparative Politics Model for the Study of Foreign Policy Formulation Structures" (Paper presented at the 1969 Annual Meeting of the International Studies Association, San Francisco, March 1969). Our point in making these distinctions among different qualities of participation is essentially the same as that made by these authors.

23. See, for instance, Ulf Torgersen, "The Trend Towards Political Consensus: The Case of Norway," in Allardt and Rokkan, *Mass Politics*, chap. 2.

24. Strong support for our assertion that affective and/or existential purposes are salient in participation in this type of polity can be found in Ronald Inglehart, "The Silent Revolution in Europe: Intergenerational Change in Post-Industrial Societies," *American Political Science Review* 65, no. 4 (December 1971): 991–1017. It and such other analyses of emergent ideological divisions in Europe—based on large-scale cross-country survey data—as Paul R. Abramson, "Social Class and Political Change in Western Europe: A Cross-National Longitudinal Analysis," *Comparative Political Studies* 4, no. 2 (July 1971): 131–55, have bearing on our model. First, they lend appreciable support to the argument that "traditional" socioeconomic class-based ideology has declined. Second, they point to the likely source of new ideological divisions in these countries. We return to the second point toward the end of this chapter.

socioeconomic ideologies have become less important as those ideologies lost some of their issue-defining significance.

Affective or existential participation (B_2) varies within and between European systems. But, in general, the behavior it represents does not have much practical effect on the substance of political outputs. As Ulf Himmelstrand has suggested, "rituals of intensification" (affective or existential participation) by supporters of Sweden's bourgeois parties—important at election time as mechanisms of unity—have little consequence for the day-to-day politics in the interim between elections.[25]

Participation that leads to adjustments in the roles and/or role incumbencies of the decision-making subsystem (B_3) is of little consequence in the shifting of personnel. Elites are usually of one mind in terms of goals, and a replacement of one man by another has the effect of replacing one technician with another.[26] Moreover, as we shall show in more detail shortly, the structural parameters constituting the decision-making system and the nature of the decisions to be made leave little room for innovation by whoever is selected to fill the position.[27]

During the last two decades these and related characteristics of participation in modernized societies have been the subjects of a vigorous, if sometimes less than stimulating, controversy among social scientists: has there or has there not been a "decline of ideology" in the West?[28] Since virtually every writer who has treated the question, or, indeed, merely used the phrase, has provided a formulation that differs in some degree from all others, it is difficult to formulate a synthesizing summary statement of the "decline" hypothesis that is at once cogent and representative. An excellent distillation of the essential features of the affirmative case can be found in a recent essay by Mostafa Rejai:

---

25. Himmelstrand, "Depoliticization and Political Involvement."

26. Egil Fivelsdal and John Higley, "The Labor Union Elite in Norway," *Scandinavian Political Studies*, vol. 5, ed. Olof Ruin (Oslo: Universitetsforlaget, 1970), pp. 165–208.

27. For a discussion of selection procedure, see Kvavik's paper on Norway, chap. 3 in this volume.

28. For a comprehensive bibliography on the phenomenon and on the controversy surrounding it, see M. Rejai, ed., *Decline of Ideology?* (Chicago and New York: Aldine/Atherton, 1971), pp. 317–22. In addition to the items listed there, the reader is directed to Daniel Bell, *The End of Ideology* (rev. ed; New York: Free Press, 1965); Himmelstrand, "Depoliticization and Political Involvement"; and Georges Vedel, ed., *La dépolitisation: Mythe ou réalité?* (Paris: Librairie Armand Colin, 1962). Note that the evidence supporting the decline-of-ideology hypothesis extends to elites. That is, while most of the supporting material deals with mass political phenomena, substantial evidence indicates that "European elites have turned from ideology to pragmatism, from nationalism to transnationalism, from parochialism to pluralism" (Daniel Lerner and Morton Gorden, *Euratlantica: Changing Perspectives of the European Elites* [Cambridge, Mass.: MIT Press, 1969], p. 5). This development (i.e., a decline in the saliency of ideology among European elites) is particularly important for the "cartel of elites" and cooptive policy-making structure elements of our model. It serves as a partial explanation of why it was possible for such structures of policy and decision making to come into being in certain systems.

The decline of ideology hypothesis refers to either one of two proposi-tions: (1) a relative modulation over the last two decades of the ultimacy with which ideological goals are stated, or (2) a relative attenuation of the emotive intensity with which ideological goals are pursued. . . . The hypothesis does not suggest the total disappearance of ideologies. The notion of an "end" of ideology is simply a euphemism. What the hypothesis does convey is an ending of "apocalyptic," "total," or "ex-tremist" ideologies—that is to say, a decline of ideology. . . . There is no question that the decline writers consider ideology a permanent factor in human affairs.

The hypothesis of ideological decline is stated within certain explicit limits: specifically, it is both time-bound and space-bound. The hypothesis is time-bound in that it embraces ideological politics in the postwar period only. It is space-bound in that it applies primarily to advanced, industrial, Western societies. . . .

The most important [changes in societies manifesting a decline of ideology] revolve around economic development and its attendant conse-quences: an increasing general affluence; an increasing reliance on science and expertise; and increasing attenuation of class and party conflict; a gradual attainment of political and economic citizenship by the lower classes; a gradual emergence of a vast, homogeneous, professional-mana-gerial middle class; a gradual transformation of laissez-faire capitalism into the welfare state; and *a gradual institutionalization of stable political processes for resolution of political issues.*[29]

Himmelstrand, referring to this phenomenon, stated that society has changed to such a degree that a national consensus on goals emerges and is transformed, in turn, into a set of administrative technologies, to be imple-mented by a managerial elite.[30]

In summary, direct mass participation of the instrumental type (B_1) does not crystallize into distinct policy positions on a regular, patterned basis. To the degree that such activity does not provide structurally differentiated inputs into the decision-making subsystem,

C. *European polities manifest such a "decline of ideology"—on the input side.*[31]

29. "Political Ideology: Theoretical and Comparative Perspectives," in Rejai, *Decline of Ideology?*, pp. 18–19. Italics added.

30. Himmelstrand, "Depoliticization and Political Involvement," p. 65.

31. We note, below, some indications of the "repoliticization" of the output side of the system in the European polity. Cf. the argument against the "decline of ideology" hypothesis by Dahl, suggesting that new ideological divisions may be created by dissatisfied (and satisfied) clients of the technocratic regimes that are emerging in the very systems in which the "de-cline" phenomenon has been most noticeable. See Robert A. Dahl, ed., *Political Oppositions in Western Democracies* (New Haven and London: Yale University Press, 1966, p. 400.) See also the discussion by Rejai, *Decline of Ideology?*, pp. 21 ff.

Related to, and in part derived from factors A, B, and C,

D. *a degression of the relative institutional roles of parliaments is evident in European polities.*[32]

Taken together, these four characteristics (A through D) denote the distinctive change on the "input side" of the political system we noted above. They do not, however, provide a new basis for distinguishing a particular type of polity; for these conditions—in some form and in some degree—are noticeable in most "Western industrialized societies," or in polities classifiable through some similar gross criteria already in evidence. In itself, the observation of a lesser saliency of input-side activity is akin to the universal proposition that "In some systems it is more important, and in others it is less important."

Structural Parameters: Access, Decision Making, and Output Legitimation through Widespread Cooptation

The first pattern allows little more than the grouping of European polities in one segment of a particular (universalistic) continuum; but the two remaining patterns help to delineate the type more sharply.

The shifts in input-side activity in European polities have been accompanied by the development of

E. *highly articulated pluralistic structures, representing multifarious political, social, and economic cleavages of comparatively high intensity and thorough politicization.*

Viewed as a whole, these structures approach

F. *a scheme of sectoral representation akin to neocorporatism, or perhaps more accurately, corporate pluralism.*[33]

The increased saliency of such "corporatist politics" is, of course, linked with the decline in the importance of the more traditional channels

32. Much has been written over the past ten to fifteen years about the degression of the influence of parliaments vis-à-vis other branches of government—and perhaps even in absolute terms. While this literature contains varying appraisals and prognoses, there seems to be no noticeable contradiction of the pattern. See Alfred Grosser, "The Evolution of European Parliaments," in *A New Europe?*, ed. Stephen R. Graubard (Boston: Beacon Press, 1967), pp. 236, 242–43, and 219–43, passim; and Karl Dietrich Bracher, "Problems of Parliamentary Democracy in Europe," in ibid., pp. 245–64. See also Gerhard Loewenberg, ed., *Modern Parliaments: Change or Decline?* (Chicago and New York: Aldine/Atherton, 1971); and Kornberg, *Legislatures in Comparative Perspective.*

33. Cf. Stein Rokkan, "Norway: Numerical Democracy and Corporate Pluralism," in Dahl, *Political Oppositions in Western Democracies*, chap. 3, esp. pp. 105 ff.

for political activity. As Karl Dietrich Bracher has observed, "Beyond all national differences [in Europe], two main tendencies are discernible: the growing importance of pressure groups, tending even to a *Verbände-Staat* [corporate state]; at the same time, the decline of ideological parties."[34]

Within this system, spokesmen of voluntary associations, religious denomination-based groups, agencies of socioeconomic representation, governmental bodies, mixed or quasi-governmental agencies, and expressly political entities (such as parties) participate in the decision-making process on a continuing basis. Access is established and structured. The consequent decision-making structure has been described by Lijphart as

G.   a "cartel of elites."

The phrase "cartel of elites" was first used by Ralf Dahrendorf, to describe a condition (in Germany) in which

> . . . elites behave as if they had agreed to cease from all initiative, to distribute social power according to a certain rule and not to dispute this rule. The "cartel" in this social-political sense is a conceptual implication, not a real institution, nor is its background necessarily the same as that of economic cartels.[35]

Dahrendorf then proceeded to elaborate the concept in a direction which may, in some ways, be closer to the formulation we utilize than is the construct developed by Lijphart. For, as Dahrendorf saw it,

> . . . political multiformity does not become effective by means of a competition of interests and persons; instead elites of divergent interests combine in what we described as the cartel of anxiety. Each interest seeks security and protection for the position it has already acquired, and together they rob political conflict of its dynamics.[36]

Dahrendorf's fascinating application of this formulation to the Federal Republic has a twofold relevance for the European polity. First, this pattern of elite behavior is operative in the European polity: faceless and self-effacing groups of leaders—who shun the status of leader—are authorities without visible authority; there exists, in a sense, a "headless authoritarianism," according to Dahrendorf. Second, there is a growing dissatisfaction with this pattern by those who do not regard all forms of political conflict as undesirable—and, who, for diverse reasons, would prefer to reintroduce a modicum of political conflict in the form of challenges to the prev-

34. "Problems of Parliamentary Democracy in Europe," p. 264.
35. Ralf Dahrendorf, *Society and Democracy in Germany* (Garden City, N.Y.: Doubleday, 1967), p. 269.
36. Ibid., pp. 277–78.

alent regime norms. We note this phenomenon in our comments on the emergence of a new ideological cleavage in some countries that approximate the European polity model.[37]

Factors E, F, and G are the central features of Lijphart's "consociational democracy" model and they also characterize (to be sure, somewhat less comprehensively) Lehmbruch's "non-competitive pattern" and Lorwin's "segmented pluralism" constructs. They characterize a type of system that coheres in spite of the centrifugal tendencies[38] that deep-cutting cleavages in the society induce. This in large part reflects the efforts of the government, in effect an elite cartel, the members of which consciously strive to transcend the polity's major cleavages. Elites can succeed in overcoming fissiparous tendencies found in societies with fragmented political cultures if the politically salient divisions of the society are vertically structured, and if the divisions (or pluralistic structures) are led by persons who agree among themselves—tacitly or explicitly—that the persistence of the larger system might be jeopardized, should any of the sectoral interests be pushed to "victory at any price."[39]

The cartel of elites operates in the manner depicted only when it has an effective monopoly in cross-segmental communication. At the heart of the consociational democracy and segmented pluralism models is the dual assumption that (1) political or politicized social cleavages fragment the society, and that (2) the cleavage-demarcated subsocietal groups are structured vertically (from members to leaders, i.e., from followers to the sector's elite), so that aggregation and (both upward and downward) communication can occur within the sector. (A further assumption of the consociational democracy model, of course, is that communication at the cross-sectoral level is likely to be restricted—for politically important purposes, at any rate—to the various sectors' elites. This last characteristic of the pluralistic infrastructures of consociational democracies, segmented pluralist systems, *and European polities* entails an encapsulation of sectors or segments, so that different interpretations of interests or conflicting goals or cultural antipathies militate against systematic communication among members of two or more segments, except at the leadership level.)

In Norway and Sweden, the vertical structuring within sectors is demonstrated by the linkages between interest groups in specific economic

37. For Lijphart's formulation of the concept of "cartel of elites" see his "Consociational Democracy." See also Lorwin, "Segmented Pluralism," p. 158; and Lehmbruch, passim.

38. Lijphart categorizes "fragmented and unstable" democracies without the consociational mechanism as "centrifugal," and cites the Third and Fourth French Republics, Italy, the Weimar Republic in Germany, the First Austrian Republic, and the Spanish Republic as illustrations. He associates ideological cleavages among the masses with immobilism. See Lijphart, "Consociational Democracy," pp. 222–23.

39. The concept of "persistence" is used in its formal Eastonian sense here. The viability of the system at its most extensive—i.e., community—level may be brought into question if secession or civil war are possible consequences of the breakdown of the consociational structure.

sectors. All groups within farming, for example, perform a specific task—economic, cultural, etc.—for the sector. At the top of the sector is a peak organization which coordinates the activities of the functionally more specific units below. Accordingly, one has a structuring of individuals who work in the farm sector, as well as of the organizations. Membership by individuals is generally limited to organizations within the economic sector. If horizontal or cross-cutting relationships develop, it is between the elites of each sector. Membership patterns are cumulative—to use LaPalombara's term—and serve to intensify the vertical structuring of the system.

While this also holds for the Netherlands, in lesser degree, the Dutch, Belgian, and Austrian systems are probably more accurately characterized as possessing vertical structures that developed (historically) in terms of ideological, denominational, and, in the case of Belgium, most recently, "linguistic" or ethnic cleavages, rather than economic sectors (although the latter played varying roles in each case, as well). Perhaps the most appropriate concept in terms of which the vertical encapsulation and structuring can be thought of in these three systems is *verzuiling* ("pillarization").[40]

Regardless of whether the economic sectoral or the "pillarization" perspective is taken, the structural consequences remain essentially similar: encapsulation of activity and orientation through the role-structuring effects of horizontal division and vertical ordering shapes the attitudes and interrelationships of the population. The structural outcomes of the two types of processes have the same impact on the polity.

Two additional conditions are needed if the cartel of elites is to succeed in countervailing the centrifugal impetus imparted by political cultural fragmentation. First, there should be agreement among the elites that the resolution of problems of systemic scope be pursued at the cross-sectoral elite level, by transcending cleavages, even if that is feasible only in an ad hoc manner.

(By qualifying the scope of the problems in question, we seek to distinguish the level at which the "cartel" structure is operative. The threshold will become more evident once the nature and operation of the structure have been depicted, in the pages that follow. In general, the purpose of calling attention to this level is analogous to Easton's intent in qualifying his conceptual definition of politics as "the authoritative allocation of values *for a society*": the decision-making structure with which we are concerned in this model may or may not influence political life at all subordinate levels. The type we seek to delineate is established at the level of the whole system.)

Second, a horizontal, cross-sectoral leadership structure—as inclusive

40. For a discussion of the concept, see Lorwin, "Segmented Pluralism," pp. 142 ff.; among other important Dutch works on this phenomenon, see J.P. Kruijt and W. Goddijn, "Verzuiling en ontzuiling als sociologisch process," in *Drift en Koers*, ed. A.N.J. Den Hollander (2nd ed.; Assen, 1962) pp. 227–63; and Hans Daalder, "The Netherlands," in Dahl, *Political Oppositions in Western Democracies*, chap. 6.

as possible but, ideally, much wider than necessary to sustain the bases of specific support—must be established and sustained.[41]

Such a decision-making structure serves to mitigate the stress-producing effects of cleavages and simultaneously manages to help the regime escape—or at least minimize—tendencies toward *immobilism*.[42] When successful, it keeps the contending actors from locking themselves into a bargaining arena that—in terms of their perceptions, at any rate—resembles a zero-sum confrontation. It converts decisions into a mold in which an incremental-satisficing calculus dominates.

In its simplest terms, the social-psychological condition of perceiving the bargaining context as a zero-sum relationship consists of the assumption that gains registered by any actor must have come at the commensurate expense of one or more of the other actors in the system.[43] The most direct escape route from such a condition (regardless of whether it is perceptual or objective) is through maximizing common advantages or benefits: consociational decision making seeks to raise the common denominator among the competing actors.[44] Participants in such a system are seen as "sharers" rather than as "winners" or "losers."

While in the past system-type characteristics E, F, and G have been identified in the Netherlands, Belgium, Luxembourg, Switzerland, Austria, and Lebanon,[45] we submit that they are also relevant for the analysis and

41. See Lorwin, "Segmented Pluralism," p. 158; Daalder, "The Netherlands," pp. 188–236; Lehmbruch, "Non-competitive Pattern of Conflict Management" and Lijphart, "Consociational Democracy." On this point, Lijphart cites Claude Ake, *A Theory of Political Integration* (Homewood, Ill.: Dorsey Press, 1967), p. 113; his own treatise, *The Politics of Accommodation: Pluralism and Democracy in the Netherlands* (Berkeley and Los Angeles: University of California Press, 1968), pp. 1–15, 197–211; Frederick C. Engelmann, "Haggling for the Equilibrium: The Renegotiation of the Austrian Coalition, 1959," *American Political Science Review* 56, no. 3 (September 1962): 651–52; and Val R. Lorwin, "Constitutionalism and Controlled Violence in the Modern State: The Case of Belgium" (Paper presented at the Annual Meeting of the American Historical Association, San Francisco, 1965).

42. Lijphart, "Consociational Democracy," p. 212. Cf. Lorwin, "Segmented Pluralism," pp. 158–59. See also Heisler's paper on Belgium, chap. 5 in this volume.

43. Lijphart distorts somewhat the notion of the zero-sum game condition when he stipulates that it obtains only in "societies with completely homogeneous political cultures and . . . societies with completely fragmented political cultures" ("Consociational Democracy," p. 215). In social relationships (of which political relationships are a subset) the zero-sum condition can never obtain fully in actual practice—in fact, it is rarely approached. Rather than being an actual contextual condition of bargaining, it is more appropriately thought of as a set of perceptions which leads to assumptions about the bases of distribution of scarce values or commodities. On the syndrome as a concomitant of political or politicized social cleavages, see M. O. Heisler, "Political Community and Its Formation in the Low Countries," (Ph.D. dissertation, University of California [Los Angeles], 1969), pp. 288–312; and idem, *The Low Countries* (Englewood Cliffs, N.J.: Prentice-Hall, forthcoming), chap. 6, passim. Associated with the social-psychological (i.e., perceptual-behavioral linkage) phenomenon of the zero-sum game syndrome is the notion of "*Lager* psychosis" used by Rodney Stiefbold in his essay on Austria, chap. 4 in this volume.

44. See, for instance, Lijphart, "Consociational Democracy," passim.

45. Note that the three writers upon whose theoretical contributions we seek to build have treated these six countries in an overlapping fashion. Thus, Lorwin ("Segmented Pluralism") was concerned with Austria, Belgium, Luxembourg, the Netherlands, and Switzerland;

explanation of the essential character of political life in Scandinavia. To be sure, in the six systems listed above, the fundamental dimensions of cleavage can be traced to social, cultural, and denominational sources as well as economic structuring; while in Scandinavia there is markedly less cultural heterogeneity, and many of the important divisions found there are more distinctly economic in origin. Our reasons for focusing on the structural manifestations of segmentation rather than on its underlying culture-bases are discussed at length below as well as in the preceding chapter. For the moment, it should suffice to note that the structural phenomena discernible in Norway, Sweden, and Denmark are very similar to those observed in the Low Countries, Switzerland, Austria, and Lebanon.

In the Scandinavian polities we find economic sectors—e.g., labor, employers, farming, fishing, shipping—that are highly organized and enjoy substantial self-government. Within each sector, a centralized and bureaucratized network of interest groups serves as the principal means for the advancement and coordination of sector interests. Most groups are in a position to develop and implement policy in many or most of the issue areas that have the greatest importance for them. The institutionalization and coordination of the resulting quasi-corporate arrangements occur within a network of more than one thousand committees that are attached to the governmental administrations. Such committees regulate the activities of the interest groups on the cross-sectoral level. They imbue with legitimacy the quasi-public activities of interest groups that have been coopted into the committee systems, while providing a decision-making arena suitable for the accommodation of highly organized and effective interest groups. In Norway, for instance, a functionally established elite, recruited from interest groups and the governmental administration, is responsible for the formulation and implementation of a great deal of policy.[46]

The European polity also exhibits characteristics E, F, and G. The major differences in this regard between the actual consociational democracies and Scandinavian systems on the one hand and the European polity model on the other occur in the development of the decision-making structures, the degree of the formalization of those structures, and, to a lesser extent, in their primary functions and styles of operation. That is, the differences are noticeable more in the explanations of how and why the structures in the models came about than in their observable features and consequences. Historical, social, and socioeconomic explanations (such as those offered by Lijphart and Lorwin) of the advent of the "cartel of elites"

Lijphart ("Consociational Democracy,") dealt with those five countries and Lebanon; while Lehmbruch's attention was occupied by Switzerland, Austria, and Lebanon. Not only do the empirical referents overlap; but, as we have sought to show, so do the theoretical frames of reference.

46. For a detailed discussion of the Norwegian phenomena, see Robert B. Kvavik, "Interest Groups in Norway: A Study of Corporate Pluralism" (Ph.D. dissertation, Stanford University, 1970).

and similar decision-making structures are not central to our concerns, however; nor do we wish to stress the main function (assigned it by Lijphart) of cleavage amelioration. Rather, we would emphasize as a characteristic of the European polity, a common denominator of all the polities noted above:

H.   *a decision-making structure characterized by continuous, regularized access for economically, politically, ethnically, and/or subculturally based groups to the highest levels of the political system—i.e., the decision-making subsystem.*

Access for group actors is regularized, established in the European polity; and *such access takes a structured form.*[47]

This pattern, essentially one of *cooptation*, is not new to European politics. As early as the middle 1800s, interest groups were coopted into administrative commissions in Norway mainly for their technical expertise, but also to bind them to public decisions in advance of their implementation.[48] These committees have continued to function throughout the last 120 years. The real expansion of the committee network and the cooptation of most societal groups occurred with the emergence of the Labor government in the 1930s. One could argue that the early experience with cooptation provides an important and supportive precedent for modern arrangements, especially in polities where economic liberalism did not completely undermine the guild system and its corporate privileges.

47. Our meanings for "structure" have varied across a narrow but perceptible range in the last few paragraphs. Our general meaning follows Levy's usage: "The term *structure* as used here means a pattern, i.e., an observable uniformity of action or operation. The general form of this concept is deliberately left in to cover a wide range of possibilities from highly stable uniformities to highly fleeting ones" (Marion J. Levy, *The Structure of Society* [Princeton, N.J.: Princeton University Press, 1952], p. 57).

Fred W. Riggs provides an elaboration of this concept in which the crucial relationship between the general notion of structure and its special form "institution" is presented with lucidity and simplicity: ". . . structures tend to survive despite changes in their functions. . . . A well-established structure becomes entrenched or enculturated. It is then reinforced by the attitudes and norms of those directly involved. When a structure becomes thus entrenched we speak of it as an *institution.* Thus institutionalization involves the relatively permanent or persistent establishment of a structure, or of a set of interrelated structures" ("Systems Theory: Structural Analysis," in *Approaches to the Study of Political Science,* ed. Michael Haas and Henry S. Kariel [Scranton, Pa.: Chandler, 1970], p. 214.)

At a later point in our discussion, we utilize the more commonplace, role-theory-derived meaning of "structures," especially in describing the impact of output and output-implementation saliency in shaping the role-perceptions (and role-structures) and behaviors of members of countries that closely approximate the European polity model. See also Kvavik's essay on Norway, chap. 3 in this volume, on "structured access."

48. A historical perspective of the cooptation of Norwegian interest groups is demonstrated by W. Haffner, who has compiled a list of all committees and their participants—especially the early committees. See W. Haffner, *Innstillinger og Betenkninger* (Oslo, 1936). There is also a discussion of the development of the committee system and group participation in Jorolv Moren, *Organisasjonene og Forvaltningen,* Skrifter fra Norges Handelshøyskole i rekken almene emner Nr. 3 (Bergen: Garnæs Boktrykkeri, 1958).

Lars Foyer outlines the various cooptive forms that have developed in Sweden. Most notable is the committee system which incorporates all "private" sectors, the administration, and the government.[49] Mention is also made of the *remiss* system—now used in Norway as well. A *remiss* is a response made by a societal agency such as an interest group to a piece of pending legislation affecting the group. A *remiss* is routinely requested by the administration or a committee of all groups that could possibly have any interest in the issue. *The practice, in effect, incorporates all organizations into the decision-making process.*[50]

A less formalized but equally important form of cooptation brings together the leadership of voluntary associations and members of the government at periodic intervals. Under the Swedish Social Democratic government of Tage Erlander, the arrangement came to be called *Harpsund Demokrati*—after the locale where the meetings took place. In Norway, organizations such as *Norges Industriforbund* have cosponsored lunches with the government at regular biweekly intervals for similar purposes.

Most European countries have had some experience with cooptive arrangements of the sort outlined for Norway and Sweden. Variations occur on the level, the extent, and formalization of cooptation. Familiar examples of coordination at a top level include France's *Conseil Économique et Social*, the Netherlands' *Sociaal Economische Raad*, Weimar Germany's *Reichswirtschaftsrat*, and Norway's *Økonomiske Samordningsråd*.

Cooptation occurs both within and across sectors. In Norway both forms are in evidence. After the establishment of minimum and maximum prices for all farm products—essentially a cross-sectoral issue with representatives of farming, labor, government—the implementation of the details devolves upon a "private" organization, *Landbruketssentralforbund*. In the style and consequences of the latter's implementation of price policy, it becomes difficult to tell whether one is viewing a "private" or "public" institution. Similar arrangements exist for the labor market, fishing, etc.

The following observations regarding the Swiss and Danish systems have general applicability to the systems that closely approach the European polity type:

In Switzerland . . . one can speak of a corporatist society. Economic and social organizations are charged with public tasks and, thus, permitted to

---

49. Lars Foyer, "Former för Kontakt och Samverkan Mellan Staten og Organisationerna," *Statens Offentliga Utredningar 1961:21* (Stockholm, 1961). See also Hans Meijer, "Bureaucracy and Policy Formulation in Sweden," *Scandinavian Political Studies*, vol. 4, ed. Olof Ruin (Oslo: Universitetsforlaget, 1969), pp. 103–16. Meijer gives a good overview of the Swedish committee system.

50. Foyer, "Former för Kontakt." See also Nils Elvander, *Interesseorganisationer i Dagens Sverige* (Lund: CWK Gleerup Bokförlag, 1966).

exercise their influence. Above all, they are very active in the preparation of all kinds of legislation. Among other things, they are well represented in the expert commissions. These commissions usually resemble miniature parliaments of interest groups; they include academic and administrative experts as a mere appendage. . . . According to the federal constitution, the interest groups must be "heard" in the course of legislative proceedings—but then, to be heard, also means to influence the general direction of a bill.[51]

In Denmark we find interest groups performing a similar role; we can discover a committee system that incorporates the groups on both the cross-sectoral and the intrasectoral levels. According to Miller,

. . . interest organizations play an important role in Danish public administration. "The groups are quasi-public bodies responsible for various administrative tasks and rule-making functions. They constitute, therefore, a branch of state administration."[52]

Such entities retain many or most of their characteristics as private actors in the polity. The sense in which they have come to constitute a "branch of state administration" is that they have been coopted: they do some of the work of public administration and policy formulation, while possessing only a modicum of the political system's authority; and yet, by playing such a role, *they have become responsible* to an extent that is comparable to (formal) state agencies.[53] This interesting and important development began in the first and second decades of the present century, so that, by the 1930s,

. . . traditional administrative techniques often seemed inadequate to cope with the vast number of detailed executive and supervisory functions which governments were now expected to discharge, and the governments not infrequently sought in desperation to devolve some of their new burdens upon private bodies in various fields while retaining, at least in theory, the general functions of policy determination and oversight.[54]

51. Hans Huber, "Swiss Democracy," in *Democracy in a Changing Society*, ed. Henry W. Ehrmann (New York: Frederick A. Praeger, 1964), p. 106.

52. Kenneth E. Miller, *Government and Politics in Denmark* (Boston: Houghton Mifflin, 1968), p. 169. Miller attributes the quote within the quote to William E. Laux, *Interest Groups in Danish Politics* (Ann Arbor, Mich.: University Microfilms, 1963), p. 297.

53. In Norway, the "public" vs. "private" distinction has been blurred even more through changes in roles and the institutionalization of groups into the committee network. Denmark, the Netherlands and other polities that closely resemble the European polity model adhere somewhat more to notions of economic liberalism, which militate in favor of the (greater or lesser) retention of such distinctions.

54. Ralph H. Bowen, *German Theories of the Corporative State* (New York: McGraw-Hill, 1947), p. 4.

An interesting variant of the phenomenon is offered by Knut Dahl Jacobsen. Studying the relationships of the Norwegian farm administration with the private farm organizations, he discovered that *the government initiated the formation of private organizations to perform public tasks.*[55]

We consider this "cooptive" policy- and decision-making structure to be one of the salient features of the European polity model.[56] From the analyst's vantage point, it is critical to understanding how the political system operates and why it works as it does. From the perspective of practical politics as well as of analysis, it provides a rudimentary introduction to the "rules of the game" of politics in the European polity.[57]

In pluralistic societies (disregarding for the moment the relative intensity and nature of the divisions) the legitimation of outputs is complicated by the likelihood that some sectors will be dissatisfied with particular decisions that satisfy others. Two alternative means have been suggested for overcoming the difficulties of gaining broad-based acceptance of, and generating diffuse support through, outputs in democratic pluralistic societies. (This paper assumes throughout that we are dealing with what can be classified in gross terms as "democratic regimes." The literary and empirical referents upon which our model is constructed clearly militate in favor of such an assumption. Further, we think it is no longer necessary to stipulate with specificity the meaning of "democratic" as a qualifier of regime type, although the danger of arbitrariness in making unsupported assignments of

55. Knut Dahl Jacobsen, *Teknisk Hjelp og Politisk Struktur* (Oslo: Universitetsforlaget, 1963).

56. Easton's conceptual lexicon contains two associated meanings for the term "policy." The first is a synonym for decision or output. The second "is . . . used in a . . . broader sense to describe the more general intentions of the authorities of which any specific binding output might be a partial expression. As such, the statements of policies are not binding for the members. But by revealing the intentions of the authorities, they do help to interpret the meaning and direction of authoritative outputs and to this extent may encourage or discourage their acceptance by the membership" (*Systems Analysis of Political Life*, p. 358).

The policy-making structure can be distinguished from the decision-making structure, in that the former houses the activities of *advisers* and "policy influentials"—those who have direct access to and are regularly consulted by the authorities; the latter, in its narrowest sense, is restricted to the authorities themselves. In practice, it is often hard or impossible to locate the threshold between the two levels. However, since we shall suggest that in the European polity many or most sectors are continuously, regularly represented (in fact, have their leaders present) in the former *and* the latter, it is important to make explicit the nature of these two structures.

57. Cf. the partially related sense in which Lijphart, *Politics of Accommodation*, chap. 7, presented the "rules of the game" in the Dutch system: Lijphart's point (pp. 123–24) that the "game" is in fact "serious business" is more than merely the rejection of a metaphor; and it is a point that is applicable to the European polity in general. The distinction between the game orientation—which perhaps characterized the Fourth French Republic (see Nathan Leites, *On the Game of Politics in France* [Stanford: Stanford University Press, 1959])—and the businesslike approach is not only one of style, but of political culture and regime norms as well: the preoccupation is with results ("outcomes" in Easton's terminology) rather than with political advantage as a means toward some unspecified close-at-hand or future goals or ideological victories.

systems to this rubric remains. For example, elsewhere in this essay we felt obligated to point up what appeared to us both an arbitrary and an erroneous exclusion of Lebanon from the realm of "modern democracies." It should go without saying that the placement of any particular political system into the "democratic" category should depend on empirically verified possession of type-characteristics; and it should be remembered that the democratic nature of regimes is not an immutable trait.[58] Were we to consider nondemocratic alternatives as well, a monopolistic or hegemonic style for resolving these problems of pluralism would also have to be noted. Such a style is exemplified by the approaches of the USSR, South Vietnam, and South Africa to the problems in question.)

First, it is possible to aggregate differing policy preferences into alternative blocs which have the potential and the opportunity for capturing—through electoral or parliamentary or recombinational means—control of the decision-making apparatus. Once in office, each bloc will presumably work its (constitutionally or otherwise limited) will. For the sake of identification, we shall label this response to the challenge the *adversarial* style.[59] Second, we can identify a pattern of response in which conscious efforts by elites to avert systemic crises (generally associated with the centrifugal tendencies of the cleavage-structured social and political processes) result in outputs that are more satisfying than would be decisions reached on the basis of "splitting the difference" among the contending groups. This is the consociational democracy pattern already identified.

The number of conditions required to make either of these alternatives effective means to their ends—i.e., facilitating the legitimation of outputs and generating diffuse support through those outputs—is great enough to bring into question the viability of either structure. Thus, for instance, the adversarial style is premised on (1) the capabilities and/or inclinations of the leaders of most sectors (a) to compromise with adequate regularity and (b) to sell the bargains they made with each other to their followers; (2) making possible the coalescence of two or three (but not too many!)[60] sets of

---

58. For our general meaning of "democracy," we refer the reader to the theoretical usages of, inter alia, Dahl, Lijphart, and Rejai. See M. Rejai, ed., *Democracy: The Contemporary Theories* (New York: Atherton Press, 1967) for a broad range of formulations which, nevertheless, share a basic internal consistency.

59. Almond (see "Comparative Political Systems"), Lijphart, and others have associated this style with the "Anglo-American" type of regime: broadly aggregative parties, operating in (relatively) homogeneous political cultures, fashioning alternatives which, in fact, alternate in power. (That the type is a gross oversimplification of what obtains in the systems to which it refers—Canada, Australia, New Zealand, the United Kingdom, and the United States—is to be suspected, especially in light of the "incremental" hypothesis which states that the proportion of outputs that can be effectively changed from government to government is slight, in comparison with the bulk of the business that *any* government operating within the established regime norms has to perform.)

60. A number of writers (Almond and Duverger come to mind most readily) have associated the presence of a large number of parties with ineffective performance of the tasks of aggregation.

groups around differing policy positions and office-seeking factions; (3) a widespread, predictable willingness of the members of each coalition to limit the pursuit of political advantage, so that the group out of power retains the minimal capability to challenge the officeholding coalition in the next round; (4) the willingness of the losers to accept defeat, and to continue to contest the game according to the rules—i.e., to defer to the winners while waiting for another opportunity to gain control; and, perhaps most important, (5) the effectiveness of the regime of adversarial coalitions in extending and sustaining the aggregating umbrella over a large enough segment of the political society to keep alienation, protest, and "rule-violating" antiregime behavior within manageable limits—that is, in Easton's terms, to minimize the debilitation of the sources of diffuse support.[61]

If a political society is segmented to an appreciable degree (though not necessarily as deeply cleaved as the segmented pluralist regimes in Lorwin's model), such assumptions may not be warranted. In particular, aggregation across sectors at the member or mass (rather than elite) level is problematic; the ability of the leaders to convince their followers that the compromises they negotiate do not entail the yielding of vital group positions; and moderation in victory and patience in defeat cannot be routinely expected.

Like the adversarial pattern, the regime in the consociational democracy depends upon the ability and inclination of the cross-sectoral elite to play by the rules. The rules are different, but the necessity of adherence to them by the elite is indispensable for satisfactory system performance—i.e., for the system to produce outcomes acceptable to the "players." Lijphart evaluated the recent records of the systems he treated and found them to be relatively free from immobilism. But, although he may be generally correct insofar as the immediate past is concerned, most of those systems have, in fact, experienced serious periods of that political ailment in this century—either as a consequence of the failure of leadership or because of the heightened politicization of one or more dimensions of cleavage or both. The *dynamic* stability found in most such systems at present is hardly assured for any of them in the future.

The cooptive model posited in this paper is not premised on either the adversarial style or on the abilities and predispositions of cross-sectoral elites (although the existence of some type of cross-sectoral leadership structure at the system level is presumed)—at least not to the same degree. The cohesion of the system of the European polity depends less on a particular pattern of elite behavior and predisposition than does the cohesion of the consociational democracy, because the former has several other but-

61. Three studies that address the problem of government managing the pluralist arrangement—its successes and failures—from a related perspective are Theodore J. Lowi, *The End of Liberalism* (New York: W. W. Norton, 1969); Grant McConnell, *Private Power and American Democracy* (New York: Alfred A. Knopf, 1966); and Adolf A. Berle, *Power Without Property* (New York: Harcourt, Brace & World, 1959).

tresses. One of the most important of these consists of another facet of cooptation: the establishment of *structured access*.

H_1. *By being brought into the policy-making structure, the various sectors are given a vested interest in the continued successful operation of the structure—regardless of the satisfaction or dissatisfaction of any particular sector with short-term outcomes.*

The strongest stimulus for the support of this arrangement—even by those actors who may disagree with particular outputs—is the continuation of access. The necessity and advantages of continued access motivate representatives of the various segments to

$H_{1.1}$. *moderate their challenges to or rejections of specific outputs;* and
$H_{1.2}$. *(except in rare and extreme cases) abstain from the legitimation process rather than directly challenge the legitimacy of either a specific output or the manner in which it was produced.*[62]

Continued access puts the representatives of sectoral interests in a position from which it becomes virtually impossible for them to challenge the decisions produced, since they have come to be regarded as participants in making those decisions. They have assumed a "share of the responsibility." Consequently, to criticize an output becomes tantamount to criticizing oneself.

The participants are bound to the cooptive policy-making structure at several points; and, while they retain a nominal prerogative to opt out at any of those points, the nature of the regime behooves them to adhere. Thus, although a nominal option exists at the initial stage of "joining" the cooptive structure, in practice it is usually difficult to find a meaningful alternative to participation—especially when the central structure moves to incorporate all visible sectors, either through the committee network or by extending the opportunity to participate through a *remiss* or similar structure. Nor is the choice, at a subsequent juncture, between "quitting" and

62. It is impractical to seek great precision in delineating this trait in the European polity. Intragroup disagreements may result in a situation in which the formal leadership is split or a division occurs between the formal and the informal or lesser leaders on the question of whether the group's interests would be better served by challenging publicly an already articulated output or by waiting silently for a future opportunity to recoup within the bounds of the rules of the game. Further, the qualification "except in rare and extreme cases" is nearly tautological, insofar as the systems that most closely approach the polity type are concerned: in Norway, Switzerland, and the Netherlands overt challenges have been rare indeed—and these can be readily classified in terms of the qualification, or as "exceptions that prove the rule." (Thus, in the illustration of a Dutch riot, quoted below, if the group in question had been coopted in the manner in which virtually all others of its kind had been, the drastic actions would probably not have occurred.)

"continuing to play" a real one for most groups; as we shall illustrate forth-with, it would be tantamount to political suicide for one actor to withdraw while all others continued to participate.

Viewed from the system level, an actor participates simply by virtue of being recognized—i.e., coopted. For, once access is established for a par-ticular entity, its rank and file, the government, the bureaucracy, and the public all assume that its elite does in fact participate in the policy-making process. It is in this sense that cooptation entails the sharing of responsi-bility for the outputs generated. Observers outside the policy-making milieu attribute responsibility for outputs to a coopted sector's elite, whether in fact it was or was not a party to the decision, and regardless of the specific policy position articulated by those who represented it in the interelite bargaining process.

The dynamics of factors H_1, $H_{1.1}$, and $H_{1.2}$, as well as the group actor's sensibility to the notion of "sharing responsibility" are illustrated by the ac-tions of some Norwegian economic groups. Five years after the National Economic Coordinating Council came into being (in 1945), several groups perceived themselves to have become captives of the government—hos-tages at the mercy of an administration intent upon implementing a set of proposals clearly derived from a single source—the Norwegian Labor party's platform—rather than from the corporate mix. The groups withdrew from the cooptive arrangement. They gave up their access when they perceived it to have become meaningless—an encumbrance rather than a medium for exerting influence. Interestingly, however, with the resultant demise of the National Council, organizations set about constructing new, smaller councils within the government— entities that were more limited in scope but similar in purpose to the defunct National Council. The new structure preserved the advantages of the cooptive ar-rangement, while it minimized the possibility of a threat from the "politicians."[63]

To be sure, membership in the cooptive structure does not mean that an actor dissatisfied with the policy product must accept it with good grace—or, for that matter, accept it at all. In Norway, for instance, a dissatisfied group could challenge an output at one of the final stages of the policy-making process—the parliamentary level. In Rokkan's terminology, groups have an "out" on the first tier of a two-tiered decision-making system.[64] In the Netherlands, Belgium, Sweden, and Austria (and, in general, in all the countries to which the European polity can be deemed

63. In Sweden the "nonparticipants" have ignored the implications of "sharing responsi-bility" by challenging the government as well as the leadership group of their own sector—as witnessed by the wildcat strikes in Kiruna. But such cases are exceptions.

64. The existence of an alternative tier may provide psychological support for the organiza-tion, with the effect of keeping it committed to the administrative structure longer than might have been the case had no such "out" been present.

applicable) the politicization of specific issues or even particular outputs is possible, and the challenge may be communicated in the streets as well as in the partisan parliaments.[65]

But, clearly, the inclinations of dissatisfied groups—especially established groups with organizational continuity that have participated in the cooptive structure—are to avoid such strategies. To challenge the technocratic governmental process by politicizing an issue is generally regarded to be counterproductive in the European polity, in the sense that such action tends to undermine good working relations with administrators—who are generally presumed to be more influential in the long run than are parliamentarians. Thus, the benefits associated with continuing presence in the decision-forming milieus are sufficient to moderate the forms and expressions of disapproval, with the consequence that the likelihood of regime maintenance and system persistence becomes greater than it would be if the pluralistic political society were to experience immoderate clashes over outputs, their contents, and the manner of their production.[66]

Other benefits derive from the cooptive pattern. Structured access may become a substitute for ideologically circumscribed group integrity in pluralistic societies in two ways. First, if "victory" in the form of group hegemony is an unrealistic or dangerous aspiration (dangerous from the perspective of regime stability or even system persistence), and if minimal coalitions promise too little in returns or threaten to degenerate into immobilist stagnation, then it is possible that corporate participation or even merely systematic consultation prior to the making of decisions will suffice to provide assurances of group representation and as promises of real or potential group influence. In any event, structured access has the supreme virtue (for such systems) of providing the opportunity for constantly monitoring "the others." It also allows the monitoring of the government.

Structured cooptation transcends the government or the governing coalition, if these entities are formally viewed. That is, the parliamentary (and electoral) oppositions—and even ideological, class, religious, ethnic,

65. E.g., street riots in Amsterdam in 1966; massive manifestations of direct political action in Belgium, associated not only with the pervasive and deteriorating "linguistic question" (i.e., the ethnic cleavage), but also with the "Royal Question" of the late 1940s and early 1950s (see Heisler, "Political Community and Its Formation in the Low Countries," pp. 187–92) and with labor and other economic issues (most recently, in October, 1972, storekeepers demonstrated in Brussels over the nuisance and expense of administering the value added tax); recent incidents of young people and housewives taking direct action as means for demonstrating dissatisfaction with food prices and the chopping down of trees in Sweden; and similar manifestations in a number of polities that closely approximate our model. Our point here is that, while as a tendency or general pattern, the European polity exhibits a marked capability for ameliorating political conflict through cooptation and the provision of structured access, it does not preclude either the manifestation of dissatisfaction or the challenge of regime norms.

66. For a useful distinction between regime maintenance and system persistence, as those processes are intended here, and remaining consistent with Easton's conceptual terminology, see Donald J. Devine, *The Political Culture of the United States* (Boston: Little, Brown, 1972), pp. 19–21, 31–32. Cf. chap. 5 in this volume.

or language-group opponents—are frequently coopted, in ways and with consequences noted above. Meijer's study of Sweden, Lijphart's analysis of politics in the Netherlands, Wolfe's discussion of *Blockpolitik* in the German Democratic Republic (and less directly, his description of the roles played by the corporatist Senate of Bavaria), and to a degree Rokkan's appraisal of the Norwegian case demonstrate that in the type of system with which we are concerned political groups may be incorporated as simply another component—an equal one—in the cooptive policy-making structure.[67]

Second, in its extreme form, structured access in effect grants monopolies to the recognized spokesmen of particular blocs. Potentially new and competitive groups representing similar blocs or interests are barred from entry into the decision-making structure—government will neither recognize them nor give them access—and consequently they wither away, assuming that they form at all in such an environment.[68] (Such extreme cases are rare.)

Structured cooptation becomes particularly important as more and more politically active groups—using the rubric loosely enough to subsume all formally organized and at least some informal agglomerations of people that articulate group preferences regarding "authoritative allocations" of goods and values at the societal level—are *drawn* (coopted) *into* the policy-making milieu, or the decision-making subsystem itself. The European polity model exhibits a high level of development along this dimension: most such groups have already been coopted—*virtually without regard to their supportive or opposing orientations to the regime and its norms.* Further, both the scope attained in the process of coopting group-actors and the length of time that groups have worked through the cooptive structure tend to enhance the likelihood (1) that groups already linked will continue to adhere; and (2) that entities not yet coopted will be.[69]

To this point we have been concerned with some of the salient forms that structured access takes in the European polity—with questions about *who* is incorporated and in *what ways* into the policy-making milieus. We have suggested that once access is established, its value becomes apparent to representatives for the established societal sectors, causing them to moderate their challenges to the system. But, while we raised in general terms some implications of structured access and cooptation for the stability of the regime—particularly through the sharing of responsibility—most of our discussion has focused on what, in Easton's terminology, is the level of the "authorities," and only secondarily have we considered the "regime

67. See Meijer, "Bureaucracy and Policy Formulation." Rokkan gives a good example of the attenuating effect of the cooptive arrangement upon the Labor Government (see Rokkan, "Norway," p. 108).

68. See Lijphart, *Politics of Accommodation*, passim.

69. See Lijphart, "Consociational Democracy," pp. 216–17.

level." We now turn to the "regime" and, to a lesser extent, "system levels."

Cooptation is a means for channeling specific demands directed toward the authorities, and all but the most extreme demands aimed at the regime level, into directions that assist in regime maintenance and contribute to system persistence.[70] But,

I.   *cooptation is also an important source of change in the generation of specific outputs and in regime norms, because it brings into the policy-making milieu actors for whom access was, previously, sporadic or nonexistent.*

The most important quality of cooptation from the perspective of participation is that access is not directly dependent on electoral, parliamentary, or government coalition positions or on interest-groups' lobbying successes; but, rather, it is an alternative to translating one or more societal cleavages into political currency.[71]

The divisions that undergird the cooptive structure cannot be presumed to vanish with the advent of that structure. Thus, it follows that

I₁.   *the entry of important sectoral or group actors occasions parametric and structural changes at the policy-making and decision-making levels.*

Both the process of being coopted—an "entry phenomenon" but one which may be sudden and clearly identifiable or prolonged and characterizable as "blending in"—and the participatory condition present the opportunity to alter the preexisting structure. Entry may be accompanied by a "bargain" or renegotiation of the processes and norms through which policy is made or in substantive shifts in outputs.

Influence in the policy-making milieu and participation in the central decision-making subsystem may be determined by such "external" (i.e., input-side) support factors as parliamentary and/or electoral position, the

70. Extreme demands at the regime level may consist of attacks on one or more of the "three components: values (goals and principles), norms, and structure of authority" (Easton, *Systems Analysis of Political Life*, p. 193). Attempts to change drastically and suddenly any of these components—but most particularly the second and the third—may preclude the kinds of relationships that cooptation seems to require. Indeed, a purposefully cultivated, symbolically charged "antiregime" image is often a concomitant of such demands; and it precludes cooptation. Thus, Communist parties or parties of the extreme right may not be successfully coopted in systems that are at some distance from the European polity type (e.g., Italy, France, and the Federal Republic of Germany). In systems that closely approximate the ideal-type model, however, such groups are very small or nonexistent; and virtually all elements have been or can be (potentially) coopted. Belgium is a deviant case; see chap. 5.

71. For a concrete example of this phenomenon, see Rokkan, "Norway," pp. 107–9. Belgium is a deviant case. See chap. 5 below.

proportion of the population or sector represented by a corporate actor or the political skills and energies of particular leaders. Unlike coalition governments, however, cooptive polities do not as a rule exhibit adherence to any precise formula of proportionality in the distribution of influence. In their extreme forms, they may have recourse to some formal division of labor and the recognition of functional or even territorial jurisdictions to determine participation and "spheres of influence."[72] But such manifestations, if they occur, are characteristics of particular systems. In effect, some systems use rather rigid quotas for the allocation of positions—and, occasionally, of outputs as well—by language group, religious denomination, ethnic group, or other nominal population categories.[73] What is important is that the distribution of influence within the policy-making structure of the cooptive polity is determined more by the internal dynamics of that structure and by prevailing balances in the political system at large than by the cleavages that are so common in such polities. In this sense, the cooptive polity's core is *trans*-sectoral rather than *cross*-sectoral:

I_2.   *cooptation reorients the thrust of the new entrant toward the system level, even though it may continue to pursue particularistic ends inside the policy-making structure. The structure often yields to impetus; it alters, but it binds.*

This quality of the European polity's central structure is most readily evident in the transmutation of private interests into public interests and the contributions that are made to the latter by nongovernmental actors. (To be sure, the obverse also obtains: government officials may emerge as champions of "private interests." The important point to note here is that, when the latter is observed, it is rarely suspected and virtually never proved that "corruption" exists—in the form of self-aggrandizement by public officials. Rather, public officials may be advocating the strengthening or protection of private interests *as a means of advancing systemic goals.* In other words, part of the public interest may require the protection of private interests; and, if private actors lose sight of the latter in some instances, then it behooves public officials to take an active part.) More precisely,

J.   *distinctions between public and private may become blurred when formal public roles are assigned to private agencies or when "mixed" public and private bodies come to play active parts as advisers or actual policy makers and/or implementers.*

72. Switzerland, Austria, Lebanon, Belgium, and the Netherlands provide particularly good illustrations of this phenomenon. See, e.g., Lehmbruch, "Non-competitive Pattern of Conflict Management," p. 3; and the essays by Stiefbold and Heisler, chaps. 4 and 5 in this volume.
73. Ibid.

An interesting manifestation of these phenomena can be found in the restructuring of elite roles in the decision-making process. In Norway, for example, in response to a question testing for cross-pressures exerted by public and private interests upon interest-group representatives serving in government councils, officials averred the propriety of a middle stance. That is, their task, as they saw it, was the accommodation of public and private interests. This compromising stance was not inconsistent with their positions as bureaucrats or elected officials. Rather, it was seen as a position necessitated by the nature of the decision-making process in which they were involved.[74] Similar perspectives characterize the blurring of distinctions between public and private interests in this sense in a number of other European systems. In fact, characteristic (J) of the policy- and decision-making patterns in the European polity is one of the distinguishing hallmarks of the system-type.

The key to understanding this feature is the existence of a very high level of *trust* in the political culture. As Anton has observed, with reference to Sweden, citizens expect and believe that their leaders—especially the administrative elite—will faithfully perform the jobs for which they were selected.[75] The leaders' day-to-day work is seldom monitored by the public. Such trust is based on a long history of responsible administration—administration with an operative tradition of high standards for adhesion to formal responsibilities. The public bureaucracy has demonstrated a willingness and an ability to regulate itself in the best interests of the society. Corruption has been virtually nonexistent.[76]

Trust is also demonstrated by the population's presumption that "public" representatives on mixed advisory, decision-making, and administrative bodies actually represent the public at large rather than the government; and "private" representatives are not expected to pursue private interests to the detriment of common interests.[77] This sense of trust is accompanied by a general expectation that self-interest will be

---

74. Kvavik, "Interest Groups in a 'Cooptive' Political System: The Case of Norway," chap. 3 in this volume.

75. Thomas J. Anton, "Policy-Making and Political Culture in Sweden," *Scandinavian Political Studies* 4 (1969): 97.

76. While we do not assert that the bureaucracies of systems that closely approach our model are free from self-aggrandizing behavior and old-fashioned graft and corruption, we do believe that such behavior is markedly lower in the countries within the type-cell. This dimension of the model will be tested, using data from the public prosecutorial files. (In Scandinavia, the role of the ombudsman has both minimized and shed light on the rare instances of such behavior. See note 99.)

77. A marked contrast is provided by the recent experience of the United States (1971–72) with public and sectoral representatives on the pay and price boards. Perhaps it will suffice for the present purpose to associate our notion of *trust* with Easton's formulation of the concept of "diffuse support" as "good will" (see *Systems Analysis of Political Life*, pp. 276–77). Easton identified such support as that which "is not directly linked to specific material rewards and satisfactions or coercion (negative rewards)." He associated three types of response with diffuse

pursued only to the point of satisficing.[78] And, in general, the bargaining and administrative processes are not accompanied by a public sense of deprivation.

It is interesting to note that the European polity manifests high levels of (what can be regarded in Easton's terms as the equivalent of) diffuse support, notwithstanding the presence of cleavages that, in Easton's implicit theory, militate against such support and induce stress through the erosion of support.[79] The reason for this, we submit, is that feedback-induced responses generate regular, predictable inputs of specific support at consistently high levels—and the expectation that the system will continue to satisfy specific demands has generated reservoirs of diffuse support. The support-sapping effects of cleavages have been mitigated by the effective operation and thorough legitimation of the cooptive mechanisms: *the members and leaders of most sectors of the European polity expect the regime to continue to exhibit and expand responsiveness to their demands.*[80]

Easton, in a somewhat diverging analysis, anticipated the relationship between outputs and the generation of diffuse support:

> Although I have been restricting my remarks about outputs to their effect for fostering specific support, it is clear that outputs may also be discussed in the light of their consequences for diffuse support. The authorities may become aware of the role that sentiments and beliefs about legitimacy, the common good, or the community play in the input of support at the regime and community level. Where information feedback alerts them to the fact that the state of mind of the members in the system

---

support: "first, those that seek to instill a deep sense of legitimacy in the members for the regime as a whole and for individuals who act on behalf of it; second, those that invoke symbols of the common interest; and third, those that promote and strengthen the degree to which members identify with the political community" (ibid., 277).

Our concerns would lead us to focus on the first and second types of response noted by Easton—although the third, diffuse support at the community level, would not be entirely irrelevant.

78. For the concept of "satisficing behavior" as we use it, see Herbert A. Simon, *Models of Man* (New York: John Wiley, 1957), pt. 4. Briefly, such behavior entails settling for outcomes that are deemed adequate, rather than pressing for maximal results. This expectation is directly contrary to the analytic values present in most modern "pluralist" and "political economy" theories of American democracy. In the latter, groups seek to maximize their benefits—and it is accepted that they should. See James M. Buchanan and Gordon Tullock, *The Calculus of Consent; Logical Foundations of Constitutional Democracy* (Ann Arbor, Mich.: University of Michigan Press, 1962), pp. 295, passim, but esp. chap. 19. A brilliant critique of the theory is to be found in Olson, *Logic of Collective Action.* Normative as well as theoretical criticisms are plentiful. See, for instance, William E. Connolly, ed., *The Bias of Pluralism* (New York: Atherton Press, 1971).

79. See Easton, *Systems Analysis of Political Life,* chaps. 14–15.

80. Anton, "Policy-Making and Political Culture in Sweden," provides an excellent illustration of this phenomenon—at least for Sweden. We suggest that this characteristic typifies the European polity in general; and it can be found in high degrees in the three Scandinavian systems with which we are concerned, as well as in the Netherlands, and in Switzerland.

is such that diffuse support is on the wane, positive and deliberate counter-acting efforts may be taken.[81]

Responding to a perceived drop in support is one way the authorities can seek to avoid stress; *anticipating* such an occurrence is another. Easton recognized the capability to anticipate, but he associated it with the level of the authorities and with the generation of specific supports.[82]

K.   *In the European polity, members of the system associate the antici-patory capability with the cooptive regime structure—and, conse-quently, the support generated in this manner is directed toward the cooptive mechanisms (at the regime level); and it is diffuse rather than specific support.*

These effects of the cooptive structure help the European polity to cope with and overcome the cleavage-induced fissiparous tendencies of the political society. They are structural parameters which define roles, guide behavior, beliefs and expectations toward the regime level; and, at the same time, they sustain sectoral or group identities and loyalties for most aspects of most members' lives. The structural parameters favor widespread and constantly increasing access. The legitimation of outputs emanating from the decision-making subsystem is greatly facilitated by the cooptation of im-portant group or sectoral actors (while the particular identities of such actors are sustained or even reinforced, rather than challenged). The use of coop-tive strategies for such a purpose is noticeable even in systems that are peripheral to the European polity type. Thus, in his inaugural address in 1964, former Lebanese President Charles Helou characterized the regime as one of "a framework of brotherly cooperation. Rule is consultative, and the consultative system in Lebanon is one of the conditions of cooperative and stable life."[83] Further impetus is provided for the legitimation process by the confidence and trust instilled in the regime as a consequence of the cooptive structure's effectiveness in continuously meeting and anticipating demands.

The development of the cooptive structure has been accompanied by a shift in the locus of decision making in the European polity from the parlia-ment and parties to the administrative agencies. Authority to formulate and implement public policy has been delegated in substantial degree to the ad-ministrative subsystem which, in turn, has passed some of its responsibilities

81. Easton, *Systems Analysis of Political Life*, pp. 464–65.
82. Ibid., pp. 385–87.
83. Michael C. Hudson, "Democracy and Social Mobilization in Lebanese Politics," *Comparative Politics* 1, no. 2 (January 1969): 245.

to the "private sector." Concomitantly, the parliament has come to resemble a rubber stamp in many of the most important policy areas.

This phenomenon has been widely discussed by scholars concerned
with politics in postindustrial societies, mainly in terms of the themes of
"the decline of parliaments"[84] and the "waning of oppositions."[85] Until
very recently, however, virtually no systematic treatments of the nature of
the structural and behavioral changes in the administrative arena had been
associated with the lessening of the political prominence of the input side.[86]
It is not our intention to describe all the relevant changes that have occurred in the administrative subsystems of such polities; and limitations of
space prevent detailed discussion of the cases we shall use as illustrations.[87]
Rather, our purpose is to present an overview of the general phenomenon of
the heightened politicization of administrative activity and to relate these
manifestations to the alterations in inputs and the cooptation of segmental
and sectoral elites—the first and second patterns in European politics we
discussed above. Thus, we now turn to a brief overview of the third, and
final, pattern we associate with politics in Europe: the increased *political*
significance of administration in the daily lives of Europeans.

Administration by Cooptive Structure: The European Polity's Form for Reintegrating Politics and Administration[88]

The most important manifestations of cooptation have not brought
elites into parliament or party. Functional representation of the kind found
in the Irish or Bavarian parliaments[89]—although not without relevance for
the concerns at hand, nor lacking in intrinsic importance—has been the
exception rather than the pattern-shaping case. The dominant pattern consists of the emergence of commissions, permanent and ad hoc, as extensions
of the formal governmental bureaucracy. (In fact, it may be more accurate
to characterize this process as the growth of the formal bureaucracy through

84. See the works cited in note 32.

85. See Dahl, *Political Oppositions in Western Democracies;* and the seminal article by the
late Otto Kirchheimer, "The Waning of Opposition in Parliamentary Regimes," *Social Research* 24, no. 2 (Summer 1957): 127–56.

86. Some chapters in this book treat this subject; and a somewhat oblique treatment of the
general phenomenon, as it is manifested in Belgium and in France, can be found in the symposium "La Politisation de l'Administration en Belgique et en France," *Res Publica* 13, no. 2
(1971): 165–242.

87. For a more detailed treatment, see Kvavik's essay on Norway, chap. 3 in this volume. See
also Heisler's discussion of Belgium, chap. 5 in this volume.

88. See the essay by the editors that introduces the section, "The Application of Public
Policy," in *European Political Processes: Essays and Readings*, ed. Henry S. Albinski and
Lawrence K. Pettit (Boston: Allyn & Bacon, 1968), pp. 355–67. See also the essays that com-
prise the section, esp. pp. 368–433.

89. See Wolfe's discussion of Bavaria, in chap. 9 of this volume.

the adhesion of "mixed"—governmental, private, and public—and private bodies.)

In Norway (where there are more than one thousand of them), such commissions administer schools, manage public corporations, draft legislation, and, to some degree, economically manage the various functional sectors of the society. These powerful committees are comprised of members of parliament (MPs), government administrators, interest group leaders, corporation bureaucrats, professors, scientists, etc. Some commissions are made up solely of the representatives of private groups—a situation that can constitute, in effect, a delegation of authority to the private sector; other bodies, in order to achieve balance, are cross-sectoral in composition.

Among the numerous parallels in Belgium, we can cite as an example the *Conseil National des Charbonnages* (National Council of Collieries), founded in 1947, which underwent many changes but retained its essentially mixed character. Thus, after its 1958 reorganization, it was comprised of corporate ownership, workers, consuming industries' representatives, bureaucrats concerned with mining, labor, public consumption and other governmental responsibilities, and representatives of financing agencies— which were "mixed" public and private entities themselves![90] The council was called upon to plan, implement, and seek to mitigate the dislocative consequences of the phasing out of inefficient and marginal mines in the southern provinces of Belgium in the 1950s and early 1960s. Because no coalition government in Belgium was strong enough to withstand the political consequences of terminating subsidies, putting out of work tens of thousands of miners and workers in associated industries, it fell to this broadly representative entity to seek to implement the economic decisions. (It should be noted that the dislocation caused by the closing of coal mines proved politically so stressful that neither mine owners nor workers could be kept in the fold through the entire ordeal.)

For more than a decade now, the work of many ministries and public and mixed commissions has been coordinated at the highest level by Belgium's Ministerial Committee for Economic and Social Coordination. While the activities and spheres of formal responsibility of such bodies vary greatly in Belgium, individually several of them are the dominant forces in their own sectors; and collectively they are the most important agencies of policy planning, the delineation of policy alternatives, and the overseeing of policy implementation.

Our references above to studies by Foyer (Sweden), Huber (Switzerland), and Miller (Denmark) provide some indication of the manifestation of this general phenomenon in other systems. In sum, then,

90. See Maurice Masoin, "Les instruments de la politique économique," *Res Publica* 3, no. 3 (1961): 197–204; and Jean Meynaud, Jean Ladrière, and François Perin, eds., *La décision politique en Belgique* (Paris: Librairie Armand Colin, 1965), pp. 268–86.

L.   *cooptation has been accompanied by the development of a new type of decision-making structure—essentially a network of committees— adjacent to the central administration.*

The degree to which the new network of committees is institutionalized as a distinct decision-making subsystem varies within the European polity type. The Scandinavian systems and the Netherlands, for example, operate with committees that adhere to articulated bureaucratic principles; and their policy jurisdictions are demarcated by an agreed upon division of labor. The participants in the structure—administrators, MPs, group representatives, scientists, and others—are most appropriately viewed as technocrats with shared or common purposes. The congruence of their expectations, goals, and behavior is striking.[91]

Thus, the new decision-making structure serves as a "linkage structure":[92] we can now say that in the European polity, unlike in Lijphart's consociational democracy, the cross-sectoral structure transcends the agglomeration of factional elites (and its government by "elite cartel").

L₁.   *In the European polity the cross-sectoral linkage function is performed in the administrative or output-implementation phase as well as the decision-making phase; and linkage roles are played by governmental and private administrators as well as by sector leaders.*

By viewing the decision-making structure in the European polity as a linkage structure, we wish to convey a picture of an established, rigorously structured—perhaps even institutionalized (see the quote from Riggs in note 47)—entity. The decision-making subsystem that characterizes the European polity is in no way ad hoc. It undergirds the "elite cartel" with massive bureaucratic infrastructures, comprised not only of the governmental administration formally viewed (i.e., the civil service), but of the nu-

91. For a discussion of the style of decision making, see Anton, "Policy-Making and Political Culture in Sweden." See also Torodd Strand, "Expertise, Innovation and Influence," *Scandinavian Political Studies* 4 (1969): 117–32.

92. The concept of "systemic linkage" is useful in considering this type of decision-making structure, because it brings together the institutional, attitudinal and behavioral components of the structure. Sociologist Charles P. Loomis developed this formulation, and defined it as "the process whereby one or more of the elements of at least two social systems is articulated in such a manner that the two systems in some ways and on some occasions may be viewed as a single unit. [The 'social systems' need not be whole systems, of course. Subsystems or even subsocietal segments can occupy that position.] . . . [T]he convergence of ends is common in systemic linkage, but norms, sentiments, status-roles and other elements may be involved. . . . The process of systemic linkage refers to the organizational arrangements for group interdependencies. . . . Whole organizations sometimes have the sole function of systemic linkage" (*Social Systems* [Princeton, N.J.: D. Van Nostrand, 1960], pp. 32–33. See also Heisler, "Political Community and Its Formation in the Low Countries," pp. 54–57. The overall policy- and decision-making structures are, we suggest, the linkage structures that help to hold the pluralistic systems of the European polities together.

merous admixed commissions and committees as well. Inasmuch as the role sets that comprise the decision-making subsystem are so numerous, diverse, and broadly encompassing (in terms of the society as a whole), the linkage structure forms a substantial segment of the overall political structure in the European polity.

The "group interdependencies" and the "convergence of ends . . . norms, sentiments [and] status-roles" that make up the structure are, therefore, pervasive and quite wide in scope. It is useful, consequently, to conceive of the decision-making structure in the European polity as more pervasive than a "cartel" limited to elites.

The European polity's decision-making subsystem is especially effective when the issues involved can be visualized as economic in substance or as conforming with broadly based, legitimized central plans. It works well particularly where political debate, as observed in Sweden by Anton,

> . . . is almost totally devoid of ideological or philosophical symbolism, fo-
> cusing instead on specific proposals to deal with specific problems—usu-
> ally economic in content. Should the children's allocation be raised to
> 1,100 or 1,200 crowns? Should rent controls be abolished for some or all of
> Stockholm's apartments?[93]

Such issues are readily converted into technical formulas. Further, they are issues that can be settled in such ways that all affected by them can regard themselves and each other as "sharers" rather than "winners" or "losers."[94]

The structure of the decision-making subsystem and the capability for formulating issue positions in nonzero-sum terms facilitate the discovery of acceptable outputs. This characteristic is particularly evident in European polity type systems that exhibit economic and interest organizational pluralism (e.g., Norway, Sweden, Denmark, and Luxembourg). In systems that manifest deep, reinforcing societal cleavages—for instance, Belgium, Austria, and Lebanon—it may be more difficult to treat even intrinsically economic and technical matters in a detached manner. Indeed, such political and administrative affairs often become charged with a symbolic significance that tends to politicize the routine and make into a crucial issue a detail in day-to-day administration.

The conception of sharers is made possible by the existence of a national consensus. Such consensus does not always accompany the institutionalization of an effective cooptive structure. In systems in which deep

---

93. Anton, "Policy-Making and Political Culture in Sweden," p. 98.

94. Fenno points out an interesting consequence of economic issues for the Appropriations Committee of the U.S. House of Representatives: the fact that one is dealing with issues that can be handled in a nonzero sum way is beneficial to the consensual approach that prevails among otherwise diverse and sometimes contentious individuals (in goals and style). See Richard F. Fenno, Jr., *The Power of the Purse* (Boston: Little, Brown, 1966).

societal cleavages divide the population, elite bargains may be accepted by the masses but a broadly shared supportive predisposition (a function of consensus) may be lacking in some instances. In such circumstances, the operation of the central linkage structures may be modified at the implementation stage, through the assertion of segment-level prerogatives—in effect, the assertion of a limited autonomy. The *dédoublement* of some Belgian ministries, discussed elsewhere in this book, provides an apposite illustration of this variant: the budgets of some functionally identified sectors are split between Flemish-language and *francophone* ministries—most notably in education and culture. The basic expenditure levels, value priorities and goals are established at the system-level for these sectors—budgetarily the most important; the apportionment of the overall allotment reflects the Flemish-*francophone* relationship's institutional accommodation of the day; while the spending of the money reflects, to a substantial degree, segmental rather than system-level criteria.

Put briefly, the European polity's structure is a manifestation of accommodation to divisions within the society, and it cannot be presumed to fuse the society into a monolith. While the linkage structure may serve to ameliorate divisive tendencies,

L_2.   *the retention and institutionalization of some divisions may prove useful in minimizing conflict-induced stress through compartmentalization.*

Thus, in systems in which the underlying sources of pluralism are more economic interest or issue oriented than they are societal, the cooptive structure may serve to ameliorate the divisions in general. But even in those instances in which compartmentalization at some subsystem level undergirds the elite consensus, another technically shaped feature of the European polity can be supported:

M.   *European polities exhibit comprehensive economic planning at the system level.*

The activities of representatives of group actors in the European polity are guided by central economic plans; and they are largely occupied by trying to implement or modify such plans. The tasks of value allocation that are entailed in drafting and pursuing the plans shape the system-wide consensus. As Gunnar Myrdal has observed,

> one interesting aspect of [the] gradual perfection of the modern democratic welfare state is that many divisions of opinion, once of burning importance, now tend to fade away, or to change character and thereby to become much less important. . . .

[There is] a trend towards convergence of attitudes and ideologies [which] point[s] to the increasing political harmony that has come to exist much more generally between all the citizen groups in the advanced Welfare State. The internal political debate in those countries is becoming increasingly technical in character, ever more concerned with detailed arrangements, and less involved with broad issues, since those are slowly disappearing.[95]

Lode Claes has observed the operation of this process in Belgium:

In other countries, there is a great deal of disagreement as to how the socio-economic struggle between left and right will evolve in the welfare state. But once unanimity has been reached regarding the goals and over-all structure of the welfare state itself and the system is functioning, that is to say, is assuring a continually increasing amount of prosperity to all social classes—and these premises are fulfilled for the Belgium of today— the socio-economic debate is transferred from the political to the technical plane. A corollary phenomenon is a growing apathy and passivity towards socio-economic questions on the part of the masses of the population. A political vacuum is created which may be filled by other issues.[96]

But, while the allocation process can operate in terms of technical criteria, its operation has consequences for people—and people evaluate those consequences in terms that often differ sharply from the rationalistic criteria used by the administrators. Different interpretations of the parameters of equity are possible, and conflict may be the result. The responses of affected population groups may take highly political forms, especially if such groups are not as effectively included in the structure as others against which their members measure their condition. In other words, there can be no assurance that "routine" and technical administration will not result in extraordinary political action—especially at the periphery of the cooptive structure. For, even in the European polity, in relative terms a center-periphery distinction exists. In modern times the distinction does not portend the cleavage of which Rokkan has written with profundity,[97] but perceptual as well as material gaps may exist. Lijphart, after indicating that the processes we have been concerned with are in fact operative in the Dutch setting, noted one of the dramatic

95. Gunnar Myrdal, *Beyond the Welfare State: Economic Planning and Its International Implications* (New Haven: Yale University Press, 1960), pp. 72, 77.

96. Lode Claes "The Process of Federalization in Belgium," *Delta* 6, no. 4 (Winter 1963–64): 49.

97. See Rokkan, *Citizens, Elections, Parties*, pts. 1 and 2; and Seymour M. Lipset and Stein Rokkan, eds., *Party Systems and Voter Alignments: Cross-National Perspectives* (New York: Free Press, 1967): chap. 1, by Lipset and Rokkan, "Cleavage Structures, Party Systems, and Voter Alignments: An Introduction"; and chap. 8, by Rokkan, "Geography, Religion, and Social Class: Crosscutting Cleavages in Norwegian Politics."

manifestations of dissatisfaction by a group, the members of which perceived themselves to be underrepresented and wronged:

> The end of ideology has facilitated elite cooperation and their negotiation of compromises, and will probably continue to do so. On the other hand, the further growth of the welfare state for which there is widespread support, will probably also increase the amount of dissatisfaction about the *administration* of the welfare state. Complaints about excessive governmental power and arbitrary bureaucratic action are likely to grow in intensity. The serious riots in Amsterdam in June 1966 were triggered by such a relatively minor but indeed rather arbitrary action: a 2 per cent reduction in the vacation pay of nonunionized construction workers in order to cover administrative expenses.[98]

Parallels to the Amsterdam riots can be found in the recent histories of all the systems that approach the European polity model. One class of them can be traced to administrative error or lack of foresight—or, in the plain terms used by Lijphart, bureaucratic arbitrariness. While such shortcomings of the regime type in question will probably never disappear, there is reason to believe that they will not pose serious problems for the maintenance of the regime in the European polity.

While some exceptions have occurred, generally centralized or coordinated planning has resulted not from programmatic thrusts, but rather from the collation of ad hoc or piecemeal interventions by the central authorities in specific, sectorally delimited problems. In a number of modern systems such interventions do not lead to concerted central planning.

N.   *In the European polity, however, the ad hoc, case-specific intervention of public authorities tends to be coordinated into sector-specific and even system-wide programs.*

The direct citizen actions (such as riots, street demonstrations, and rallies) manifested in the class of systems with which we are occupied constitute a type of *political* response to decision making by administration. The regime has sought to cope with the actual and potential stress-producing consequences of such action through two structural means: (1) the erosion of the periphery, by providing access to all sectors in the implementation and administrative oversight phases; and (2) the creation of such "public" overseers of the bureaucracy (broadly conceived) as the ombudsman.[99]

---

98. Lijphart, *Politics of Accommodation*, p. 185.

99. Citizens' advocates and/or independent, nonpartisan overseers of public bureaucracies exist in several countries. They are most firmly institutionalized in Denmark, Finland, Norway, Sweden, and New Zealand. On the operations and problems of the ombudsman system, see

The population in the European polity is concerned primarily with "what is done," rather than "how it is done." It is, as Anton has observed for Sweden, concerned with "the outputs of the system, rather than inputs." In sum, most citizens are not likely to question the nature of the cooptive structure, so long as the structure produces outcomes that satisfy:

> Swedish popular emphasis on what the government, parties and interest groups do for them, rather than how they do it, may help to account for the shifts in support given to the bourgeois parties, whose vote totals and legislative representation move up and down as they seek to find programs that can motivate voter and member loyalty. Such fluctuations in support, together with the continuous search for program improvement among government agencies, underline what appears to be the highly tentative and conditional nature of citizen involvement in governmental support. . . . If service standards go down, what else is there to motivate support?[100]

If it is regarded as an undifferentiated mass (rather than a population structured into sectoral or otherwise organized group actors in a pluralistic regime), then

O.   *the influence of the mass public in the European polity can be said to have been effectively removed from the making of decisions.*

As Alan Arian has observed, with reference to Israel,

> Politics in Israel is largely party politics and party politics is played by the party elite. The populace is rarely brought into play. Public opinion almost never enters the political arena in a meaningful sense. Pressure groups fight it out among themselves and with the government and administrative agencies, with only infrequent appeals and activation of

---

Walter Gellhorn, *Ombudsmen and Others: Citizens' Protectors in Nine Countries* (Cambridge, Mass.: Harvard University Press, 1966). The indigenous analytic and case literature is extensive.

100. Anton, "Policy-Making and Political Culture in Sweden," p. 96. Similarly, in Israel it is the quality of governmental performance that is valued by the public, rather than who achieves the desired outcomes or how they attain them: "It has been argued . . . that the very essence of Israeli democracy is threatened by the continuing dominance of one party (once Mapai, now Labor). Rejecting the line of reasoning that the forms of democratic decision making can be maintained within the context of the give-and-take between groups in the dominant party, this argument asserts that an actual changeover of the ruling party is a necessary condition of democratic government. Two-thirds of the population does not accept this argument. They are quite willing to see the dominant party stay in power so long as it is doing a good job. This datum is especially interesting, since only 46 per cent of the voters voted for the dominant party. At least an additional 20 per cent of the population who did not vote for the Labor-Mapam Alignment are willing to concede that parties should be judged on performance and not on length of time in office" (Alan Arian, *Consensus in Israel* [New York: General Learning Press, 1971], p. 6).

public opinion. Power is sharply focused at the center and so is the pressure of interest groups. . . . The data seem to indicate that the Israeli citizen is fundamentally a passive political animal, identifying with democratic forms, confident that the politician is concerned with his opinion, yet basically unconvinced about his own ability to influence policy.[101]

The actually and potentially stifling consequences of this trait of the polity type have been recognized by citizens of some of the countries that most closely resemble the model; and there have been expressions of frustration and dissatisfaction by small but growing numbers of politically sensitive persons—especially in Sweden and in the Netherlands. Such reactions raise a number of questions which are important in consideration of the future of the European polity type system. Answers to these will probably be most fruitfully pursued along two paths—the developmental and the normative. Given the constraints of knowledge and space with which we are working, we cannot explore these paths in this essay. Consequently, we must content ourselves with merely pointing them out, so that they might be considered at a subsequent stage of European political studies.

Before taking up questions of the consequences of the European polity in operation and of its place in developmental sequences, however, it seems imperative to project a configurational overview of the model. For, as indicated, the special nature of the system type cannot be discerned from a mere inventory of traits; rather, the European polity is distinguishable from other types of systems principally because of the manner in which those traits interrelate: the essence of the type is the configuration in which the characteristics are arrayed.

A Configurational View of the European Polity

The European polity has been sketched principally in terms of its structural features. That is, we have stressed patterned—indeed, more or less institutionalized—governmental and political interactions and parameters of behavior. With this emphasis, *we have sought to highlight the preeminence of the political:*

P.   *in the European polity intra-(political) systemic phenomena provide better clues to understanding the political process than do environmental—i.e., "input-side" or prepolitical—factors.*

Whether this overall characteristic is described as the degression of the input side, or as the predominance of withinputs over inputs, or as the

101. Arian, *Consensus in Israel*, pp. 5–7.

salience of the political structure, its source and explanation are the same. The European polity's structure is, as we have suggested, an accommodation to politically relevant divisions in the society. Such divisions may be socioeconomic, religious, linguistic, or occupational. So long as they have been politicized sufficiently to lead to the formation of more stable than ad hoc group political actors, *under particular circumstances* a policy- and decision-making structure type—one we have labeled "cooptive"—is likely to emerge.

This structure will shape (strongly influence, rather than "cause") the role structures, norms, and value orientations in the society to an appreciable degree. As the Swiss learning theorist Jean Piaget has observed: "In the social context, structures . . . express themselves sooner or later in the forms of norms and rules to which individuals are, to a greater or lesser extent, subject."[102] This, we assert, is the manifestation of the autonomy of the political culture of the European polity: to understand how and why people in the European polity express political concerns and pursue aims in the political system, one should look first to the orientation and behavior-shaping forces exerted by the political structure.

Upon first reading, this may appear to be a straightforward—indeed, a platitudinous—proposition, but we suggest that it constitutes a sharp departure from the conventional patterns of thought in contemporary political theory. Unlike general models of political systems and unlike most special theories, our model militates in favor of seeking to understand political phenomena in terms of what is already inside the system, rather than through what is put into it from its environments.[103] This is our emphasis on withinputs rather than on inputs. That is, in the type of system under discussion, the political structure exerts a greater influence on

102. *Structuralism*, trans. and ed. Chaninah Maschler (New York: Basic Books, 1970), pp. 102–3.

103. In general, we share the growing impatience of political scientists—especially those involved in comparative research—with the continuing preoccupation with prepolitical or environmental factors that characterizes much of the work in the field. For excellent criticisms along these lines, and for cogent pleas to shift priorities in political science so that the focus is again on the political, see Roy C. Macridis, "Comparative Politics and the Study of Government: The Search for Focus," *Comparative Politics* 1, no. 1 (October 1968): 79–90; and La-Palombara, "Parsimony and Empiricism in Comparative Politics."

As noted in chap. 1, a focus on European referents militates in favor of according primacy to political processes and structures; perhaps those concerned with the study of political life in other types of systems should retain different priorities. In our system type, withinputs make up a larger share of the workload of the political system than they might in other types. This system characteristic should not lead to an ignoring of or insensitivity to environmental factors—as influences, inputs, and outcome-induced effects. The last category of environmental factors is of particular interest, because "policy impact" and "system performance" measures, appraising the influence of political and governmental variables upon the society, promise the most fruitful paths toward operationalization of the European polity model. See Peters' study, chap. 7 in this volume, and discussion in this chapter, "Uses of the Model."

politically pertinent orientations and behavior than is likely to be the case in other types (in which social, socioeconomic, and other structures occupy equivalent positions of importance in shaping the political culture). Additionally, the interactions of members who play continuous—but not necessarily formal—political roles account for a greater share of the totality of politically relevant interactions in the European polity than they would in other system types. These two characteristics—the first dealing largely with "mass behavior," while the second is restricted in some degree to "elite behavior"—underline the relative autonomy and saliency of the political system in the European polity's overall social system.

We consider the manner in which outputs are generated and the means by which they are implemented to provide better clues to understanding the political process in the European polity than would clues gleaned from such mass-participation phenomena as voting and party activity or from such elite activities as party leadership and coalition formation. For we believe that a particular type of ideological conflict is no longer present in most European systems: no important debates take place over who ought to participate (directly or through representation) in basic political processes or over gross questions of distribution of wealth. In the period since the end of the Second World War, channels of participation have been opened to all those who have wanted to avail themselves of such opportunities for political expression, and the grossest inequities in the distribution of wealth have been eliminated—or, minimally, they have been approached earnestly with a view toward their amelioration. (The basic redistributive mechanism has been a complex of notably progressive taxes.)

To be sure, ideology is not dead in the European countries that are the principal referents for our model. Intergenerational differences in value orientations and in the foundations of political behavior are very much in evidence.[104] Furthermore, challenges to the operating regime norms may emerge, on the ground that the cooptive mechansim works *too well*: there are more and increasingly more truculent criticisms leveled at the elites of a number of countries, arguing that the regime stifles sharply deviating aspirations and that access and demand-satisfaction are restricted by structural gatekeepers to goals and behaviors that are essentially regime-maintaining.[105] The most important class of gatekeepers in the European polity is intrasectoral: the sectoral elites shunt aside demands from their

104. See, for instance, the data and analyses in Abramson, "Social Class and Political Change," and Inglehart, "Silent Revolution in Europe."

105. For the concept of structural gatekeeping, as used in this paper, see Easton, *Systems Analysis of Political Life*, pp. 86–88, and 86–97 passim. We adhere to Easton's usage but disagree in part with his empirical allusions regarding the operation of the process in actual systems.

own members, if they deem such demands to embody a potential for disrupting the regime. Put another way, the amplitude of participatory access is not always perceived as openness to all value orientations. (We return for a brief look at these and related concerns when we consider the normative implications and developmental locus of the model.)

The focus of our attention to this point has been the internal or societal aspect of the country. Such a preoccupation is justified in the case of the European polity type, for two major reasons. First, many of the European polity's distinctive features—especially the operation of the broadly inclusive, segment-linking policy- and decision-making structures; the mixed advisory and administrative bodies, with their legitimizing potential; central economic planning; and the penchant for converting political issues into technical, rationally approachable problems—militate in favor of an inward perspective. Such elements tend to work most effectively if they have an incremental, reductive impetus. That is, they favor the reduction of new problems to effective, already proved formulas (i.e., the linking of such problem-resolving efforts to the existing, operating structure); and new challenges are taken up with the aid of the results of past (successful) efforts. Thus, dissident factions are more readily coopted if most other groups have been coopted already; and politically sensitive issues are more easily converted into technically articulated problems if success with similar or analogous issues can be demonstrated. "Progress," in terms of a society's self-perceptions, militates in favor of operating within a finite, definable universe—a manageable environment.

Second, *the system-type's empirical referents all appear to be relatively small countries that have largely withdrawn from confrontations with other states and tend to shun power politics in the global arena—or, for that matter, in their regional international subsystems.*[106] It is not, we suggest, an insulation from other societies or international relationships that these countries seek.[107] (On the contrary, most of them have extensive multifarious networks of interactions with other countries—bilaterally, multilaterally, in intergovernmental organizations, and, usually, in supranational bodies, such as the European Communities of the "Nine." In fact, as noted forthwith, one characteristic of the European polity is that it has intensive interactions of certain kinds with symmetrically structured neighbors.) Rather, the goal is to minimize particular kinds of actually or

---

106. Lorwin considers "smallness of population and power" an important factor in the emergence of segmented pluralist regimes. See his "Segmented Pluralism," pp. 149–51.

107. Such insulation was prescribed by Plato and Rousseau for the populations of their ideal-state constructs in, respectively, *The Republic* and "Constitutional Project for Corsica." But they were concerned with keeping the less-perfect world from tainting the populations of the ideal states; while we suggest that the association of this tendency with the European polity is due more to the desire to control the demands made on the system's scarce resources and on its cleavage-linking capabilities.

potentially stress-inducing interactions—interactions that might over-burden the systems' capabilities to cope and to persist.[108]

Intensive interactions among some European countries have led to a characteristic of European polities that has (1) reinforced their structural similarities, and (2) militated in favor of regarding Western Europe as the principal locus of the "European polity phenomenon." Thus, we suggest that

Q.   interactions among sectoral and system-level actors in European polities have led, over time, to the reinforcement of like charac-teristics in several systems.

Such interactions have resulted, in some instances, in the formation of institutional linkages of sectors across systems—enhancing the intra-system autonomy of sectors, and bolstering their political efficacy within their respective systems. They have also militated in favor of structural symmetry across systems. That is, the opportunity (need?) to participate in multicountry ventures at the sector level has been related by participants to the existence or development of parallel structures within and between systems.

Parties, labor unions, and employers' organizations in the European Communities have provided illustrations of this tendency. Thus, for instance, Socialist and Christian Democratic labor unions have formed cross-national organizations at the level of the Communities. The seating of members of the European Parliament is by party, rather than by nationality (even though the members are formally delegates of their respective national parliaments). These and corresponding arrangements for other types of actors reinforce domestic or internal positions, and they

---

108. For this view, see Trygve Mathisen, *The Functions of Small States in the Strategies of the Great Powers* (Oslo: Universitetsforlaget, 1971), esp. chap. 11. See also Annette Baker Fox, *The Power of Small States* (Chicago: University of Chicago Press, 1959); and Peter J. Lloyd, *International Trade Problems of Small Nations* (Durham, N.C.: Duke University Press, 1968).

Several smaller European countries have experimented with some form of neutrality or nonalignment, and *all the direct referents of the European polity model have been neutral during most of their modern histories.* Thus, Sweden and Switzerland maintain an armed neu-trality: save for nuclear attack or total conventional war with one of the superpowers, their de-fensive capabilities provide them with credible deterrents. Austria has been neutral since regaining its autonomy in 1955, by edict of the major powers. Belgium, Denmark, Luxem-bourg, the Netherlands, and Norway moved away from a general orientation toward nonalign-ment only following the bitter experiences of World War II.

The populations and elites of all of these countries are vigorous supporters of arms reduc-tions and the lowering of the level of military confrontation in Europe between the United States and the Soviet Union. Clearly, in terms of their power positions, these small countries are not self-sufficient; and their leaders and populations do exhibit from time to time a sense of frustration over the lack of control (or, for that matter, of appreciable influence) of this vital variable that affects their destinies.

may exert influence toward the growth of structural symmetry across country frontiers.

It is in large part for this reason that we have labeled the system type with which we are concerned the *European* polity. For, through such cross-country organizations—at the heart of which is the European Community system itself—the peculiarities or special characteristics of the type are likely to be sharpened, and, over time, it is conceivable that dissimilarities between systems that are part of this interactional framework and systems that are outside it are likely to grow. We do not suggest that some political systems that do not participate in the European Community system might not exhibit all or most of traits A through P. Rather, the point is that if they do not also share in characteristic Q then, *over time*, their structural configuration may come to be unlike that of systems which do have reinforcing linkages with each other. Logically, then, system trait Q is more a developmental than simply a descriptive attribute of the European polity type. Clearly, the European milieus for interaction among systems that exhibit the type characteristics we have identified are important not because they comprise a setting in which all or most of the traits will be found, but because they designate a *nexus* for those features:

> . . . *relationships between variables will be different for data from different geographic or cultural contexts.* [109]

We are, thus, primarily concerned with a "configurative regionalism."[110]

The European polity, then, is likely to be approximated by a small country that is striving to minimize conflictive relationships with other countries and is involved in multicountry undertakings that tend to complement and reinforce its structural characteristics. It provides access to the policy- and decision-making centers for virtually all organized groups within the society; and it seeks to coopt group actors from all segments or sectors. The political society's divisive ideological predispositions—where such exist—are not transferred directly into the political system. Rather, the identification and resolution of issues tends to be technical and "rational"— not political. Clearly, however, the decision-making process is political by definition. It is not, as a rule, politicized in mass opinion or ideological cleavage terms; and it is this kind of politics that we find downgraded in importance in the European polity's decision-making core. The processes of output implementation, on the other hand, are likely to be highly politicized.

109. Hayward R. Alker, Jr., "Regionalism Versus Universalism in Comparing Nations," in *World Handbook of Political and Social Indicators*, ed. Bruce M. Russett et al. (New Haven: Yale University Press, 1964), p. 323.

110. Ibid., pp. 322–40.

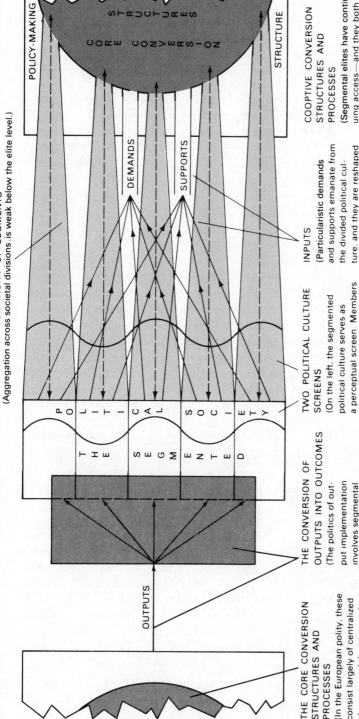

Figure 1. Flow Model of the European Polity

CONTINUITY OF SEGMENTS
(Aggregation across societal divisions is weak below the elite level.)

POLICY-MAKING

CORE CONVERSION STRUCTURES

STRUCTURE

DEMANDS

SUPPORTS

THE SEGMENTED POLITICAL SOCIETY

COOPTIVE CONVERSION STRUCTURES AND PROCESSES
(Segmental elites have continuing access—and they both influence the making of binding outputs and are, in turn, bound to accept the legitimacy of the output-generating processes.)

INPUTS
(Particularistic demands and supports emanate from the divided political culture, and they are reshaped by the general political culture.)

TWO POLITICAL CULTURE SCREENS
(On the left, the segmented political culture serves as a perceptual screen. Members perceive outcomes through a particularistic subculture. On the right, the general or societal political culture molds demands and supports into inputs that are processable by the system.)

THE CONVERSION OF OUTPUTS INTO OUTCOMES
(The politics of output implementation involves segmental actors at some points. Note that the impact of outcomes is segmentally perceived by the members of the system.)

OUTPUTS

THE CORE CONVERSION STRUCTURES AND PROCESSES
(In the European polity, these consist largely of centralized planning and decision making, performed in terms of technically defined issues.)

The emergence of the European polity—in a logical rather than a historical developmental sense—can be traced through three stages. First, elites at the system and group levels seek to cope with the divisive effects of groups that manifest predispositions to assert particularistic or narrowly perceived interests. The elite's response is to coopt the leadership of such groups. Second, once coopted, the group leaders begin to formulate their concerns less in distributive and zero-sum game terms and more in terms of technical problem solving, satisficing, administrative amelioration of problems, and maximizing stabilizing conditions at the system level. Third, the effectiveness of the system—and subsequent, feedback-induced public response to its operation—is judged largely in terms of the effective delivery of desired values and things. This last aspect points the way toward the operationalization of our model: can we, in fact, trace backward through time—with the aid of longitudinal analyses of quantified data on policy impact and system performance—the emergence of the structure type we have depicted? Further, would "the study of ecological correlation, Lazarsfeld's well-known technique of elaborating a relationship, and the multivariate statistical technique known as the analysis of covariance,"[111] together with other tests performed on aggregate data, show a geographical "Europeanness" in conjunction with the heuristic Europeanness we have postulated?

This, then, is a brief sketch of the European polity. It—or, more precisely, the actual systems that approach it most closely in the "real world"—is susceptible to a number of criticisms and doubts. The two most important among these are, in our estimation, the normative and the developmental. We now turn to these lines of attack, in two very brief notes. These are followed by an equally abbreviated note on the "Uses of the Model," in which the broad outline sketched in the paragraph above is related to some actual systems.

A Note on the Normative Implications of the Model

Cooptation should not, of course, connote consensus. The political stress-producing aspects of cleavages and conflicting outcome preferences may be ameliorated by the extension of structured participation by group actors in the policy-making process; and the mechanism of cooptation may—if it works effectively and if its preconditions obtain—enhance regime stability. Conflict is mitigated in the operative European polity; but is that, in itself, good? In an important sense, the cooptive polity preempts: effective political action, whether directed toward specific policy outputs, or toward the values in terms of which authoritative decisions are made, or toward the "rules of the political game," seems possible only through the

---

111. Ibid., pp. 323–24 and passim.

existing regime's structures and in terms of its operative norms. Alternative policy positions are clearly realizable, but implementing these—i.e., developing and using alternative means for generating policy and decisions—appears to be outside the regime's effective scope.

When meaningful participation in the political process is dependent on effective organization—organizational effectiveness being determined by the prevailing structural arrangement—a real danger exists that interests less rigorously or less harmoniously (vis-à-vis the structure) organized will find themselves excluded from the decision-making subsystem. (Among the illustrations cited above, the case of the unorganized Dutch workers' riot in 1966 is perhaps the most dramatic.) To assume that the dynamics of the structural features of the cooptive system and its technical "rules of the game" will incorporate such groups through some invisible or automatic processes would be naive indeed. Technological standards exclude demands that are or appear to be nonrational. Yet, such demands may well be legitimate; they may involve important human values—and democratic societies commonly expect that such demands will, indeed *must*, be heard.

Further, the delegation of powers to functionally established and legitimized agencies can blur the responsibilities of constitutionally accountable leaders. Functional rather than substantive accountability makes decision makers responsible only in terms of expert criteria, to experts, not to the public—which is thus shut out from the decision-making process in yet another way. This possibility is particularly crucial in societies in which the sectors themselves are not internally homogeneous.

Next, does this type of polity embody the values of stability, rational discourse, moderation and harmony; or does it stifle healthy—even essential—political disputation, renewal through dynamic competition, and the possibility for significant changes in the political lives of these societies? Clearly, these and similar considerations are important to the student of politics, and by assigning them to a marginal position in this paper we do not wish to indicate either an unawareness or a disregard of them.

There are, it seems to us, three major aspects of the overall normative dimension of the European polity that need to be considered even in a cursory overview. First, whether the amelioration of conflict between large subsocietal groups is viewed as good or as undesirable generally depends on one's perspective—whether it is that of the whole system or that of an aggrieved group. Thus, for instance, if the latter's perspective entails negative expectations with regard to long-range aspirations and the adjustment of value scales at the level of the system as constituted, then intergroup conflict may prove more desirable (for some members of the group in question, at any rate) than would its circumvention.[112] If, on the

---

112. See Georg Simmel, *Conflict*, trans. Kurt H. Wolff (New York: Free Press of Glencoe, 1955); Lewis A. Coser, *The Functions of Social Conflict* (New York: Free Press of Glencoe, 1956); and idem, *Continuities in the Functions of Social Conflict* (New York: Free Press, 1967).

other hand, the question is approached from the vantage point of the whole system, then its persistence may militate in favor of the avoidance of conflict. (We note some instances of such conflictive situations below, when we touch briefly on those ethnic and linguistic conflicts that lead to group demands for altering the shape or level of the political community.)

Second, as noted, the institutionalization of the cooptive regime norms curtails the growth and viability of alternative norm-sets—that is, of multifarious existing and potential oppositions. This is, of course, a conservative tendency. The most important safeguards against the possibility that such a tendency will move the regime toward a state of entropy are (1) the introduction of new actors and new value orientations—as noted in type characteristic (I), (I_1), and (I_2) above; and (2) the planning rationality, foresight, and ability of the leaders.

The conservative tendency of the regime may also detract significantly from the system's capability to respond appropriately and in good time to environmental challenges that differ appreciably from those already experienced. This is so because a system that operates through a broadly participatory, ever-compromising decisional mechanism will be less likely to adjust swiftly—especially if the degree of adjustment needed is substantial. The existence of, or opportunity for, markedly differing alternatives to the operating regime would seem to provide a higher potential for appropriate responses to new or drastic environmental inputs. All of this is to say that by increasing the efficiency and sensitivity of the system to respond to "withinputs," the European polity has sacrificed to a degree the efficiency and sensitivity of the system to (environmental) inputs. This loss of capability in coping with extrasystemic challenges may, of course, jeopardize the prospects for regime maintenance—and even for system persistence.

Finally, a third normative consideration centers on the fact that, in the European polity, the group is the basis for political representation. While the processes of interest articulation and aggregation tend to give similar roles to interest groups and political parties in most other types of systems, in the European polity the encapsulation and "pillarization" of social, political, and economic life through segmented role structures makes it much more difficult for individuals either to be selective in their acceptance of a role set (i.e., to behave in an idiosyncratic manner or to exhibit status inconsistency by choice) or to reject in toto the particular role set into which they had been socialized.

This last normative consideration may, in fact, be a contributing factor in the intergenerational ideological divisions that Abramson and Inglehart have noted (and upon which we comment below). It is also manifested in the eschewing of group-based participation in favor of individual participation. Olof Ruin recently commented on this phenomenon, as it occurs in

Sweden.[113] An increasing demand—particularly on the part of young people—is noticeable in Sweden (and in Norway and the Netherlands, to a lesser degree) for direct personal involvement in policy processes. This demand is quite independent of the capability of the cooptive mechanism to generate satisfactory outcomes.

The capability of the system that approximates the European polity model to coopt elements that are radically and explicitly opposed to the prevailing regime norms is truly impressive. Thus, for instance, the Amsterdam town council had elected to its membership and participate constructively in its normal governing activities members of two of the most radical social and political dissident groups. Young protesters—in the mid- and late 1960s the *Provos* (from *provocatie*, "provocation"), and in the early 1970s the *Kabouters* ("gnomes")—engaged in sometimes violent, generally massively disruptive acts of civil disobedience, while ideologically challenging the regime; and yet, their core elements were (relatively) successfully coopted! (It can in fact be argued that the *Kabouters* arose as a consequence of the cooptation of the *Provos*, since the latter appeared to have been tamed within less than two years of their appearance.)

While this capability of the regime demonstrates its "openness" and flexibility, it also raises a distressing question: how, if not through direct, extralegal confrontations with the political system's authorities and the society's values, can the individual or the dissident faction step outside the regime norms—for whatever purpose? It becomes difficult, in such circumstances, to fix or locate the regime along a number of value continua. It may also become difficult for the dissident to visualize a scenario for important regime-level change, short of an attack on the society itself—that is, short of change at the system level. These difficulties may well lead to frustration in attempts to evoke change and to the development of a sense of political impotence. Such consequences of the cooptive polity's efficient operation may well result in highly dislocative or disruptive behaviors and orientations. Such orientations may underlie the intergenerational ideological diffierences that Abramson and Inglehart have noted and analyzed, and the participatory demands discussed by Ruin. They may also contain the seeds of change for the system type.

The advent of new ideological divisions in the type of system under examination and the necessity to contemplate change in the type puts into sharp relief the rather static nature of our model. This is a concomitant of ideal-type modeling, we submit. For when the analytic foci are the ac-

---

113. "Participation, Corporativization, and Politicization: Trends in Present-day Sweden" (Paper presented at the Sixty-second Annual Meeting of the Society for the Advancement of Scandanavian Studies, New York, 5–6 May 1972).

centuated characteristics and peculiar configurations of some systems, then the muted, less pronounced manifestations of the systems' traits—manifestations more likely to be found in the stages of "coming into being" and "waning"—are not of central interest. Yet, clearly, no system type has existed in its current shape in all time, nor is it likely to persist unchanged. It came to possess its traits and configuration; and it will, in all likelihood, evolve different traits and shape. Although it is outside the scope of this paper to outline the developmental framework of the European polity, we now take note of some of the more immediate questions concerning the possible futures of the systems that approach the model.

The Developmental Perspective: Is the European Polity a Phase?

It will be recalled that one argument against the "decline of ideology" hypothesis noted above—an argument most notably advanced by LaPalombara[114]—is that, while one kind of ideological thinking and behavior may be declining, other forms of ideological division may be coming to the fore in the same systems. Our response to that argument was, in essence, that the point we sought to make by accepting the "decline" hypothesis as a working premise did not deal with ideology per se, but with the structural consequences of one particular ideological cleavage in the latter portion of the nineteenth century and the first part of the twentieth century in Europe—the division of rapidly mobilizing political societies into socioeconomic classes. We suggested that, in the European polity type of system (which, in developmental terms, was past the ideological age noted above), political structures were no longer shaped by conflicting world views based on clashing socioeconomically founded ideologies, and operating through parties and interest groups in an atmosphere of hostility and suspicion characterized by the perception of the political arena as a zero-sum game setting.

We have also indicated that, while the question of how the "consociational democracy" and "segmented pluralism" types came into being was of major interest for Lijphart and Lorwin, respectively, at this juncture in the construction of the European polity model we are more concerned with similarities in structure among a larger number of countries. For, as Lorwin's historical analysis and Lijphart's allusions to political culture traits indicate, there are important *developmental* differences between a number of the systems that exhibit marked structural similarities. The developmental differences, we submit, are of more legitimate interest to the historian, while

---

114. Joseph LaPalombara, "Decline of Ideology: A Dissent and an Interpretation," *American Political Science Review* 60, no. 1 (March 1966): 5–16. This article is reprinted in, among other places, Rejai, *Decline of Ideology?*

political structural similarities should be the primary concerns of students of politics.

This is not to say that we concede the argument that the developmental or historical differences between two or more sets of the countries that are our referents are substantial or that they have had lasting consequences. We could, in fact, construct a strong case for the argument that the Scandinavian systems, the Low Countries, and Switzerland partook of a common developmental pattern. (It will be remembered that the major difference between the scope of our model and that of the Lijphart and Lorwin constructs is that we conjoin three Scandinavian countries with the Low Countries, Switzerland, and Austria, while they exclude the Scandinavian systems.) As an illustration of one strong line of argumentation, we cite as one possible point of departure the profound observation of Hans Daalder that "European states fall *prima facie* into at least three distinct groups: (1) countries which developed slowly from oligarchies into consistently stable democracies: e.g. Britain, the Scandinavian countries, The Netherlands, Belgium, and Switzerland. . . ."[115] From that observation, we could proceed to argue that the sectoral representation manifested in the cartel of elites in the European polity has been made possible by the historic oligarchic structures (in late medieval and early modern city life, in guilds, in the churches—Protestant and Catholic alike, etc.). The longevity of such structures and the historic predisposition to accept them and work through them could then be regarded as an important underpinning of their legitimacy, and so forth.

But while it may prove fruitful to return to the historical perspective (especially in the context of the longitudinal studies we propose to use at the operational stage of the model), at this juncture of the modeling we are more concerned with the present structure and the most likely courses it might follow in the near future. Two forces that carry the potential for important change in the European polity are readily evident at this time, and we now note these very briefly.

One powerful force for change is manifested in an increasingly virulent and spreading attack on what is perceived by many younger citizens to be an incremental approach to public problems—an approach they deem both inadequate for coping with new challenges and, given its indwelling conservatism, normatively questionable. The other force with a potential for altering the nature of the polity type is a two-pronged drive to change the level at which the political systems of European countries operate. A shift toward a more inclusive system level may occur, if the European Commun-

115. Hans Daalder, "Parties, Elites, and Political Developments in Western Europe," in *Political Parties and Political Development,* ed. Joseph LaPalombara and Myron Weiner (Princeton, N.J.: Princeton University Press, 1966), p. 44.

ity of the "Nine" makes substantial progress toward supranational unification.[116] Alternatively—and probably with more immediacy—in some systems that approach the European polity model, politicized social cleavages (in particular those that combine to take the form of emerging nationalisms) may militate against the retention of the existing state structures—and may lead to some form of regional autonomy.

One possible interpretation of the emerging intergenerational ideological cleavages—in terms that are consistent with our model—is that ventured by Lammers, at the conclusion of his assessment of student unionism in the Netherlands through a social-class (i.e., "pre-European polity") model. Lammers suggests that student protest and activism (in many Western European countries, not only in the Netherlands)

> is in all likelihood not primarily centered around economic interests but rather around power and privilege interests, interests such as the loosening of tight bureaucratic rules, getting better educational service from a mainly research-oriented faculty, or generally showing University, Administration, and Faculty that students do not like to be shoved around or dealt with as a closing entry in the time budgets of these authorities.[117]

Two sets of concerns are embodied in the "power and privilege interests" Lammers notes. One of these derives from the cloture that characterizes the effectively operating cooptive structure. Students are being processed *as a class;* consequently, individuals may be alienated, because they are not being considered as individuals. (This form of individual reaction may, significantly, form the object of collective representations. The irony of a group forming in order to protest the absence of individual attention parallels the seeming incongruity of anarchists organizing into political parties.) The second concern is with the *quality* of the outputs provided by the system.

In effect, the former is a new type of participation demand; while the latter is a new focus on the quality of life—replacing the previous generation's preoccupation with distributional or quantitative outputs. At this point in time, whether the cooptive regime has the capability to provide the psychological satisfaction that can prevent or ameliorate the alienation to

116. See Lindberg's essay, chap. 6 in this volume. The "Nine" of course, consist of the original six signatories of the Paris and Rome treaties that established the European Coal and Steel Community (1951) and the European Economic Community and Euratom (1957)—Belgium, France, West Germany, Italy, Luxembourg, and the Netherlands; and the three members that recently joined them (effective 1 January 1973)—Great Britain, Denmark, and Ireland. Norway's status, following a negative vote on a referendum, will remain uncertain for some months or years.

117. Cornelis J. Lammers, "Student Unionism in the Netherlands: An Application of a Social Class Model," *American Sociological Review* 36, no. 2 (April 1971): 261–62.

which we have alluded is an open question. We would venture that mass participatory means—such as elections—will probably not suffice. Rather, it will probably be necessary for the components of the segmental or group infrastructure to adapt to the new demands by evolving new and appropriate forms.

There are numerous indications of an already widespread and rapidly growing awareness at all levels of planning, policy making, and policy implementation in most European countries of the shift from quantitative to qualitative value priorities on the part of many citizens. Thus, to cite some specific illustrations, urban planners in these countries have become deeply concerned with ambience, aesthetic environment, and other qualitative aspects or urban life in a modern society.[118] Labor unions are now more likely to bargain for improved working conditions instead of (or in addition to) simply for more money; and their leaders strive to satisfy the membership by developing more attractive leisure-time activities and facilities. Nutrition is discussed not in terms of the availability of foodstuffs, but in terms of the health and aesthetic values of comestibles. Indeed, it is interesting to note in this connection that virtually all Western and Northern European countries must import substantial numbers of foreign workers from less affluent societies (e.g., from Greece, southern Italy, Spain, and North Africa) to fill unskilled, menial and other low-status positions, since their own citizens are increasingly placing the value of *how* income is earned ahead of *how much* they are able to gain.

The size and social and functional scope of the state changes over time. This century has offered perhaps the first widespread opportunity for people to question the appropriateness of the size and nature of the units in which their political lives unfold.[119] European systems are affected both by drives for increasing the size (though not necessarily the functional scope) of the basic political system and by separatist or particularistic movements that seek greater social and/or political homogeneity and autonomy, at the cost of smaller size. From the perspective of the developmental prospects of the European polity type, the question we must ask is, How, to what extent (if at all), would new units that might emerge differ from the type?

118. Such concerns formed the theme of a "Conference on European Urbanism," sponsored by the Council for European Studies, Los Angeles, 18–21 June 1972. Most of the papers addressed the theme of "the quality of urban life" in Europe. European participants indicated that academic students of urban planning as well as practicing planners (and policy makers) had shifted their attention to questions of the quality of urban life in recent years in most Western European countries. (The United Kingdom, the Netherlands, Sweden, Norway, Denmark, and France were cited in particular.)

119. For the raising of this point, as well as for a brilliant essay on changes in the size and nature of political systems (and concomitant evolutions of political philosophy), see Karl W. Deutsch, *Political Community at the International Level* (Garden City, N.Y.: Doubleday, 1954), chap. 1.

While Lindberg and other students of European integration have speculated with cogency about the structural shape of the European Community's political system, it is probably more difficult to estimate the range over which the structures of, for instance, a confederal Belgium (in which the four Walloon provinces, the four Flemish provinces, and the Brussels *agglomeration* possessed not only cultural but also juridical and fiscal autonomy), or an Austria with the addition of South Tyrol, or a Switzerland with an autonomous canton of Jura might vary. The important point with regard to fissiparous movements is that their success would be in some measure an indication of the failure of the cooptive structure to sustain the original system. In the final analysis, the question of whether the original level should or should not be retained must be confronted; and the answer to such a question is largely a normative one.

Clearly, then, the European polity does not represent a final—or, for that matter, possibly even a particularly stable or lasting—stage of development. It is, as a model, a relatively static representation of the present structural configuration. We are aware of the limitations that accompany such a static model, but would suggest that this is an indispensable first step in the derivation of a dynamic—and, hence, more satisfactory—theory of European politics. The next stage in the development of such theory consists of applying the model; and, thereafter, it becomes appropriate to contemplate an operationalization that permits dynamic analysis.

A Note on the Uses of the Model

The European polity model presented on the preceding pages is an ideal-type construct. The principal utility of such a model is that it permits the identification of similarities among concrete ("real") phenomena, with the model serving as the standard of comparison. As indicated, the model has two dimensions for comparative analysis: (1) the type characteristics (A through Q) and (2) the configuration of those characteristics or the shape of the overall political structure. Before we would contemplate the task of application, it is useful to retrace the manner in which the model itself was derived.

We did not derive the type characteristics from an empirical examination of all or most extant political systems, or even of all (geographically or culturally) European systems. Clearly, there is nothing inductive about the model. Rather, we began with relatively impressionistically distilled *patterns* that we noted—in readings, field research, in perusal of whatever empirical data we encountered—in most of those European systems with which we have some familiarity. The three patterns identified early in the paper seemed to us both prevalent and important as characteristics of politics in most Western and Central European countries. We then sought to explain in a deductive fashion (1) the occurrence of those patterns and (2) their interrelationships. It was this endeavor that led us to the positing of the (highly accentuated) type characteristics.

Based on our general familiarity with the systems in question and a relatively thorough examination of the secondary literature, we have tentatively identified eight systems that seem to us to possess all the characteristics and to exhibit configurations that are quite close to those of the model. Additionally, we stipulate two other polities as being peripheral to the type: (1) they share most of the characteristics—but not all; and (2) they exhibit some slight congruity with the type's configuration. Finally, we see some important system-type characteristics exhibited by three other polities.

Prior to a systematic examination of relevant data, we consider Austria, Belgium, Denmark, Luxembourg, the Netherlands, Norway, Sweden, and Switzerland to fall within the European polity type-cell. Israel and Lebanon exhibit a substantial number of the type's traits; consequently, we tentatively classify them as "peripheral" to the type—i.e., borderline cases. The system of the European Communities can also be analyzed through the model. Finally, France, the Federal Republic of Germany, and the United Kingdom seem to share the three general patterns and exhibit a few of the system-type characteristics. Thus, we think it permissible—in the sense of avoiding "the travelling problem" noted by Sartori—to make limited comparisons between these three larger systems and members of the type.

Throughout the text, we have used illustrations from the systems we have classified as members of the European polity type-cell. In this way, we sought to transmit the impressions (via impressionistic "evidence") that helped to shape our preliminary judgments. On such bases, we would consider Norway, the Netherlands, and Sweden to be somewhat closer to the ideal type than are Belgium and Austria. (The remaining members of the type fall between the closest and most distant.) Essentially, the degree to which profound cleavages are politicized in these two polities is great enough to bring into question the stability of the cooptive structure and the pervasiveness of the political culture's norms for satisficing behavior.

Clearly, the next step in moving this rudimentary pretheoretic framework toward the status of theory is to operationalize it, formulate testable hypotheses, identify pertinent indicators, generate and analyze data, and formulate and interrelate the propositions thus derived into empirical theory. Only then will it be possible to say whether (1) this model is useful for the study of politics in European societies, and (2) if it offers a helpful explanation of what European systems do and do not have in common with each other—as well as with other systems. A number of scholars—including several of the contributors to this volume—have begun such work.

Summary

By focusing on the output-generating (i.e., policy and decision making) and implementing structures and processes, our model makes possible two theoretical improvements over previous constructs. One of these is in the realm of analytic approach, while the other consists of a substantive theoretical benefit. The first consists of a break with the long-employed, established preference for giving primary importance to "input-side" factors in the development of typologies and in the evaluation of structural means for improving system performance and enhancing regime viability or maintenance. Beginning with Almond's distinctions between "Anglo-American" and "Continental European" democracies, and continuing through Lijphart's and Lorwin's constructs, gross characterizations of political culture and of party subsystems served as the basic dimensions of classificatory analysis. While Lijphart's concern with overarching or cross-sectoral elites (in the consociational democracy model) opened a window on the structural core of the system, the view of the essential structural features was still, in large part, obscured by a preoccupation with political cultural fragmentation; and only the relatively tenuous element of leadership ability and intent served as the central structural anchor.

Without denying the importance and pervasiveness of political cultural heterogeneity in some of the countries in the European polity type-cell or the existence of politicized social and economic pluralism in all such systems, we nevertheless maintain that such and similar features (and differences in the variables of which they are comprised) *do not* determine the nature of the polity. Rather, we suggest that the processes by which the various sectors of the political society are coopted (through their leaders) into the systemic structures of output generation and the habits of (advisory or quasi-authoritative) consultation that help to blur the distinctions between public, quasi-public, and private responsibility and interest combine to mitigate the destabilizing potential of the cleavages.

While it is probably true that the scope, pervasiveness, legitimacy, and stress-reducing capability of such a structure moves with political cultural homogeneity, we suspect that the output-structural and political-cultural variable sets do not covary with precision. We recommend (and shall in part follow up in work now in progress and planned) that the input-side analytic and research emphasis be partially superseded by an emphasis on formal and informal structural configurations at the level of the whole system and at the subnational level as well, with special attention accorded to output generation and implementation, the impacts of public policies, and the assessment of system performance.

The most important substantive theoretical contribution that may be derived from the European polity model is related to the structural emphasis recommended above. We believe that the identification of the cooptive structure leads to more accurate and broader explanations—and, perhaps, with the empirical testing of hypotheses of the sort that can be derived from our pretheory, to predictions—of politics in most of the countries of Western and Central Europe than is possible through the more limited consociational democracy and segmented pluralism models. In projecting our model on a more general plane than Lijphart and Lorwin deemed appropriate for theirs, we have sought to construct (pre)theory in an orderly and cumulative fashion; but we have also endeavored to extend the explanatory umbrella only as far as the theoretical and empirical resources presently available would warrant.

The next task in this ambitious and clearly long-term enterprise is the generation of an operationalized version of the model. Such a model will make possible the formulation of hypotheses that can be tested through empirical indicators. A coordinated effort by a number of scholars in the social sciences—working on both sides of the Atlantic—has been launched toward that end.

Part II

EUROPEAN POLITY-LIKE SYSTEMS: Illustrative Cases

3

Robert B. Kvavik

Interest Groups in a "Cooptive" Political System: The Case of Norway

An analysis of interest groups in the political process generally proceeds from a normative paradigm of group interaction and participation which suggests that public policy is—or ought to be—the product of an unencumbered competition among societal groups seeking to realize the articulated private interests of their membership.[1] Together with structural-functionalism and Easton's conceptualization of the political process, the above model of interest groups and the interest group system has skewed—one could say limited—the study of groups toward "input politics," i.e., "the politics of being heard." Typical studies define, implicitly or explicitly, interest groups as agencies which articulate the special interests of societal subsectors, e.g., farming, fishing, shipping, religious sects, etc. The studies show how groups effectively vie with each other for the attention of policy makers and implementers; demonstrated are methods by which a group's "private demands" are realized. In effect, one explains the causal sequence of "inputs" upon societal "outputs."

Several factors undermine the applicability of the above paradigm or admixture of conceptual ideas in a non-American or comparative setting. First, interest groups are undergoing complementary changes in structure and societal role. Ultimately, the articulation of special interests by groups (input activity) in certain polities may be less important than their partici-

---

1. The most often cited sources of the paradigm include Arthur Bentley, *The Process of Government* (Chicago: University of Chicago Press, 1908); David Truman, *The Governmental Process* (New York: Alfred A. Knopf, 1951); and Earl Latham, *The Group Basis of Politics* (Ithaca: Cornell University Press, 1952).

pation as policy makers or public administrators (conversion or output activity).[2] Second, the conception of groups in essentially competitive relationships to one another is inaccurate for political systems such as Norway, Sweden, the Netherlands, and to a lesser extent, Denmark and Belgium. In the European polities noted, public policy is not the result of an unencumbered or even partially controlled competition among diverse societal groups but rather a product of highly routinized and deliberate proceedings between government and bureaucratized interest groups—many of the latter enjoying virtual monopolies over distinct issue areas. Samuel Beer emphasizes similar trends in his discussion of the changing structure and relationships of economic groups in Great Britain:

> In the past two generations or so, certain structural changes have taken place—reaching a further point of development in Great Britain than in the United States—that depart radically from this model. These developments, which we may call "collectivism," can be summarized under four headings. One is the tendency to a concentration of economic power among a few large buyers or sellers in a particular industry or complex of industries. Along with the increase in size of units has gone a change in internal structure that is referred to by terms such as bureaucracy and managerialism. Moreover, where such large units have grown up, they tend to deal with one another by a process of "bargaining"—or perhaps it is better to say "collective bargaining." Finally, while bargaining tends to be confined to the relations of producers—whether business firms or trade unions—in their dealings with the mass of ultimate consumers, large units have learned to shape, even to create, the very "wants" that presumably they have come into existence to satisfy.[3]

Beer's description has broader application. For our purposes, three points need to be emphasized: (1) monopoly increasingly characterizes the relationships of interest groups (particularly economic groups) to issue areas; (2) concomitantly, the terms bureaucracy and managerialism best describe the participants and decision-making style affecting policy content and focus; and (3) the relationship of citizen to government with groups as intermediaries (as idealized in pluralist models of society) is undermined by agencies which create—on an elite level—the wants of the citizens they represent.

The phenomenon in question—sometimes referred to as neocor-

2. See, esp., Samuel Eldersveld, "American Interest Groups: A Survey of Research and Some Implications for Theory and Method," in *Interest Groups on Four Continents*, ed. Henry W. Ehrmann (Pittsburgh: Pittsburgh University Press, 1958). Studies also question the effectiveness of groups as articulators of special interests; see Raymond A. Bauer, Ithiel DeSola Poole, and Lewis Anthony Dexter, *American Business and Public Policy* (New York: Atherton Press, 1963).

3. Samuel Beer, "Group Representation in Britain and the United States," *Annals of the American Academy of Political and Social Science* 319 (September 1958): 131.

poratism or corporate pluralism—takes an extreme form in Norway.[4] Monopolization of distinct issue areas by networks of interest groups is an accepted and common occurrence; the articulation, modification, and implementation of public policy is increasingly left to a "functional elite" operating without the constraints of constant public surveillance; the monopolistic or corporate arrangement is substantially institutionalized. Accordingly, Norway becomes an interesting case study for the delineation of dimensions of corporate pluralism, particularly those aspects of the system that govern the interrelationships of interest groups to interest groups, interest groups to citizens, and interest groups to government. The sections that follow describe in detail the phenomenon as it occurs in Norway. In so doing they (1) present dimensions to be considered in an alternative model of interest group interaction and (2) develop a better understanding of how public decisions are made in Norway.

Data

In 1967 Amanuensis Jorolv Moren of the University of Oslo and I constructed and administered two questionnaires. The first, a mail questionnaire, investigated the role of representatives—from government, interest groups—on over eight hundred law-making and advisory councils listed in *Odelstingsmelding Nr. 3*.[5] The questionnaire assessed degrees and kind of participation by public and private sectors of the society; it determined the purpose and patterns of decision making of the committees—royal councils, boards, and directorates. The questionnaire provided basic data for a description of the marginally studied complex of committees central to the making of public policy in Norway. The second questionnaire consisted of a battery of open-ended questions on the role of interest groups and their representatives. Questions were designed to determine which decision-making arenas groups sought access to, where they were effective, whether they were satisfied with existing arrangements, etc. The questionnaire was administered to twenty-seven leading representatives of Norwegian interest groups. A follow-up study by Moren collected descriptive data on six thousand participants in the committee system. The present analysis of groups in Norway benefits from the availability of all three bodies of data and by the research and findings presented to date. To facilitate the description, comparisons are made with the United States to highlight Norwegian patterns

4. See esp. Stein Rokkan, "Norway: Numerical Democracy and Corporate Pluralism," in *Political Oppositions in Western Democracies*, ed. Robert A. Dahl (New Haven: Yale University Press, 1966), chap. 3.

5. *Odelstingsmelding Nr. 3* is a government document cataloging administrative councils and their participants. As a locational device, it greatly facilitated research and guaranteed that the study encompassed the entire committee network.

of group behavior, group structures, and their interrelationships with one another and the government.

Traditional Group Politics: The Problem of Access

Interest-group behavior in the United States has generally been characterized as a politics of inputs consisting of two sets of behaviors: (1) gaining access to political decision makers; and (2) effecting group demands through influence on public officials by means of a variety of "pressure techniques" once access has been attained, e.g., after the group is an established clientele of some governmental agency.[6] Realization of group goals (the object of group participation in the political process) is determined by the success of the interest group's strategies and behavior on each of the two stages.

The proposition of group political behavior as two-staged input politics is best stated by David Truman: "Toward whatever institution of government we observe interest groups operating, the common feature of all their efforts is the attempt to achieve effective access to the points of decision."[7] But this is only the minimum or first requisite objective in the attainment of group goals. "Once achieved, access provides an opportunity to maneuver, a chance to use established relationships and procedures of the legislative body to give effect to group claims."[8] That is to say, once access is achieved, groups provide additional inputs (of varying kinds—information, threats, bribes) to the system which are designed to get the decision maker to act favorably in the group's behalf. In this second stage, group goals are successfully or unsuccessfully effected through decision-making behavior of the "pressured" officials. The politics of inputs, especially the gaining of access, is considered the most critical set of group behaviors relating to interest-group goal attainment in the political system. The competitive behavior of groups, either of stage 1 or stage 2, yields the result—public policy.

Political scientists accept the almost universal principle that interest groups in all political systems seek access to decision-making arenas. Groups especially seek access to those arenas wherein power resides and which offer the least resistance to group participation. In the United States such critical arenas for decision making are many, as evidenced by the wide and varied access points groups effectively utilize. Group studies indicate the access of voluntary associations to the president, the administration, both Houses of

6. "Pressure techniques" may not be the best of terms. It is only partially descriptive of the behavior of interest groups and their representatives. Conceptually it implies a mechanistic model of group interaction.
7. Truman, *Governmental Process*, p. 264.
8. Ibid., p. 353.

Congress, the federal courts, and to similar arenas on the state and municipal levels of government.[9]

The Norwegian Pattern of Access

A competition among interest groups for access to public officials, a basic necessity and first step in group politics of the American system, is noticeably absent in the Norwegian polity. Instead, interest groups find themselves established participants in the decision-making process with an institutionalized set of communication channels continually open to them. They are expected to and do utilize these channels on a regular basis. One means of communication, the *remiss* system, uniformly incorporates most organizations into the policy-making process. Many groups obtain access through cooptation or penetration into the decision-making process, particularly into the large administrative committee system—to be described together with the *remiss* system in the following sections. Within the committee system access is an established reality because of earlier efforts by voluntary associations or the initiative of public officials to make the formation of public policy an informally institutionalized and cooperative

9. For studies focusing on interest groups on the state level, see Harmon Zeigler, "Interest Groups and the States," in *Politics and the American States*, ed. Herbert Jacob and Kenneth N. Vines (Boston: Little, Brown, 1965); Harmon Zeigler and Michael Baer, *Lobbying: Interaction and Influence in American State Legislatures* (Belmont: Wadsworth, 1969); Kenneth Janda et al., *Legislative Politics in Indiana* (Bloomington, Ind.: Indiana University Press, 1961); John C. Wahlke, Heinz Eulau, William Buchanan, and LeRoy C. Ferguson, *The Legislative System* (New York: John Wiley, Inc., 1962); Samuel C. Patterson, "The Role of the Lobbyist: The Case of Oklahoma," *Journal of Politics* 25, no. 1 (February 1963): 72–92; Ronald D. Hedlund and Samuel C. Patterson, "Personal Attributes, Political Orientations, and Occupational Perspectives of Lobbyists: The Case of Illinois," *Iowa Business Digest* 37, no. 11 (November 1966): 3–11. Studies of group activity on the Congress include Lester W. Milbrath, *The Washington Lobbyists* (Chicago: Rand McNally, 1963); Bauer, Pool, and Dexter, *American Business and Public Policy;* Albert Somit and Joseph Tanenhaus, "The Veteran in the Electoral Process: The House of Representatives," *Journal of Politics* 19, no. 2 (May 1957): 184–201; Luke E. Ebersole, *Church Lobbying in the Nation's Capital* (New York: Macmillan, 1951); Robert A. Dahl, *Congress and Foreign Policy* (New York: Harcourt, Brace, 1950). For a study of groups and political parties, see Hugh A. Bone, "Political Parties and Pressure Group Politics," *Annals of the American Academy of Political and Social Science* 319 (September 1958): 73–83. Studies of groups and the executive-administrative branch include Theodore J. Lowi, *The End of Liberalism* (New York: W. W. Norton, 1969); Grant McConnell, *Private Power and American Democracy* (New York: Alfred A. Knopf, 1966); J. Leiper Freeman, "The Bureaucracy in Pressure Politics," *Annals* 319 (September 1958): 10–19. Group activity and the courts is discussed in Clement Vose, "Interest Groups, Judicial Review and Local Government," *Western Political Quarterly* 19, No. 1 (March 1966): 85–100; Lucius Barker, "The Supreme Court as Policy-Maker: The Tidelands Oil Controversy," *Journal of Politics* 24, no. 2 (May 1962): 350–66. There are numerous other examples of group activity on various levels of government in the United States. Case studies, for example, trace the activity of a group on multiple levels of government and in different arenas. For the most part, all focus on "input politics." For an extensive bibliography on groups, see Truman, *Governmental Process*. For a description and evaluation of various approaches, see Eldersveld, "American Interest Groups."

effort by all individuals and institutions (public and private) that in any way have some vested interest in a particular outcome.[10]

As a matter of course, all recognized interests in Norway are incorporated or coopted into the decision-making process in one or more of three ways.[11] For all groups access is established by the *remiss* system. A *remiss* is a written response—generally by an organization—to a request from an administrative department concerning evaluation of policy decisions of import to the organization. *Remisser* are given in response to department (ministry) drafts of legislation and also to formally written bills of official committees *(offentlig komitéinnstilling)*. In recent years, the administration has asked for a *remiss* from all groups they feel can legitimately react to a particular piece of legislation.[12]

A more significant form of cooptation is direct participation on administrative committees where important policies are formulated and which often serve as implementing agencies for the policy they write. Rokkan says of these agencies and their work:

> The crucial decisions on economic policy are rarely taken in the parties or in Parliament: the central area is the bargaining table where the government authorities meet directly with the trade union leaders, the representatives of the farmers, the smallholders, and the fishermen, and the delegates of the Employers' Association. These yearly rounds of ne-

10. An effort toward formal incorporation of groups into administrative bodies came after World War II with the establishment of the *Økonomiske Samordningsråd* (Board of Economic Coordination, an organization similar to the *Sociaal-Economische Raad* (Social Economic Council) of the Netherlands, Weimar Germany's *Reichswirtschaftsrat* and *Le Conseil Économique et Social* of France.

11. Criticism of regularized access occurs in McConnell, *Private Power*, and in Lowi, *End of Liberalism*.

The cooperative behavior of interest groups and the Norwegian administration are not unlike the relationships that have been developing between certain American organizations and administrative departments. Organizations such as the American Medical Association and the U.S. Chamber of Commerce have long had a clientele relationship with particular departments—clientele relationships being related to official cooptation. According to Lowi and McConnell, particular groups—notably farming, labor and business—have long been coopted for administrative decision-making functions. For a discussion of clientele relationships, see Aaron B. Wildavsky, "Budgetary Strategies of Administrative Agencies," in *Readings in American Political Behavior*, ed. Raymond E. Wolfinger (Englewood Cliffs, N.J.: Prentice-Hall, 1966); Robert Engler, *The Politics of Oil* (Chicago: Phoenix Books, University of Chicago Press, 1961). One critical difference between the two political systems is that the Norwegian pattern takes place with a set of expectations and norms congruent with monopolistic behavior. This is not true of the United States. The incongruence of competitive norms and monopolistic behavior is the basis for the normative objections of Lowi and McConnell.

12. For information on the *remiss* system, see Lars Foyer, "Former för Kontakt och Samverkan Mellan Staten och Organisationerna," *Statens Offentliga Utredningar 1961:21* (Stockholm: Justiedepartementet, 1961); Nils Elvander, *Interesseorganisationerna i Dagens Sverige* (Lund: CWK Gleerup Bokförlag, 1966). *Remisser* received, pro and con, are usually reported with the recommended legislative draft sent to Parliament by an administrative unit.

gotiations have in fact come to mean more in the lives of rank-and-file citizens than the formal elections.[13]

The degree of cooptation of groups, the institutionalization of the negotiations, and the role of committees is explained in the next section. A third form of cooptation is the delegation of public responsibility to "private" organizations. This is common in the farming and fishing sectors where organizations such as *Landbruketssentralforbund* (The Central Federation of Norwegian Cooperatives) implement or administer the details of the contract between government and the large organizations representing the farm sector.[14] General enabling legislation gives the organization substantial leeway in the application of legislation or negotiated contracts.

The development of the *remiss* system and the increased participation of interest groups in administrative committees has been accompanied by a lessening of interest-group activity with political parties and the legislature. The shift in foci and style of participation distinguishes the Norwegian polity from the American. Several recent studies amplify the apolitical orientation of voluntary associations and their technocratic leadership. Egil Fivelsdal and Knut Dahl Jacobsen report on the neutrality of most organizations in Norwegian elections.[15] A content analysis of organization journals demonstrates that few take a public, partisan stand (labor unions being an exception). The authors conclude that an informal norm militates against partisan activity. Valen and Katz, working with Fivelsdal and Jacobsen's data, support the finding. In 1957 organizations urged their members to go to the polls, but few organizations specified which party their members should support. This behavior was true even of some labor unions. Parties carried no advertisements in organization journals; organizations contributed no funds to party campaigns. Valen and Katz comment on the phenomena as follows:

> Apparently it is an official policy of all . . . organizations to avoid taking a partisan stand. The minimum requirements for such neutrality seem to be that they (1) do not support any party financially, and (2) do not encourage their members to vote for any particular party. Implicitly, however, they may take a stand, e.g., by commenting upon political decisions or policies of relevance for their own interests.[16]

13. Rokkan, "Norway," p. 107.
14. For a detailed discussion of the "public" activities of the farm organization, see Central Federation of Norwegian Cooperatives, *Norwegian Agriculture and Its Organizations* (Oslo: Central Federation of Agricultural Cooperatives, 1966).
15. Egil Fivelsdal and Knut Dahl Jacobsen, *Interesseorganisasjoner og Stortingsvalg* (Oslo: Institutt for Samfunnsforskning, 1962).
16. Henry Valen and Daniel Katz, *Political Parties in Norway* (Oslo: Universitetsforlaget, 1964; London: Tavistock, 1964), p. 310.

The journal of the Federation of Norwegian Commercial Associations, *Næringsrevyen*, is a good example of what Valen and Katz suggest. *Næringsrevyen* makes extensive commentary on public officials and political parties. Nevertheless, *Næringsrevyen* does not seem to limit its criticism to any one department or any one party. The journal takes a neutral, nonpartisan stand.

Regi Enerstvedt, in a longitudinal analysis of the top economic stratum in Norway, discerns an unmistakable downward trend in the political activity and orientation of organization leadership.[17] Comparing activity in the modern period to earlier decades (1890, 1900, etc.), he shows that only 29 percent of the top economic stratum as compared with 63 percent of the earlier leadership group participate in partisan activities. He suggests that the political entrepreneur as an organization representative is a phenomenon of an earlier age.[18] Enerstvedt's findings are reinforced by the statements of the twenty-seven interest-group representatives I interviewed in 1967. Partisan activities reflected the personal preferences of the representative—they were considered "private," i.e., the activity in no way obligated or affected the organization. Ranking the percentage of time spent on behalf of the organization with public institutions, all representatives ranked the administrative committees highest—parties and partisan activity were considered unimportant.[19]

Relationships between parties and interest groups do exist and I do not mean to imply they are insignificant. But they must be seen in the perspective of the broader decision-making process in which there is extensive cooptation of interest groups on the administrative level. Valen and Katz point out that groups are related to parties as follows:

> Informally . . . parties are tied to social groups through two devices: (1) overlapping leadership, and (2) the operation of informal groups within the party structure. In the relationship between the Labor Party and the trade union movement two additional ties exist, which are more formal in character: (3) liaison committees between the party and the unions and joint managership of enterprises like the Labor press, and (4) collective affiliation, a procedure through which local labor unions can have membership and representation in the party at the local level.[20]

17. Regi Th. Enerstvedt, "Toppskiktet i næringslivet. Politisk deltakelse og partipreferanse 1890–1940," *Tidskrift for Samfunnsforskning* 4 (1967): 269–91.

18. The existence of lobbies as found in American state capitals and Washington, D.C., and as defined by Milbrath—so essential for the transmission of information requisite for effective decision making in the American system—are virtually unknown in Norway. Valen and Katz indicate that the Norwegian Temperance Union may be an exception. Valen and Katz, *Political Parties in Norway*, p. 304. The existence of a "political entrepreneur" (Milbrath's term) never occurs in Norway.

19. Robert B. Kvavik, "Interest Groups in Norway: A Study of Corporate Pluralism" (Ph.D. dissertation, Stanford University, 1970).

20. Valen and Katz, *Political Parties in Norway*, p. 313.

The relationship of groups and parties may partially explain the failure of interest groups to focus in parliament and parties. They can be shown (in some instances) to be constituent members of parties, or "aligned." When action is required through the parliament, interest groups have established channels to utilize. But such action is seldom required. Lately, there has been pressure within the unions to dissolve their "informal" ties with the Labor party, given the recognition by the union leadership of the following significant factors: (1) more and more legislation is being settled outside parliament; and (2) the Labor party is not as strong as it once was. It appears to the union that its effectiveness can be increased by acting in a politically neutral fashion with the administration. The administration gives weight to arguments that are stated in apolitical and technical terms.

The tendency away from parties and toward the administration by interest groups is a general system-wide phenomenon in Norway. Partial causes of the change include the lessening role of the legislature in the formulation of public policy, and of late, the realization that no one party is likely to emerge with a majority in the Storting—as implied above. No interest group can afford to link its fortunes with those of a political party in such circumstances. What is preferred and supported is a dual arrangement, a two-tiered system, as Rokkan calls it. In such a system, established interests are protected through affiliations with parties and hence the legislature (tier 1) as well as through durable arrangements with the national administration (tier 2).[21] The strategy is to participate heavily within the administration in a politically neutral fashion (as required by the administration) while still maintaining good relations with any government that may be formed.

Support for the assertion of a refocusing of group activities—for the minimal use of parties and the legislature—is reflected in the comments of the twenty-seven representatives. Most of the organization representatives felt that there was little they could do on the parliamentary level and preferred to keep at a distance. Most often, contact was made with a member of parliament only if the member initiated the contact, i.e., asked for advice or requested the organization to make a statement about its feelings on a particular bill presently before the parliament. In most cases, if organizations such as the Norwegian Federation of Industries or the Federation of Norwegian Commercial Associations contacted the parliament directly, it was as a last resort after all other possibilities had been exhausted. Never, for example, would a case be brought up simultaneously to the parliament and the administration. Such action would not speed up or positively influence an outcome. Rather, given the procedures for drafting public policy and the norms of the system, such behavior would be exceedingly detrimental to all the important group relationships on the administrative level. It would upset the administration's

21. Rokkan, "Norway," p. 106.

ability to control the bill; it would make a political issue of a problem that in most cases could be handled as a technical matter; it would make public a matter that could be solved in cooperation with the concerned private and public parties; it would cause suspicion.

At this point we would summarize certain distinguishing characteristics of the Norwegian polity presented thus far:

1. Access is not a goal of organizations that are *established* participants in the decision-making process. In Norway, most organizations are established organizations. How established they are is demonstrated in the next section.

2. Access is maintained primarily within one decision-making arena and is not sought in arenas traditionally considered foci of group activity. Participation is limited to the administrative sector and is not diversified—directed at multiple decision-making arenas.

3. The shift in levels of participation from parties and the legislature to the administration together with the cooptive form the shift has taken must be considered a major characteristic of the Norwegian polity.[22] It has been accompanied by a change in style of participation, in organization structure and organization leadership. Bureaucrats, technically trained representatives, have emerged as the leading spokesmen of interest groups. Political entrepreneurs are nonexistent. "Managerialism" best describes the activities and objectives of interest groups.

4. An additional characteristic is that the cooptation results in substantial control over distinct issue areas by the groups most affected by the activity of the administrative committees. In its extreme form, one organization is entrusted by the government with a monopoly over its own quasi-public and private affairs.

Interest Groups in the "Conversion Process"

It is misleading to focus on a politics of access in Norway. First, interest groups do not transmit demands to parties and the legislature to the same degree and with the same import as found in the United States. In the case of political parties, the interaction between parties and interest groups may be characterized as a one-way relationship. That is, while parties try to gain the support of interest groups, the groups do not reciprocate the attention and concern. Second, interest groups are established participants in the administration's central decision-making apparatus. In the latter arena, interest groups must be seen as "insiders." They behave as insiders as their representatives fulfill public or quasi-public roles in a decision-making process where distinctions between public and private have been obfuscated. As I shall demonstrate, Norwegian groups perform a developed and

22. The "European polity" type demonstrates this phenomenon as well; see the Heisler-Kvavik essay, chap. 2 in this volume.

formalized role in the conversion of inputs to outputs; i.e., their representatives fill official decision-making positions in one of two arenas: (1) the committee structure, and (2) managing the various publicly recognized monopolies of the corporatelike economic sectors. In each case, organizations contribute substantially more to the making of public policy than simply articulating demands and presenting technical information; their representatives take on roles which suggest they are more than articulators of private interests.

As of 1971 there were 1,069 committees formally attached to one of four levels of the Norwegian administration and within which groups played a significant role. The four levels include: (1) the fourteen regular departments (ministries), (2) independent agencies, (3) partially dependent agencies, and (4) public corporations. Most common are the committees attached to regular departments. The committees are categorized according to function by Jorolv Moren as shown in table 1.[23] Of the six types of com-

Table 1. Types of Norwegian Committees: Distribution as of 1967

Type	Number
1. Boards and commissions responsible for the management of various public services	215
2. Commissions for inquiry (permanent and ad hoc); for the formulation of public policy	180
3. Councils and committees for coordination of various branches of the public administration. The committees are generally limited to consultative functions, but on occasion wield actual authority	80
4. Advisory bodies primarily designed to provide the civil service with the viewpoints of interest groups	110
5. Advisory bodies with expert status	80
6. Control commissions handling matters of appeal from clients	135

mittees, numbers 2, 4, and 5 are oriented toward the clarification of issues, while numbers 1, 3, and 6 have as their main task the making or enforcement of decisions.

Boards are highly independent committees acting on their own responsibility in a wide variety of issue areas: export policy, labor market problems, agricultural marketing, regulation of schools and hospitals, etc. These problems are often political matters appropriately handled by parliament and the parties. But in Norway, these problems—to a substantial degree—have been delegated by traditional political institutions to bureaucratic agencies. Boards are institutions representative of what has been

23. Jorolv Moren, "Organization Theories and the Study of Boards, Councils and Commissions in Public Administration," in *Contributions to the Theory of Organizations II*, ed. Torben Agersnap (Copenhagen: Munksgaard, 1968), pp. 64–65.

called the "depoliticization" phenomenon, especially when a particular private group or set of groups dominates board membership. *Commissions for inquiries,* according to Jorolv Moren, are generally not permanent organizations.

> They can, however, be considered the principal tool for the preparation of new legislation and also for the investigation of policy questions at an early stage. The more important and far reaching the problems, the more indispensable such search activities are thought to be.[24]

Group participation on these committees is extensive. It is routinized and established for groups representing functional sectors of society. *Councils for coordination* are essentially bureaucratic mechanisms for the stipulation of administrative responsibility. The committees manage or coordinate bureaucratic services. *Councils for the representation of interests* are essentially advisory bodies consisting of representatives from the government and interest organizations. The government plays a mediating role between groups seeking the implementation of rules or private demands by administrative agencies. The administrative agencies affected by decisions of the advisory bodies are generally those that enjoy a wide spectrum of interpretative discretion granted to them by the legislature. As a rule, these committees coincide with economic sectors usually controlled by Norway's most important interest groups. Participation on advisory bodies is generally fixed by committee statute or existing informal norms. *Councils of experts* "operate like the foregoing category as advisory agents within loosely programmed sectors of the administration, where the information they provide rather than the written rules, make up the most important criteria for policy decisions."[25] They encounter the policy-making process at a later stage. The experts are often members of voluntary associations. *Bodies for control and appeal* enforce principles stipulating administrative ethics or fairness and efficiency. To some degree, they clarify any ambiguities in existing legislation.[26]

---

24. Ibid., p. 73.
25. Ibid.
26. Jorolv Moren is more explicit about the characteristics of the committee system. He is presently engaged in research that will investigate in detail the entire network of boards and councils. A body of literature is emerging to clarify the role of administrative bodies in the making of Scandinavian public policy. The major research includes Jorolv Moren, *Organisasjonene og forvaltningen,* Skrifter fra Norges Handelshøyskole i rekken almene emner Nr. 3. (Bergen: A. Garnæs Boktrykkeri, 1958); Bent Christensen, *Nævn og Råd* (Copenhagen: Gads Boktrykkeri, 1958); a government document of the Norwegian government entitled *Innstilling for Komitéen til å utrede spørsmålet om mer betryggende former for den offentlige forvaltning* (Oslo, 1958); Hans Meijer, "Bureaucracy and Policy Formation in Sweden," *Scandinavian Political Studies,* vol. 4, ed. Olof Ruin (Oslo: Universitetsforlaget, 1969); C. J. Hansen, *Guide to Decisions: The Royal Commission* (New York: Bedminister Press, 1965). A study is presently under way on the Danish system by Egil Fivelsdal and Torben Beck Jørgensen of the Institut for Ledelsesforskning, Copenhagen.

Composition of Committees, Tasks of Committee Representatives, and Implications

The composition of Norwegian committees is described in table 2. We find politicians filling 3 percent of all positions; administrative officials, 20 percent; public officials such as police, military, court personnel, 22 percent; educators, 13 percent; and representatives from interest groups, 42 percent. The table suggests broad participation by all societal agencies (public and private) in the Norwegian policy-making process.[27] I would emphasize the extensive participation—or cooptation—of representatives from voluntary associations. If we incorporate universities into the interest-group representatives category, then the percentage of interest-group representation swells to better than half of all the participants in the committee system. Table 2 also demonstrates the division of labor in the committee system, i.e., the tasks and the participants assigned to specific jobs. About 61 percent of the positions belong to committees dealing with the clarification of issues (committee types 2, 4, and 5—see table 1); 39 percent enforce public policy (committee types 1, 3, and 6). The table shows that groups supply the largest percentage of manpower to type 1 and more naturally type 4 committees.

Table 2 does not demonstrate patterns of representative concentration. We can estimate that 15 percent of the organizations—particularly peak organizations—fill 93 percent of the positions occupied by interest groups. The trade unions, employers' organizations and industrial groups each hold close to 10 percent of the positions allocated to interest groups. Similar concentration occurs in the administrative sector where Hoven and Hallenstvedt, using Moren's data, have determined that 272 representatives hold 623 positions on 351 committees.[28] The "concentration" phenomenon raises the question of balance of interests on committees. If the system tolerates the concentration of positions by several organizations, how—or why—can public policy be acceptable to the society as a whole? First, the organizations that participate extensively are peak organizations—organizations that represent most organizations in the same economic sector (62 percent of all Norwegian organizations are economic organizations).[29] All the major economic sectors have a peak organization. If peak organizations are representative of their sector's interests, then the problem of extensive participation—or concentration—by a small percentage of the groups is not as disturbing as it might otherwise be. The concentration factor is a charac-

27. The figures in table 2 are different from the figures presented by Meijer for the Swedish system. Organization participation is substantially less in Sweden—22 percent as compared with 42 percent; participation by members of parliament is higher (18 percent). In Norway, members of parliament play a minor role. Representation in the Norwegian system would seem much broader and diverse. Meijer, "Bureaucracy and Policy Formation in Sweden."

28. Abraham Hallenstvedt and Finn Holmer Hoven, "Den Kollegiale Administrasjon" (unpublished ms., December 1971).

29. Kvavik, "Interest Groups in Norway," p. 68.

Table 2. Committee Composition by Type of Committee

Representative Type Committee	Politicians N = 171 (3%)	Administration N = 1,221 (20%)	Public officials N = 1,359 (22%)	Educators N = 799 (13%)	Interest Groups N = 2,625 (42%)	Total 6,175
Type 1	43	225	264	156	639	1.327 (21%)
Type 2	20	144	118	101	120	503 (8%)
Type 3	22	90	67	1	37	217 (4%)
Type 4	33	188	178	116	1.263	1.778 (29%)
Type 5	28	486	261	337	388	1.500 (24%)
Type 6	10	40	132	31	91	304 (5%)
Other	15	48	339	57	87	546 (9%)

teristic of the Norwegian interest-group system. Groups are ordered functionally within economic sectors. At the top of each sector sits a peak organization, the function of which is to coordinate the activity of groups within the sector and also to represent the sector on committees incorporating other sectors and the government (cross-sectoral problems) [30] Second, groups that do not have formal representation in the committee system can participate—if they choose to—through the *remiss* system.

The representatives answering the mail questionnaire were asked to assess the "balance of interests" as found on committees. Table 3 shows their response:

Table 3. Evaluation of Whether Concern Is Shown for Balancing Interests in the Selection of Committee Members

Committee members who believed that:	Percentage of Total
Balance of interests is stressed	50
Balance of interests is not stressed	31
Not ascertained	19

We find that 50 percent of the committees reflect a balance of interests. That 50 percent of the committee representatives interviewed did not affirm the presence of a concern for the balance of interests may be explained by the fact that half of the committees are: (1) dealing with apolitical issues; (2) concerned with factual rather than valuative problems, i.e., a technical as opposed to a partisan approach is the accepted manner for making decisions; and (3) on occasion, members are not cognizant of the recruitment procedures for committee participants. In interviews with twenty-seven representatives, satisfaction was expressed for the present selection procedures to administrative committees. Organization leaders felt that if their requests suggested a legitimate interest in an issue, they would be granted membership on the appropriate committee automatically.

Functional Determinants of Participation in the Committee System: The Absence of a Competitive Politics of Access

The balance-of-interests problem is better understood when the selection procedure to committees is explained together with the style of decision making on committees—"technocratization" and "managerialism."

30. See the Heisler-Kvavik discussion of the cartelization of elites as a distinguishing characteristic of the "European-polity" type, chap. 2 in this volume.

Utilizing data from the mail questionnaire plus the detailed twenty-seven interviews we find that functional determinants affect the selection of interest-group representatives to administrative committees. First, group representatives are chosen because of their position within an organization. Individuals who head organization bureaucratic sections are invariably selected to represent the organization on administrative committees dealing with their sector's issue areas, i.e., to represent them on issues as the organization's "expert." In other words, technically oriented bureaucrats are routinely chosen to sit on corresponding technical administrative committees. This selection procedure conforms with the expectations of both group representatives and administrators; it is premised upon the belief that effective decision making requires specialists from both sides. This is especially the case when committees deal with "technical problems." Second, the committee's explicit purpose (a functional one, generally) limits who is eligible to participate on the committee. Committees deal with functionally distinct issues for functionally distinct sectors of the society. Representation on these committees correlates with the interests affected by committee jurisdiction.

Responsibility for particular interests is divided among leaders in accordance with a rational division of labor related to issue content. There is also a division of labor among organizations comprising a distinct economic sector. Assignment of issues to an organization is dependent upon the organization's function within the economically defined sectors (e.g., farming, industry, shipping, fishing, etc.). For example, in the farming sector, issues dealing with the farmers' cultural problems and general welfare are referred to the general farm organizations, the Norwegian Farmers' Union and the Norwegian Smallholders' Union; issues concerning sale, prices, and production of farm goods are assigned to specific cooperative organizations, such as the Egg Producers Sales Organization; problems dealing with general economic coordination within the farm sector are handled by the Federation of Norwegian Cooperatives. The result is that when any particular issue or problem, especially of an economic variety, is to be negotiated, it is easy to determine not only which organization will be concerned, but who in the organization will represent the interested parties. There is little fragmentation organizationally of a societal interest and little deviation from the selection process constrained by the functional organization of the private sector.

The responses of twenty-seven group officials demonstrate the organization's internal division of labor. Twenty-two representatives identified themselves with a particular set of issues; five, all of whom were of the top elected echelon, identified themselves with a broad range of issues. A characteristic response from the latter category was as follows: "A president has to deal with a broad range of technical and sometimes political issues. It is not his job to handle matters in any great detail. That is for the organization's specialists." The president proceeded to name those to whom control was delegated over particular sets of issues in the organization. Typical responses of the issue specialists included their limited activity to issue categories as follows: taxes, regulations (granting of licenses, import and export controls), prices or wages, subsidies, training and education, national legislation affecting the group as a whole (e.g., vacations for farmers), legal problems. In each case, the individuals had long experience and appropriate training in the issue area for which they were responsible. Most had been members of the organization for fifteen years or more. All considered themselves experts or knowledgeable through experience and personal interest in the particular areas. Many had become active in the organization because of their experience in the area. Also, they wanted to take a more active part in the formulation of their area's public policy. On occasion, they had been recruited by the organization or government for the particular position because of their technical expertise. Normally, very few individuals have the credentials requisite for participating on committees responsible for an issue area. Thus, the number of people who might actually participate on a given issue were few and well known by the organization, the administration, and other voluntary associations.

Within each organization, then, one finds an elected or appointed bureaucratic specialist responsible for a set of issues that constitutes goals of the organization and its membership. The specialist becomes a type of functional representative responsible, *generally*, for the aggregative and articulative procedures requisite for the realization of the group's goals. The assignment of issues and the qualifications of assigned representatives reflect the functional structure of the organization. The representatives, when viewed as a whole, appear as a functionally "established elite."

Utilizing the functional organization of interest groups and the interest-group system, we can see that it is a relatively simple matter to determine who will participate in the congruent structure of the administrative network. One finds that it is not political entrepreneurs (lobbyists) who by friendship or money participate;[31] rather, participants are limited to established organization specialists. These people are chosen in accordance with statutes (formal and informal) of the committes or the administration. Administrative norms do not allow nonspecialists to participate. In such a system a competition for access seems meaningless.[32] Participation in the

---

31. I use entrepreneur here as distinguished as a distinct political actor by Milbrath, *Washington Lobbyists*, p. 36.

32. The system is not so perfect that we find all groups to be accommodated by it. If dissatisfied, excluded groups can seek redress on Rokkan's first tier (the parliament). But it must be made clear that such groups are few in number and also, when political pressure has been applied, the solution invariably incorporates the excluded group into the administrative system. A good example of the phenomenon occurred during the student uprisings when the student organization and its leadership was effectively coopted into the administrative structure.

political process is not dependent upon constant success in a competitive political game; instead, it is established within administrative decision-making procedures that acknowledge certain organization positions as requisite and legitimate voices of a collective interest. *Participation is structured by functional or technical rules of the game.*

Group Participation on Committees: A Function of Representative Roles

An assessment of interest-group representative roles and role performance in Norway is perhaps the clearest manifestation of the changes that have taken place between interest groups and government and between groups and their membership. As I shall demonstrate, the roles are hardly those envisioned by Milbrath—related to transmission of information—nor do they correspond with the roles outlined by Wahlke et al. or Zeigler and Baer. Rather, roles reflect the cooptation of groups, the change to technocratization—which governs issue resolution—and the modified relationship of citizen to government with the group as an intermediary. I first present the perceived contribution of groups to the government by virtue of their participation on committees—essentially one of technical expertise; second, I attempt to define some role types applicable to the Norwegian system. The role types suggested here are just that—suggestions. Much more comparative work needs to be done with a more substantial data base to fully construct appropriate role "types."

Norwegian interest-group leaders describe their contribution to committee work in at least four ways. All reflect their perception of themselves as integral parts of the "conversion" process. First, they envision themselves as supplying the technical expertise the administration does not have but requires for making responsible policy. The representatives recruited and sent to committees by private groups are the most knowledgeable individuals in their respective fields and serve as invaluable aides to the administration. Second, participation by organization representatives makes possible a far wider evaluation and hence, better and more stable legislation. Organizations effectively aggregate varied demands and present them in a negotiable fashion. Both of these contributions, by virtue of the groups' regularized participation on committees, constitute a "withinput" function—in the United States, an "input" function. Third, groups are seen as speeding up the decision-making process. As a result of their constant and formal presence on committees, information is made available immediately as to the effect and acceptability of legislative modifications. In other words, organization viewpoints are integrated conjointly with those of the administration. Action is not taken separately and drafts can never be developed in any sufficient manner apart from any of the recognized participants. Hence, no time is spent drafting an extensive, potentially unacceptable proposal. Fourth, group leaders perceive that organizations come to share responsibility for legislation; that this guarantees the government little adverse reaction to legislation once effected; that reaction, if it comes, would be directed not toward the government, but at the participants—the interest groups and their representatives—who accept the legislation in behalf of the organization membership. Whether intended or not, this latter factor further develops the organization as the middleman between the government and a functionally organized public. Factors three and four—the speeding up of decision making and the sharing of responsibility—occur as a result of interest-group participation as decision makers in the formulation of public policy.

Supporting the perception of organizations as integral parts of the "conversion process" by virtue of their contribution to committee work is the self-evaluation of the twenty-seven interest-group representatives of their *role* in committees. Three basic roles emerge: (1) the expert, (2) the advocate, and (3) the trustee. All the roles relate to participation in the making of public decisions. In this respect they differ from the roles described by Milbrath which relate to the transmission of interests.[33]

The expert (*fagman*) role is by far the most common. Individuals adhering to this role present their arguments in technical terms and accept a conclusion, whether good or bad for the organization, on the basis of technical arguments relating the present case to accepted long-range societal goals. The reasoning behind the continued and necessary use of this role is as follows: (1) The representative is asked to participate on these committees by virtue of his technical skills and expertise. (2) The ultimate decision is determined by the soundest argument in any event; hence, there is no basis or reason for arguing otherwise. Moreover, not to argue in technical terms is to embarrass oneself in the eyes of practicing colleagues, thereby effectively barring oneself and perhaps one's organization from future participation in a committee. The expert plays his role on both advisory and negotiating councils (although to a lesser extent on the latter where, often, the issue contains less technical considerations). An attempt is made, as far as possible, to convert all problems into technical language.

The expert role comes naturally to the technicians of the Norwegian interest-group bureaucracies. The members are well-trained, knowledgeable men in their respective fields. They hold their positions in the organizations in great part because of their technical skills. Movement upward in the organization has been concomitant with increased practice and experience. Their approach to problems is similar to those of administrators. They have learned through time and through socialization on many of these committees (most have had extensive experience within the committee net-

33. Milbrath, *Washington Lobbyists.*

work) that argumentation on the basis of fact achieves the most satisfactory results in terms of realization of group goals.

The trustee role, more common among elected officials than among the organization bureaucrats, is a second and less frequent approach to the representing of interests of organizations on committees. It is often combined with or justified on the basis of expertise. Essentially the two arguments for its use are as follows: (1) The organization's goals and the representative's goals are one and the same. If they are not and a representative is acting contrary to his inclinations, he is acting dishonestly and should therefore leave the position. One cannot be an "errand boy" and be effective in committee work. The danger here, of course, is to undermine the representative relationship between the group representative and the organization member. (2) For committee work to succeed, it is important that all participants be able to negotiate, to be able to decide on and accept the best strategy. If all members, or even some, are bound in any way (by mandate or by one's conception of representation), then no acceptable compromise is likely to be reached.

The advocate role is the role least mentioned and least adhered to. Few consider themselves organization "mouthpieces" except on the most important and critical of issues or where the membership's point of view is so clear as to preclude alternative action. All organizations, on occasion, give their representatives an explicit mandate. When this happens, the representative must function as an advocate. Only one of the twenty-seven representatives interviewed was an advocate in an ideal sense—making a point of always finding out what the organization's executive committee or the membership intends before acting. He was a new man chosen specifically from the rank and file for one representative task on behalf of the organization (this occurs as the organization's staff can no longer participate on all the committees that request them). He was asked to report back to the organization and to confine any negotiations to the limits set by the mandate formulated by a parallel committee within the organization. Few of the established leadership are confined by such strictures.[34] In recent years, as the organizations have come to play a larger role in the committee network, the commitments have become so varied and so numerous that the elected and appointive organization leadership can no longer satisfy the demand for participation alone, hence the recruitment from the membership and the resulting restrictions. To the extent that such individuals (rank and file) do participate on committees, committee work is delayed in that advocates constantly halt proceedings by having to defer to organizational wishes or by their insistence on clearing any changes with the leadership before agreeing to them on behalf of the organization.

34. It is possible that the rejection of the advocate role is a cultural factor in that it goes against Norwegian political norms.

The Technocratic Behavior
Pattern of Cooptive Groups

The behavior of Norwegian interest groups on committees is characterized by an emphasis on technical argumentation realized by sending technocrats as representatives and by presenting statements in a well-researched technical format. How much technical information can be presented in a technical format by a well-known and respected specialist is the key to success. Accordingly, technical factors are the criteria for success ranked most highly by the organization's representatives.

Table 4[35] indicates the factors that committee members considered as requisite for the acceptance of group reports. Technical skills was by far the

Table 4. Ranking of Factors Determining Acceptance of Committee Reports by Parliament

Ranking	Factors Facilitating Acceptance of Committee Decisions
1st	Committee members had technical skills
2nd	All opposing sides were present
3rd	All interested parties were present
4th	Prior agreement between committee and administration
5th	Issue is noncontroversial
6th	Committee deals with procedural issues
7th	Practice is customary

most important. Factors seldom used and considered of little weight in an argument on a committee include numbers of members in the organization, the organization's economic resources, ability to affect public opinion, ability to persuade and influence the parliament. The factors, how well established the organization is vis-à-vis the administration, the percentage of the total eligible population represented by the organization, how affected the organization is by a particular outcome, are weighted somewhat higher. This ranking of factors in Norway is contrary to the criteria for implementing demands in a more competitive system. While technical facts and presentation are very important in the competitive system, so are the implications of actions at the polls and in a politician's district. The latter are seen to be directly related to the resources an organization can muster, e.g., money, total number of voting members. Bluff and threat are far more critical in the American system. Because of the degree to which decisions are made apart from the Norwegian Parliament, many of the above factors need not be considered.

35. Table 4 is based on open-ended questions in the committee questionnaire. It must be noted that only 150 of 454 respondents answered these questions. Accordingly, the table represents tendencies present in the responses. The first two factors were by far the most mentioned. Other factors were suggested less often. The table is intended as an indication of a pattern (an important one), no more. Karen Feste organized much of the materials for the table.

Kenneth Janda's study of politics in Indiana demonstrates the significance of differing group resources in an American state system; his findings make an interesting comparison with the Norwegian data. When asked to evaluate the reasons for the power of interest groups, the American respondents (legislators) mentioned size and electoral influence most often, followed by organization and leadership, financial resources, importance of issues, skilled lobbyists, information and facts, the influencing of public opinion, and prestige of group, in that order.[36] In other words, resources seemingly useful in competition were most often emphasized. Technical skills, representativeness, etc., received substantially less mention, if any.

The organization's representatives in Norway were asked to evaluate various types of behavior in terms of their being used and their effectiveness in the formulation of public policy. The results were interesting. All the representatives agreed that no member of the committees had any extra weight because of his status outside the group or the power of the organization he represented. This is, of course, consistent with the emphasis on expertise. About 87 percent felt that the success of a committee's work depended upon the willingness of the participants to compromise. The deviant cases included the representatives adhering to the advocate role. One should note, however, that even the "advocate" felt that some compromise was necessary. Reciprocity or vote trading was frowned upon, although a small percentage admitted to its use on a rare occasion. Presentation of arguments in a format agreeable to a strong committee chairman was considered by 80 percent of the representatives as either not applicable or improper. The notion that representatives were present on committees only to supply information and to leave the formulation of the bill to the committee chairman or the department's representative was rejected by 75 percent of the representatives outright. Again deviation is explained by those representatives who consistently participate on fact-finding boards where legislation is drafted within the department on the basis of expert committee findings. All representatives agreed on the impossibility of making demands solely in terms of private interests. All requests had to be related to long-term goals of the society as a whole.

The attitudes and expectations of organization representatives vis-à-vis participation and the role of organizations in the conversion processes further clarifies the characteristics of the Norwegian interest-group system. Organization representatives felt that their participation in the decision-making process was a positive and meaningful contribution to the formulation of public policy. For example, only five representatives felt that

36. Janda, *Legislative Politics*, p. 18. I am aware of the problems of the comparativeness of the above data, especially since legislators may see the "political game" differently from interest-group representatives. However, to the extent the comparison is valid, the competitiveness vs. the noncompetitiveness is partially supported. The findings of Bauer, Pool and Dexter, *American Business*, regarding the role of groups as links in a communications process suggest that the American pattern is less competitive than generally believed.

the development of councils by the administration had been initiated for the purpose of binding organizations to administrative decisions and making them share the responsibility of public acts. They were not pawns in the political process. Group-government cooperation was a meaningful dual venture. Regardless of which government or party was in power, the process would not differ. Groups did not necessarily perceive the government as the opponent, and organizations were not simply defensive bodies protecting the individual from the state. Norway's high standard of living was not perceived as the result of the free play of market forces, but was integrally tied to the planned economy and the cooperation between organizations and the government. In short, the making of public policy was seen as a cooperative venture; interests were reconciled in terms of nationally accepted long-term goals. One might speculate that the existence of a national consensus is requisite for the cooptive pattern in Norway to work. Without it, groups would argue about "ideological" issues rather than implementing essentially an administrative plan in a bureaucratic fashion.

An argument could be made that interest-group representatives would find themselves in a conflicting role situation. Specifically, the requirements of their job as presently defined would require them to reconcile criticism from the public accusing them of pressing one-sided interests and complaints from the membership in their being too much state civil servants. In reality, organization representatives recognized the public vs. private dilemma and rationalized the problem as follows: (1) If the problem arises, we know we are on the right track. (2) We cannot bring up something that is one-sided and without public significance. (3) Arguing on a technical basis can hurt the membership in the short run but not in the long run. (4) We are doing the best we can, and hence, the criticism is unjustified. For these reasons, the representatives were unimpressed by an argument that danger to democracy lay in removing so many issues from the public eye. It can be argued, as Eldersveld does, that the leadership of interest groups is becoming a management group with many publics (e.g., the administration, the membership, the press, the public in general), and with a role in the political system far more complex and varied than was earlier understood.[37] The resolution of the private-public conflict as stated above is perhaps the clearest manifestation of the technocratization or managerialism phenomenon as it has developed in Norway.

Summary

The formulation of public policy in Norway is predominantly the product of group-government interaction in an extensive network of committees. Within that network, the central decision-making arena in Norway, decisions are made in accordance with a rationalized, "technicalized" de-

37. Eldersveld, "American Interest Groups," p. 193.

cision-making procedure. Participants and the problems they deal with are related to functional considerations. The recruitment of experts, facilitated by the functional structuring of voluntary associations, is critical for the working of the system. Their experience and background, as well as the roles they adhere to, complement the methods for making decisions. Groups and group representatives accept their role as public officials serving both a public and private constituency. They are satisfied with the results of an established "cartel-like" arrangement for making public policy. These are not the relationships we have come to expect from the existing group literature but they must be considered before any comparative study of groups can be made and before any attempt at a universal model of interest-group interaction applicable in a comparative setting can be made.

4

Rodney P. Stiefbold

Segmented Pluralism and Consociational Democracy in Austria: Problems of Political Stability and Change*

Introduction

Modern Austrian political development—from the inception of mass-party politics in the late stages of the decaying multicultural Habsburg Empire in the 1880s, to the late stages of the decaying Red-Black "Great Coalition"

*This is an entirely revised version of my earlier paper, "Elite-Mass Opinion Structure and Communication Flow in a Consociational Democracy (Austria)," presented at the 1968 Annual Meeting of the American Political Science Association, Washington, D.C., September 2–7. It also incorporates portions of my 1970 monograph, *Elites and Elections in a Fragmented Political System* (Stony Brook, N.Y.: Department of Political Science, and Cologne: Westdeutscher Verlag, forthcoming). Unless otherwise stated, references to elite attitudes and behavior are based on interview evidence contained in my *Surveys of Austrian National Elites* (cited as *S.A.N.E. Interviews*) conducted in 1965–66, 1967, and 1968. For a full report, see Stiefbold, *Segmented Pluralism, Consociational Democracy, and Austrian Electoral Politics: A Theoretical and Empirical Case Study of Austria under Great Coalition, 1945–1966* (Ann Arbor: University Microfilms, 1973), esp. chaps. 1, 6 and appendix 1 (cited as Stiefbold, *Austrian Electoral Politics*).

Research and writing were facilitated by support from Columbia University, the University of California at Berkeley, and the State University of New York at Stony Brook. Field work in 1965–66 was supported by the Foreign Area Fellowship Program administered by a Joint Committee of the American Council of Learned Societies and the Social Science Research Council, and by the Institute for Advanced Studies and Scientific Research in Vienna. Subsequent field work in 1967, 1968, and 1970 was supported chiefly by the International Study of the Politics of the Smaller European Democracies under a grant from the Ford Foundation. I would like to thank friends and colleagues who commented extensively on an earlier draft of this study: G. Bingham Powell, Arend Lijphart, Kurt Steiner, Giuseppe Di Palma, Eric A. Nordlinger, and Duncan MacRae, Jr. I have also benefited from detailed constructive criticism by Kenneth Erickson, Gordon Adams, Douglas Chalmers, Mark Kesselman, Juan Linz, Val Lorwin, and Gerhard Lehmbruch. Austrian friends, contacts, and colleagues who helped me in my research are too numerous to mention individually; I hope to thank them, however inadequately, in a forthcoming book.

which served as the midwife to an increasingly culturally integrated nation-state in the 1960s—has been characterized by what Val Lorwin has described as "segmented pluralism." Under segmented pluralism social, cultural, and political activities are organized along the lines of ideological blocs or "segments" (subcultures). Within each segment individuals carry on most of their meaningful communications, social relations, and group memberships; although a high degree of communication and interaction takes place within segments, there is relatively little movement across subcultural or segment boundaries.[1]

The hypothesis that a direct link exists between a nation's political culture and the performance of its political system is well established in contemporary political science. In accord with this hypothesis, empirical democratic theory has long ascribed several basic weaknesses to political systems characterized by "segmented pluralism," that is, by "mutually reinforcing" or "superimposed" social, organizational, and attitudinal cleavages. The first weakness is decisional ineffectiveness, or immobilism, which undermines a regime's legitimacy; and this, in turn, sets the stage for potentially destabilizing political movements or coups d'etat.[2]

Moreover, countries fragmented into political subcultures lack what are said to be essential moderating influences promoting homogeneous political cultures and hence stable and viable political systems. These influences are psychological cross-pressures, which act at both the mass and the elite levels. At the mass level, there are no overlapping individual memberships in organizations that have competing outlooks and make divergent claims on individual loyalties. At the elite level (in the absence of overlapping memberships by individual citizens), organizational leaders are not faced with the task of having to accommodate widely divergent views of heterogeneous members. Instead, influences such as family, church, interest groups, and political parties all tend to reinforce one another, leading, under hypothetically extreme conditions, to what Sidney Verba has described succinctly as

> a political system made up of two closed camps with no overlapping of membership. The only channels of communication between the two camps would be at the highest level. . . . Politics comes to resemble negotiations between rival states; and war or a breakdown of negotiations is always possible.[3]

1. Val Lorwin, "Segmented Pluralism," mimeographed. Center for Advanced Study in the Behavioral Sciences, Stanford, Calif., 1967; revised version published in *Comparative Politics* 3, no. 2 (January 1971): 141–75.

2. Gabriel Almond, "Comparative Political Systems," *Journal of Politics* 18, no. 3 (August 1956): 391–409, esp. 408.

3. Sidney Verba, "Organizational Membership and Democratic Consensus," *Journal of Politics* 27 (August 1965): 470; see also Gabriel Almond and Sidney Verba, *The Civic Culture: Political Attitudes and Democracy in Five Nations* (Princeton, N. J.: Princeton University Press, 1963), pp. 133–34.

Interwar Austria—the so-called First Austrian Republic, born of the destroyed Habsburg Empire and supplanted, after a brief civil war between Catholics and Socialists in 1934, by an indigenous clerical-fascist dictatorship, which was itself absorbed by Nazi Germany in 1938—corresponded closely not only to the classic fragmentation model, but even to the extreme situation hypothesized by Verba. Val Lorwin succinctly describes that interwar setting as follows:

> From the three "camps" or Lager of prewar days society and politics became polarized when the smallest and least widely organized of the three, the German Nationals, threw much of their support to the "Blacks" against the "Reds." Class and geographical alignments deepened those of religion and ideology: Catholic businessmen, artisans, and farmers versus Socialist workers; rural areas versus industrial cities; the Black hinterland versus the Red capital.[4]

In addition, moderate leaders of both the clerical-conservative *Lager* and the anticlerical socialist *Lager* lacked either the autonomy or security of position which might have permitted a bridging at the elite level of divisive conflicts of interest deeply rooted in the subcultures. Mass loyalties ran to the ideological blocs and their parties, whose flags, anthems, and private armies accurately reflected the reality of an Austrian state totally lacking in national unity or identity.

In the face of this gloomy history of instability and decisional ineffectiveness, however, the Second Austrian Republic offers the social scientist a challenging deviant case. It is neither immobilist nor unstable, despite its historical legacy and its still fragmented political culture, in seeming defiance of political theorists.

In terms of the highly original fourfold typology of democratic political systems recently proposed by Lijphart, Austria is a near-perfect

4. Lorwin, "Segmented Pluralism," p. 144. *Lager* is the Austrian word for "camp" or "armed camp" (in connotation). On the organizational and ideological development of the *Lager*, see Adam Wandruszka, "Oesterreichs politische Struktur: die Entwicklung der Parteien und politischen Bewegungen," in *Geschichte der Republik Oesterreich* ed. Heinrich Benedikt (Vienna: Verlag fuer Geschichte und Politik, 1954), who is generally credited with establishing the *Lager* frame of reference for the analysis of Austrian Politics. See also Rudolf Schlesinger's comparative analysis of *Central European Democracy and Its Background: Economic and Political Group Organization* (London: Routledge & Kegan Paul, 1953). Peter Pulzer, "The Legitimizing Role of Political Parties: The Second Austrian Republic," *Government and Opposition* 4, no. 3 (Summer 1969): 324–44, applies the SSRC Committee on Comparative Politics model of successive crises in the course of political development, while Stein Rokkan sets the Austrian case in broad comparative perspective in his "The Structuring of Mass Politics in the Smaller European Democracies," *Comparative Studies in Society and History* 10, no. 2 (January 1968): 173–210. For an empirical study using statistical time series of major parties' development, with special attention to urban-rural and regional cleavages, see R. Stiefbold and T. P. Koppel, "The Three 'Lager' in Austrian Electoral History . . ." (Paper presented at International Political Science Association, Specialist Meeting on Electoral Research, Seventh World Congress, Brussels, 18–23 September 1967).

example of "consociational democracy."[5] The central characteristic of this type lies not in any specific institutional arrangements, but rather in elite attitudes and behavior when confronted with the condition of a fragmented political culture. Its defining feature is "overarching cooperation at the elite level with the deliberate aim of counteracting disintegrative tendencies in the system." Thus the consociational democracy is a paradoxical form of government in terms of older empirical theory: despite the burden of being a "conflict society"[6] characterized by social, organizational, and attitudinal fragmentation, it is both stable and decisionally effective. Lijphart posits a number of preconditions and facilitating conditions for the success of consociational democracy (i.e., for its persistence and decisional effectiveness), which are discussed more fully below. For the moment we are concerned with simply the basic definition: the possibility that elite collaboration at the top of the system *can*, by rational choice and through development of supportive decision-making procedures, negate the hypothesized direct link from fragmented political culture (or "conflict society") to poor system performance.

The Institutionalization of Consociational Democracy in Postwar Austria

Primary focus in this chapter is on Second Republic Austria during the period from 1945 to 1966 when the Catholic Conservative People's party (OeVP) and the Socialist party (SPOe) joined in a carefully circumscribed

5. Arend Lijphart, "Typologies of Democratic Systems," *Comparative Political Studies* 1, no. 1 (April 1968): 3–44 passim. Lijphart differentiates chiefly among three types of democratic systems: the centrifugal (competitive elite behavior, fragmented political culture, as in Italy); the centripetal (competitive elite behavior, homogeneous political culture, as in the Anglo-American countries); and consociational (coalescent elite behavior, fragmented political culture, as in the Netherlands, Austria, Belgium, and Switzerland). He later adds a fourth type, depoliticized democracy (coalescent elite behavior, cultural homogeneity, as in the emerging "model democracy of the New Europe"). The specific theoretical work of Arend Lijphart used in this brief summary includes his *The Politics of Accommodation: Pluralism and Democracy in the Netherlands* (Berkeley and Los Angeles: University of California Press, 1968), esp. chaps. 7–10; his "Typologies" and his "Consociational Democracy," *World Politics* 21, no 2 (January 1969): 207–25 passim. There is considerable overlap in these three works.

6. In an article on "The Study of French Political Socialization," Fred I. Greenstein and Sidney G. Tarrow have recently summarized the propositions associated with the notion of "conflict society" as follows: "(1) attitudes are widely held, sharply crystallized, and intensely felt in the mass public; (2) individuals hold internally consistent attitudes (i.e., revolutionary or reactionary attitudes on issue 'a' will be matched by parallel attitudes on issue 'b'); (3) attitudinal disagreement is high and cumulative (i.e., disagreement on one issue is bolstered by disagreement on the next); and (4) agencies of socialization and membership inculcate and reinforce these attitudinal patterns." (*World Politics* 22, no. 1 (October 1969): 115). Thus the conflict-society model combines segmented pluralist political organization and sociological distinctiveness with polarized public policy preferences that are rooted in ideological differences and characterized by intense involvement and great partisan hostility.

contractual agreement to form a Great Coalition to govern Austria.[7] Many of our observations also characterize Austria under the single-party conservative government formed after the elections of 1966 and the single-party Socialist government that replaced it in 1970. But a thorough investigation of elements of continuity and discontinuity between the two regimes—dissolution of the Great Coalition in 1966 amounted to a change not merely of governments but, to a great extent, also of regimes—deserves separate treatment exceeding the scope of this chapter.[8]

Despite its historical legacy of intensely ideological class, ethnic, and confessional cleavages which had contributed *internationally* to the country's engagement in two world wars and *domestically* to sporadic outbreaks of physical violence between the *Lager* terminating in a brief but serious civil war in 1934, Second Republic Austria proved to be durable, capable of significant decision making, and apparently legitimate in the eyes of its population. Stated differently, instead of instability, Austria under the Great Coalition recorded an enviable record of dynamic political stability characterized by a remarkable capacity for gradual peaceful change. Instead of immobilism, it demonstrated decisional effectiveness. It proved capable of resolving, or at least defusing by subjecting to incremental adjustment through collective bargaining, many basic issues, some invested with high current or previous ideological content, that were contentious between the major subcultures or *Lager*. Among these were mutually acceptable wage-price regulation and control; fiscal policies that successfully counterpointed both socialist and conservative concerns; agreement on both the extent and the method of operation of Austria's large complex of nationalized industries; and renegotiation of the 1934 Concordat with the Vatican.

Several factors helped to establish and sustain a Great Coalition government between the two major *Lager* a scant twelve years after their

7. On Austrian politics, see R. Stiefbold et al., eds., *Wahlen und Parteien in Oesterreich*, 3 vols. (Vienna: Oesterr. Bundesverlag, 1966); F. C. Engelmann, "Austria: The Pooling of Opposition," in *Political Oppositions in Western Democracies*, ed. Robert A. Dahl (New Haven: Yale University Press, 1966); U. Kitzinger, "The Austrian Election of 1959," *Political Studies* 9, no. 2 (June 1961): 119–40; O. Kirchheimer, "The Waning of Opposition in Parliamentary Regimes" (1957), now in Kirchheimer, *Politics, Law and Social Change* (New York: Columbia University Press, 1969), pp. 292–318; Kurt Steiner, *Politics in Austria* (Boston: Little, Brown, 1972); and Gerhard Lehmbruch, *Proporzdemokratie* (Tuebingen: Mohr, 1967). The specific notion of rational contract as the basis of the coalition regime has been particularly emphasized by Kirchheimer. The somewhat awkward phrase "contractarianism" is used by political theorist William T. Bluhm to underscore the same point. See his fine essay, "Nation-Building: The Case of Austria," *Polity* 1, no. 2 (December, 1968): esp. 153 ff.

8. For a comprehensive study of the Austrian political system, see Rodney Stiefbold, ed., *The Political System of Austria* (Stanford University Press, forthcoming), a volume in the cross-national research project on The Politics of the Smaller European Democracies, under the editorial direction of Stein Rokkan, Robert Dahl, Val Lorwin, and Hans Daalder. See also the literature cited in note 7.

civil war confrontation at the barricades: (1) the Soviet occupation after World War II and the threat to Austria's independence; (2) the need to pool resources in a common effort to oppose and finally to free Austria from all the occupation powers; (3) the demands of postwar reconstruction (applying the energies of both *Lager* to the solution of concrete common problems); (4) the influence of the United States and the Marshall Plan on planning and policies for economic growth; (5) shared experiences by many elites as concentration camp cellmates; (6) a previous, although brief, First Republic experience in joint coalition; and (7) the desire to avoid doing anything that might again plunge Austria into civil war.

Two other closely interrelated factors were perhaps even more important for stabilization. The first was the purposive depoliticization of the decision-making environment through creation of a new set of procedural rules designed to minimize interelite rancorousness and avoid conflict over basic values (which in many cases remained highly divergent but generally latent). The second was the creation of new institutional resources designed to increase the capacity of the SPOe-OeVP coalition regime to cope with problems whose mere existence had overburdened the fragile First Republic.

> —The former clerical-conservative Christian Social Party was recast as a federated "People's Party" (see table 1) appealing to a somewhat more diverse theological and sociological clientele. Modeled on postwar Christian Democratic parties throughout Western Europe, it provided a flexible, adaptive organization capable of accommodating an increasingly representative cross section of the Austrian electorate.
> —A single Trade Union Congress was created, and a system of corporatist chambers of interest group representation was devised. Endowed by Austrian constitutional law with both administrative and advisory functions, the Black (clerical) Chambers of Commerce and Agriculture and the Red (Socialist) Chamber of Labor and TUC provided for a uniquely stabilizing mixture of both "multipolar" and "bipolar" interest aggregation and decision making. These chambers functioned as a paracoalition of interest groups, paralleling the related government ministries which "belonged" to each member party in the coalition.
> —An extraconstitutional body, called the Coalition Committee, was instituted for the purpose of bringing together the top leaders of both the paracoalition and the Cabinet ministries, i.e., the top socioeconomic and political elites of both *Lager*.

Thus the Austrian political system artfully bifurcated "political" and

Table 1. Coalition and Paracoalition: *Lager* Aspects of Austrian Political and Socioeconomic Bargaining

Bargaining or Conflict Structures	Socialist (SPOe) Lager (or "segment," or subculture)	Conservative (OeVP) Lager (or "segment," or subculture)
Political party organizations	SPOe, Socialist party of Austria	OeVP, Austrian People's party: actually a federation of three occupational group peak associations: OeBB, OeWB, and OeAAB, with party secretariat as "roof" or "glue"
Corresponding government ministries which were dominated by a single party during Great Coalition period (1945–66)	Social Welfare (Labor) Justice Interior Transport, Nationalized Industries, and Electricity	Agriculture Education Defense Commerce and Reconstruction Finance
Major associated interest groups (voluntary associations)	OeGB, Austrian Trade Union Congress (TUC)	OeBB, Farmers' (Agrarian) League OeAAB, Catholic Workers' and Employees' League OeWB, Businessmen's League VOel, Union of Austrian Industrialists
Major associated Chambers (*Kammern*, the corporatist bodies of occupational representation)	Chamber of Labor	Chamber of Agriculture OeAAB *Fraktion* in Chamber of Labor Chamber of Commerce

(Left margin brackets labeled: Coalition, Paracoalition)

"socioeconomic" interest aggregation and decision making into a "coalition" and a "paracoalition," then reunited them in an extraconstitutional body whose primary purpose was to mitigate potential, incipient, or actual party or group conflict.[9]

Under this unique governmental arrangement the two major political

9. On the Austrian "paracoalition" see Rodney Stiefbold, "Parties, Groups and Chambers in the Political Bargaining Process: Pluralist Democracy in Austria" (Paper presented at the Annual Meeting of the American Political Science Association, 1967); and Herbert P. Secher, "Representative Democracy or 'Chamber State': The Ambiguous Role of Interest Groups in Austrian Politics," *Western Political Quarterly* 13, no. 4 (December 1960): 890–909.

parties monopolized, along with their client interest groups and party-related ancillary organizations, the political life of the Austrian state. The two parties not only divided between themselves governmental posts such as Cabinet ministries (as indicated in table 1), but they also parceled out among their adherents most of the significant administrative posts in the civil service and in the nationalized banks, industries, and communications network.

Parliament, as one might expect, was virtually emasculated as a separate decision-making site. Legislation took place only by mutual consent between the coalition partners; legislative drafts might be elaborated in the interest groups and party organizations, or chambers, or government ministries, or combinations of all of these, as in any other political system. But before the Nationalrat, the lower House of parliament, could act on a prospective bill, that bill had to be approved by the extraconstitutional Coalition Committee. Thereafter it was binding under the terms of the parties' "Coalition Contract" upon the members of both the Cabinet and the respective parliamentary fractions of the two parties. Members of the two coalition parties could exercise their normal parliamentary functions only with the permission of the partner party, permission which rested in each particular case on an agreement between the party leaders. Essentially, therefore, the entire system amounted to the elimination of major political opposition through government by party cartel, but within a system that allowed for the expression of limited opposition through new channels. Each coalition partner was simultaneously government and opposition.

The critical question concerning the balance of power between the two coalition partners turned on the ratio by which principal governmental and administrative posts were shared, a ratio determined by the relative electoral and parliamentary strength of the two parties. Thus, despite the fact that the Austrian electorate was in effect not called upon to choose between rival potential governments, the electoral process retained a clear-cut meaning: the shift of votes between the two parties decided the conditions of their collaboration. It furnished a revised index of strength between the opposing coalition partners, and therefore heavily influenced the resolution of the administrative and legislative issues that were controversial between them.

The two coalition parties normally divided close to 90 percent of the popular vote almost evenly between them; hence the slightest change was noted emphatically on either side, and sometimes led to significant revision of the formal coalition pact. In 1959, for example, the Socialist party (SPOe) raised its share of the popular vote by 1.2 percent to 41.8 percent, and gained three additional seats in the Nationalrat (still one seat short of the People's party [OeVP] parliamentary plurality). By the rules of coalition politics, the election amounted to a "decisive" victory for the Socialists, and resulted in transfer of the Ministry of Foreign Affairs, the nationalized industries, and wage-and-price policy making from control by the OeVP or bipartisan commissions to control by the SPOe.

The Waning of Ideology: The Austrian Case

Virtually every scholarly source, and most of the politicians, opinion leaders in the mass media, and lay public would agree that substantial deideologization has taken place in Austria, as throughout Western Europe, since World War II. These changes have occurred along several relevant dimensions as both a planned and a natural outgrowth of the Great Coalition experiment. One can speak of a progressive ideological dilution of the conflicts of interest between the major *Lager*, in the sense of ideological convergence on some previously contested issues (e.g., the Austrian state and nation); in the sense of growing functional dissociation of political ideology and practical politics; and finally, in the sense of a decreasing impact of traditional ideology as a guide to political action.[10] (This last development was facilitated by the withdrawal of the Catholic church from partisan politics in 1945, and by the adoption of a new Socialist party program in 1958 specifically renouncing anticlericalism and sharply reducing the salience of traditional Austro-Marxist phraseology.)

But this general picture of an Austrian political culture bedeviled by segmented pluralism yet able to generate and support a political system that was somehow stable and viable and characterized by a substantial reduction in its ideological baggage is at least partially misleading. Despite all these developments, ". . . the two major subcultures remain separated socially and psychologically; *Lagermentalitaet* [*Lager* feeling and identification] persists. It has lost much of its philosophical basis, but retains its psychological reality; having lost much in ideology, it yet remains as mentality."[11] Thus did one of the most astute observers of Austrian politics summarize the situation in 1965. And indeed, numerous indicators of continued psychological apartness, of the tendency to perceive Austrian

10. Our differentiation of these aspects of deideologization is based on Ulf Himmelstrand's provocative essay, "A Theoretical and Empirical Approach to Depoliticization and Political Involvement," *Acta Sociologica* 6, nos. 1–2 (1962): 83–110, esp. 87. The often successful effort by Austrian political elites to play down differences in values in the interests of solving common problems according to commonly accepted procedural rules was, of course, self-reinforcing: as the behavior gained results, the results reinforced the motivation to continue to subsume, insofar as possible, conflicting values to a "partisan mutual adjustment" scheme of decision making. Relevant here is the book by Charles E. Lindblom, *The Intelligence of Democracy: Decision-Making through Mutual Adjustment* (New York: Free Press, 1965), esp. chap. 15. See also Verba's thoughtful article, "Some Dilemmas in Comparative Research," *World Politics* 20, no. 1 (October 1967): 111–27, esp. 127.

11. Engelmann, "Austria," pp. 267–68; cf. p. 276.

politics in terms of still hostile camps in coalition out of mutual mistrust, could—and can still—be found.

In short, there are two quite different and equally valid perspectives from which one can view the Second Austrian Republic. One set of scholarly studies has emphasized the caricaturelike nature of Austria's paracoalition, which amounted to the institutionalization of the politics of corporatist interest-group bargaining several years before it became fashionable for scholars to applaud and analyze similar decision-making trends in the rest of Europe. In this literature writers have usually emphasized the rational, pragmatic bargaining among interest-group and chamber elites, which led frequently to concrete, mutually acceptable, and beneficial results in socioeconomic policy questions during the period of rebuilding postwar Austria.

The second genre of scholarly literature has tended to emphasize a seemingly incongruous opposite situation related to the nexus which connects political parties, electoral politics, parliament, and governmental decision making, where political life was dominated by a highly "expressive" or "ideological" verbal style. In that part of the political spectrum, according to this branch of the literature, decisional effectiveness and even political stability depended almost exclusively on the practice of the "politics of accommodation" by a cartel of top subcultural elites. In this second view, Austria was pictured as a still highly politicized and hostile society divided along subcultural lines, densely organized, and ruled from above by enlightened elites who perceived their society as conflictful, and who therefore benevolently imposed a kind of "mechanical solidarity" upon their beleaguered countrymen—from the top down, but ostensibly in everybody's best interests. Bargaining behavior in which participants each give a little in order to reach compromise decisions was only intermittent and, in any case, limited to a handful of top party leaders. It certainly was not characteristic of the politics of middle- and lower-level party functionaries.

Elections, Ideology, and Consociational Democracy

Particularly at election time, the Austrian political system seemed to reveal itself in what many authorities considered its true light—as not only *organizationally segmented*, but also as *highly polarized and politicized* from top to bottom. As Robert Dahl has pointed out, conflicts involving politically distinct subcultures are frequently too explosive to be managed by such devices as ordinary parliamentary opposition or election campaigning or winning elections. Thus it is hardly surprising that Arend Lijphàrt, in discussing various conflict-avoidance strategies available to consociational elites, specifically contemplates the possibility that elites will try to neutralize latent public anxieties and hostilities by eliminating or obscuring from public view political processes that are inherently rancorous. Indeed,

Lijphart argues, "The desire to avoid political competition may be so strong that the cartel of elites may decide to extend the consociational principle to the electoral level in order to prevent the passions aroused by elections from upsetting the carefully constructed and possibly fragile, system of cooperation," as they have occasionally done in consociational democracies such as Lebanon, Colombia, the Netherlands, or Belgium.[12]

But in Austria such a solution was impossible: election returns provided the principal objective standard by which the two major Austrian political parties periodically reallocated spheres of political power, patronage, and influence between them within their Great Coalition. Hence a certain incompatibility between the requirements and practices of "electoral" democracy and those of "consociational" democracy existed in Austria throughout the Great Coalition period. For it is clear that if a society were so divided that it required consociational rule, it could hardly afford divisive elections; and if a society were not so divided, it would not need consociational rule. Indeed, exacerbative elections might so deeply politicize and mobilize the mass public as to pose a threat to government by elite cartel. Conversely, "integrative" or "catchall" electoral tactics of the type which the literature on postwar European trends posits as increasingly "normal," involving "centrist" (as opposed to "Right" or "Left") appeals by each major political party to a cross section of the entire electorate (as opposed to a homogeneous segment of it) would undermine segmented pluralism, promote the development of a more homogeneous political culture, and ultimately lead to transformation of crisis-based consociational rule into either a consensual coalition or alternating government-and-opposition political formula.

It is important to underscore both the pervasiveness of the stereotype of Austrian mass political culture that lies at the heart of Engelmann's observation concerning "Lagermentality," and the point that this stereotype condition was most clearly visible under electoral conditions. It is precisely the interaction of elites with nonelites in the electoral arena, and the contrast with elite-mass interaction at other times, that structured the balance between costs and benefits in Austria's version of consociational democracy. This interaction necessarily turned on the question of whether or not Austria was a "conflict society"—polarized, ideological, politicized, partisan—and on the degree to which mass attitudes and elite perceptions of mass attitudes were congruent. The next three sections deal with elite and mass opinion structure under both electoral and nonelectoral circumstances and with elite-mass interaction in each case. By extrapolating from our own Austrian case study we are then able to raise important questions in

---

12. Lijphart, "Consociational Democracy," p. 214; cf. his "Typologies," p. 22. The points made by Robert A. Dahl are advanced in his *Political Oppositions in Western Democracies*, p. 358.

the final section about the conditions that facilitate or impede political change in consociational democracy in general, and hence to reflect on certain types of developmental problems that exist not only in Austria but in other industrially advanced societies as well.

Mass Opinion Structure

This section examines several dimensions of mass political culture in Austria, in an effort to ascertain to what extent Austria corresponds to the model of a "conflict society," and to what extent Austrian political culture—or more simply, the structure of Austrian public opinion—might affect elite electoral conduct or outcomes or otherwise contribute to the systemic consequences of the democratic election process in Austria. We also want to adumbrate the important question considered in the next section, whether elite electoral behavior is influenced more by objective realities of the mass political culture or by elite perceptions of those realities, and how congruent these two things might be.

Unfortunately, the data are limited and real tests of all facets of the so-called conflict-society model are unavailable, but we can, by using less direct evidence, arrive at a reasonably complex understanding of our subject. Despite the relatively crude nature of available survey research and related data, we are able to marshall evidence that seems, at first glance, somewhat startling and unexpected. Thus the data do not betray a "conflict society" in the Austrian setting; quite the contrary, in most respects. They suggest instead the following summary propositions about Austrian political culture—about mass opinion structure in the electoral arena:

1. the majority of the electorate may be characterized as partially *depolarized,* endorsing the existing party system and the consociational political regime, in basic agreement on the legitimate ends of governmental endeavor, and "pragmatically" oriented to what are essentially bargainable bread-and-butter issues (rather than to traditional ideological and/or symbolic issues contentious between the *Lager*);
2. as relatively *depoliticized,* exhibiting moderate (neither especially high nor low by worldwide standards) levels of political interest and information, and moderate frequencies of political discussion; and finally,
3. as also reflecting relatively *limited* intergroup *partisan hostility* in the sense that there appears to be a relatively low level of emotional commitment on the part of most citizens to the partisan *Lager* organizations, coupled with an apparently

minimal impact of political partisanship on individuals in their "nonpolitical" roles or spheres of activity.[13]

In short, while we cannot confront directly the thesis that the Austrian mass public exhibits continued attitudinal fragmentation corresponding to the great, sociologically and organizationally distinct, *Lager*—that the masses' orientations to substantive solutions of public issues are widely held, sharply crystallized, and intensely felt or that these are internally consistent from one issue to the next in harmony with the catechisms of the principal *Lager*—we can present a variety of evidence which suggests that the Austrian mass public, taken as a whole, exhibits limited polarity, considerable pragmatism, a relatively low political temperature, and certainly a much lesser degree of partisan hostility or concern than authorities on Austrian politics assert or imply.

Nonetheless, there are some indications of continued psychological apartness and distrust between the major camps; and perhaps capitalizing on these factors, national elections have tended to repolarize the electorate as they intensify mass political involvement, and increase public awareness of, attention to, and concern for the great ideological (symbolic) issues contentious between the *Lager*. At the same time, the political parties' campaign appeals have usually raised the specter of fundamental change in the political regime (or at least in its modalities). As a result of all this, elections tended to underline the "necessity" (or at least the elite's perception of necessity) of continuing existing consociational practices between the major political parties qua *Lager* through the mechanisms of Great Coalition and paracoalition.

Basic Consensus

Basic consensus, in the sense used by Easton and Hess, means the congruence of basic value and attitudinal orientations, not necessarily at the level of the government, but at the level of the regime and/or the political

13. For tabular presentation of many of the data on which the analysis in this section is based, and for further elaboration of key findings, see Stiefbold, *Austrian Electoral Politics*, chap. 5. While individual scholars may quarrel with my usage of such terms as relatively, basically, partially, etc., all who are familiar with the body of writings on Austrian politics would no doubt agree that the traditional picture of Austria—albeit usually without much empirical supportive evidence—was one of a highly polarized, ideological instead of pragmatic in issue delineation and problem-solving orientation, highly politicized, and severely partisan people; in short, of a country that would rank near the bottom of any group of democratic systems compared on these terms. This kind of interpretation was especially prevalent in scholarly writings of the 1950s and 1960s. A primary example, which both reflected and continued the prevailing analytical tone, was the first major effort by a political scientist to analyze the coalition political system: Herbert P. Secher, "Coalition Government: The Case of the Second Austrian Republic," *American Political Science Review* 52, no. 3 (September 1958): 791–808.

community.[14] Such a consensus existed in Austria under the Great Coalition, at least in two crucial respects, covering not only the regime itself but also—to a surprising extent—the designation and degree of urgency of the jobs to which that regime was expected to devote itself.

Public Support for the Austrian Party-Coalition System

In Republican Austria political parties have been traditionally and popularly perceived as tantamount to the state. The literature of Austrian politics abounds with references to the unique role that parties have played—institutionally and organizationally—in structuring Austrian political life.[15] Hence the public's view of the party system and the modes of interparty collaboration becomes a crucial indicator of the support it accords the political regime. As Jack Dennis has pointed out in his persuasive article on "Support for the Party System by the Mass Public," one can approach the question of mass support for public institutions at two rather different levels. (1) public support may be construed and measured in terms of the observable "specific" returns (e.g., "the economic security of patronage, the pleasures of association with like-minded people, or perhaps the symbolic pursuit of preferred policy programs and leadership") the supporters obtain from it; or (2) it can be "diffuse," that is, "endorsement of the party system as a whole and of the general norm that partisan spirit and activity is allowable in political life." Specific support is exchanged for gratification of immediate demands, while diffuse support constitutes a reservoir of favorable attitudes or goodwill toward existing forms of political authority; it is thus relatively independent of the effects of daily system outputs.[16]

While the extraordinarily high Austrian ratio of members to voters in both the SPOe and the OeVP suggests a high degree of party-system support in return for specific benefits, what seems to be a more remarkable finding is the traditional widespread support for *the existing party system*, despite (because of?) the persistence of the *Lager* as mutually exclusive segments of political society. This was indicated by a 1956 finding that four-fifths of Austrian men and two-thirds of Austrian women supported the notion of a multiparty system, and by a 1962 disclosure that more than four-fifths of both men and women favored the then existing party system ("no

14. David Easton and Robert D. Hess, "Youth and the Political System," in *Culture and Social Character*, ed. S. M. Lipset and R. Lowenthal (Glencoe, Ill.; Free Press, 1961), pp. 229–37.

15. See Herbert P. Secher, "The Problem of the Austrian State: The Post World War II Experience" (Ph.D. dissertation, University of Wisconsin, 1953), and the literature cited in this study.

16. Jack Dennis, "Support for the Party System by the Mass Public," *American Political Science Review* 60, no. 3 (September 1966): 600–601.

additional parties").[17] The "no additional parties" answer is not exactly a "democratic" response in quite the same sense as is support for a multiparty system, of course; rather it may suggest approval of the Black-Red political balance, coupled with a desire not to see that precious balance compromised by the addition of more parties.

Clearly these findings indicate that—whether for positive or negative reasons—a wide measure of diffuse support existed for the party system and the Austrian political regime as then constituted. Previous analysis of Austria as a "segmented pluralist" society shows that a high level of specific support exists for political parties within each major subculture. But diffuse support can apparently coexist with a high level of segmentation. This does not necessarily imply that organic solidarity based on growing functional interdependence across blocs was developing within the bosom of the mechanical, normative solidarity imposed on Austria by the Great Coalition. On the contrary, as noted in a paper on cross-national patterns of political socialization,[18] it is important to point out that diffuse support of political pluralism may mean something much different for the life and perspectives of the citizen of a high-consensus society, such as Britain, than it does where dissensus is ingrained in socially reinforced subcultures, as in Austria. The citizen of the latter system may well tolerate and even support a multiplicity of parties because he knows realistically that such must exist to represent divergent interests—and to protect groups and individuals from their political adversaries. Such diffuse support may also be a reaction to previous unhappy experiences under authoritarian regimes (Dollfuss, Nazi) that violated the political and legal rights of some individuals and groups.

There is no intrinsic or logical reason why a funtioning democratic regime cannot be built, as was perhaps true in the postwar Austrian case, on suspicion, distrust, and organizational apartness, as long as sufficient institutional arenas remain for bargaining, and there are a sufficient range and number of important issue areas that require and obtain minimal consultation or even cooperative decision making across subcultural lines. Perhaps sophisticated enough to recognize this need, along with the probability that such intercultural contact occurs with least friction and most promise of success at the "top" of the political system, between corresponding elites,

17. Computed from data supplied by the Austrian Gallup-Institut, Vienna, and collected as part of Survey No. 960, a representative quota sample of 2,500 Austrian men and women 18 years of age and over, interviewed in December 1962. (Hereinafter cited as Nachwahlstudie 1962)

18. Jack Dennis, Leon Lindberg, Donald McCrone, and Rodney Stiefbold, "Political Socialization to Democratic Orientations in Four Western Systems," *Comparative Political Studies* 1, no. 1 (April 1968): 82, 87, 96. See also Rodney P. Stiefbold and Hans N. Weiler, "Political Socialization in West Germany: Tolerance of Conflict and Dissent" (Paper, Annual Meeting of the American Political Science Association, Los Angeles, 1970), passim.

the public may come to support—consciously or not—the particular institutional arrangements that make this possible. New members of the political system, obviously less intimately aware of the political conditions that led to or necessitated such developments, may well internalize the same norms, without, however, being as consciously wedded to them. Thus the norms may persist, at least for a while, even after whatever objective needs gave rise to them have disappeared. Taken together, these various factors may help to account for the widespread "diffuse support" accorded the party system and the Great Coalition regime by the Austrian electorate through the middle of the 1960s.

Issues and the Jobs of Government

Although survey data on the issue orientation of the Austrian public leave much to be desired, in that they do not normally tap the respondents' feelings concerning what makes a given issue important or how it ought to be resolved, there *are* data concerning what Austrians perceive as the "jobs" or "issues" or "problems" most requiring governmental attention. From an examination of the frequency with which partisans of one party or the other spontaneously enumerate specific issues, or with which they single out specific issues from lists of potential issues submitted to them, it is at least possible (1) to establish that there is substantial inter-*Lager* and interparty consensus at the level of the electorate as to what the issues are, and (2) tentatively to characterize mass issue orientation as essentially pragmatic and cautious, in that public attention is directed primarily to bread-and-butter (rather than to traditional, symbolic, or ideological) issues.

Thus, for example, when asked to select from a list of tasks facing the new government after the 1962 election those they regarded as most important, more than half of the respondents in a national sample chose "Stable Currency"; more than a third each checked "Stable Prices" and "Neutrality"; and about one-fifth, made cognizant by the election campaign of the increasing extent to which Austria's future prosperity might hinge on the modalities of the proposed association with the Common Market, checked that option. Issues such as the operative rules of the Great Coalition or South Tyrol interested no more than one in ten of those who had voted SPOe or OeVP in the preceding election. Moreover, except for a single issue—higher wages and salaries—the big-party supporters were in substantial agreement both on the rank-ordering and on their levels of endorsement of particular issues.[19]

19. Nachwahlstudie 1962. Obviously agreement on what are the issues is not tantamount to agreement on what the solution should be or even on how to go about reaching it. There is no substantive or procedural consensus with respect to solutions implied by consensus in defining the relevant problems. What I am arguing is that those problems on which the elites have been most capable of establishing decision-making machinery and finding middle-range, pragmatic "solutions" are also precisely those issues defined by the masses as the most important tasks of

But perhaps of greatest significance, from the point of view of this chapter, is the fact that some issues found to be most salient and to discriminate most sharply between the political elites of the two chief *Lager*— such as the Habsburg question, educational reform, organization of the mass media, planning and nationalization, worker co-determination, influence of the church, the contemporary significance of Austria's Austro-Marxist, clerical-fascist and Nazi pasts—rate little or no measurable spontaneous enumeration by the public. Other issues salient at the elite level— neutrality and the questions of trade with Eastern Europe and association with the Common Market—are evoked at the mass level only in response to direct questions.

Intensity of Political Involvement

Not only does the Austrian mass public exhibit diffuse support for its political regime and considerable consensus on the centrality of the specific problems that happen to have proved most amenable to resolution by consociational practices, but by exhibiting a healthy measure of apathy toward day-to-day political affairs it also provides the regime with substantial operational freedom, which is important for the reduction of day-to-day stress on the political system.

Political Interest, Information, and Discussion

There are few extant data that bear directly on the level of day-to-day political interest in the Austrian population. When asked directly, "Are you interested in politics?" a recent national sample divided as follows: one-fourth designated themselves as "very" interested, one-half as "somewhat" interested, and the rest as "not at all" interested. Pollsters scoff at the relevance of such direct questions, noting that "to be Austrian is to be political" and that more than two out of every ten Austrians are card-carrying members of political parties, and that media attention to political matters as well as frequency of political discussion suggest political interest is substantial.[20]

Yet national survey data which tap the "information" dimension of political interest paint a more ambiguous picture of political intensity: although newspaper readership is high, the proportion of the population that

---

government. I do not mean to infer substantive consenses on policy outcomes or precise procedures among the masses, but I do infer—based chiefly on elite interview responses—that agreement on the essential tasks of government at the mass level was a powerful constraint on top elites to get results that would reinforce mass-level support for the coalition regime. (Stiefbold, S.A.N.E. Interviews, 1965–66.)

20. Interviews with the directors of the three most important commercial polling institutes, and with the director of the Social Science Study Group (SWS), a semi-independent, Socialist, and trade-union-oriented volunteer organization conducting periodic national surveys of differential technical quality. Vienna, 1965–66.

reads political material regularly is relatively low—even in Vienna, where the political process is close at hand and where the population is consistently more attentive to political news. One-third of the national population watch the news daily on television, and about one-half listen to the news on the radio, but most of these cannot recall specific news items.[21] Finally, when asked such questions as, "Who makes the laws?"—even in the days following an election campaign, when the salience of politics and the institutions of Nationalrat and government can be assumed to be at their peak—one-fifth of the respondents confessed total ignorance. In the judgment of Frank Pinner, expert observer of Austrian affairs and analyst of Austrian survey data, "Public opinion polls attempting to probe voter attitudes and information reveal a condition rather common in the Western world: most voters are singularly uninformed and unmotivated"; moreover, "the voter's knowledge of issues, events, and personalities is in general so low that it is not possible to attribute to him a system of political beliefs."[22]

Pinner has somewhat overstated his case to make his point; having "a system of political beliefs," at least at a very general level, seems perfectly compatible with depoliticization and with having relatively little precise knowledge of issues, events, or personalities. This is an empirical question, of course. Nevertheless, following Samuel H. Barnes' insightful argument in his "Ideology and the Organization of Conflict: On the Relationship between Political Thought and Behavior,"[23] I prefer to use the term *belief system* as an open term referring to the set of political attitudes held by an individual whether or not these attitudes exhibit "constraint," while reserving the term *ideology* to "a belief system that is internally consistent *and* consciously held."[24] As Barnes points out, this formulation does not necessarily imply an absence of constraint in the belief systems of mass publics; in fragmented polities, individuals "are often socialized into subcultures rigidly separate from one another, and may belong solely to organizations reflecting the belief systems of that particular subculture."[25] Under such circumstances the individual citizen "may be functionally isolated from deviant beliefs."[26] Or political organization, especially when it is as

21. Based on survey data made available to me by Karl Blecha, director of IFES, whose time and generosity I greatly appreciate. Blecha has pioneered in the empirical analysis of the relationship between politics and the mass media in Austria, and has several forthcoming publications based wholly or partly on the extensive IFES and SWS data files on the mass media during the 1960s. One of Blecha's collaborators, Rupert Gmoser, has analyzed some of these data in "Herr and Frau Oesterreicher vor der Entscheidung: Die Nationalratswahlen 1966 im Spiegel der Meinungsforschung," *Die Zukunft* 7 (April 1966): 11–15.

22. Frank A. Pinner, "On the Structure of Organizations and Beliefs: *Lagerdenken* in Austria" (Paper presented at the Annual Meeting of the American Political Science Association, 1967), p. 8.

23. *Journal of Politics* 28 (June 1966): 513–30.

24. Ibid., p. 514.

25. Ibid., p. 524.

26. Ibid., p. 520.

salient a feature of the political landscape as in Austria, may "provide the functional equivalent of ideology, or 'ideology by proxy.' " [27]

The analytical point, in the Austrian case, may be this: if organizational segmentation persists, interelection political apathy among the mass public may be more apparent than real; mass apathy may be rather easily translated into intense mass electoral engagement by elites who capitalize on the organizational weapons and traditional ideologies at their command. The high electoral turnout—between 94 and 97 percent of the electorate in the Second Republic—may reflect, in part, the confluence of these factors.

On another indicator of politicization, however, the frequency of engaging in political discussion, Austrians show a higher aggregate level of political participation than, say, West Germans or Italians. [28] If we compare data from the 1961 West German *Wahlstudie* with what is probably the most detailed Austrian study to date, the IFES study of 1965, we find substantial differences in the levels of face-to-face political communication in the two countries. Thus, 28 percent of Austrians, and one-third of those declaring a party preference, admit to multiple weekly discussions of politics, while in Germany only about 15 percent of both party and nonparty respondents could meet the much less rigorous requirement of discussing politics once a week. Talking politics in Austria may, of course, amount to little more than a kind of "expressive efficacy" on the part of individuals who find release for civic tensions (or merely behave according to longstanding cultural habits) in political gossip, without desiring personal responsibility and without perceiving themselves as any more "relevant" to actual political decision making than individuals who rarely talk politics. Nonetheless, knowledge of such patterns of communication about politics affords some insight into the potential effect of campaign propaganda: the masses are depoliticized, but with a high, if latent, mobilization potential. The saliency of politics may be "low" on a daily basis, but, since communications patterns are organizationally fixed and nonoverlapping, particularly among those major sectors of the electorate who support the OeVP or the SPOe, the saliency of politics can rather quickly bubble to the surface under extraordinary (e.g., electoral) circumstances.

Pervasiveness of Political Partisanship

It is widely assumed and argued in the literature on Austrian politics and society that political partisanship—the self-conscious identification of an individual with a particular *Lager*, coupled with individual commitment to and concern for the integrity of that relationship—pervades nearly every nook and cranny of Austrian society. As evidence one usually cites not only

27. Ibid., p. 516.
28. See Almond and Verba, *Civic Culture*, p. 116, for comparable data on Germany and Italy which suggest that Austria actually falls between Germany, where 39% never talk politics and 60% sometimes do, and Italy, where the percentage is 66% to 32%.

the organizational segmentation of Austrian society, but also the highly negative images said to be held about one party by supporters of the other party, as well as the high stability of voting patterns. Responsibility for the alleged continuing pervasiveness and intensity of the traditional *Lager* is attributed to highly homogeneous and intensely partisan patterns of political socialization supposedly prevalent in the Austrian family.[29]

Two pieces of evidence derived from a 1968, post-coalition survey of the Austrian electorate (which I use in the absence of data from the coalition era, although I am aware that there may have been relatively significant changes in the patterns and/or intensity of political partisanship after two years of a working noncoalition government) tend to cast some doubt on both the pervasiveness and the intensity of political partisanship. They suggest instead that both are much lower than assumed, that, while the *Lager* are not yet mere "shells" psychologically speaking, it is primarily the organizational components that make the *Lager* such formidable factors in Austrian politics (e.g., under electoral conditions, when the *Lager* organizations become powerful instruments of mass political mobilization).

Tables 2 and 3 show the data for two indicators of the impact of politics on individuals' personal lives: respondents' degree of concern about the political like-mindedness of their associates in different social contexts, and their feelings regarding the hypothetical situation of the marriage of a daughter across party lines. The first case (table 2) seems a striking commentary on the alleged level of politicization and partisanship in the Austrian family: a mere one-third of the respondents exhibit any concern at all when members of their own families hold political orientations different from their own, and 60 percent report themselves as experiencing no displeasure whatsoever in that event. Also interesting is that 70 percent do not care at all about their friends' political persuasion, and over half of the respondents do not care if their work colleagues or superiors hold different views (with another one-quarter to one-third having "no answer," perhaps because they have not had occasion to consider the matter).

Table 3 also refutes somewhat the notion of finely honed, highly manifest political partisanship extending even into the personal lives of average Austrian citizens: large percentages of either major party's supporters would view the marriage of their daughter to someone from the opposite party's ranks with indifference. The point is not that there is no evidence of the cumulative impact of group affiliations (e.g., family, religion or occupation, or party); there is. But in Austria today, as in West Germany, concern over the partisan affiliation of one's future son-in-law "is more frequently expressed positively as pleasure over marriage *within* the party

29. See the review of the literature by F. O. Heyt and L. A. Vaskovics, "Sozialforschung und Soziologie in Oesterreich," *Koelner Zeitschrift fuer Soziologie und Sozialpsychologie* 18 (1966): 94–116, esp. 117–18. See also Steiner, *Politics in Austria*, chap. 7.

Table 2. Degree of Concern by Respondents in the Event That Their Associates in Various Milieus Would Have a Political Orientation Different from Theirs, in Percentages of Total Sample (1968)

Type of Associates	Degree of Concern[a]					
	High	Substantial	Some	None	Don't know	No answer
Family members	14	5	15	59	2	4
Good friends	5	4	16	69	2	4
Work colleagues	2	2	8	57	3	28
Work supervisors	1	1	5	57	5	31
Salespeople	1	1	5	79	6	8
Sports, conversation	1	2	7	77	5	9
Churchgoers	1	1	4	75	6	14

[a]Due to rounding, percentages do not always add across rows to 100%.

Source: Engelmann-Schwartz survey. Sample was multistage random probability of 1,741 Austrian men and women over 20 years old. Study carried out by the Institut fuer empirische Sozialforshung (IFES, Vienna; Director, Karl Blecha), April 1968.

Table 3. How Supporters of Major Parties Would View Marriage of Daughter Within or Across Party Lines in Austria, in Percent (1968)

Attitudes toward inter- or intraparty marriage	OeVP = OeVP	OeVP = SPOe	SPOe = OeVP	SPOe = SPOe
Pleased	53	2	—	36
Displeased	1	19	14	—
Indifferent	43	72	81	62
Other, Don't know, No answer	3	7	5	2
N =	372	372	567	567

Source: Engelmann-Schwartz survey; see table 2. I am greatly indebted to Professors Mildred Schwartz and Frederick C. Engelmann for use of these data.

rather than displeasure over marriage *out* of the party."[30] Only in the case of a Communist entering the family is there a striking variation on the general patterns; whereas three-quarters of the total sample indicate indifference regarding marriage of a daughter to someone supporting the OeVP, SPOe, or FPOe, 40 percent would experience displeasure over a Communist son-in-law and fewer than half, indifference. Perhaps the very contrast between concern over Communists and concern over others illustrates the extent to which the two dominant *Lager* (at least at the level of public opinion) now *accept* each other *within* the Austrian political system.[31]

Political Attitudes of Youth

Austrian youth attitudes merit our special attention. They best reveal the trends in the attitudinal bases of the *Lager*, and help delineate more sharply the profile of the changing popular arena in which elite-mass electoral campaign interaction unfolds. What is of particular interest is the degree of concordance between youthful and adult attitudes, given the potential significance of any differences for the timing and direction of political change.

Study of both published and unpublished data suggests that basic political orientations and levels of political involvement among Austrian youth differ substantially from those among adults.[32] Thus, the younger

30. Almond and Verba, *Civic Culture*, p. 137; see, more generally, pp. 132–39 for a discussion of marriage within and across party lines as an indicator of psychological distance between parties. (The data are not exactly equivalent: the Almond and Verba data have to do with the hypothetical marriage of either a son or daughter across party lines, the Austrian data with daughters only. However, this would not seem to be a serious difference.)

There is a difference between the OeVP and the SPOe; my statement in the text, quoting Almond and Verba on Germany, applies to both Austrian parties but in particular to the OeVP. The Austrian Socialists, on the other hand, come closer to the Italian counterparts who are less often indifferent and more often express displeasure. The Socialist data are quite interesting: as compared with the OeVP data, I would interpret them as reflecting the slower pace of modernization and the still greater prevalence and tenacity of *Lagermentalitaet* to be found on the Austrian Left in the 1960s—perhaps as a result of the more comprehensive and more tightly articulated organizational infrastructure of the Socialist *Lager* (with its greater cumulative "political socialization" impact) perhaps as a result of the general similarity in the traditional nature of the Austrian and Italian Left ("revolutionary and anticlerical" in Almond and Verba's words), perhaps as a combination of both.

31. Anticommunism, despite the tendency of the OeVP's campaign managers and functionaries—whom I designate as "middle-level political elites" later on in this analysis—to try "red scare" electoral tactics (by evoking the Popular Front or Austro-Marxist spooks), has been a cornerstone of Austria's limited inter-*Lager* consensus since World War II. Hence it is not surprising that 63% of the OeVP supporters would feel displeasure over the prospect of a Communist son-in-law (compared to 19% in the event of a Socialist entering the family), or that 36% of SPOe supporters would feel displeasure at a Communist marriage (compared to 14% at an OeVP marriage). Source: Engelmann-Schwartz Survey, 1968.

32. Highly suggestive data on youth orientations toward the political system have been collected by Karl Blecha; they are partially reported in a series of internal IFES studies, notably "Jugend und Demokratie," 3 parts, 1967, and "Die Jungwaehler des Jahrganges 1945," 1966. Another important but unpublished study is the Austrian Gallup Institute's Survey No. 608 (February and March 1959). Several published studies are relevant to an under-

Austrian is less deeply attached to the given political system and its principal actors. He may agree that coalition was necessary and extremely useful in the rebuilding of the Austrian state, but he is less certain of its utility for the future. He has less knowledge than older persons of the origins of the party system, a weaker image of the current party competitors, and is more attracted to personalities than to programs. If he is a party member, it is likely to be out of pragmatic considerations—it is good insurance "if you want to get ahead in Austria" or if you want an apartment in Vienna.[33]

The younger Austrian is also less intensely involved in political life than are his elders. In an IFES survey conducted just prior to the 1966 parliamentary election, from one-half to three-quarters of first-time voters in four election districts considered themselves less interested in politics than their parents. Only a small proportion of those interviewed reported frequent political discussion.[34] Supportive data have been reported by several commentators; for example, when a representative cross section of the Austrian population was asked in 1962 (before the parliamentary elections) whether they read newspaper articles dealing with the election, a mere 23 percent of the youngest voters and just over one-third of those aged 22–30 said yes, whereas about half of all those over 30 years of age reported reading such articles.[35] And in 1966 the national polling institutes found that indifference to the election outcome was considerably greater among first-time young voters than among any other age group.[36] Earlier data (1956 and 1959) had indicated greater political involvement by youth. For example, it was found that an overwhelming majority considered the right to vote important, and, moreover, that less than half of those under 25 years of age were prepared to state that the mere act of voting fulfilled one's obligation to participate in politics. Obviously, one must be cautious in drawing inferences from such disparate evidence, but scrutiny of unpublished Gallup poll data suggests a similar waning of political involvement and electoral concern among youth in recent years.[37]

All the data reported or cited above indicate that the level of politiciza-

---

standing of the various kinds of specific and diffuse support accorded the Austrian political system by its younger citizens. See, e.g., Karl Blecha, "Wo steht Oesterreichs Jugend politisch?" *Sozialistische Erzichung*, 10 October 1965, pp. 226–34; Leopold Rosenmayr, *Familienbeziehungen und Freizeitgewohnheiten jugendlicher Arbeiter* (Vienna: Verlag fuer Geschichte und Politik, 1963).

33. Blecha, "Die Jungwaehler," pp. 17–21, 38–40.

34. Ibid., pp. 10–13.

35. Blecha, "Wo steht Oesterreichs Jugend politisch?," p. 230.

36. Gmoser, "Herr und Frau Oesterreicher," p. 13; Blecha, "Die Jungwaehler," pp. 14–16.

37. I am indebted to Dr. Fritz Karmasin for the opportunity to review these data at length, and for cooperation in performing various computations at Gallup's Vienna headquarters. For an annotated list of political surveys, together with a short sketch of the contents of standard interview schedules and identification of principal sponsors (parties, pressure groups, govern-

tion may be quite unrelated to continuing segmentation. The former acquires electoral significance when its embers are reignited by ideological fear-evoking election propaganda of party organization cadres and managers who intentionally utilize the organizational bases of segmented pluralism to reinforce partisanship, in order to crystallize, solidify, and mobilize their party's traditional ghetto bloc of voters in the perpetual quest for the 1 to 3 percent swing that would spell victory and bring appropriate spoils. Otherwise, among broad sectors of the electorate, political involvement (in terms of the pervasiveness of partisanship, and in the sense of having political interest, being informed or talking politics) seems relatively low and is generationally decreasing. Politics, in short, seems to have become less salient to the average American.

Indicators of Continuing Political Relevance of the Austrian Lager

On the other hand, these findings should not obscure the central fact that abundant evidence exists to support the proposition that the *Lager* remained throughout the coalition era (and for several years beyond, for most people) the central structural, social, and "cultural" realities affecting the style and patterns of elite-mass political interaction. As the Introduction to this chapter already indicated, and as we shall argue (see pp. 159 ff.) in a later section, the relevance of the *Lager* "mentality" tenaciously persisted among certain *elites* of both parties. From the perspective of *mass* political culture, abundant unpublished data confirm not merely the continuing social and organizational distinctiveness of the *Lager*, but also point to a hard *residuum* of strong subcultural (not merely party) identification coupled with feelings of distrust and apartness between adherents of different *Lager*.

Based on my familiarity with both published and unpublished survey data for the coalition period, I would identify at least the following elements as part of the general atmosphere, in the 1960s, of perceiving political affairs in *Lager* terms. I am *not* arguing that these are analytically part of a *Lager* psychosis or even necessarily part of what Engelmann called a *Lager* "mentality." I am, however, reporting, on the basis of considerable field research, that elite *and* mass respondents to interviews identified these features of Austrian politics (in field interviews conducted in 1965–1966 before the collapse of Great Coalition in April 1966) as being—in the words of the last chancellor of Austria under the Great Coalition—"various aspects

mental agencies, individuals), see Rodney Stiefbold, "Politische Meinungsforschung in Oest-terreich, 1954–1965," in *Nationalratswahl 1966*, ed. Peter Gerlich, Georg Ress, and Rodney Stiefbold (Vienna: Verlag f. Jugend u. Volk/Oesterr. Bundesverlag, 1968), pp. 249–51. I am indebted to the major polling organizations for permitting me at least limited access to many of these data. The directors are Dr. Fritz Karmasin (Gallup-Institut), Dr. Walther Fessel (Fessel-Institut), and Karl Blecha (Institut fuer empirische Sozialforschung, IFES), all of Vienna.

of a traditional *Lager*-centered framework for viewing the political world." These features, then, include:

1. the widespread tendency to view the SPOe or the OeVP as distinctly class parties, sociologically and ideologically reflective of, and bound to, their own particular ghettos of mutually exclusive support;[38]
2. the high degree of organizational membership in both the Socialist and Conservative (Catholic) subcultures, the relatively slight electoral fluctuation among social groups or between the major camps, and a level of voting participation which is consistently high even by European standards;[39]
3. the long-prevalent notion of so-called equilibrium voters (those voters who, trusting neither side, waited to see which party seemed likely to win, then voted for the other in a conscious effort to maintain Black-Red parity), a thesis claiming considerable support by leading authorities on Austrian politics[40] and with some, if inconclusive, empirical underpinning;
4. the complaints of Austrian survey research organizations, especially a few years ago, that political distrust and alienation from political life—even among some party members— resulted in high percentages of refusals to state party preference, or to report past party voting;[41]
5. and finally, some evidence of political insecurity, in the form of pessimism concerning the outlook for Austria in the event of dissolution of the Great Coalition between OeVP and SPOe.[42]

38. See the "images" data reported in Karl Blecha, Rupert Gmoser, and Heinz Kienzl, *Der durchleuchtete Waehler: Beitraege zur politischen Soziologie in Oesterreich* (Vienna: Europe Verlag, 1965), pp. 88–126. On the social distinctiveness and cohesion of Austrian parties during the Coalition era, see Dwaine Marvick and Rodney Stiefbold, "Sozialstrukturelle Merkmale der Waehlerschaft der OeVP und SPOe, 1961–1962," *Koelner Zeitschrift fuer Soziologie und Sozial-Psychologie,* 19, no. 4 (1967): 708–20; and Klaus Liepelt, "Esquisse d'une typologie des electeurs allemands et autrichiens," *Revue française de Sociologie* 9 (1968): esp. 16 and 23.

39. For a summary of these points, consult Stiefbold, *Austrian Electoral Politics,* chaps. 2, 3, and 5; Stiefbold et al., *Wahlen und Parteien in Oesterreich,* vol. 2, sections B-22 and B-56; and Karl-Heinz Nassmacher, *Das oesterreichische Regierungssystem* (Cologne: Westdeutscher Verlag, 1968), chap. 2.

40. See, e.g., F. C. Engelmann, "Haggling for the Equilibrium: The Renegotiation of the Austrian Coalition, 1959," *American Political Science Review,* 56, no. 3 (1962): 657, 662, 653; Kitzinger, "Austrian Election of 1959," p. 120n.

41. This is a general phenomenon, confirmed repeatedly in my interviews of personnel in major and minor survey research institutes, and their clients, throughout Austria. In fact, this was one reason why the OeVP, in frustration over the fact that many of their eventual voters would not describe themselves in surveys as party identifiers, thus complicating party efforts to explore the political culture and policy preferences of its clientele, decided in 1966 to reduce its expenditures for survey research and to rely more extensively on a party and interest-group–based organization similar to the SWS on the Socialist side.

42. Stiefbold, "Elite-Mass Opinion Structure," p. 14 and table 5.

Summary of Findings and Implications

Generally speaking, this analysis of some of the contours of mass opinion in Austria has suggested that the public's broad day-to-day political dispositions are characterized by regime support, considerable pragmatic agreement concerning the jobs of government, political apathy, and a low impact of political partisanship on the individual in his nonpolitical roles—but that Austria's continuing organizational segmentation into Catholic-Conservative and Socialist subcultures is complemented by lingering elements of psychological distrust and apartness. What makes these "lingering elements" significant is the political organizational component of Austrian life. Segmented pluralist organizations are a formidable potential instrument of mass political mobilization—particularly, one would suspect, in a relatively unintegrated polity under conditions of an ideological campaign in a close election.

Still, the Austrian electorate in the coalition era possessed essentially the same political dispositions as "electoral cultures" in much of the rest of Western Europe. Austrians appeared to have a vested interest in the existing system; they did not exhibit a high level of ideological commitment or political interest or involvement, but were concerned chiefly with bread-and-butter issues. No doubt the diffuse support for the status quo and the apparent resistance to open-minded experimentation and innovation restricted the possibilities of change, the extent of disintegration, the magnitude of fluctuation, and the depth of postelection disaffection that might be induced by inflammatory campaign rhetoric. And it condemned splinter parties to insignificance.

The Conduct and Consequences of Election Campaigns

According to Janowitz and Marvick, a truly democratic election ought to promote attitudes of political compromise and further social consensus. This belief is apparently based on the assumption, shared by Downs, that under conditions of two-party competition, the votes at the center of the political spectrum are decisive in the struggle for power, forcing each of the major contestants to focus its appeals on the uncommitted votes in the middle, halfway between either pole in the system.[43]

But in Austria under the Great Coalition, despite some halfhearted steps in the direction of catchall appeals by parties mindful of changing socioeconomic conditions, election campaigns operated somewhat differently.[44] They were not primarily catchall in character, nor did they

43. Morris Janowitz and Dwaine Marvick, "Competitive Pressure and Democratic Consent," *Public Opinion Quarterly* 19 (Winter 1955–56): 381–400. Anthony Downs, *An Economic Theory of Democracy* (New York: Harper & Brothers, 1957).

44. For an analysis, see Rodney Stiefbold, *Elites and Elections in a Fragmented Political System* (Cologne: Westdeutscher Verlag, 1973) chap. 4. My generalizations in these and

contribute to the development of a catchall national political style. For several reasons—the tiny size of any genuinely "floating" vote, the narrow margin needed to "win" an election and with it important concessions by the opposing coalition partner, the extremely high level of voter turnout, and the continued perception by campaign elites of Austrian political parties as components of monolithic *Lager*—election campaigns Austrian-style turned into "scare" exercises in extremist political propaganda and organizational mobilization of the voters. Hence the villains of each successive campaign were Dollfus and clerical-fascism, Austro-Marxism and the hoax of a Communist-Socialist Popular Front, the threatened return of the Habsburgs, and the allegedly invidious intention of the other party to change the rules of coalition conduct and thus sabotage coalition work as it was accused of having tried to do in the past.

This "blatant evocation of historical fear,"[45] intended to drive home the urgent necessity for the Great Coalition in the fragile Austrian setting— coupled with a sinister warning that electoral victory by the other party could wreck that coalition—was, of course, designed less to attract floaters or detach and convert potential switchers than it was to mobilize each party's "ghetto vote." That is, it attempted to awaken *Lager* sentiments and to evoke *Lager* reflexes among each bloc's apathetic partisans, to eliminate any possibility of dissidence and defection among bloc militants and ideologues, and to get both these groups to the polls on election day.

The impact of elections in a democracy is felt at both mass and elite levels. With respect to the mass level in Austria under the Great Coalition, some (still classified) survey data suggest that the *effect* of election campaigns corresponded closely to campaign elites' *intent* of recrystallizing and reinforcing distinct lines of social, organizational, and attitudinal cleavages between the Red SPOe and the Black (OeVP) subcultures. But most of the extant published materials (and most of the still classified data) point to little more than a kind of "pulsation" of the system of social cleavages as a result of campaign stimuli, i.e., to the normal but temporary increase in intergroup awareness and apartness which one probably finds in any electoral democracy.[46] There is no evidence that these pulsation effects had deleterious long-term consequences at the mass level.

On the other hand, elite *perceptions* of the mass-level impact of elections contrast sharply with the above picture. Detailed interviews which I

following paragraphs are based on interviews with campaign elites in Vienna and provincial capitals, 1965–66, and descriptions of past campaigns in ·the popular press, on numerous internal memos of the campaign units of the national political party organizations, and on the available scholarly literature. Cf. Stiefbold, *Austrian Electoral Politics*, chap. 3.

45. Kitzinger, "Austrian Election of 1959," p. 120*n*. passim.

46. See Bernard Berelson et al., *Voting* (Chicago: University of Chicago Press, 1954), p. 144, for a classic statement.

and my associates conducted with 131 Nationalrat deputies elected in 1966, and with public opinion pollsters, campaign staffs, and campaign managers of both major political parties, indicate clearly that (1) the campaign exacerbated Austria's subcultural cleavages; and (2) these cleavages were in any case "durable constants on the Austrian political scene." In short, Austria still remained, in the eyes of her electoral elites, very much a "conflict society," polarized, politicized, partisan, ideological at nonelite level.

My interviews suggest further that the reason for this apparent misperception of mass political culture was to be found in the interlocking of three factors. *First,* the slide-rule faithfulness with which election outcomes were translated into periodic revisions of the inter-*Lager* balance of coalition power placed a high premium on achieving incremental gains and avoiding incremental losses. *Second,* the easiest and safest way of accomplishing these ends, given the small number of potential "floating voters," was to be more efficient in mobilizing "your" *Lager* adherents than your opponent was in mobilizing "his" *Lager* adherents. *Third,* the "conflict society" perceptions harbored by those elites responsible for the conduct of election campaigns were nurtured by self-serving public opinion pollsters who emphasized in their written (and especially in their oral) briefings of these elites throughout the campaign those data which indicated that the more highly politicized components of the electorate were reacting to the campaign with increasing feelings of insecurity, apprehension, and subcultural distinctiveness. *Thus the chain of electoral interaction seems clear: deliberate elite politicization of the masses, selective perceptions by the elite that such is the true state of the masses, and consequently reinforcement of the elite's previous views and "validation" of its previous efforts. At this point in our analysis, therefore, it appears plausible to argue that the electoral process under the Great Coalition may have served basically to reinforce traditional features of Austrian politics; and that misperceptions by elites, or some elites, may have artificially prolonged the life of crisis-consociational rule beyond any "objective" necessity* (in the sense that the data presented do not support the notion that Austria was really a "conflict society" in need of crisis-consociational rule; at most these data suggest a certain cultural and organizational hangover from an earlier era).

Italian political scientist Giovanni Sartori has argued, in a persuasive line of reasoning followed by such other contemporary scholars as Samuel Barnes and Giuseppe Di Palma, that mass political beliefs are part of the basic raw material of political democracy, a limiting or constraining factor but not a determinant one in structuring the behavior of political elites.[47]

47. Giovanni Sartori, *Democratic Theory* (New York: Frederick A. Praeger, 1965), pp. 78–79 and chaps. 5 and 6, passim; Barnes, "Ideology and Organization of Conflict," p. 530; and especially Giuseppe Di Palma, *Apathy and Participation: Mass Politics in Western Societies* (New York: Free Press, 1970), passim.

Both published and unpublished Austrian data from the coalition era, some of them reviewed above, appear to underscore the limited explanatory power of mass political beliefs in describing or predicting political outcomes in the Austrian variant of Western industrial society. In fact, one might argue, they carry us a step further, suggesting that it is elites' *perceptions* of mass belief systems—rather than the mass belief systems themselves—that are ultimately most important in determining whatever influence mass publics have in policy formulation, review, or control via electoral and other political processes. Thus, in a peaceful and affluent context, which we might expect would encourage the competing political parties to devote their efforts to catchall electoral tactics, we find instead that campaigning has as virulent an "ideological" edge as can be found in contemporary Europe. Furthermore, despite apparent public satisfaction with the coalition regime, a survey of electoral outcomes during the coalition era would show that substantial costs were exacted at the elite level by the electoral process, often including long postelection periods of decisional ineffectiveness while laborious efforts were made to re-create a minimal pool of interelite trust, renegotiate the coalition, and find a common set of programmatic goals which might allow a new government to get moving forward again.

Obviously these seeming paradoxes in the Austrian case are not resolved by examining political culture and public opinion data at the mass level. While that examination does now provide us with some clues as to why the Austrian system survived the change of regime from coalition to government-and-opposition in 1966 with little or no mass-level disruption, it is still not at all clear why crisis-consociational rule *persisted so long* but was then *transformed so easily* at the elite level. What prevented a growth of mutual trust and confidence between the *Lager* in political spheres, when those commodities seemed abundantly available in arenas dominated by interest groups and chambers? Why wasn't the original, 1945-based crisis-consociational rule "self-devouring" under conditions of peace, prosperity, and prolonged political stability?

The next section seeks answers to these questions. First, however, we must review some of the principal features of the mildly authoritarian and elitist model of "consociational" democracy proposed by Arend Lijphart as a viable alternative in divided societies to prevailing competitive and pluralistic models of democratic politics and government. Then we shall turn to an examination of pertinent Austrian data on elite opinion structure, role differentiation, and both inter- and intra-*Lager* communication patterns. Armed with the information and insights thus provided, and having appraised their consequences, we can at last focus on the complicated problem of persistence and change in consociational democracy, and in so doing raise some broader questions of political development theory as well.

Elite Opinion Structure

Consociational Democracy: A Critique of the Lijphart Model

The keystone in Lijphart's analysis of consociational democracy is the role played by political elites in the face of fragmented political cultures, in trying to neutralize whatever immobilist or destabilizing tendencies exist. For Lijphart, the elites cannot afford to behave ideologically, or at least not toward each other. Instead, consociational elites must be able to recognize the dangers inherent in a fragmented system, be committed personally to the system's maintenance, be strong enough to transcend the divisive subcultural cleavages at the elite level, and be able to forge appropriate solutions for the demands of the subcultures (by developing institutional arrangements and specific rules of the game for the accommodation of differences). If the leaders of the rival subcultures lack any one of these four "behavioral" attributes the system will not work: they are the prerequisites for consociational democracy.[48]

If the first brick in the structure of consociational democracy is interelite behavior at the top of the political system across subcultures, the second is the relationship between elites and masses within the same subculture. Thus, subcultures must remain as mutually exclusive as possible: there must be "distinct lines of cleavage" (sociologically and organizationally) between subcultures, which will be further enhanced if masses are psychologically committed to their subcultures—if they evince high partisanship or what Lijphart calls "high internal cohesion." [49]

The success of the consociational venture will ultimately depend not only on the establishment of fruitful interelite cooperation, but also on the retention of the support and loyalty of the separate subcultures. Elites must be more tolerant than followers, yet able to carry them along. Thus, while the key features of consociational democracy are conciliatory intentions, attitudes, and behavior of subcultural elites, Lijphart does not discard the premise of direct linkage between political culture and system performance: for the politics of accommodation to work effectively, subcultural elites must be secure in their positions of leadership and relatively unencumbered by intraparty directives. And this combination of elite security and autonomy depends in turn on a particular admixture of mass-level at-

---

48. Lijphart's summary of these propositions is found in "Typologies," pp. 24–25, and "Consociational Democracy," p. 216, and *The Politics of Accommodation*, pp. 111, 179, 204, 197–211.

49. "Typologies," pp. 26–27; cf. pp. 36–37. See also "Consociational Democracy," pp. 219–21.

tributes—namely, on the sociological distinctiveness, firm partisan attachment, and organizational mobilizability of separate groups of followers, or subcultures, combined with intrasubcultural attitudes of deference toward incumbent leaders and substantial diffuse support by all nonelites of the regime of government by elite cartel.[50]

The Lijphart model is an intriguing explanation for the apparent success that such divided societies as Austria or the Netherlands have had in achieving and maintaining stable, effective, and legitimate political regimes under consociational elite rule. Nonetheless, several troublesome problems remain unresolved in Lijphart's model. Two of these are particularly thorny, yet vitally important: (1) the dynamics of elite-mass interaction in consociational democracies; and (2) how, once established, consociational regimes are sustained, modified, or transformed. High partisanship, reinforced by ideological posturing of elites within their subcultures,[51] is apparently useful at the intrasubcultural level to help maintain the organizational and sociological distinctiveness and cohesion of separated subcultures; but the elite cartel system of decision making depends also on substantial mass support and avoidance of destabilizing mass involvement which ideological posturing by elites might produce.[52] Do elites in consociational democracies behave both ways? at different times? for different purposes? No answers are supplied.

Just as Lijphart does not concern himself with the precise linking mechanisms that operate between the level of individuals and groups and the level of elite behavior and system performance, he likewise leaves unresolved the question of how crisis-consociational regimes evolve, although he is quite explicit about the probable outcomes of such evolution in Europe. Lijphart apparently believes that prevailing Western European conditions of prosperity, peace, and the growth of public planning at national and pan-European levels will lead increasingly toward an altogether different type of democratic regime: the "depoliticized democracy," in which consociational practices will reflect consensus rather than cleavage. He foresees a direct and linear evolution in which growing, Europe-wide "depoliticization" and "deideologization" of mass publics will reduce frag-

50. Strictly speaking, Lijphart differentiates between the previously enumerated "behavioral" characteristics of elites, which he calls "essential," and the mass-level attributes and elite-level consequences enumerated, which in his various analyses are labeled "facilitating conditions." It takes little effort to realize that the "essential" conditions can be met only when the mass-level attributes discussed here are also present. For a critical theoretical discussion and elaboration of these points, see Stiefbold, *Elites and Elections in a Fragmented Political System*, esp. chaps. 4 and 5; and Stiefbold, *Austrian Electoral Politics*, chaps. 1, 5, 6, 7.

51. Lijphart, *Politics of Accommodation*, pp. 144, 141.

52. Ibid., chap. 7, "The Rules of the Game." See also my discussion on pp. 126–28 of this chapter, in the section on "Elections, Ideology, and Consociational Democracy," and the references there to Lijphart's "Consociational Democracy," p. 214, and his "Typologies," p. 22.

mentation, which in turn will reduce the need for resorting to elite-imposed "crisis" consociational practices. At the same time these changes at the mass level will allow development of "natural" consociational practices based on the growth of functional interdependence of groups in society and on a correspondingly increased reliance on "normal" patterns of industrial society decision making which emphasize the interaction of bureaucratic and interest-group elites.[53] *But we still do not know how—by what linking mechanism or process—a politics of stable suspicion among a cartel of subcultural elites gets transformed into a politics of trust among those same elites. Nor, conversely, do we know from Lijphart's analysis, by what mechanisms such evolution is prevented.* Again, if we are to go beyond mere description, beyond a mere snapshot of political regimes at one point in time and at a later point in time, *we must focus on the dynamics of elite and mass interaction which facilitate or impede change in the locus and pattern of decision making.*

Empirical data suggest that elite-mass interaction in many countries, particularly under electoral circumstances, is characterized by considerable acerbity and ideologism. Moreover, an accumulating body of empirical evidence suggests "that the belief systems of mass publics seldom exhibit constraints among elements, and that elites are the hosts of ideologies," as Barnes observes.[54] Thus, McClosky et al. found that "Whereas leaders of the two [American] parties diverge strongly, their followers differ only moderately in their attitudes toward issues"; that it is more accurate to assert "that the natural cleavages between the leaders are largely ignored by their followers"; and that leaders (compared to the great mass of their supporters) are more articulate, informed, and highly partisan.[55] And the data reported by Converse and Dupeux[56] for the French electorate and by

53. Lijphart, "Typologies," pp. 27, 28, 32, and 35 ff. The assumption here, of course, is that advanced industrial societies manifest increased consociationalism as a result of their increased reliance on patterns of decision making that emphasize the interaction of bureaucratic and interest-group elites, a phenomenon associated with the growing importance of the output side of government. See, on these points, the theoretical discussion by Heisler and Kvavik, chap. 2 in this volume. Focusing on Western Europe as a whole, Di Palma and Stiefbold have provisionally identified the more important general "rules of the game," which hold for consociational democracies as well: see their "Conflict and Elites in Western Industrial Societies: A Theoretical Reassessment and a Proposal," mimeographed (Department of Political Science, University of California, Berkeley, and Faculty Committee for the Study of Industrial Societies, 1969), and Di Palma's "Project Description: Political Conflict and Conflict Regulation in Western European Societies," mimeographed (Department of Political Science, University of California, Berkeley, 1968).

54. Barnes, "Ideology and the Organization of Conflict," p. 522. See also Philip Converse's superb article, "The Nature of Belief Systems in Mass Publics," in *Ideology and Discontent*, ed. David Apter (New York: Free Press, 1964), pp. 206–61.

55. Herbert McClosky et al., "Issue Conflict and Consensus among Party Leaders and Followers," *American Political Science Review* 58 (June 1964): 372–73.

56. Philip E. Converse and Georges Dupeux, "Politicization of the Electorate in France and the United States," *Public Opinion Quarterly* 26 (Spring 1962); reprinted in Angus Campbell et al., *Elections and the Political Order* (New York: John Wiley, 1966), pp. 269–91.

Duncan MacRae, Jr.,[57] for French legislators also support the primary notion that polarization of political opinion is more pronounced at the elite level, as well as the concomitant notion that polarization of public opinion seems, to a considerable degree, to be an elite-induced phenomenon. In stable and legitimate political systems, this may not pose a problem to system stability, since these elites are also likely to be highly committed to the given regime and more tolerant and more accepting of democratic norms than those whom they lead.[58] But in a subculturally divided society, political elites, according to Gabriel Almond, tend to exhibit a "general alienation from the political market. . . . The political actors come to the market not to exchange, compromise, and adapt, but to preach, exhort, convert, and transform the political system"[59]

In short, neither traditional empirical democratic theory of the Almond variety nor the leaders-followers data that can be adduced from various empirical studies make credible Lijphart's depoliticized, pragmatic, and cooperative "consociational" elites, especially in fragmented societies. But Lijphart's examples of functioning consociational democracies also refute the claim that polities with fragmented political cultures are inherently immobilist and unstable at least in part because of the recruitment and socialization experiences, and consequent political behavior, of subcultural elites. Particularly baffling is the case of Austria— which Engelmann specifically identifies as an example of the kind of "continental European" system that Almond was ostensibly describing[60]— where the observer can find ample evidence of both ideological behavior by elites, with polarizing and destabilizing consequences, and of consociational behavior with its stabilizing and integrating consequences.

The difficulties of meshing the two possible interpretations of subcultural elites as assets or obstacles to political stability would appear to lie in the specific *level* of elites we are talking about. It is at this point that an important insight from Karl Deutsch concerning "the decisive 'middle level' of communication and decision" becomes relevant. Writes Deutsch:

> The strategic "middle level" . . . is that level of communication and command that is "vertically" close enough to the large mass of . . . citizens . . . to forestall any continuing and effective direct communication between them and the "highest echelons"; and it must be far enough above the level of the large numbers of the rank and file to permit effective "horizontal" communication and organization . . . on its own level.[61]

57. Duncan MacRae, Jr., *Parliament, Parties, and Society in France 1946–1958* (New York: St. Martin's, 1967), passim, esp. pp. 326 ff., 333 ff.

58. See, e.g., Almond and Verba, *Civic Culture*, pp. 486–87.

59. Almond, "Comparative Political Systems," p. 407.

60. Engelmann, "Haggling for the Equilibrium," p. 654.

61. Karl W. Deutsch, *The Nerves of Government: Models of Political Communication and Control* (New York: Free Press, 1963), p. 154, and more generally, pp. 154–57.

In Deutsch's words, these are persons who "usually received very little publicity." They are the men behind the scenes in the sense that they are the "men who do the work of making, permitting, and executing the largest number of strategic decisions."[62] Admittedly, the concept of middle-level elites is difficult to operationalize. Deutsch himself quickly decides that the group he is really concerned with—in the government, parties, mass media, armed forces, and pressure groups—is best characterized as "*upper* middle level."[63] Obviously, middle or upper-middle level in these various contexts encompasses a very broad range of levels and types of elite roles which for theoretical clarity and empirical utility need to be rigorously distinguished from one another.

Unfortunately, there is not a very systematic, empirically based literature on middle-level elites or on intraelite relationships. As Dwaine Marvick has pointed out, in modern theory about political systems, two components—top elites and mass publics—receive most of the attention; what is largely missing is behavioral evidence of how the interstitial components, the cadres, or middlemen of politics, do function, why, and with what consequences.[64] Hence, much of the real process and motivation of political and socioeconomic decision making still remains relatively obscure for most political systems. Nonetheless, there is a sufficient core of studies to suggest, as Marvick does in his excellent summary of the available literature, that cadres, or middle-level elites, are key units in explaining top elite behavior, for a number of reasons:

> Top elites depend upon, often derive from and not infrequently are coerced by those who may be called middlemen, or cadres; top elite deliberation is routinely shaped by cadres; top elite survival and success are commonly dependent upon cadres.[65]

Thus we might hypothesize that in any given political system elite acceptance and practice of the "new" politics of collective bargaining and pragmatic adjustment in decision making,[66] or of "catchall" electoral strategies,

---

62. Ibid., p. 156.
63. Ibid., p. 155. Italics added.
64. Dwaine Marvick, "The Middlemen of Politics," *Approaches to the Study of Party Organization*, ed. William Crotty (Boston: Allyn & Bacon, 1968), p. 341.
65. Ibid., pp. 343–44. Marvick summarizes also the various meanings of such terms as "elite" and "cadre," and identifies a number of key research areas for both inter- and intra-elite analysis. For a similar effort to map what we know of top elites, see Lewis J. Edinger, "Political Science and Political Biography: Reflections on the Study of Leadership" *Journal of Politics* 26, no. 2 (August 1964): 648–77, and the Introduction to his edited volume, *Political Leadership in Industrialized Societies: Studies in Comparative Analysis* (New York: John Wiley, 1967).
66. See Robert A. Dahl's Epilogue to his *Political Oppositions in Western Democracies*. Cf. Di Palma and Stiefbold, "Conflict and Elites," passim. The next few paragraphs draw on Di Palma's and my formulations in this paper, and on the discussions in the graduate seminar on conflict regulation in Western Europe that we jointly taught at Berkeley in Spring 1969.

will depend on the type of elite role differentiation, the nature of elite recruitment and role socialization, and the communications and other relevant linkages among roles which obtain in that society.

In keeping with the Deutsch-Marvick thesis concerning the decisive significance of middlemen in communication and decision structures—and with a frequently observed distinction, as for example in Haas's formulation, between elites whose aims and behavioral style are "dramatic-political" and those whose aims and style Haas characterizes as "incremental-economic" (pragmatic, oriented to bargaining over largely technical economic issues)[67]—we posit a trio of principal elite roles that will be found in all national political systems. These are: (1) *top elites* who share major responsibility for overall system stability and regime performance and in whom is vested major decision-making authority; (2) party organization cadres, or *partisans*, whose tasks include making daily partisan propaganda and conducting election campaigns and whose deep ideological or philosophical commitment leads them to issue threats, demands, and emotional appeals on behalf of their party and its programs; and (3) interest group, chamber, media, and bureaucratic elites, or *technocrats*, who are responsible for day-to-day operation of major socioeconomic, governmental, and cultural institutions, and who practice the politics of "distributive bargaining," rendering decisions by the process of incremental adjustment, by engaging in pragmative give-and-take with their counterparts in related organizational-elite roles.

In general terms, the principal hypothesis relating system or regime performance to elite role structure is simply this: *the more partisan elites place constraints on the personal values, organizational role definitions, and decisional autonomy of top political and governmental elites, and on their communications with nonpartisan technocratic elites pursuing "incremental-economic" goals, the greater will be the strains upon accommodationist and bargaining politics, and hence the greater the total "load" on the political regime.*

Linked to this master hypothesis are a number of subsidiary assumptions and hypotheses. Thus, for example, we should expect to find that accommodationist attitudes and bargaining behavior will be most widespread at the upper level of elites (i.e., among the consociational top elites in a country such as Austria). The organizational roles of these individuals are

67. Ernst B. Haas, "The 'Uniting of Europe' and the Uniting of Latin America," *Journal of Common Market Studies* 5 (June 1967): 328–29 f. Obviously not all real-life political or economic actors can be so neatly classified, since in any given issue area the dramatic-political and incremental-economic distinction may well be ranged along a continuum in the same plane. Nonetheless, I would maintain that, if measurement problems are properly and carefully dealt with, most real-life actors could be classified as more nearly corresponding to the one or the other of these analytical distinctions. Finally, on the politics of "distributive bargaining," see Richard E. Walton and Robert B. McKersie, *A Behavioral Theory of Labor Negotiations: An Analysis of a Social Interaction System* (New York: McGraw-Hill, 1965), esp. chap. 2.

likely to expose them to the interests of diverse groups within the society, and their constituencies (clienteles) are more likely to be heterogeneous than those of lower-level elite members. We also hypothesize that partisan elites are less likely than governmental or technocratic elites to embrace the politics of accommodation and sacrifice traditional ideological views. Party leaders have an organization to maintain and ideological appeals are likely to solidify the support of rank-and-file party activists. In addition, party leaders below the top level are more likely to interact with like-minded individuals. Their environment is probably politically homogeneous and the communicative stimuli to which they are exposed therefore reinforce ideological attitudes. Because top elites require the allegiance of the party organizations in order to mobilize support for policies or at election time, the impact of partisan elites on top elite attitudes and behavior may occasionally be severe, leading under some circumstances to a possible reduction in consensus at this higher level—especially among those upper-level elites whose early careers had exposed them chiefly to party organization needs which socialized them to perceive the world through a systematically distorted partisan lens.[68]

The hypotheses advanced in this brief discussion become particularly problematic in "segmented pluralist" societies where rigid patterns of elite and activist recruitment and socialization through mutually exclusive organizational and associational channels may impose great de facto burdens on the day-to-day operational freedom of top decision-making elites. Despite commitment of these top elites to consociational politics, the historically derived structures of cleavage and access to the political market retain their relevance.[69]

Even if objective cleavages and inequalities decline and policy differences become attenuated, partisan organizations preserve many of their subcultural features; hence the significance of Barnes' argument for researching ideology in its organizational context. He writes: "The important question, What is the impact of the ideological preferences of elites on the goals of their political organizations? is often asked. But this is only half of the relationship. The opposite but related question is of at least equal

68. These functions of party organizations are stressed by many writers, few so forcefully as Barnes, "Ideology and the Organization of Conflict," esp. pp. 521–24. Dwaine Marvick has written persuasively on these matters in "Communications in Political Parties," mimeographed (UCLA, 1969). The "distorted partisan lens" idea is also treated in Murray Edelman's insightful essay "Myths, Metaphors and Political Conformity," *Psychiatry* 30, no. 3 (August 1967): 217–28.

69. Among scores of studies which emphasize the points in this paragraph, see inter alia: William A. Gamson, *Power and Discontent* (Homewood, Ill.,: Dorsey, 1968); G. Bingham Powell, Jr., *Social Fragmentation and Political Hostility: An Austrian Case Study* (Stanford: Stanford University Press, 1971); Leon N. Lindberg, "Europe as a Political System: Measuring Political Integration" (ms., Center for International Affairs, Harvard University, April 1967); Walton and McKersie, *Behavioral Theory of Labor Negotiations;* Samuel P. Huntington, *Political Order in Changing Societies* (New Haven: Yale University Press, 1968).

significance: What is the impact of political organization on the ideologies of the elites?"[70] Almond and Verba make a corollary point concerning the significance of different elite "role cultures" to the operation of democracy. They argue that "elite attitudes may be characterized by cultural heterogeneity, and thus 'seriously affect the performance of political systems,' if the elites are recruited from particular subcultures' or if 'the process of induction and socialization into these roles produces difference values, skills, loyalties, and cognitive maps.' "[71]

If the top elites are recruited through socioeconomic organizations (e.g., major interest groups and chambers), they may already be socialized to a type of elite "role culture" that combines emphasis on a set of strict procedural rules with a set of general conflict-avoidance orientations by rival parties to a bargaining situation. They are used to practicing a politics of incremental adjustment of divergent policy positions, a process that allows decision makers to proceed as soon as they agree on *what* needs to be done, even if they do not fully agree on *why* it needs to be done or on what specific *outcomes* are being sought.[72] On the other hand, if top elites are recruited from political party organization jobs in the political subcultures they are likely to continue to share with middle-level partisan elites similar attitudes and perceptions and to respond with special attention to cues emanating from them, especially under circumstances (e.g., elections) which emphasize "political" as opposed to "technocratic" goals. But both the professional role and life-style situation of such medium-level party officials is one of substantial partisan isolation coupled with distrust and distorted perception of the opposition parties. As Frank Pinner suggests, explicitly partisan organizations can thus become "powerful blockages to the free flow of information" from elite to mass and mass to elite; and under highly politicized circumstances, medium-level party officials may come to have extraordinary influence. "They may prevent or fail to transmit unorthodox thought at the organization's base," and they may give top elites "the impression that, in order to keep the confidence" of their rank-and-file membership, "they must at all cost avoid too close an association with their opposite numbers in the other party" or subculture.[73]

To paraphrase a remarkable recent study of hostile behavior among foreign-policy decision makers,[74] a world perceived as hostile and threatening could cause a decision maker to opt for an aggressive move in

70. Barnes, "Ideology and the Organization of Conflict," p. 520.

71. Lijphart, "Typologies," p. 32, quoting Almond and Verba, *Civic Culture*, pp. 29–30.

72. For data and theory on the pragmatic decision-making process in Western democracies, see Lindblom, *Intelligence of Democracy;* Walton and McKersie, *Behavioral Theory of Labor Negotiations;* David Braybrooke and Charles E. Lindblom, *A Strategy of Decision* (Glencoe: Free Press, 1963); and Ralf Dahrendorf, *Class and Class Conflict in Industrial Society* (Stanford: Stanford University Press, 1959), chap. 6.

73. Pinner, "On the Structure of Organizations and Beliefs," pp. 20ff.

74. Dina A. Zinnes, "A Comparison of Hostile Behavior of Decision-Makers in Simulate and Historical Data," *World Politics* 18 (1966): 474–99, esp. 474.

the face of a political crisis; he might be led by his perception, as filtered through middle-level elites, to believe that he must strike before being struck—that he must engage in publically dramatic rancorous or even disruptive political behavior, lest similar prior behavior by elites of the other side place him at a disadvantage. In short, an important, perhaps critical area for research must be the perceptual framework of the strategic elites in divided societies. The opportunities afforded by election processes for mass political mobilization, and the dependence for political stability in countries such as Austria on complex patterns of elite behavior, make the nexus between elite perceptions and behavior under electoral circumstances a critical one for students of political life in divided societies.

Exactly how useful these insights are in helping us to achieve a more multivariate (and more accurate) understanding of elite opinion structure and elite-mass interaction in a consociational democracy becomes clear when we consider Lijphart's formulations in the light of some of our empirical data on Austrian elites.[75]

Data on Austrian Elites

The data reported below were collected in conjunction with my study of electoral politics, cultural pluralism, and the dynamics of elite-mass interaction in postwar Austria, and in conjunction with the Smaller European Democracies/Austria Project I directed.[76] The interview data discussed here or reported in tabular form all derived from an original elite sample of 450 persons chosen as respondents on the basis of their reputations and positions in national politics or social and economic policy making. Some local and provincial elites were also included on the basis of their national decision-making relevance and influence as judged by fellow decision makers and/or established scholars and experts on Austrian politics.

The 300 respondents included 112 members of the Austrian Nationalrat (lower House of parliament), 50 officials of the two major parties, 40 officials of the chambers and chief interest groups, 15 high-ranking federal

75. In reviewing an earlier draft manuscript of both the theoretical and empirical sections of this chapter, Arend Lijphart (in a letter to the author dated May 6, 1969) writes: "I think you show the importance of critical additional variables on the elite level. . . . You strengthen the model of consociational democracy a great deal. . . . Your theoretical elaboration also means that I shall have to rethink my explanation of the 'Dutch paradox' in these terms."

76. My primary debt in structuring this research is to my former mentor and friend at Columbia, the late Otto Kirchheimer, under whose direction I began the "electoral politics/elite/mass" project, and with whom I was collaborating on the SED/Austria project. I am also indebted to Professor Dwaine Marvick of UCLA, my collaborator on *Wahlen und Parteien in Oesterreich*, for many useful suggestions. The research design, procedures, and various methodological considerations are thoroughly discussed in Stiefbold, *Elites and Elections in a Fragmented Political System*, Appendix 1; and Stiefbold, *Austrian Electoral Politics*, chaps. 1 and 6.

civil servants, 40 officials of local and provincial governments, 20 academic personnel or other "outside consultants" serving as political advisers to one of the two major political parties at the time of the interview, and 23 important personal staff assistants serving higher officials in governmental, party, and chamber or interest-group positions. Most interviews were concluded prior to the dissolution of the Nationalrat over a budget crisis in November 1965, and prior to the absolute majority victory by the OeVP in the March 1966 national parliamentary elections (which led in April to the universally unanticipated failure to renegotiate the Red-Black Coalition).

Interview length varied widely, ranging from a minimum of twenty minutes to two hours or more; most interviews exceeded one hour. Although interviewers covered a roughly standard range of topics, all but four items were programmed as open-ended questions, and in most cases no other notes were taken during the interview. The closed questions included one designed to measure respondents' perception of interparty differences on a list of sixteen issues; another to measure distributions of "ideologism" and "pragmatism" in the respondents' basic approach to politics; and two designed to measure *Lager* penetration of private life (concern over cross-party marriage of daughter and son, whether party affiliation is considered a relevant factor in choosing one's friends). The unstructured (or semistructured) part of the interview dealt with various political issues in depth, dimensions of interelite and intraelite and elite-mass political communication and perceptions, and political efficacy, among others.[77]

We also experimented with a relatively complex system by which the individual interviewers (thirty specially schooled graduate students, young men in Austrian professional life, and university professors) could rate respondents in terms of "ideologism" or "pragmatism" depending on the semantics used by the respondent in open-ended discussion of the aforementioned sixteen specific issues. After first identifying about fifty words, phrases, or expressions most frequently used in the parties' public "correspondence" or in ten widely read party newspapers (sampled over a "normal" three-month period in the spring of 1965) to characterize a

---

77. We also collected standardized personal and social background data for all respondents as part of the structured questionnaire. After the formal questionnaire was administered (which took an average of 20 to 30 minutes) the remainder of the interview was conducted informally. (In the case of members of parliament we did a separate substudy involving a second questionnaire and a shorter period of semistructured interviewing.) During this informal part of each interview usually few or no notes were taken and the data derived from this part of the interview were based chiefly on interviewer notes made immediately afterward. This procedure was adopted after pretests had shown elites' unwillingness to respond to more lengthy questionnaires coupled frequently with a willingness to expound "off-the-record." Respondents were, of course, guaranteed anonymity. Another major consideration in opting for this mixed interviewing strategy was that we were free to pursue in more natural fashion those questions and areas on which a given respondent evinced particular interest and loquacity. We gained a rich fund of comparable information in this way, though obviously with fewer respondents per coded item. Half the respondents were reinterviewed in 1967/68.

policy, tactic or other form of public behavior by the opposing party (its partner in coalition), we then divided these into three categories: *ideological* (including chiefly references to values and symbols prominent in Austrian political ideologies), *pragmatic* (factual, technical, oriented to problem solving by collective bargaining methods), or *eclectic* (ambiguous word or phrase involving the "joint and integrated appearance of these two types in one and the same context"). Interviewers used these categories, derived from the work of Ulf Himmelstrand,[78] quite successfully; agreement between their ratings of respondents and respondents' scores on a four-point agree-disagree scale designed to test the ideologism-pragmatism distributions from another perspective was over 80 percent.[79]

Elite Role Structure and Communication Patterns: Principal Findings and Implications

Alerted by previous studies contrasting Austria's unique system of functional representation with its regular political structures, and by Deutsch's hypothesis concerning the significance of the middlemen in a communication system, we sought to overcome the tangle of overlapping jobs in Austria's parties, groups, chambers, and governmet ministries and probe for differentiated "pragmatic" and "political" roles among elites.

To be sure, such differentiation scarcely existed at the very apex of the

78. Himmelstrand, "A Theoretical and Empirical Approach to Depoliticization and Political Involvement," esp. pp. 88ff., and passim. Also of some utility in adapting Himmelstrand's work to our purposes were Albert O. Hirschman, *Journeys Toward Progress: Studies of Economic Policy-Making in Latin America* (New York: Twentieth Century Fund, 1963), esp. "Digression: The Semantics of Problem Solving," pp. 248–49, and B. Douglass Jansen, "A System of Content Analysis by Computer of International Communications for Selected Categories of Action," *American Behavioral Scientist* 9, no. 7 (March 1966): 28–32. I benefited greatly from Murray Edelman's provocative analysis *The Symbolic Uses of Politics* (Urbana: University of Illinois Press, 1964), and from his later "Myths, Metaphors, and Political Conformity," pp. 217–28.

There are, of course, various problems with interviewer ascription of such categories. Political rhetoric is often inflated for dramatic effect and bargaining advantages; words and phrases shift their meanings over time and once meaningfully violent rhetoric may retain merely symbolic overtones, if that; political leaders, especially top leaders, may alter their vocabulary to suit the role they are playing. Especially in the "segmented pluralist" society ought the foreign researcher pay careful attention to such problems.

79. Research literature on ideologism-pragmatism as a way of characterizing the basic conceptual approach and verbal and behavioral style of political leaders is meager. Theoretical statements of relevance to this focus may be found in various works of Sartori, Kirchheimer, Tingsten, LaPalombara, Verba, and Dahl, among many others. Some useful material may be found inter alia in Himmelstrand, "Theoretical and Empirical Approach"; Himmelstrand, "Social Pressure," *Attitudes and Democratic Processes* (Stockholm: Almqvist & Wiksell, 1960); Angus Campbell et al., *The American Voter* (New York: Wiley, 1960) chaps. 9–10; Samuel H. Barnes, "Leadership Style and Political Competence," in *Political Leadership in Industrialized Society*, ed. Lewis J. Edinger (New York: Wiley, 1967), pp. 59–83; and Wendell Bell, *Jamaican Leaders: Political Attitudes in a New Nation* (Berkeley and Los Angeles: University of California Press, 1964). For a recent effort that appears to be conceptually similar

political regime.[80] The top subcultural elites cumulated as many roles as possible, the better to consolidate their power and to assure their operational freedom in summit bargaining with each other. An aggregate data study of top elites by Engelmann and me[81] revealed that a mere nine men held the half dozen most important positions in party and state throughout the entire era of Great Coalition on the OeVP side, while eight men held four analagous positions for the SPOe. For the OeVP the positions were party chairman, general party secretary, chancellor, the first and third presidents of the Nationalrat and the *Klubobmann* (chairman of the parliamentary caucus). For the SPOe the principal positions were the party chairman, the vice-chancellor of the government, the second president of the Nationalrat, and the *Klubobmann* of the party caucus. However, it would be a gross exaggeration to argue that these few elites were *the* people who "governed" Austria: given the structural bifurcation of decision making in the Austrian political system, which we recounted briefly in our previous section on the institutionalization of the Austrian consociational regime, top-elite status must also be ascribed to the leaders of the key chambers (commerce, labor, agriculture) and interest groups (trade union congress, union of Austrian industrialists).[82] We were, of course, aware of this, and despite the tangled role-overlapping we thus obtained thirty interviews with party, group, and chamber members of these strategic top elites and ascribed them, for analytical purposes, to a separate "top-elite" category.

At levels below that involving "top" elites, while overlapping roles and competencies still made for occasional difficulty in categorizing this or that

---

in focus to my study (on this point at least) see William E. Wright, "Ideological-Pragmatic Orientations of West Berlin Local Party Officials," *Midwest Journal of Political Science* 11, no. 3 (August 1967): 381–402. See also Robert D. Putnam, "Studying Elite Political Culture: The Case of 'Ideology,'" *American Political Science Review* 65 (September 1971).

80. "A typical Austrian politician," writes English political scientist Uwe Kitzinger, "will combine a function in a voluntary organization, a position in an official Chamber, a party position, a parliamentary seat, an executive post and, if he is high enough on the ladder, a seat on the Coalition caucus: if he does not hold all these simultaneously he may pass from one combination of them to another without any particular sense of a break between voluntary and official, legislative and executive functions." Uwe Kitzinger, "Austria: The Corporatist Coalition," in *Britain, Europe and Beyond: Essays in European Politics* (Leyden: A. W. Sythoff, 1964), p. 86. Kitzinger's "typical" politician is very near the top of the system, but at that level of the polity the description is trenchant.

81. For our joint chapter on "Cabinet Government," mimeographed (Vienna, 1967) in Stiefbold, ed., *The Political System of Austria*. Both Nassmacher, *Das oesterreichische Regierungssystem*, p. 48; and Steiner, *Politics in Austria*, chap. 8, accept our designation of this handful of roles as the most critical ones.

82. One of Austria's leading political commentators, Alexander Vodopivec, repeatedly emphasizes the significance of these "interest group and chamber" elites in his two important books: *Wer regiert in Oesterreich?* (2nd ed.; Vienna: Verlag f. Geschichte u. Politik, 1962), and *Die Balkanisierung Oesterreichs: Folgen einer grossen Koalition* (Vienna: Molden, 1966). Cf. Engelmann, "Austria: The Pooling of Opposition," and Secher, "Representative Democracy or 'Chamber State.'"

respondent, we generally had little difficulty in establishing whether a respondent was a middle-level "partisan" or "technocrat" (see below). When individuals in these middle categories held overlapping positions, they usually did not do so at precisely the same level: for example, a major trade union secretary held a comparatively lower-status party job, if any.

The S.A.N.E. interviews provide striking empirical evidence of the theoretical utility of the middle-level elites hypothesis in arriving at a more satisfactory explanation of the internal workings of consociational democracy than has heretofore been possible. In particular, these Austrian data illuminate the structure and modalities of intersegment and intrasegment interaction patterns among elites, and of elites with nonelites. Thus, from these data we can extract a great deal of information about the *overall day-to-day capacities for and constraints on rational decision making operative in a consociational regime*. Moreover, these data allow us to arrive at a satisfactory explanation of *how, once established, consociational democracies are sustained, modified, or transformed over time*.

In the paragraphs below, and in tables 4 and 5, we have first summarized briefly the principal findings relevant to this study, then elaborated on some of their more important implications, particularly with respect to the Austrian version of consociational democracy. We have saved most of our discussion of political change for the concluding section, where we shall try to relate our material to broader questions of political development in Western Europe.

The principal points revealed by the S.A.N.E. data (drawing on both the structured and unstructured responses) are these:

1 There is not a single group of elites; rather, there are three functionally distinct groups. The smallest of these, comprising no more than 25 or 30 persons, is responsible for the overall pattern of consociational politics. These "top" elites provide the system with a steady guiding hand on a day-to-day basis, guaranteeing operational freedom to the middle-level socioeconomic elites, generally agreeing with them on issues, and inclined to support them in policy disagreements with middle-level political elites of the same *Lager* under all but electoral conditions.

2. These top elites are highly pragmatic in their approach to politics, tend to see all but political (coalition-style) issues as bargainable. Inter-*Lager* contacts at this level are often more cordial than relations between top elites and partisan middle-level political elites in the same *Lager*. They exhibit surprisingly little role conflict except at election time, when they become the "captives" of their own political elites.

3. Under the duress of elections, there is thus substantial distor-

tion of normal intra-*Lager* (and interelite) communication flow; the top elites tend to perceive mass opinion as both politicized and polarized, thus complicating the subsequent (postelection) capacity of top elites to "get back together," and further inculcating the *Lager* mentality whose pervasiveness at the mass level they overestimated in the first place.

4. *The most striking differentiation within Austria's ruling elite* (see tables 4 and 5) *is that between the socioeconomic elites, or technocrats, of both* Lager, *and the political elites or "partisans," of both* Lager. Only on certain symbolic issues is there some erosion in the essentially "centripetal" tendencies of the socioeconomic elites, while the partisan elites exert almost continual "centrifugal" pressures on the political system. Since socioeconomic elites work chiefly at technical matters behind closed doors, while political elites carry much of the responsibility for day-to-day definition and discussion of whatever issues happen to be current, daily Austrian politics wears a conflict-laden "public" face while behind-the-scenes decision making is characterized by conflict-avoidance strategies and behavioral norms of restrained partisanship, about which the Austrian mass public learns little.

5. The basic political style of the *partisan elites* is expressively ideological, with frequent references to values and symbols prominent in Austrian political-ideological history; vituperative and rancorous, characterized by frequent *ad hominum* remarks and accusations about personalities prominent in the other *Lager;* and publicly uncompromising on most issues, often expressing belief in neither the possibility nor desireability of inter-*Lager* compromise. There is no role conflict or cross-pressuring for partisans; they talk only with each other most of the time. They actually express fear of the opposing *Lager,* imputing to it a secret desire to win majority parliamentary power and then utilize it to eliminate, forcefully if necessary, the opposition. They see the coalition as a "safeguard" against Austro-Marxism or clerical-fascism.

6. The *technocratic elites* engage almost constantly in some form of politics of collective bargaining. Their political style is moderate, their rhetoric subdued and nonrancorous. They generally approach pending public policy issues empirically and pragmatically. They consider the inter-*Lager* compromise both possible and desirable on most subjects (excepting certain symbolic items, as is clear from table 5). Technocrats are relatively unconcerned about such "trivia" as cross-party marriage of their offspring or their friends' partisan

Table 4. Some Distributions of "Pragmatism" and "Ideologism" Among Middle-Level Elites in Divergent Organizational Milieus, by Selected Issue Areas (S.A.N.E. Interviews, 1965-66)

Issue Area	Social-Economic Elites (chambers, interest groups) N = 90			Political Elites (party organizations) N = 75		
	Responses to questions concerning issue area in column at left were predominantly:[a]					
	I	E	P	I	E	P
Social-economic[b]		+	++	++	+	
Political style and performance[c]	++	+		+	++	
Foreign policy[d]		+	++	++	+	
Social-cultural and symbolic[e]	++	+		++	+	

[a] Coding categories: I, ideological; E, eclectic; P, pragmatic. Derived from Ulf Himmelstrand, "A Theoretical Empirical Approach to Depoliticization and Political Involvement, *Acta Sociologica* 6, nos. 1–2 (1962; special issue on "Approaches to the Study of Political Participation," ed. Stein Rokkan), pp. 83–110, as described in text. A single plus sign (+) means at least one-third of the responses in the total sample (including both *Lager*) fell into that cell of the table. A double plus sign (++) means that from one-half to two-thirds of the responses were allocated to that cell by the interviewers. Interviewer scoring was on the basis of Austrian phrases and words used most frequently to define the opposing party's position on an issue or to contrast the two parties' positions, as described in text.

[b] *Social-economic issues*
1. wage-price problems
2. fiscal problems
3. housing problems
4. collectivism (e.g., operation of the nationalized industries)

[c] *Political issues*
1. necessity for coalition
2. internal coalition strains and coalition performance
3. party leadership succession and conflicts
4. current or past public scandals

[d] *Foreign policy*
1. EEC association
2. closer East European ties
3. "neutrality"
4. South Tyrol

[e] *Cultural and symbolic issues*
1. mass media organization
2. the past: Habsburg, Nazism
3. church-state relations
4. educational reform

Source: The patterns reported in this table are based on data derived from depth interviews with 90 middle-level decision makers in the major social-economic organizations (the three chambers, the Union of Austrian Industrialists, and the Trade Union Congress), and 75 in the two major political parties (Socialist, SPOe; Conservative, OeVP). See text for discussion of original sample components. We arrived at these "middle-elite" subsamples by eliminating from the total S.A.N.E. sample (*N* = 300) the 30 respondents ascribed to the "top elite" category; 22 of the 112 Nationalrat deputies interviewed by us and identified by us as not owing primary occupational allegiance to a political party, interest group, or chamber; the 40 nationally prominent "local and provincial" elites interviewed by us; the 20 special consultants and the 23 special assistants to other S.A.N.E. respondents.

preferences (in both cases in strong contrast to middle-level political elites who care deeply about both). While technocrats may distrust certain adherents of the "opposing" *Lager,* they do not fear the other *Lager* per se nor impugn its democratic motives. Both coalition and paracoalition are viewed as matters of habit, convenience, and sound management practices. Considerable cross-segmental contact occurs between the middle-level economic elites of each of the *Lager* in their professional roles. Even their informal contact patterns are much more flexible; personal and social interaction across sectoral lines, for fun, is described as commonplace.

Political socialization and recruitment processes served to guarantee the continued "integrity" of this trifurcated national-elite role structure. New elites internalized the norms of their predecessors, especially in the sharply diverging middle-level roles, thus sustaining the duality of types of conflict and accommodation, cleavage and integration that characterized

Table 5. Relative Rankings of Three Elite "Role" Groups by Average Frequency of "Pragmatic" Responses to Questions Concerning Various Dimensions of the Political Culture Attributes of "Polarity" and "Politicization" (S.A.N.E., 1965–66)

Attribute/Dimension	Top Elites (N = 30)	Middle-level Socioeconomic, or "Technocrats" (N = 90)	Middle-level Political, or "Partisans" (N = 75)
Polarity			
1. re. the consociational coalition regime itself	2nd	1st	3rd
2. re. issue areas:			
—social-economic issues	2nd	1st	3rd
—political issues	3rd	1st	2nd
—foreign policy issues	2nd	1st	3rd
—cultural and symbolic issues	(2nd)	(2nd)	3rd
Politicization			
1. basic approach to politics and decision making	2nd	1st	3rd
2. cross-*Lager* marriage of daughter or son	2nd	1st	3rd
3. concern over friends' political affiliations	2nd	1st	3rd

Source: Same as table 4. "1st" is a group rank for that category of elites compared to the group ranks of either of the other elite role categories; the rank is dictated by the average of all individual scores on that item.

the coalition and paracoalition subsystems, and that so strongly affected the manner in which political conflict in post-World War II Austria arose at various decision-making sites and was then resolved or "regulated."

Top elites were "role-socialized" into the key "consociational" jobs transcending either the "technocratic" or "partisan" organizations from which these various elites had been recruited. Given the conditions of normal daily politics, top-level elites recruited from middle-level political roles generally assumed the much more accommodating and cooperative norms of their new "consociational" roles, while relinquishing much of the hardness and partisan rancorousness associated with their previous roles. Top elites recruited from middle-level "technocratic" jobs in the interest groups or chambers were already, by previous career training, socialized to norms of civility and depoliticization in interpersonal relations, and to the practices of collective bargaining politics with compromise outcomes. They were relatively "isolated" structurally and were psychologically detached from the expressively ideological styles of behavior that characterized more partisan political milieus. On the other hand, those top-level elites who had previously been party "cadres," that is, middle-level political men in the political party organizations, were prone to lapse back to bitterly partisan behavior during "crisis" circumstances—for example, at election time.

Ulf Himmelstrand has drawn attention to, and expressed concern about, the problematic consequences of an elite that is depoliticizing faster than and is more genuinely depoliticized than an electorate which retains organizationally reinforced ideological components and which might be mobilized to the detriment of the system on a periodic basis.[83] We would suggest that in the Austrian case (throughout the Great Coalition period from 1945 to 1966) the elites were those who remained most problematic, not the mass electorate. Particularly at election time the middle-level political and repoliticized "top" or "consociational" elites perceived "issues" (often unperceived by the masses) and "hostilities" (often not felt by the masses) and acted according to these in ideologically relevant fashion, thereby repolarizing the political system and reducing its conflict-regulating capabilities.[84]

We asked elite participants in the S.A.N.E. interviews (both in 1965–66 and in follow-up interviews in 1967 and 1968) to identify, from their perspectives, some of the basic reasons for the problematic interplay of

83. Himmelstrand, "A Theoretical and Empirical Approach to Depoliticization and Political Involvement," p. 119.

84. Cf. on these points Lehmbruch's insightful speculations in *Proporzdemokratie* (Tubingen: Mohr, 1967), pp. 30–31. Fragmentary data from a case study of Viennese party officials support my general line of argument (see Pinner, "On the Structure of Organizations and Beliefs," esp. pp. 19ff.). Many arguments advanced here are also supported by G. Bingham Powell's careful case study of the single western Austrian community of Hallein: *Social Fragmentation and Political Hostility; an Austrian Case Study* (Stanford: Stanford University Press, 1970), esp. chaps. 4, 5, and 8.

"ideologistic" and "pragmatic" political styles in the Austrian system of government by elite cartel. Four basic explanations emerged, which we may describe succinctly as: (1) the partisan channel bias in the recruitment of "top" elites throughout the coalition era; (2) clogged top elite/mass public communication channels; (3) the predominance of an ideologistic, rancorous style of elite-mass political communication; and (4) the continued *instrumental* significance of the parliamentary election process throughout the twenty-year period of Great Coalition.[85] Let us elaborate briefly on each of these.

Biased Elite Recruitment Processes

Political recruitment to national elite roles in Austria is primarily by advancement on candidate lists at parliamentary elections, and all the advantages in the processes of candidate recruitment and selection lie with party organizational elites. Entry to the small class of top and near-top national elites for individuals who make their careers in interest groups or the corporatist chambers of occupational representation, on the other hand, is not basically a process of gradual vertical mobility; it comes more frequently "laterally" relatively close to the top of the political system, after the individual has already had a successful career in a paracoalition organization. Particularly during the Great Coalition (1945–66), this meant that at all levels below the top, those jobs or roles identified as preparatory for national political leadership roles were, essentially, themselves "partisan" roles. This had understandable consequences at the top of the system, because it meant that at any given point in time the majority of the country's top governing elites had more than likely had their political socialization experiences in milieus characterized by a high incidence of traditional *Lager* mentality.

Hence the tendency to momentarily lapse from consociational norms and practices into bitterly rancorous forms of behavior was not only recurrent. There was a widespread susceptibility of upper elites to set aside everyday norms of restrained inter-*Lager* partisanship precisely because of the persisting and cumulative impact on them of the extended political

---

85. These explanations were either identified directly, by the 1965–66 S.A.N.E. respondents, or emerge from careful scrutiny of the interview protocols. Although our paraphrasing of the four basic points throws them into somewhat sharper relief than did any given respondent, most of the technocrats and more than two-thirds of the top elites provided very similar composite analyses in open-ended discussions about the characteristics of the Austrian consociational regime—and these interviews took place prior to the demise of Great Coalition between OeVP and SPOe. Remarkably, by 1967 and especially by 1968 (summer) all three types of elites—top, technocrat, and partisan—not only were willing to discuss openly such questions of "how" and "why" the Austrian coalition system had worked the way it did, but also tended to identify, retrospectively, the same four congeries of explanations elaborated here! To a certain extent, particularly among the better-educated members of the three elite groups, these four explanations were internalized as conventional wisdom within a fairly short period following the transition from consociational rule to a new regime of alternating government-and-opposition.

party apparatuses through which they'd been recruited to top elite status in the first place. This lag, this regressive behavior pattern, tended to occur with ever-greater frequency, becoming virtually an obstacle to continued regime stability, the longer the Coalition lasted. The explanation is really quite simple. The 1945 "Founding Fathers" generation of consociational elites had shared experiences of civil war, Nazi rule, and political incarceration during which they had sometimes shared jail cells with their previous political enemies and from which they had emerged with cross-subcultural friendships and the common goal of trying to rid their homeland of foreign occupying powers. Younger elites—those who came to positions of power in the late 1950s and early 1960s—had fewer shared memories rooted in the trials of the distant past or the shotgun marriage of 1945. Moreover, given their predominantly partisan-track socialization and recruitment, the new top elites usually had fewer cross-*Lager* friends than their predecessors. They were probably less ideological in the sense of how deeply they embraced abstract value ideas historically important to their *Lager*, but they were also somewhat less consistently consociational (and were more often ideologistic) in their cross-*Lager* behavior than the Founding Fathers had been. They might have been more "modern" in their thinking and in their general approach to problem solving, as one political scientist has recently argued, preferring "the efficiency of long-range calculation based on survey research data" to the ad hoc, intuitionist, wineglass politics of the 1945 leaders.[86] But this in no way reduced the salience or intensity of their partisan identification, nor did it eliminate latent feelings of inter-*Lager* hostility imparted during their early political careers.

Clogged Top Elite/Mass Public Communication Channels

A critical dimension of the Austrian coalition regime's problem of long-term "institutionalization" was its failure to develop top elite/mass public communication channels that were genuinely independent of the mediating partisan elites at the middle levels and of the grass-roots' party organizational cadres. This led to systematic distortion of top elites' perceptions of nonelite political culture. Top elites simply misperceived the emerging, tamer mass culture, i.e., the reality, and saw instead the image of continued intersubcultural mistrust and hostility nurtured by the political middlemen who served the top elites as the latter's "eyes" and "ears." This deception occurred both because of (1) the organizational isolation and intensely negative partisan affect of the variously positioned political middlemen, and because of (2) the top elites' absolute reliance on these middlemen for basic "knowledge" and "understanding" of the mass public. To Franz Olah, then TUC president and a caustic antiideologue, the top elites' deception was obviously self-inflicted:

86. Bluhm, "Nation-Building," pp. 158–59.

". . . the party leadership which utilizes the functionaries to explore public opinions obtains instead the opinions of the functionaries, and the one is not always identical with the other." [87]

Many of my respondents in the S.A.N.E. interviews not only stressed this very point, they also stressed a further point made by Olah: on many issues there was probably substantially more real agreement between the top consociational elites and the general Austrian mass public than there was between the top elites and their own middle- and lower-level partisans, in socialist and trade-union segmented pluralist organizations. What is interesting here is that most top elites did not realize this congruence existed; most assumed the continued existence—in the mid-1960s!—of at least a dormant "conflict society." In short, they did not really understand—as Olah and relatively few others did—that their perception of the realities of mass political culture was being filtered through a partisan lens which systematically distorted those realities.

Rancorous Style of Top Elite/Mass Public Political Communication

But biased recruitment processes and partisan editing of mass-to-elite information—both involving the culpability of the political party apparatuses—were not the only factors sustaining the sharply etched duality of elite behavioral styles in Coalition Austria. A third reason identified by our respondents as having contributed to both the durability and the interactive consequences of the "ideologism-pragmatism" phenomenon involved, at least in part, a rational choice by top elites to employ an acerbic *Lager*-oriented style of public discourse. Although they basically shared the empirico-pragmatic orientation to government that characterized socioeconomic elites and the nonelite masses, their behavior in public forums contributed more often than not to the ideologically expressive and conflict-laden public atmosphere so typical of Austrian politics. In some ways this "inflammatory" behavior in nondecision-making settings merely involved a necessary tradeoff between the diverse needs and relative importance of the top elites' nonelite and two subelite clients.

Top elite respondents in the S.A.N.E. interviews claimed emphatically that there was nothing sinister or unusual in this behavioral discrepancy. Not only does their argument accord with what we know is generally true of elite political behavior, regardless of the political system; it is especially understandable in a country of slender electoral and parliamentary majorities where one does not dare risk the disaffection of the party faithful on whom fall the burden of recurrent popular mobilization. Hence the apparently rancorous and "hostile" public rhetoric of top elites can be read as reassurances to their most dedicated followers and especially to the middle-level political subelites that their party is not about to risk its virtue and identity by "selling out" to the evil-intentioned coalition partner. The Aus-

---

87. Franz Olah, "Der Proporz des Mistrauens," *Forum* [Vienna], June 1959, pp. 211 ff.

trian historian Robert Schwartz has neatly captured this point; most of the time, he writes, one need not be overly concerned by such public outrage:

> Vitriolic words, coming from lips or the pen, are reminiscent of the partisan gulf of the first Republic, but only if one does not know the precise conditions of present-day [1959] Austria. . . . The picture which comes to mind . . . is one of each coalition partner with one arm across the other's back, the other gesticulating wildly for the benefit of the watching audience.[88]

One particularly impressive piece of evidence which tends to support the notion that the top elites engaged in such behavior as a kind of charade is reported by Kurt Shell in his now classic book on The Transformation of Austrian Socialism: namely, the frequency with which SPOe party functionaries complained that their national leadership failed to consult or even inform them on specific *policy* matters.[89]

But no matter how functional top elites' deference to middle-level political elites in "reading" the public mind or reassurance to those same elites by public displays of "ideologism" might be, in terms of maintaining the firm boundaries around subcultures posited by the consociational democracy model, there is also a more problematical consequence of such behaviors. We have already pointed out above that a cardinal precept of consociational rule is the norm of restrained partisanship, to use Manley's term.[90] Violation of this norm, either continuously or recurrently, could conceivably lead to system disruption; what at one time is mere rhetoric might at another time become a self-fulfilling prophecy. Or, as Schwartz puts it, "the gesticulating is often harmless enough but sometimes there is a tightening of the fist which has the mark of authenticity."[91] The S.A.N.E. interviews suggest that this is a crucial point, and I shall have more to say about it in my concluding section, when I discuss the significance of the Austrian experience in light of more general problems of political development in advanced nations.

88. Robert Schwartz, "The Contemporary Austrian Press and the First Republic: A Study in Political Journalism," Western Political Quarterly (1959): 1038–56; the quote is from p. 1055. See also the insightful analysis by Steiner, Politics in Austria, chaps. 7 and 9, passim. Theoretical analysis of the "hortatory language style" as a device for conflict management is provided by Murray Edelman, The Symbolic Uses of Politics, chap. 7; see esp. p. 149. See also Edelman, Politics as Symbolic Action: Mass Arousal and Quiescence (Chicago: Markham, 1971), esp. pp. 80–83.

89. Albany: State University of New York Press, 1962, p. 101. See also the excellent chapter on political communication in Steiner, Politics in Austria, chap. 9.

90. Manley finds the "norm of restrained partisanship" important in the reduction and management of conflict of interest in an American legislative committee, and provides an excellent theoretical analysis; see his "the House Committee on Ways and Means," American Political Science Review 49 (1965): 927–39.

91. Schwartz, "Contemporary Austrian Press," p. 1055. See his further discussion, p. 1056, on the resurgence of *Lager* mentality and some genuine fear in association with the electoral campaign of 1959.

The Continued Instrumental Significance of the Parliamentary Election Process

To some extent of course, elections in any national political system, even in the age of "catchall" electioneering, may give rise to destabilizing periods of high "ideological" saliency and sharpness. But the potential for dangerous consequences in a fragmented system such as Austria's is increased because of the relatively sharper crystallization of negative affect along social and organizational fault lines that are historically derived and still terribly potent.

Moreover, to the extent that elections have been reduced to grandiose exercises in political-preference census taking, as Tingsten suggests, and perform chiefly ceremonial or at most "diffuse support" functions, as Nordlinger and others might argue, recurrent electoral contests are harmless enough.[92] However, as Rose and Mossawir point out, the answer to the question, What is the functional significance of democratic elections in democratic regimes? is that it depends greatly on the configurative context.[93] My research suggests not only that Austrian elections retained instrumental significance, and did not undergo the relative decline in terms of instrumental functions so often observed for other political systems. My elite interviews also clearly demonstrate that the parliamentary election process was explicitly dysfunctional for the Austrian political regime once consociational rule had fulfilled its initial purpose of enforcing mechanical solidarity on a badly fragmented people. Parliamentary elections produced an extremely problematical interaction between the political party organizations and the principal units of the paracoalition, and hence a rather disjunctive pattern of overall political development: growing functional integration, abetted by the chambers and giant interest groups, and led by what we have called middle-level socioeconomic elites (technocrats) received periodic setbacks whenever parliamentary elections occurred.

This was not just a normal case of democratic election fever: a political system which *normally* contained a high level of negative partisan affect, or rancor, was virtually swamped in ideologism during election campaigns. It would hardly be surprising if, under these conditions, the political regime of Great Coalition were not so badly overloaded it could not recover afterward. I would argue that this is precisely what happened in later elections, particularly in those of 1959 and 1966, and that the formal consociational regime was the eventual victim.[94]

92. Herbert Tingsten, "Stability and Vitality in Swedish Democracy," *Political Quarterly* 26 (1955) 140–51; Eric A. Nordlinger, "Representation, Governmental Stability, and Decisional Effectiveness," in *Representation*, ed. J. Roland Pennock and John W. Chapman (New York: Atherton, 1968), p. 124; A. J. Milnor, *Elections and Political Stability* (Boston: Little, Brown, 1970), chap. 1.

93. Richard Rose and Harve Mossawir, "Voting and Elections: A Functional Analysis," *Political Studies* 15 (1967): 173–201. This article is an excellent summary of the literature.

94. For a full analysis of these complex phenomena, see Stiefbold, *Austrian Electoral*

Summary and Conclusions

At the outset of this study, we set ourselves two principal objectives. The first was the task of resolving the "Austrian paradox" by explicating how stable, democratic, and decisionally effective government could be combined—as the literature suggests and as we originally assumed—with a highly polarized, politicized, and organizationally fragmented political culture. The second was the task of elaborating, on the basis of the Austrian case, the hypothetically prerequisite and/or supportive conditions favoring (or compelling!) the long-term maintenance of what Arend Lijphart has recently described as "consociational democracies." In both cases we addressed ourselves to the relationship we posited as most crucial: that between elites and the mass public. In so doing we have taken care to focus on mass opinion structure and political culture; on elite role and opinion structure, and related patterns of inter- and intraelite political communications and patterns of decision-making behavior; and on the interaction of elites and masses under "crisis," i.e., electoral conditions. In general we may summarize our principal findings, which help to resolve the reasons for the peculiar simultaneous existence of an "ideological Austria" and a "pragmatic Austria," and to explain their problematic interactions, as follows:

Public Opinion. Survey data reveal the Austrian mass public as highly supportive of the established consociational political regime and its authorities, and as being in basic interparty agreement concerning the centrality of the specific problems to which governmental endeavor should be directed. Moreover, both major-party phalanxes exhibit a sufficiently low level of intensity of political involvement (on such indicators as interest, information, frequency of discussion) so that the political authorities are left with substantial day-to-day operational freedom. Finally, two indicators of the pervasiveness of political partisanship indicate that the impact of political considerations on the individual in his nonpolitical roles is much lower than has been widely assumed heretofore. And yet, some indications of psychological distrust and apartness remain, and despite the surprising homogeneity of day-to-day views on the issue-objectives of government policy, at election time, the traditional ideological "camps" or *Lager* seem to reappear in more sharply delineated form.

Elite Opinion. With similar probing, elite interview data reveal sharply dichotomized elite opinion structures, with three principal sets of actors: *"top" elites,* whose cooperation and accommodation made the Great

---

Politics, passim; and Stiefbold, *Elites and Elections in a Fragmented Political System,* chaps. 4 and 5. The difficult bundle of propositions concerning tradeoffs between elite norms of restrained partisanship and elites' occasional undermining of system capabilities through rancorous conflictual behavior is analyzed in G. B. Powell, Jr., and R. P. Stiefbold, *Social Structure and Political Conflict in Fifty Austrian Community Systems: A Preliminary Report* (Munich: International Political Science Association, Eighth World Congress, 1970), esp. pp. 6, 7, 19 ff., and notes 31 and 32.

Coalition between mutually antagonistic subcultures work; *middle-level "socioeconomic"* elites, who made the paracoalition system of chambers, wage-price mechanisms, and the like work also; and *middle-level "political"* elites, whose diehard ideological orientations and *Lagermentalitaet* (or *Lagerdenken*) mortgaged the political system to strains to which it eventually succumbed. To these latter political elites were entrusted most day-to-day political speechmaking, nearly all of the important party organizational work, much of the electoral effort, and even the public definition of many principal issues.

Interaction of Elites. While top elites communicate politically relevant signals to and receive them from both middle groups, they are generally more attuned to the middle-level socioeconomic elites, or "technocrats," whose role culture (oriented to pragmatic decision making, with low salience of ideologically divisive issues) they share. Their principal interaction with the middle-level political elites, or "partisans," is under the duress of election campaigning, at which times the top elites—particularly those recruited from among the partisans—may lapse back into ideological style, with much higher intensity of partisanship and hence, great polarization on issues affecting the work and decisional effectiveness of even the highest level of consociational politics, the Coalition Committee.

Stability of Consociational Democracy. Thus, in the Austrian variant of consociational democracy, whatever developments there were toward a rapprochment, toward pan-*Lager* organic solidarity, suffered periodic set-

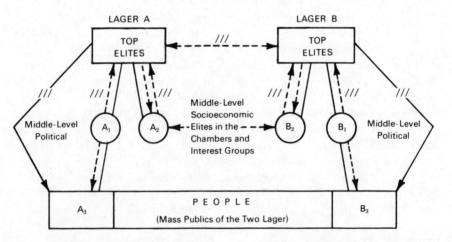

- - - = Lines of principal professional and private contacts
(Arrows indicate predominant direction of
flow of political communication)

/ / / = Interrupted two-way communication or
exacerbated one-way communication under imp
of parliamentary election campaigns

Figure 1. The Relationship Between Elite Structure and Inter-Lager Political Communication

backs; and the political system did not tend, in its basic features, to evolve toward a centripetal democracy. Given the periodic electoral opportunity to emphasize their outmoded concepts of political reality—perception of interparty goals as incompatible, of policy disagreements as fundamental *Lager* cleavages—the partisans forced both the mass public and the top elites back into the consociational stance, while effectively, and for a long postelection period, neutralizing the technocratic elites. The latter continued to communicate with each other and hence to make the system operate, but the scale of their meaningful interaction with top elites was severely reduced.

If we were to construct from the above findings and analysis a hypothetical model of the flow of relevant political communication in Austria's version of fragmented but consociational democracy, it could be schematically portrayed as in figure 1.

Consociational Democracy and The Austrian Case: Toward Empirical Refinement of the Lijphart Model

Lijphart's analysis of the elite-mass relationship most supportive of consociational democracy, as well as his model of political change, may be restated in terms of four principal propositions or groups of propositions ("propositional sets"), corresponding to the empirical Austrian data just summarized above.

Propositional Set 1: The Mass Level. There must be distinct lines of cleavage between subcultures accompanied by high density of subcultural organization, high partisanship (identification), and high mass support for elite-level consociational forms and practices.

Propositional Set 2: The Elite Level. There must be overarching elite commitment, cooperation, and demonstrated ability to resolve contentious issues often and well.

Propositional Set 3: Interaction of Elites. Overarching elite accommodation becomes and remains institutionally and behaviorally possible *because of* the relatively quiescent mass political culture postulated in propositional set 1.

Propositional Set 4: Stability and Change in Consociational Democracies. Decrease of both organizational and psychological distinctiveness may lead, over time, to a distinctly different type of democratic political system, the depoliticized democracy. In that case, consociational practices would result from consensus and the convergence of ideologies, not as a deliberate response to the tensions of a fragmented society. Moreover, there would be a change in the locus of principal decision making from the highest actors (party leaders) to lower levels (where interest group representatives and bureaucrats predominate).

If we refine this analysis on the basis of our empirical study of the Austrian case, we can restate the conditions that may be supportive of (contribute to or compel maintenance of) consociational democracy as follows.

Lijphart's Propositional Set 1. Our study generally confirms Lijphart, with one important caveat. While significant levels of partisanship must be present, the political stability and vitality of consociational systems are served best if that partisanship remains *potentially* mobilizable but *generally* latent, and if it is combined with a high degree of depoliticization sufficiently extensive to permit top elites and technocrats day-to-day bargaining flexibility. Thus centrifugal tencencies in the system are subverted at the same time that enough subcultural divisiveness is preserved to allow electoral subversion of whatever centripetal tendencies may exist.

Lijphart's Propositional Set 2. Our study also supports Lijphart as far as the "top elites" are concerned. However, our empirical and theoretical analysis of the Austrian case indicates the existence and functional utility of a *trio* of elite types and roles in consociational political systems.

Lijphart's Propositional Set 3. Elite accommodation at the top of the system is possible not only because of the mass-level situation posited in propositional set 1, but also because of the *division* of elites noted in propositional set 2. Specifically, in a country in which the principal competing groups are entrenched in economy, society, and polity in such a way that electoral victory by one side would not represent a de facto physical threat to the loser, it is possible that the trichotimization of elite roles described in this study may be a functional prerequisite of continued consociational democracy—that without such a division, the political system would evolve willy-nilly toward a centripetal or centrifugal type.

To restate the gist of the argument: our discovery of dual-track communication channels and specialized elites at the middle ranges provides us with an empirical explanation of why consociational democracy is not, under such deceptively docile conditions as existed in Austria in the late 1950s and early 1960s, self-devouring. One set of subsidiary elites, the partisans, "defends" consociational democracy against the "threat" of centripetal democracy, e.g., seizing on the latent *Lager* bases of the political system and mobilizing them under the aegis of electoral necessity. These partisans create or maintain the psychological conditions that led the top elites, supported by the mass electorate, into consociational democracy in the first place. Meanwhile, another set of elites, the technocrats, "defends" the system against the "threat" of centrifugal evolution, in that it carries on efficiently and effectively the pragmatic, day-to-day business of socioeconomic decision making (with prior political ratification by the top elites when necessary).

We would be remiss, however, were we not to draw attention again to two other aspects of the Austrian political system discussed tangentially in the first section of this study, which as intervening institutional variables tended to abet the countervailing behaviors of each group (partisans, technocrats) of middle-level elites, and hence to support the preservation of status quo consociational forms and practices. I refer in particular to Austria's unique blend of "political-administrative" and "sociological" federalisms.

Let me elaborate briefly: The firm entrenchment of the separate Austrian *Lager* in "their" federal ministries or, frequently, in municipal, county, or provincial administrations amounted to a de facto "political" federalism within and between various governmental and administrative institution at various levels of the Austrian political system. Moreover, this political federalism engendered by the formally federal structure of the Austrian national state was simultaneously—to use Robert Dahl's suggestive phrase[95]—a unique "sociological federalism." The point is this: divided political suzerainty over the various administrative sectors of the state by sociologically distinct units (the *Lager* qua parties) has the effect of reducing the all-or-nothing implications of electoral victory or defeat. As one *Lager* gets entrenched at other relevant sites in the system, including some not related to electoral outcomes and others which mitigate the unfavorable effects of an electoral defeat, the incentive to continue political-consociational forms of government may be increased because of simple comfort and inertia. I would argue that this was a significant feature of postwar Austrian political stability, imparting less significance and more decision-making autonomy to consociational national elites in Vienna, and reducing the "load" on the central governmental and political apparatus of the country.

Lijphart's Propositional Set 4. As far as the points under this set of propositions are concerned, which deal with stability and change in consociational regimes, the Austrian case offers two important insights of potential cross-national relevance. First, it is not clear why both types of depoliticization, "natural" and "imposed," cannot coexist in the same system; nor that one of the types necessarily precedes or leads to the other. Austria's coalition and paracoalition provided both types simultaneously. Thus, one finds in the Austrian context that there coexisted during much of the postwar coalition period a genuinely organic solidarity and "natural" depoliticization resulting from successful collective bargaining in the paracoalition institutions among the socioeconomic partners; and a more manufactured solidarity imposed by elites in more politicized arenas; plus a combination of both at the mass level. One reason both types may exist simultaneously and develop unevenly is that the organizational bases of each, and their attendant role structures, tend to persist over time.[96]

Second, given the long history of functional representation (and espe-

---

95. As quoted in Sidney Verba, "Some Dilemmas in Comparative Research, *World Politics* 20, no. 1 (October 1967): 126.
96. Cf. Barnes, "Ideology and the Organization of Conflict," pp. 528–29.

cially the significance of the paracoalition institutions and practices) and given further the bipolar nature of government ministries, we would argue that interest-group representatives and bureaucrats made their share of the principal decisions *throughout* the period of the Great Coalition: depoliticization of elite and mass opinion did not alter the loci of various types of principal decision making.[97]

Political Change in Austria: The Problematic Interaction of Segmented Pluralism, Consociational Democracy, and Electoral Politics, 1945–66

The empirical Austrian case helps clarify and elaborate the consociational democracy model, and helps resolve some unsettled problems associated with that model. It also raises some interesting and broader questions of political development theory and allows us to reflect profitably on certain types of developmental problems that exist not only in Austria but in many other industrially advanced societies as well. In doing so, we may draw usefully on the work of a number of contemporary theorists of political change, such as Huntington, Rustow, Rokkan, and others. Let us first look at Austrian political development in the postwar period in broad general perspective, then zero in on several specific hypotheses that appear particularly useful in explicating patterns of political change in Austria, and that, conversely, are thrown into bolder theoretical relief by the Austrian example.

General Developmental Trends

In the space of two brief decades, this small Alpine democracy—a bitterly and deeply divided country without so much as an agreed-upon national identity, and with precious little democratic inclination or experience—was converted by deliberate elite design to democratic attitudes, expectations, and practices, in close approximation to the developmental scenario described by Dankwart Rustow in his perceptive article on "Transitions to Democracy."[98] A two-party system in "form" was converted to what Sartori would call a two-party system in "substance."[99] And a mildly authoritarian government by elite cartel imposed on the populace in 1945

97. On the historical development and the various loci of relevant decision making and decision-making patterns, see, e.g., Hans R. Klecatsky, "Interessenverbaende und Parlament," in Stiefbold et al., *Wahlen und Parteien in Oesterreich*, pp. 954–68. Cf. also the remarks in Gerhard Lehmbruch, "A Non-Competitive Pattern of Conflict Management in Liberal Democracies: The Case of Switzerland, Austria, and Lebanon" (Paper presented at the Seventh World Congress, International Political Science Association, Brussels, September 1967), p. 5. This paper is an English rendition of some of Lehmbruch's hypotheses and speculations in his analysis of *Proporzdemokratie*.

98. *Comparative Politics* 2, no. 3 (April 1970): 337–63, esp. 350 ff.

99. "The Typology of Party Systems—Proposals for Improvement," in *Mass Politics: Studies in Political Sociology*, ed. E. Allardt and S. Rokkan (New York: Free Press, 1970), pp. 331 ff., 336 ff., 345 ff., 385 f.

became by 1966 a British-type open regime of alternating government and opposition!

Yet, most remarkable of all, these objective realities remained unappreciated and even unperceived by the country's leadership until the almost incidental failure to successfully renegotiate the Coalition Pact after the OeVP electoral victory of 1966 stripped the emperor of all his clothes. A quick, cold shower disabused the nation's elite with startling suddenness of its twenty-year mortgage to *Lagerdenken*. Since 1966 Austria has enjoyed uninterrupted single-party rule, first by the OeVP, later by the SPOe; and *Bereichskoalition* has replaced *Bereichsopposition* as Austria's own variety of what Lowi has called "interest group liberalism." [100]

Two Hypotheses: Explaining What Happened in Austria [101]

As table 6 summarizing Austrian political development suggests, there are numerous ways in which to relate the confluence of segmented pluralism, consociational democracy, and electoral politics in Austria to more general problems of political change in Western Europe. Two of these, organizational lag and behavioral lag, we shall explore briefly, in order to suggest some of the more fruitful directions in which future research on problems of political development in advanced nations might be concentrated.

The Thesis of Organizational Lag. Between 1945 and 1966 the political-governmental problem facing Austria changed from what Huntington would call the challenge of "institutionalization" and the threat of political "decay" to what Mark Kesselman has recently and brilliantly analyzed in the French context as "overinstitutionalization and political constraint." What is involved here is the point that segmented pluralism, including the early "freezing" of partisan electoral alternatives as a result of the introduction of proportional representation electoral formulas in

---

100. T. Lowi, "The Public Philosophy: Interest-Group Liberalism," *American Political Science Review* 60 (March 1967): 5–24, is the source of the phrase. The point made for Austria is derived from Stiefbold, *S.A.N.E. Interviews, 1968*, and runs throughout the interview protocols.

101. The brief analysis which follows draws on the following studies: Samuel P. Huntington, *Political Order in Changing Societies* (New Haven: Yale University Press, 1968); Mark Kesselman, "Overinstitutionalization and Political Constraint: The Case of France," *Comparative Politics* 3, no. 1 (October 1970): 21–44; Derek Urwin, "Social Cleavages and Political Parties in Belgium: Problems of Political Institutionalization," *Political Studies* 18, no. 3 (September 1970): 320–40; Richard Rose and Derek Urwin, "Social Cohesion, Political Parties and Strains in Regimes," *Comparative Political Studies* 2, no. 1 (April 1969): 7–67; Lorwin, "Segmented Pluralism"; Rokkan, "The Structuring of Mass Politics"; Otto Kirchheimer, "The Transformation of the Western Europe Party Systems," in *Political Parties and Political Development*, ed. J. LaPalombara and M. Weiner (Princeton: Princeton University Press, 1966), 177–200; Gerhard Lehmbruch, "Strukturen ideologischer Konflikte bei Parteienwettbewerb," *Politische Vierteljahresschrift* 10 (1969): 287–313; Barnes, "Ideology and the Organization of Conflict"; Lewis J. Edinger, "Political Change in Germany," *Comparative Politics* 2, no. 4 (July 1970); Edelman, "Myths, Metaphors, and Political Conformity"; W. Howard Wriggins, "Aggregation of Power—An Approach to Politics in Emerging Countries," *Proceedings of the Sixth Annual Meeting of the International Studies Association, April 1965.*

Table 6. Segmented Pluralism, Consociational Democracy, and Electoral Politics: Some Dimensions of Political Change in Austria, 1945–66

	Principal Development Problem	Regime Solution and Effects	Type of Solidarity or Integration	Major Functions of Parliamentary Elections	Type of Partisan Competition Related to "Objective Socioeconomic Conditions"
1945	Stabilization in face of perceived "conflict society"; need for Rustow's conscious elite decision. Huntington's institutionalization. Wriggins' aggregation of power	Great Red-Black Coalition, with Coalition Committee (extralegal) as center of political power: Lijphart's consociational democracy, guaranteed by firm segmented pluralist base (Lorwin). Paracoalition of "social partners"	Mechanical solidarity, normative, based on procedural rules and centralized power imposed on mass public by top elites in perceived absence of value consensus or shared national identity	Impart formal legitimacy by masses to rulers; provide for recurrent inter-*Lager* adjustment, a modicum of flexibility in otherwise inflexible system	Firm social and organizational infrastructure of *Lager* and underdeveloped and destroyed economy provide no socioeconomic basis for recasting of partisan competition on basis of catchall umbrella-type political parties
1966	Kesselman's "over-institutionalization and political constraint"; in Lorwin's terms, failure of *ontzuiling* to occur; put differently, in Barnes' terms, simple organizational persistence disguising real substructural changes and containing them. Subcultures, which facilitated elite security and autonomy, and regime stability and efficacy, now have become obstacles to development	Coalition Committee no longer essential buckle on the system; now hindering developmental impetus provided by paracoalition. Conclusion, April, 1966: no more coalition. After brief "cold shower," an unbelievably smooth transition to a working government-and-opposition model	Organic solidarity, though not at first recognized by elites with organizational blinkers hindering their perception of new realities. New solidarity or integration based solidly on shared national identity and increased value consensus, and resulting from great increase in functional interdependence of the *Lager* or their subunits in all spheres	In early 1960s elections serving extremely "conservative" functions, i.e., sustaining "crisis" consociational rule and impeding development of "organic" solidarity and its counterpart, i.e., "natural" consociational rule	New socioeconomic base now exists for recasting of partisan competition on basis of catchall appeals. However, in initial phase it is combined with traditional ghetto mobilization, becomes ironic additional source of strain on regime until after successful switch from coalition to government-and-opposition formula, after which general European trends in partisan competition begin to be established in Austria

divided societies, has played a major role in stabilizing and rendering predictable the daily politics of low-consensus, deep-cleavage societies. As Lorwin suggests, it has been a valuable handmaiden of political modernization and social mobilization in a number of smaller European countries, including Austria. But as Kesselman and Urwin illustrate, such thoroughgoing institutionalization, originally useful in controlling the potential volatility of divided societies, may eventually become inflexible, contributing to an ossification of the system as a whole and, by thus reducing its capacity to respond to new demands, ultimately weakening it. This is precisely what happened in Austria, where elites, especially in the coalition subsystem, were simply too isolated, in partisan terms, to perceive what change was taking place and hence to respond to it.

The Thesis of Behavioral Lag. Lewis J. Edinger, drawing on another facet of the Huntington concept of "institutionalization," suggests that the institutionalization of a regime depends chiefly on a growth of congruence between regime norms and political style. As we have noted several times in this study, the consociational democracy model posits that elites will try to minimize public ideologism or rancorous interelite behavior, lest it get out of hand and mushroom into a load the system cannot tolerate. And while Powell and I have suggested that rancorous behavior itself can become a norm under certain conditions, we have also demonstrated empirically that when great conflicts of interest over preferred policy outcomes exist among competing groups of elites, there is a much greater likelihood of successfully avoiding disruptive political conflict which might be destabilizing for the political system if the contending elites practice assiduously the so-called norm of restrained partisanship in their dealings with each other.[102]

As this study has amply demonstrated, however, Austrian politics in the coalition era was characterized by a highly expressive political style. And not only do many elites, as revealed by the SANE interview data, believe the semantics anyway, but also, as Edelman warns, language forms create shared expectations and produce their own behavioral logic. The incongruence between the consociational regime norm of *nonrancorous* elite public behavior and a public style by political elites which relied heavily on *rancorous* behavior thus led to "underinstitutionalization," an effect precisely opposite from that produced by highly articulated political and governmental organizations which "refused to die" after having outlived their usefulness. It was this combination of behavioral *under*institutionalization and organizational *over*institutionalization, and especially the fateful *interaction* of the two triggered by national parliamentary election campaigns, which eventually undermined and destroyed Austria's twenty-year experiment in managing communal competition and conflict by formal consociational democracy.

102. Powell and Stiefbold, *Social Structure and Political Conflict*, pp. 19–22 and note 32.

5   *Martin O. Heisler*

Institutionalizing Societal Cleavages in a Cooptive Polity: The Growing Importance of the Output Side in Belgium*

David Easton has suggested that the principal task of political systems is to cope with stress.[1] One argument advanced by the earliest protagonists of the "behavioral revolution" in comparative politics was that different types of systems find different ways to perform the tasks that help them cope with stress, to "persist," in Easton's terminology.[2] Systems evolve specialized structures, generally at the regime level, for mitigating stress; and one of the basic premises of this book is that similar systems' structures tend to resemble each other—especially if the disturbances that induce stress in them exhibit similarities. Some analysts assign the most important places in their schema to such structures. Thus Samuel Huntington considers political order and stability (notions closely associated with success in coping with stress) to be largely dependent upon the degree of political institutionaliza-

* Research and writing were facilitated by support received from two sources at the University of Maryland: (1) the general research board of the graduate school provided a summer research grant, permitting fieldwork; while (2) the department of government and politics awarded me a "released time" grant, allowing me to read, think, and write. This paper is the precursor of two larger studies: a book-length exploration of the interfaces between societal and political cleavages in Belgium in general and the Brussels *agglomération* in particular, and a series of papers on institutional endeavors to cope with cleavage-induced stress in multiethnic societies.

    1. David Easton, *A Framework for Political Analysis* (Englewood Cliffs, N.J.: Prentice-Hall, 1965), and *A Systems Analysis of Political Life* (New York: Wiley, 1965). To attempt to define the concept *stress* more precisely would circumscribe it unduly. In general, when Easton uses the concept, he means imbalances between demands and supports, between demands and system capabilities, and failure to produce appropriate or adequate outputs. My usage follows Easton's.

    2. See pp. 11 ff.

tion (a type of structuring).[3] The principal source of stress for the system type with which this book is concerned—and, for that matter, for many other systems—is politically salient internal division.[4]

The possibility of structural variation within a type-cell has been noted earlier.[5] Given the multifarious and multicausal nature of internal divisions, such variations should be expected. Thus the structural means for coping developed in Norway, Austria, Belgium, and the European Communities are different in form but remain similar in their essential nature, and they provide a basis for classifying these systems as members of a single type. Chapter 2 emphasized the similarities. Chapters 3 through 6, by taking a closer look at specific cases, highlight some differences in the manner in which European polity-like structures actually operate.

The Setting

Viewed from this perspective, Belgium is a fascinating focus for political scientists and political sociologists. During different stages of its development, Belgium has manifested all four types of politically important cleavage commonly found in Western societies: (1) *religion*, in the Belgian case definable in large part in terms of clerical (Roman Catholic) vs. secular or anticlerical positions; (2) *socioeconomic class-based ideologies;* (3) *center vs. periphery,*[6] the least important cleavage in Belgium and generally appearing as counterpoint to the others; and, most recently, (4) *conflict between ethnic groups.*

During the first 130 years of Belgium's independence—from 1830 to 1960—a cooptive regime structure evolved in response to the need to cope with the stresses produced by the first and second types of cleavage. It dealt—sometimes handily, at other times barely—with most forms of disturbance, including ethnic conflict, until such conflict became the dominant fact of social and political life in the country.

Increasingly in the years following the Second World War, the ethnic cleavage came to define those aspects of the other divisions that remained relevant. Thus ethnic distinctions tended to reinforce differences between Catholic and secular positions, and they often influenced class-related per-

3. Samuel P. Huntington, *Political Order in Changing Societies* (New Haven: Yale University Press, 1968), chap. 1.

4. Easton considers such divisions or cleavages "a possible major source of stress on the system" (*Systems Analysis of Political Life,* p. 230). Chapter 15 of that book is entitled "Cleavage as a Source of Stress."

5. See pp. 24, 65–67.

6. Rokkan has pioneered in the conceptual and empirical exploration of this cleavage dimension. See Stein Rokkan, *Citizens, Elections, Parties* (New York: McKay, 1970), and Seymour Martin Lipset and Stein Rokkan, eds., *Party Systems and Voter Alignments: Cross-National Perspectives* (New York: Free Press, 1967), chaps 1, 8. Virtually all Rokkan's empirical referents come from Norway.

ceptions and behavior as well. Ethnicity became the salient dimension of cleavage in the late 1950s or early 1960s[7] and induced very high levels of stress in the forms of output failure and the curtailment of specific supports.

The authorities (in particular, members of successive coalition cabinets and leaders of the "traditional parties," who have come to occupy quasi-official positions) reacted quickly, but responses with long-term effectiveness required more time to develop. While certain types of regime modification were identified as the proper response, nearly a decade passed before the massive task of institutionalizing those changes was begun. That task has now been started, however: *Belgium, a unitary state since its inception, is swiftly and peacefully becoming a federation.*

Noteworthy is the fact that progress toward the restructuring of the regime was made possible by the relative effectiveness—vestigial, to be sure—of a still operating cooptive structure, although the progressive enfeeblement of that structure was obvious during the mid- and late 1960s. (An interesting question—but one not wholly within the scope of this essay—is whether the new regime will develop sufficient stress-ameliorating capabilities to assure the system's persistence before the old regime loses all its abilities to cope.)

The cooptive structure through which the regime is being reshaped approximates the European polity model. On the basis of the signs available at the time of this writing,[8] it seems reasonable to predict that the emerging regime will also exhibit most of the type's characteristics as well as its

---

The center vs. periphery cleavage is analytically unsatisfactory in the Belgian case, for at least two reasons. First, if the center is defined in terms of the commonly used indicators, then it is "Belgian," Brussels-oriented, non-Flemish, and non-Walloon. In this light, particularistic demands and sentiments might be classed as periphery-directed. But the dynamics of the ongoing regionalization drives are partly focused on the very real attraction of growing Flemish and Walloon "centers." Second—and this may be a concomitant of numerous movements toward cultural autonomy as well as toward ecological or "quality of life" improvements manifested in a growing number of Western systems—in some cases, including the Belgian, the center-periphery distinction may prove to have been a transient or generational one: movement from the periphery toward the center continues for those who are relatively less integrated, but the center seems to have lost its capacity to attract, retain, and polarize.

7. While the dating of the salience of such a cleavage is generally difficult and can rarely be precise, there seems to be consensus among commentators on the Belgian situation on this point. See, for instance, Albert du Roy, *La guerre des belges* (Paris: Seuil, 1968), pp. 110–27; Jean Meynaud, Jean Ladrière, and François Perin, eds., *La décision politique en Belgique: le pouvoir et les groupes* (Paris: Colin, 1965), pp. 214–31; Alvin Rabushka and Kenneth A. Shepsle, *Politics in Plural Societies: A Theory of Democratic Instability* (Columbus, O.: Merrill, 1972), pp. 112 ff.; Derek W. Urwin, "Social Cleavages and Political Parties in Belgium: Problems of Institutionalization," *Political Studies* 18, no. 3 (September 1970): 333; and Jean Ladrière, "Le système politique belge: situation 1970," *Courrier hebdomadaire du C.R.I.S.P.* 500 (20 November 1970): 5 ff.

8. The final draft was completed early in 1973, at a time when the three traditional parties were concluding a two-month-long "crisis negotiation" to form a new coalition. The government formation process, characterized by negotiations between the "formator" (in this instance Edmond Leburton, the *francophone* co-president of the Socialist party) and the various leaders of the regional wings of the traditional parties, labor and professional organiza-

general configuration. Thus Belgium is not becoming less a European polity as much as another form of European polity. The system's effort to cope with serious threats to its persistence—threats in the form of excessive stress induced by a highly politicized ethnic cleavage—has led to massive regime change. Here, then, is a real-world illustration of a theoretical point made earlier: a fundamental distinction exists between regime maintenance and system persistence,[9] and sometimes the former needs to be yielded in order to assure the latter.

This essay traces the development of the existing but rapidly vanishing cooptive structure; it explains—however cursorily—the reasons for the subordinacy or dormancy of the ethnic cleavage during the century in which other divisions shaped the old regime; it indicates some of the more direct reasons for the sharply heightened politicization of ethnicity during the last few years and, simultaneously, points out why this cleavage was not and should not have been expected to become institutionalized in the traditional manner, through the party subsystem; and, finally, it outlines with the broadest strokes the direction of the ongoing, and far from complete, federalization process. An important literature has come into being on Belgian politics during the last five or six years, making these tasks easier than they would have been even in the recent past. It is now possible to refer the reader to scholarly English-language materials. Nevertheless, the general level of familiarity with this interesting and important system is still so low that it seems advisable to weave some descriptive comments into the text.

The Problem

Belgium is pervasively and emotionally divided into at least three large subsocietal groups by its multidimensional ethnic cleavage: Flemings, Walloons, and Bruxellois. Yet, since the rise of that cleavage to its present position of preeminence, the country has experienced relatively few instances of group violence and has not been notably plagued by immobilism—a trait often associated with politically fragmented systems, especially in Western Europe. Further, the approaches of successive cabinets to the problem—whether one approves or disapproves of the directions taken—have been relatively reasoned, moderate, and orderly.[10] During this

---

tions, and other group actors in the cooptive regime, was utilized to hammer out the terms under which the regionalization process would be implemented. The new coalition is formed around a governmental agreement—a joint policy program.

9. See pp. 56, 78 ff.

10. Cf. Val R. Lorwin, "Cultural Pluralism and Political Tension in Modern Belgium" (Department of History, University of Oregon, 1970). Mimeographed. This is a revised version of a paper presented at the annual meeting of the Canadian Historical Association, Toronto, 6 June 1969.

period, the economy, which in comparison with other Western European systems is heavily weighted toward the private sector,[11] has been expanding at a good rate;[12] the level of public services has been sustained or raised by, for instance, the extension of social insurance and the scope and rate of pensions[13] and by the expansion of what were already some of the best public transportation systems in Europe; civil liberties and citizen participation have been maintained;[14] the rapidly expanding institutions of the European Communities have been accommodated, together with NATO and SHAPE headquarters, which moved into the country a few years ago; large numbers of foreign workers have been incorporated into the economic (and, to an admittedly lesser extent, the social) division of labor, and substantial numbers of African and Asian university students have been brought especially to the Free University of Brussels and to Louvain; and the country's vital international relationships have been enhanced. In short, *in the face of an ever-exacerbating schism, the system has more than held its own.*

Another manifestation of stability is the already noted willingness of many or most of the important group actors in the system to use the present structure in the construction of the new regime. While specific support for the authorities and for the regime has been declining—giving rise to the collapse of broadly based coalition governments in 1968, 1971, and 1972 and leading to an almost universal disinclination to put important political stakes into the defense of the present regime, creating the stress levels of crisis proportions to which I have alluded—Belgian political behavior exhibits some interesting manifestations of diffuse support at the regime level. Thus, while Belgians are turning toward parties, leaders, issue posi-

---

11. Bent Hansen with Wayne W. Snyder, *Fiscal Policy in Seven Countries, 1955–1965* (Paris: Organisation for Economic Co-operation and Development, 1969), pp. 86–93, 95–96.

12. Comprehensive figures for the period 1953–69 appear in Institut National de Statistique, *Études Statistiques,* no. 21 (1970), esp. pp. 3–7. See also OECD Economic Surveys, *Belgium-Luxembourg Economic Union* (Paris: Organisation for Economic Co-operation and Development, 1971); Robert Senelle, "The Political, Economic and Social Structures of Belgium," *Memo from Belgium* 122–123–124 (March-April-May 1970), pp. 131, 129–73 passim. For a systematic statistical survey over time (1895–1965), see Belgian Information and Documentation Institute, "Seventy Years of Modifications in Structures of Demography and Social Economy: A Statistical Inventory," *Belgian News* 2c (April 1968). *Memo from Belgium* and *Belgian News* are issued under the auspices of the Belgian Ministry of Foreign Affairs and External Trade.

13. See Senelle, "Political, Economic and Social Structures," pp. 177–256 passim; and Hansen, *Fiscal Policy in Seven Countries,* pp. 101 f.

14. Belgians vote in communal (i.e., at local level), provincial, and country-wide political elections, as well as in important union and other quasi-corporate settings. They participate in party, economic, and local congresses as well. While they may be among the most participation-oriented people in the world, the generalization made in chapter 2 with regard to the import of such participation in the European polity type system holds to an appreciable degree for Belgians: the elite milieu has set the tone of the cooptive structure, and citizen participation has not been directly instrumental (i.e., policy shaping) in most situations. The precise number of seats obtained by a party in parliament has little significance in a regime in which the leaders of one class of parties (the three "traditional" parties) participate in important discussions as a matter of course, while those of another class (the "anti-regime" or "extreme" parties) are often excluded from higher councils.

tions, and psychological postures that represent separatist views in increasingly truculent terms, they are nevertheless willing to use the ballot as a principal mode of expression for these sentiments: over 90 percent of the eligible voters continue to turn out for general (i.e., system-wide legislative) elections.[15] Other forms of diffuse support are also abundant—a general predisposition to obey laws, pay taxes, and work in public positions, and a willingness to formulate and conduct a unitary foreign policy, to operate most of the economy at the level of the overall system, and to engage in sports activities jointly and without systematically fragmenting the structures through which such activities are performed.

In other words, despite a widely shared conviction among major groups that the division of the country is so profound and irreversible that legal and institutional accommodations to that division are the only practicable way of dealing with it, the means being utilized for achieving those accommodations are essentially the same as those through which the old regime has operated for several decades. These consist of formal consultations among the leaders of the Flemish, Walloon, and Brussels organizations of each of the three "traditional" parties (Christian Social, Socialist, and Liberal); informal discussion with spokesmen for cultural, labor, employers', and professional associations and with local governmental figures; and, finally, encoding into the constitution or law or interparty agreement the broadly—though generally not consensually—based programs.

This vestigial capability of the old regime derives largely from its diffuse support. Such support emanates from the emerging regime rather than from the dying one. The sources and nature of that support provide important clues to the solution of the theoretical conundrum that evoked my initial interest in the subject of this paper: *if the schism between the Belgian communities is indeed as profound and irreversible as it appears, then perhaps one may be allowed to wonder why the processes through which the formal division of the country are being worked out are so pacific, moderate, reasoned, and orderly* (and in comparison with similarly troubled systems they assuredly are, even if they may seem to lack these virtues in the eyes of some participants or proximate observers whose perspectives are limited or distorted); *and why Belgium and Belgians have managed to flourish during these arduous times?*

Stages of Development and Loci of Institutionalization

These phenomena point to the possibility that Belgium's ethnic cleavage has become, or is becoming, successfully institutionalized—in Huntington's sense—and they contain clues to where and how that institu-

15. W. Fraeys, "Analyse des résultats des elections législatives de 1971," *Res Publica* 14, no. 2 (1972), p. 384, table 1. Tables 5–7 (pp. 390–93) provide data on the 1971 and 1968 turnouts and outcomes by region. It should be noted that voting is compulsory.

tionalization is taking place. They also militate in favor of a radical shift in the analyst's point of departure. Both the theoretical needs of social scientists pursuing generalizations of comparative applicability about politics in multiethnic societies and the more modest concerns of students of Belgian political life will be better served by shifting attention from that which is crumbling (i.e., the traditional party subsystem and the unitary state structure) to that which is persisting even under the prevailing crises. In sum, I propose that we move from a preoccupation with political phenomena on the input side of the system, treated through time-honored but no longer salient foci on electoral and interparty elite behaviors, to a primary concern with the major processes and structures that comprise the output side. Using Easton's conceptual vocabulary, this can be said to encompass the processes and structures involved in the formulation, legitimation, and implementation of authoritative decisions, regulations, and laws. It should be broadly conceived, to include—especially so when modern systems with highly elaborated bureaucracies are under consideration—administrative activity and judicial processes.

The justification for such a shift in analytic thrust can be found in changes in the real-world political situations we strive to understand. A brief look at the analytic dead-end to which the historically valid but now weak focus on party subsystems has led, coupled with a cursory review of the evolution of the present regime structure, will bring us to the current situation.

From Modernizing to Modern Systems: Changing the Frame of Reference

Several scholars who have addressed themselves to the central problems of the Belgian political system in the last few years have concluded that the ethnic cleavage has not been institutionalized in the party subsystem. Val Lorwin and Derek Urwin, in particular, have demonstrated that, unlike the historically important religious and socioeconomic class-based cleavages, the division between ethnic communities did not find its principal form of expression in the arena of the parties.[16] Urwin's comprehensive analysis, using Huntington's conceptualization of institutionalization—the process "by which organizations and procedures acquire value and stability"[17]—is particularly germane.

16. See Val R. Lorwin, "Belgium: Religion, Class, and Language in National Politics," in *Political Oppositions in Western Democracies*, ed. Robert A. Dahl (New Haven: Yale University Press, 1966), pp. 147–87; idem, "Cultural Pluralism and Political Tension"; and Urwin, "Social Cleavages and Political Parties," pp. 320–40. See also Cynthia H. Enloe, *Ethnic Conflict and Political Development* (Boston: Little, Brown, 1973), whose brief *coup d'œil* in the direction of Belgium (pp. 118–21) is entitled "Belgium: Federalism to Replace a Party System," and whose theme parallels mine.

17. Huntington, *Political Order*, p. 12.

Urwin focused on parties because he, like Huntington, believed that "the institutionalization of support for and compliance with a regime is the most important function a party can perform."[18] His analysis of the institutionalization of the religious and socioeconomic class cleavages in the party subsystem (deeming the former to have been fully institutionalized, while terming the latter "a semi-institutionalized cleavage") produces a picture of a system that resembles the European polity model to a remarkable degree. Thus Urwin stresses the importance of sharp vertical structural delineations between segments—the *familles spirituelles* or *zuilen* discussed in chapter 2. He notes the decline of the salience of ideology, viewed in traditional socioeconomic class terms, and considers the conversion of politically sensitive issues into technical questions to be treated in the context of the welfare state important prerequisites for achieving acceptable or satisficing compromises without identifiable winners or losers.[19] Urwin then concludes that the ethnic cleavage has not been institutionalized in the party subsystem[20] but does not suggest where it might be so managed.

Professor Urwin's supportable conclusion is an acceptable point at which the analysis of the institutionalization of social cleavages in the party subsystem can be terminated. But if the focus of analysis is shifted from what it was for Urwin to the question, "How, if at all, is the ethnic cleavage in Belgium institutionalized?," then his conclusion merely becomes a new point of departure. The direction in which I propose to set out was suggested by the same theoretical connection between stability and the institutionalizing role of parties—a connection developed by Huntington—that motivated Urwin.

In his book *Political Order in Changing Societies*, Huntington was preoccupied with the dynamic balance between mobilization and politicization on the one hand and the capabilities of political and governmental organizations and procedures to sustain the central patterns of the regime on the other. If those "organizations and procedures acquire[d] value and stability"—if they became institutionalized—then modernization need not represent a threat of dislocation to the regime.

Huntington's focus on parties as political organizations crucial for the channeling of potentially disruptive demands and for the generation of

18. Urwin, "Social Cleavages and Political Parties," p. 321, following Huntington, *Political Order*, chap. 7.
19. Urwin, "Social Cleavages and Political Parties," pp. 321–30 passim. Others have also characterized the outgoing Belgian regime's structure in these or similar terms, strongly supporting the conclusion that the structure closely resembles the European polity model. See Lorwin, "Belgium: Religion, Class, and Language"; idem, "Segmented Pluralism: Ideological Cleavages and Political Cohesion in the Smaller European Democracies," *Comparative Politics* 3, no. 2 (January 1971): 141–75; Meynaud et al., *La décision politique*, esp. pp. 49–70; George Armstrong Kelly, "Biculturalism and Party Systems in Belgium and Canada," *Public Policy* 16 (1967): esp. 326 ff.; and several of the *Courriers hebdomadaire* of C.R.I.S.P.—the Centre de recherche et d'information socio-politiques (Brussels).
20. Urwin, "Social Cleavages and Political Parties," pp. 330–40.

regime supports must be viewed in the context of his selected subject area, for by no means was he identifying an absolute analytic and theoretical priority. Huntington was concerned principally with "changing" or modernizing societies in Asia, Africa, and Latin America.[21] He did not extend his focus on parties to polities in which massive demands for participation were no longer pertinent—where they had been met earlier, at least in the classic sense—or to polities in which the prevailing levels of mobilization were very high *and stable*. In fact, to the extent that he dealt with modern systems at all, Huntington used them simply as contrasts to modernizing polities or to show how in their earlier careers they had modernized.

Professor Urwin and others who have treated the historical processes of cleavage institutionalization in Belgium mainly through the parties were thus consistent with Huntington's notions—*as long as they dealt with events and periods exhibiting sharply climbing rates of mobilization and rapidly increasing mass demands for participation*. The religious and, more particularly, the socioeconomic class cleavages came to the fore under such conditions. But by the time the ethnic cleavage became salient, a different set of conditions prevailed: Belgium was approaching the condition depicted in chapter 2, as a European polity. And, it will be recalled, the first three characteristics (A, B, and C) of the European polity model clearly stipulate that "very high levels of social and political mobilization, economic development, and political development," substantial political participation (although not a commensurate degree of instrumental effect from participation), and a general "decline of ideology" on the input side will be found in such systems.[22]

If the input side of the Belgian system has ceased to be salient, then, the most effective institutionalization of the most important social cleavage might not occur there. In a system in which questions of mobilization, participation, and similar sources of demands are no longer the principal forces of potential instability, it follows that political parties—the prime agencies for institutionalizing such demands in a stabilizing fashion—are no longer the crucial loci of institutionalization. For that matter, the fragmentation of the parties into a myriad of regionally and traditionally distinguished entities—the phenomenon that has occurred in Belgium during the last five or six years[23]—need have no bearing at all on the institutionalization of the ethnic cleavage.

21. See *Political Order*, p. vii.
22. See pp. 38–41.
23. Each of the three "traditional," previously system-wide parties—the Christian Social, the Socialist, and the Party for Liberty and Progress (Liberal)—has split into Flemish and *francophone* entities, and in two instances Brussels parties have emerged as well. New, "communal" or regional parties have also become important in this decade. These phenomena are touched upon in the discussion of the third phase of the old regime.

Clearly we must shift our attention to those aspects of the system where the political action is. It is there that institutionalization vital to the system's chances for persistence must take place. Those aspects are the decision-making subsystem, the norms and processes through which outputs are legitimated, and the structures and processes through which outputs are implemented and converted into outcomes.

In sum, I suggest that Belgium can be regarded as a European polity; and the systemic aspects preeminent in that type will also be found salient in Belgium. Instead of the party subsystem and the most recent election results, we need to concentrate on such phenomena as the extension and alteration of public bureaucracies, the separation of decision-making and implementing structures into ethnic components with increasing autonomy, and, finally and most dramatically, the regionalization or federalization of the country that is now in progress.

The structure of the old regime is in its third and final phase.[24] It was established in the first years of the country's independence by elites that engaged in what Lijphart has called the "consociational" enterprise: "the deliberate joint effort by the elites to stabilize the system."[25] Shortly after the attainment of independence, the religious cleavage led to the structuring of differences between the clerical and anticlerical or secular factions. The remnants of the "union of oppositions" and of the consociational beginning were incorporated into the structure, however. The new regime managed to institutionalize the cleavage through the embryonic parties that were the parliamentary factions, through the monarchy, and other institutions. These successes were no doubt aided by the very rigorous circumscribing of participation. Its adaptability was tested and proved substantial in the second phase, which lasted from the 1880s to the 1950s. During this long period, the regime coped successfully with the participation-oriented demands that accompanied the rise of the working class, the organization of labor, and the advent of the Workers' (later Socialist) party.

The third phase has been short-lived. The regime responded adequately to class-based distributional demands, and it led to the elaboration of the cooptive structure and the welfare state; but it has not managed to adapt adequately to the ethnic cleavage—unless its capability for terminating its career and pacifically launching a new regime is considered adaptability. Partly because the extension of the state's administrative apparatus during the last two decades coincided with the economic and social revitalization of the Flemish population, and partly because some decisions

24. More or less similar three-phase analyses have become commonplace in the literature on Belgian politics. My analysis of the third phase and my prognosis differ appreciably from those of other commentators, however. Cf. Lorwin, "Belgium: Religion, Class, and Language"; and Urwin, "Social Cleavages and Political Parties."

25. Arend Lijphart, "Consociational Democracy," *World Politics* 21, no. 2 (January 1969): 213.

and most aspects of output implementation lend themselves to parceling out among groups or regions, the seeds of the new regime can be said to have been sown during this period. While such a separation can be regarded as functional for the regionalized or federal regime, it was clearly stress-producing in the unitary old regime. A brief look at these three phases, with some illustrative data, should demonstrate my point regarding the relationship between stages of development and loci of institutionalization.[26]

The Establishment of the Regime Structure

Belgium came into being in 1830–31 through the fortuitous convergence of three factors. First, the "union of oppositions" brought into temporary conjunction the interests and resources of the most important political and economic forces: the provincial nobility, the clergy, and the emerging bourgeoisie. Second, the independence movement coincided with a favorable turn in the foreign policies of the major powers. Thus, the United Kingdom of the Netherlands, which had been created by the concert of great powers at the Congress of Vienna (1814–15) by giving sovereignty over the nine provinces that were to make up Belgium to the Netherlands, was not sustained by them in the face of this challenge. Third, the prevailing level of political mobilization was so low (see table 2) that the conscious efforts of the small elite could in fact be solidified in a consociational manner into such governmental and political structures as the constitution, the monarchy, and the ideological factions that became the parties.

The new regime's political and economic structures tilted the relationship between the linguistic-cultural groups sharply in favor of the *francophones*. During the nearly three centuries of Habsburg rule, the French language had enjoyed an ascending position in the provinces that were later to comprise Belgium. Then, during the French occupation (1792–1815, the Belgian provinces were formally annexed as "provinces of France" in 1795) the entire area was subjected to a policy of assimilation and francisation, and the Flemish language and culture were systematically attacked. During the brief life of the United Kingdom of the Netherlands, the Dutch monarch sought to revive the Flemish culture and language—a language consisting of dialectic variants of Dutch—in the northern provinces, while restricting the administrative and educational use of French to the area south of the historic linguistic frontier. (The linguistic frontier that divides the Flemish and French language populations—see

26. I have provided more extensive historical perspectives along these lines elsewhere. See M. O. Heisler, "Political Community and Its Formation in the Low Countries" (Ph.D. dissertation, University of California, Los Angeles, 1969), passim, but esp. pp. 126–39; and *The Low Countries* (Englewood Cliffs, N.J.: Prentice-Hall, forthcoming). The most comprehensive single volume on the socioeconomic evolution of Belgium from the mid-nineteenth century to the present is B.-S. Chlepner, *Cent ans d'histoire sociale en Belgique* (4th ed.; Editions de l'Université de Bruxelles, Institut de Sociologie, 1972).

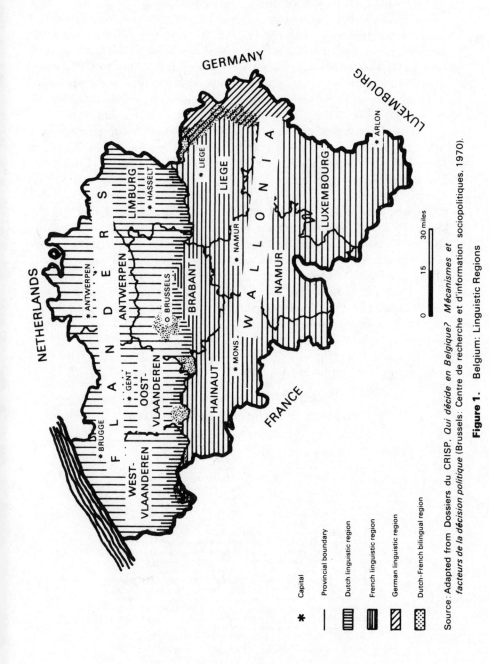

Source: Adapted from *Dossiers du CRISP, Qui décide en Belgique? Mécanismes et facteurs de la décision politique* (Brussels: Centre de recherche et d'information sociopolitiques, 1970).

Figure 1. Belgium: Linguistic Regions

figure 1—has scarcely shifted during the past fifteen hundred years, except minutely in the Brussels metropolitan area during the last two decades, a phenomenon to which I shall return. Until ten years ago, the linguistic frontier had never represented a formal political or administrative border: it was no more and no less than an interactional discontinuity, a fact of life people observed naturally or, at most, with the encouragement of social pressures. The institutionalization of the ethnic cleavage in regional terms on the output side began, in 1962–63, with the formalization of this line.)

With the advent of independence, the preeminence of *francophones* in both the political and economic arenas pulled upwardly mobile Flemings toward the French language and the *francophone* culture. This social process was responsible in large part for the siphoning off of the potential Flemish leadership element during the first century or more of Belgium's independent existence. Combined with the economic and social affects of the early, rapid, and comprehensive industrialization of the Walloon provinces (Belgium was the first continental European country to undergo thorough industrialization)—a process directed by and benefiting most the *francophone* financial and technological elites and contributing to the mobilization of the *francophone* working class through unionization—this factor helps explain why the numerically superior Flemish population (see table 1) occupied minority status in the Belgian economic, social, and political systems for well over a century.

Language and ethnicity clearly took a back seat to religion and to the center-periphery distinction as politically relevant dimensions of division in

Table 1. Distribution of the Population by Region and Language

Region and Language[a]	Population (in percent)	
	1890	*1965*
Flemish	46.6	50.7
Walloon	41.4	33.4
Bruxellois	12.0	15.9
Total	100.0	100.0

[a]The Flemish region consists of the four northern provinces of East and West Flanders, Antwerp, and Limburg, and one of the three arrondissements of the central province of Brabant. The Walloon region comprises the four southern provinces of Liège, Hainaut, Luxembourg, and Namur, and the Nivelles district of Brabant. There are fewer than 60,000 German-speaking Belgians in the eastern cantons bordering on Germany. Brussels is technically bilingual, and the legal equality of Dutch and French is maintained. In practice, however, approximately 80 percent of the population of the capital is *francophone*.

Source: Adapted from Belgian Information and Documentation Institute, "Seventy Years of Modifications in Structures of Demography and Social Economy: A Statistical Inventory," p. 2.

the nineteenth century. Nevertheless, church influence affected the ethnic cleavage during this time. It was exerted largely through the massive parochial school system. (Then, as now, approximately two-thirds of the primary school students in the Flemish provinces attended parochial schools. At present, a majority of French-speaking Belgian children attend public schools.) The church reinforced the non- or even anticosmopolitan outlook of the small-town and rural Flemish population, and it increased the gap between the *francophone*, urban, industrializing, secular center and the Flemish, rural, Catholic periphery. Communications between the Belgian communities were made even more problematic, and vestiges of the suspicions and antipathies engendered by the church-state battles still create appreciable political stress in the form of school financing arrangements—as witnessed by the crisis leading up to the *pacte scolaire* of 1958 and its renegotiation in 1972–73[27] and in debates surrounding birth control and abortion.

The church-state cleavage was institutionalized through the (Catholic and Liberal) parties, first in the parliament and then, with the extension of the franchise toward the end of the century, in the electorate itself. As Urwin observed, by 1884 ". . . the clerical-secular cleavage was fully polarized in the party system"; and "institutionalization of the religious dimension in the party system was completed after the First World War."[28]

Mass Mobilization, The Salience of Class, and
Successful Adaptation through Cooptation

If restricted political participation made the establishment of a cleavage-bridging structure easier, then the substantial demands for participation and redistribution produced by the rapid mobilization of the working class in the 1870s, 1880s, and 1890s—a phenomenon common to industrialized countries of Europe—tested that structure's adaptability.

The working-class movement in Belgium arose in an extremely hostile setting and as a consequence of very harsh industrial proletarian conditions. The catalogue of industrial capitalism's excesses in the middle and late nineteenth century is well known: inhuman working and living conditions (a workweek of 90 hours was common, families of six or eight members lived in one small, unheated room); economically compelled child labor (most children of Belgian miners were working full days in the collieries by their seventh birthday); "company stores," which forced workers to buy from them and charged prices far above those of the free market. The worker's

27. See Meynaud et al., *La décision politique*, pp. 150–76, on the earlier agreement. The recent modifications were incorporated into the "government agreement" that formed the basis of the tripartite (Socialist, Christian Social, and Liberal) Leburton government that emerged from the 1972–73 crisis. For the terms of the new pact, see Article 7 of the government agreement (reprinted in the Belgian press—e.g., *Le Peuple*, 18 January 1973, special insert).

28. Urwin, "Social Cleavages and Political Parties," pp. 324–25.

lot was made even less tolerable by the apparent lack of remedies at his disposal. The regime, whether Catholic or Liberal at any given time, was militant in its support of management: the police, the army, and the judiciary were used to keep the worker in his place; and he was denied all positions of political influence or the opportunity for political expression, including the vote. [29]

After several false starts, both the unionization process and the organization of the Workers' party gained momentum. By 1886, following a series of violent miners' strikes that elicited military as well as police action and resulted in the deaths of several miners, authorities and workers began to take each other seriously. The former tried to understand and improve the conditions of industrial and mine workers, [30] while the latter converted their rather amorphous, stress-inducing blanket demands into a program with ordered priorities, the first and initially all-encompassing goal being universal (male) suffrage. This goal was attained following an amendment of the constitution in 1893, but only after a massive and violent general strike convinced the Chamber of Representatives (which had balked at such a democratizing step on more than a dozen occasions in the preceding years) that the workers possessed real power.

Two major consequences of the extension of the franchise could be noted within a relatively short time. First, the tenfold increase in the size of the electorate brought a new major party into the political arena. (It is interesting to note, from the vantage point of the cooptation principle contained in the European polity model, that "the established elites displayed a willingness to accommodate the new party." [31]) The two-actor party subsystem, in which the Catholics and Liberals had alternated in power since the regime's origin, was converted into a three-actor situation in the early part of the twentieth century, and one-party majorities became increasingly difficult to attain. [32]

Second, partly because the Workers' party represented anticlerical

---

29. See Leon Delsienne, *Le Parti Ouvrier Belge, dès origines à 1894* (Bruxelles: La Renaissance du Livre, 1955), and *Le mouvement syndical en Belgique* (Bruxelles: Castaigne, 1936). For a look at the modern era, see Guy Spitaels, *Le mouvement syndical en Belgique* (Bruxelles: Université Libre de Bruxelles, Editions de l'Institut de Sociologie, 1967).

30. The catalogue of ills cited above was taken from the findings of a government-sponsored study commission, reporting in 1886. See Delsienne, *Le Parti Ouvrier Belge*, pp. 77–79.

31. Urwin, "Social Cleavages and Political Parties," p. 327.

32. Thus, each of the seventeen cabinets prior to the introduction of universal (male) suffrage was a one-party affair. (The first two cabinets were actually personalist or nonparty governments. They had a combined life of less than six months, and have been omitted from consideration here.) In the period 1894–1918, plural voting enabled the more conservative Catholic and Liberal parties to form homogeneous cabinets, but the need to accommodate the pressures emanating from the growing Workers' party became substantial. Since World War I, only six of forty cabinets were homogeneous, while seventeen were two-party coalitions, and seventeen (including that formed by M. Leburton at the beginning of 1973) were comprised of three or four parties.

Table 2. The Expansion of the Electorate

Year	Population (in thousands)	Voters[a] (in thousands)
1831	4,080	±46
1841	4,073	25
1851	4,473	79
1864	4,941	104
1884	5,785	126
1894[b]	6,342	1,355
1912	7,571	1,746
1925	7,812	2,081
1939	8,396	2,338
1949[c]	8,625	5,031
1971	9,670	6,271

[a]During the 1894–1914 period some voters were entitled to cast more than one vote. Thus it is important to distinguish between electors and votes. For the sake of consistency, electors are used throughout.
[b]Universal male suffrage was adopted in 1893, leading to the first of two massive increases in the electorate.
[c]As in France, women were enfranchised following World War II.

Sources: Adapted from John Gilissen, *Le Régime représentatif en Belgique depuis 1790* (Brussels: La Renaissance du Livre, 1958), pp. 188–93; and Fraeys, "Analyse des résultats," p. 384.

sentiments and partly as a consequence of the period of plural voting (1894–1919) and proportional representation, the religious cleavage remained an important factor in Belgian politics even after the socioeconomic class-based divisions had become salient. The party subsystem, operating at three levels—the electoral, the interparty elite, and parliament—had proved

Table 3. Rate of Unionization of Belgian Workers

Year	Percent of Potential Union Members in Two Largest Union Federations[a]
1910	6.88
1930	35.05
1947	40.89
1957	55.53
1967	60.87

[a]"The percentage of union workers [given here] does not include workers affiliated to other trades-union organisations such as, for instance, the General Liberal Trades-Unions Central Organisation. With no fear of exaggerating matters, therefore, it may be stated that at least 66% of all Belgian workers are members of trades-unions. This rate may be regarded as one of the highest in the European Economic Community." Senelle, p. 71.

Source: Adapted from Senelle, "Political, Economic, and Social Structures," p. 70.

effective in channeling the tide of inputs that followed rapid and substantial mobilization. Consequently, the party subsystem had become the pivot of the Belgian political system during the first half of this century. Professor Urwin summed up this development in the following terms:

> By the 1930s the three major parties had institutionalized the religious and class divisions. Through a process of structural consolidation, they had become *verzuiling* parties. The growth and scope of party organizations were extended to ancillary groups within the segments of the society whose values and interests the parties claimed to represent. [33]

Clearly the cooptive structure was operating effectively in the period between the world wars, making it possible for cleavage-derived "economic issues, like religious issues [to be] essentially resolved by bargaining around a conference table and not by an uncomplicated direct confrontation on the electoral, competitive front." [34]

But why didn't this structure similarly institutionalize the ethnic cleavage? The answer to this perplexing question can, I believe, be found in the developmental explanation I advanced earlier. Put simply, by the time the ethnic cleavage became politically critical, (1) the party subsystem had lost much of its stress-ameliorating and institutionalizing capabilities; and (2) the prevailing concerns of the Flemish and *francophone* populations were focused on matters involving autonomy or control over the formulation and implementation of policy, rather than on influencing the central policy process.

By the middle of this century, the entire population had been mobilized in a general sense, and had been divided into the *zuilen* in terms of which the society was segmented. Both Flemings and Walloons had become mobilized in political terms through the electoral system (see table 2) and in political as well as socioeconomic terms through unionization (see table 3)—Belgium is now probably the most unionized country in Europe—*before* particularistic group consciousnesses became politicized. This suggests that the ethnic cleavage was dormant from the perspective of politics until after World War II, and/or that it was crosscut by the religious and socioeconomic dimensions of division. Such was in fact the case; [35] and it ap-

---

33. Urwin, "Social Cleavages and Political Parties," p. 329.
34. Ibid., p. 330.
35. See Leo Picard, *Evolutie van de Vlaamse Beweging van 1795 tot 1950*, 3 vols. (2nd ed.; Antwerpen: Standaard-Boekhandel, 1963); Shepard B. Clough, *A History of the Flemish Movement: A Study in Nationalism* (New York: Richard R. Smith, 1930); Arie Wolter Willemsen, *Het Vlaams-nationalisme, 1914–1940* (Groningen: J. B. Wolters, 1958); Maurice-Pierre Herremans, *La Wallonie* (Bruxelles: Marie-Julienne, 1951); Meynaud et al., *La décision politique*, esp. pp. 17–147; Lorwin, "Belgium: Religion, Class, and Language," esp. pp. 158–64, 170–73; and Frank E. Huggett, *Modern Belgium* (New York: Praeger, 1969), chap. 4.

pears that the division between the Belgian communities could not become salient until structured means had been found for dealing with the basic issues of church-state relations, public vs. private realms of action, mass political participation, and social welfare.

The Cooptive Structure in Operation: The Success and Failure of the Old Regime

The current regime entered its final phase in the 1950s. This was preceded by the arraying of the body politic into vertically organized, internally more or less democratic segments representing socioeconomic interests and philosophies. The most important among these—embracing, among them, virtually all Belgians[36]—were the Catholic, the Socialist, and the Liberal. Each had its own party, its labor-union federation, its auxiliary organizations among employers and farmers, in social welfare, youth groups, sports, and the press. Each represented coherent sets of issue positions; each was, in a sense, at once a social, political, economic, and moral reference point for an important portion of the population—for a "spiritual family."

The segments and their constituent groups—varying in function, sector, size, and importance—operate in a policy-making milieu that is a specific manifestation of the general phenomenon we characterized in abstract terms in chapter 2 as the cooptive structure. Some observers find the operation of the cooptive structure dangerous, in that it can lead to barriers between policy makers and the constituencies to which they are formally accountable.[37] Others, particularly those who *are* politically accountable, often find it onerous. Thus, Paul Vanden Boeynants, then prime minister, voiced the following plaint in 1967:

> I quite realize . . . that Belgium can have only one prime minister at a time. . . . But a prime minister is surrounded by other ministers, each of whom is more or less a prime minister in his own department. And each minister is at the head of a number of civil servants whose specialized powers are, in practice, if not in name, bound up with what is commonly known as "governing." Then, outside the ministries and administrative departments, revolves a whole cosmos of more or less organized bodies with a more or less official status, usually known as "pressure groups," because, in all probability, we still have enough modesty left not to call them "governing groups."[38]

36. A good indication of the combined scope of the three major forces can be found in the combined votes received by the Christian Social, Socialist, and Liberal parties. Table 11 shows both the phenomenal coverage of the "traditional" parties in the late 1950s, before the erosion of the regime structure had become noticeable, and the progressive decline in the scope of their electoral appeal. In the 1958 legislative elections, the three traditional parties amassed 95.44 percent of all votes cast!

37. See, for instance, Huggett, *Modern Belgium*, pp. 128–29.

38. Quoted in ibid., p. 129.

Clearly, then, the cooptive structure can be a mixed blessing.[39] In Belgium some of its major assets have been that it facilitated—it might not be an exaggeration to say "made possible"—the satisfaction of both participation-oriented and redistribution-focused demands. In recent years, with remarkably slight economic structural dislocation and without significant abuses of the sort that motivated the concerns cited above, it made possible the economic democratization of the society and it contributed to the muting of socioeconomic class-based ideological conflicts. At the same time, these developments also accelerated the politicization of the ethnic cleavage and opened the door to its institutionalization on the output side of the political system. Before I take up these consequences, I shall note briefly the signs of the maturation of the Belgian welfare state.

The political influence obtained by the working class in the second phase led to substantive improvements in income and social insurance benefits, especially in the period following the Second World War. Thus, as the data in table 4 show, the real wages received by industrial workers climbed steadily from the mid-nineteenth to the mid-twentieth century, doubling approximately every fifty years; but they jumped by 63 percent in just twelve years during the third phase of the regime. The trend in the growth of the discretionary portion of workers' incomes—shown in table 5—exhibits an equally dramatic upturn in the postwar period.

Even more impressive have been expansions in the scope and increases

Table 4. The Evolution of Real Wages in Industry[a]

Year	Wage Index (1909-13 = 100)
1850	48.5
1890	83.5
1913	104.5
1921	134.2
1930	150.3
1939	165.1
1953	189.2
1965	308.2

[a] For a more comprehensive, up-to-date discussion of working-class incomes and the expansion of social security in the period 1955–71, see René Ewalenko's "Postface" to Chlepner, *Cent ans d'histoire sociale en Belgique*, pp. 428–37.

Source: Belgian Information and Documentation Institute, "Seventy Years of Modifications," p. 18, table 19.

39. See the section entitled "A Note on the Normative Implications of the Model," pp. 78–82.

Table 5. Consumption Patterns of Working-Class Families: The Trend of Disposable Income

		Consumption Category by Percent of Income			
Year	Food	Clothing	Housing	Heating and Light	Discret-ionary Income[a]
1853	67	15	8	6	4
1891	66	15	10	5	4
1908	61	5	12	7	15
1929	58	15	11	5	11
1947	44	14	11	5	26
1956	42	11	15	7	25
1961	38	11	12	6	33

[a]This rubric consists of residual income—i.e., income remaining after the four classes of essential spending specified have been subtracted from total income. Clearly it does not represent income that can be disposed of entirely according to the desires of the earner. There is, however, considerable flexibility or discretion to be exercised in its spending. Social benefits (e.g., education, earnings of retirement plans, family allowances) should be added, and contributions, taxes, etc. should be subtracted. On balance, while taxes have risen considerably in this period, social services have risen more rapidly. Thus the Belgian worker is probably better off today (in comparison with his nineteenth- and early-twentieth-century counterparts) than even the data in this table would indicate.

Source: Adapted from Belgian Information and Documentation Institute, "Seventy Years of Modifications," p. 18, table 20.

in the levels of social insurance programs. (The term "welfare" is appropriately applied to such programs only if two characteristics of most Belgian programs are taken into account: (1) they are funded almost exclusively from contributed revenues rather than general taxes; and (2) they can be drawn upon by members of all classes. Interestingly, Belgium is probably the only country in the world with a Ministry of Middle Class Affairs.) Accident and medical insurance programs—covering routine doctors' visits in many instances—are often administered by "mutuals" linked to the "spiritual families." Among the government-administered programs, the family allowance plan is one of the oldest and most generous in Europe.[40] All told, most Belgians are covered by the following programs: (1) old-age pensions, (2) paid annual holidays, (3) family allowances, (4) sickness benefits including "sickness payments" and medical attention, (5) treatment and compensation for work-connected ailments, and (6) unemployment.[41] In sum, when considering the socioeconomic progress of the last two or three decades, the gains registered by workers in the form of salary increments—impressive in themselves—should be viewed in conjunction with the extensive social welfare programs.

In the course of satisfying the redistribution demands that arose from the socioeconomic class-based cleavage, then, Belgium became a com-

40. Huggett, *Modern Belgium*, p. 197.
41. Senelle provides a full listing of coverage and schedules: "Political, Economic, and Social Structures," pp. 192–256. See also Huggett, *Modern Belgium*, chap. 11.

prehensive, highly structured welfare state. It was this development that allowed the ethnic cleavage to move to the forefront of political life and, simultaneously, opened the way for the institutionalization of that cleavage on the output side. To begin the examination of these developments, it is useful to consider the pellucid and apposite analysis made ten years ago by Lode Claes and already cited in chapter 2:

> In other countries, there is a great deal of disagreement as to how the socio-economic struggle between left and right will evolve in the welfare state. But once unanimity has been reached regarding the goals and overall structure of the welfare state itself and the system is functioning, that is to say, assuring a continually increasing amount of prosperity to all social classes—and these premises are fulfilled for the Belgium of today—the socio-economic debate is transferred from the political to the technical plane. A corollary phenomenon is a growing apathy and passivity towards socio-economic questions on the part of the masses of the population. A political vacuum is created which may be filled by other issues.[42]

The Politicization of the Ethnic Cleavage and the Collapse of the Traditional Party Subsystem

The economic democratization of the country, combined with the rapid expansion and industrialization of the Flemish provinces and the (economic) structural setbacks suffered by the Walloon region in the 1950s and early 1960s,[43] brought the Flemish population to the plateau occupied by *francophones*. The classic dilemma that had confronted Flemings for well over a century was now resolved. During the long period when economic backwardness had reinforced the social and political subordinacy of this portion of the population, becoming "Belgian" had entailed at least a tacit admission of cultural inferiority, in terms of Flemish norm structures: *"Tout Flamand qui voulait arriver devait se servir du français; comme on l'a dit: pour devenir Belge, il fallait cesser d'être Flamand."*[44] To refrain from attempts at acculturation—whether consciously, in order to preserve ethnic characteristics, or through lack of opportunity—used to mean continuing the limited (often negligible) degree of participation, opportunity, and

42. Lode Claes, "The Process of Federalization in Belgium," *Delta* 6, no. 4 (Winter 1963–64): 49.

43. For an excellent nontechnical discussion of the postwar evolution of the economy, see Huggett, *Modern Belgium*, chap. 12. For data and a technical analysis, see J. L. Litt, "Structures sociales régionales et développement économique: la population active en Belgique de 1880 à 1961," *Mutation et Région* 1972, no. 3. A profound analysis will be found in Roy, *La guerre des belges*, chap. 9.

44. Carl-Henrik Höjer, *Le régime parlementaire belge de 1918 à 1940* (Uppsala: Almqvist & Wiksells, 1946), p. 7.

benefits that the prevailing structures permitted.[45] Upward mobility, economic self-improvement, and political self-expression no longer require stepping outside the Flemish culture.

The advent of the welfare state also accelerated the termination of Flemish subordinacy. It made possible the extension of education and the accumulation of savings, since the younger generation's exclusive responsibility for meeting the needs of the old, the financial calamity of serious illness, the economic hardships of large families, and other burdens were now eased. An irony of the fortunes of war also contributed significantly to the new balance: Belgium was liberated quickly after D-Day; thus, its industrial plant escaped most of the destruction of the last months of the war. As noted, Belgian industry was concentrated in the Walloon provinces prior to World War II. Now these salvaged and repaired plants were obsolescent, and they were hard put to support the economy of the region, since they had to compete with the modern facilities that had to be constructed from the ground up in such devastated neighboring countries as the Netherlands and Germany and in the previously lightly industrialized region of northern Belgium.[46] Particularly hard hit was the coal industry, which had long been the most important base of the Walloon economy.

Economic wisdom militated in favor of channeling both domestic and foreign investment into the Flemish provinces, where a younger, more adaptable—and often cheaper and more achievement-motivated—labor pool existed. By the late 1950s the economic growth rate of the Flemish provinces was greater than that of the country as a whole, since the Walloon economy was actually contracting. In general, whether appraisals of the Belgian economy are made through formal analyses of performance measures or through informal observations, one gains a strong impression of Flemish dynamism and Walloon degression,[47] especially until about 1970, by which time both sound investment policies and politically motivated regional development programs had begun to redress the balance.

The coming of the welfare state created a need for a large bureaucracy. It would not be overly dramatic to say that *the extremely rapid growth of the (now substantial) Belgian civil service is one of the most important— and most often overlooked—forces that are determining the shape of the emerging regime. Further, this rapid growth (shown in table 6) also facilitated the institutionalization of the ethnic cleavage.* A more immediate

45. See, for example, Willemsen, *Het Vlaams-nationalisme;* and Heisler, "Political Community and Its Formation in the Low Countries," esp. pp. 182–85.

46. See, for example, T. Palasthy, "Indices bruts de prospérité régionale", *Mutation et Région* 1972, nos. 1 and 2; and Fernand Baudhuin, *Belgique 1900–1960: Explication économique de notre temps* (Louvain: Institute de Recherches Economiques et Sociales, 1961), pp. 263–66.

47. Institut nationale de statistique, "Les investissements industriels des régions linquistiques de 1955 à 1969, "*Études statistiques*, no. 27 (1972): 17–34. See also Roy, *La guerre des belges.*

consequence of this need was, however, the recruitment of large numbers of Flemish civil servants both for public contact administration in the northern provinces and for bilingual positions in the central administration. (Positions formally stipulated bilingual were generally staffed by ethnic Flemings who were more likely proficient in French than *francophones* were in Dutch. In the mid-1960s quotas were introduced, to assure ethnic parity in civil service hiring. These were not enforced uniformly and, in any event, the largest expansion of the civil service had already occurred.)

Table 6. The Expansion of the Belgian Civil Service

Year	Population Index[a]	Civil Service Index[a]
1885	100	100
1911	127	178
1920	126	191
1950	147	337
1968	163	419

[a]The base figure of 100 simply represents the number of civil servants and the size of the population in 1885. There were 28,184 civil servants at that time; and there are approximately 250,000 now—not counting the substantial number of persons employed in public agencies, such as the state police, magistrates, armed forces, and the like. Were they also counted, the civil service index, on the same 1885 base, would now be 1,007, or sixteen times the population increase during the last eighty-five years!

Source: Senelle, "Political, Economic, and Social Structures," p. 12.

Sometime in the late 1950s or early 1960s, the bureaucracy ceased to be a *francophone*-dominated establishment, although some real and much illusory "evidence" to the contrary is often cited (especially with regard to the foreign service, a branch of little interest to the concerns at hand).[48] Since the conversion of outputs (decisions, laws, rules, and regulations) into outcomes (consequences) is the bureaucracy's essential function, and since this process is crucial for the operation of the postindustrial welfare state (see pp. 63–71), this change has had a profound impact on Belgian political life. I shall elaborate on this point in the next section.

These advances were not attained by Flemings agitating politically for Flemish causes. Rather, they followed from working-class political action, personal and group initiatives, public initiatives, environmental inputs that caused structural changes in the economy, the rationally dictated system-wide extensions of social policies, and upward mobility propelled by high achievement motivation. They led to general satisfaction with the regime

48. Huggett, *Modern Belgium*, p. 165; but cf. Gordon L. Weil, *The Benelux Nations: The Politics of Small-Country Democracies* (New York: Holt, Rinehart & Winston, 1970), p. 164.

structure among Flemings, but made Walloons—who were faring less well—leery of living in a state where the formerly subordinate population had gained parity and, given its numerical advantage, might attain a position of dominance.

These developments also permitted Flemings, for the first time, to become somewhat less concerned with the substance of outputs and more with their form—and with the manner of their implementation. Economic well-being and political potency made possible the pursuit of such less tangible goals as social equality and cultural self-esteem. Huggett's observation, "Language could not become a real issue until the slow changes in society had produced more facilities of all kinds for everyone, whether Flemish or Walloon,"[49] was as valid for the first half of this century as it had been for the period for which he had originally made it—the late 1800s. Demands for "feeling at home in one's own country" replaced the classic socioeconomic and participatory demands; and the often militant expression of the newly serious Flemish goals awakened a fear of deprivation among *francophone* Belgians. The ethnic cleavage (which in the Belgian case had been identified in many minds in terms of its principal or most visible indicator—language) was rapidly politicized in the late 1950s and early 1960s. As Claes remarked in 1963,

> The conflict has been displaced from the socio-economic plane to the plane of social psychology and power. . . . The political vacuum is being filled in Belgium by two semi- or quasi-nationalisms. . . .[50]

The social-psychological dimension of ethnic confrontation is best assessed through interviews. In 1963–64 I conducted a series of interviews consisting of loosely structured informal discussions with Flemish-speaking and *francophone* Belgians of varying socioeconomic positions, and of parallel questions asked in the course of formal interviews—dealing with a broader range of subjects—with members of the Belgian political elite.[51] On the basis of these interviews I was able to distinguish important differences in the social-psychological postures of the Belgian population groups at a time when neither the erosion of the prevailing regime structure nor the eventual federalization of the state were evident.

The gains noted above encouraged the majority of Flemings to expect social and political improvements in the context of the existing structure,

49. Huggett, *Modern Belgium*, p. 38.
50. Claes, "The Process of Federalization in Belgium," p. 49.
51. See Heisler, "Political Community and Its Formation in the Low Countries," pp. 293–312. The samples were neither large enough nor selected with adequate rigor to warrant systematic generalizations for the reference groups. The findings presented in tables 7 through 10 should, therefore, be regarded as illustrative only. For a methodological note on the informal interviews and an indication of the dates, locations, and distributions of the interviews, see ibid., Appendix, pp. 386–91.

Table 7. Flemish Perceptions of
Who Controls Belgian Institutions
(in 1963–64)

Status of Respondent	Perceived Situation			Total
	Francophone/ Franskiljon[a] Control Persists	Francophone/ Franskiljon Control Is Over	Other	
Political elite[b]	7	15	1	23
Professional	9	16	2	27
Clerical	10	14	1	25
Laboring	14	12	1	27
Unclassified	6	8	1	15
Total responses	46	65	6	117

[a]*Franskiljon* is the derogatory term applied by ethnically conscious Flemings to ethnic Flemings who have adopted or who affect the *francophone* culture and the French language in Belgium.

[b]This category was distilled from the Belgian leadership groups formally interviewed on different matters in 1963–64, but who were asked to respond to the same questions used in the informal interview sequence. Of 58 individuals in leadership positions, 50 identified themselves as either Fleming or *francophone:* 23 as Flemish, 27 as *francophone.* The remaining respondents classed themselves only as "Belgian."

Source: Interviews conducted by the writer in 1963–64. See Heisler, "Political Community and Its Formation in the Low Countries," chap. 6 and appendix.

Table 8. Flemish Appraisals of the Adequacy of
the Prevailing Structure for the Pursuit of
Flemish Interests[a]

Status of Respondent	Response			Total
	Adequate	Inadequate	Other	
Political elite	18	4	1	23
Professional	16	9	2	27
Clerical	14	9	2	25
Laboring	8	18	1	27
Unclassified	10	4	1	15
Total responses	66	44	7	117

[a]Tabulated from responses to the question: "Given the present [1963–64] trends, as you see them, will the Flemish population be able to achieve satisfaction for its interests through existing Belgian institutions?"

particularly since they formed a majority of the electorate. Thus, while cultural particularism was strong, only the *Volksunie* (People's Union)—a small and relatively weak party until the mid-1960s—advocated separatism to the point of federalization on the Flemish side. The *francophone* population, on the other hand, became increasingly uncomfortable with the existing structure and the increasingly important roles Flemings were coming to play in it. It exhibited a fear of "minorisation," which represents a psychological condition, rather than an actual political or demographic

Table 9. *Francophone* Responses to the Question: "Has the Belgian State Machinery Been Captured by *Flamingants?*"[a]

Status of Respondent	Responses			Total
	Yes	No	Other	
Political elite	10	15	2	27
Professional	7	19	—	26
Clerical	8	7	1	16
Laboring	13	6	2	21
Unclassified	11	17	1	29
Total responses	49	64	6	119

[a]*Flamingant* is the term applied to militant Flemings. Impressionistically, on the basis of several subsequent sojourns in Belgium, I think the balance between "yes" and "no" perceptions on this question probably shifted in 1965 or 1966; and in the early 1970s a distinct majority of *francophones* (Walloons and French-speaking Bruxellois) would give an affirmative response.

Table 10. Francophone Responses to the Question: "Will Increased *Flamingant* Participation in Government Weaken the Political and Legal Supports of Walloon Cultural Integrity Appreciably?"[a]

Status of Respondent	Responses			Total
	Yes	No	Other	
Political elite	9	16	2	27
Professional	9	15	2	26
Clerical	9	6	1	16
Laboring	13	6	2	21
Unclassified	14	14	1	29
Total responses	54	57	8	119

[a]The attitude shift referred to in the note to table 5.9 seems to have occurred in this regard as well; and it has probably been more drastic. In the early 1970s a clear and overwhelming majority in the Walloon and *francophone* Bruxellois communities perceives such a threat—whether it is there "objectively" or not.

minority position. In essence it is a fear of *revanchist* policies or policy implemenation practices at the hands of the newly influential Flemish population—a population subordinated to *francophones* in virtually ever aspect of life for over a century.[52] It also entails the fear of becoming a permanent minority.

The attitudes reported in tables 7 through 10 indicate that working-class respondents showed markedly less satisfaction—or more insecurity— with the situations they perceived to exist in 1963–64 than did members of

52. See ibid., pp. 296–300.

the elite and of the professional class. In general, educational and occupational status varied inversely with the acceptance of the existing structure; and this underlines the social-psychological—rather than "objective"—aspect of these perceptions. However, the *francophone* political initiatives—especially in Brussels in the context of the *Front démocratique des francophones* (FDF)—toward separation soon embraced the entire socioeconomic spectrum.[53]

While movements for cultural autonomy, regional organization, and various federal arrangements are as old as Belgium itself,[54] until approximately ten years ago they were mostly restricted to the fringes of the political society. One of the direct consequences of the politicization of the ethnic cleavage was that such movements became first respectable and then "mainstream": by the late 1960s the spokesmen of the major political parties began to focus attention more on the *forms* the regionally organized state might take than on *whether* regionalization or federalization should take place. They were pushed to those positions by the remarkably swift rise of first *francophone* and then Flemish particularist parties.

The *Mouvement populaire wallon* (MPW) was formed by André Renard in 1960–61, largely on a labor-union base, with the *loi unique*—an austerity program proposed by the government for improving the generally gloomy economic situation[55]—serving as the irritant-catalyst that helped to congeal working-class socioeconomic sentiments and Walloon particularism. Perhaps because Renard's death (in 1962 at the age of fifty-one) prevented him from extending the MPW through his considerable personal and organizational resources, or because Walloons were too heterogeneous ideologically, a multitude of organizations—some of them short-lived parties, others pressure groups—was formed in the 1960s. Not until 1968 did most of these coalesce in the *Rassemblement Wallon* (RW). In the 1968 elections for the Chamber of Representatives, the RW slates obtained 10.47 percent of the votes cast in the Walloon provinces; and they stood fourth, behind the three "traditional" parties, in the southern part of the country. In the next general election, in 1971, they doubled their votes (to 20.86 percent) and edged out the Christian Social and Liberal parties, to occupy second rank behind the Socialists in Wallonia.

53. David Coombes and Richard Norton-Taylor, "Renewal in Belgian Politics: The Elections of March 1968," *Parliamentary Affairs* 22, 1 (Winter 1968–69): 67. These are also the impressions I got at meetings of the FDF and in interviews of its leaders and members during the summer of 1971 in Brussels.

54. See Rigo de Nolf, *Federalisme in Belgie als grondwettelijk vraagstuk* (Antwerpen: Nederlandse Boekhandel, 1968); and Centre de Recherches et d'Information Socio-Politique, "Tableau synthétique des projets de fédéralisme de 1931 à nos jours," *Courrier hebdomadaire* 129 (14 November 1961).

55. The best source on the *loi unique* remains Meynaud et al., *La décision politique*, pp. 214–31. On the connection between Renard's activities and the *loi unique*, see Roy, *La guerre des belges*, pp. 157 ff.

The Walloon and Bruxellois particularists (most notably, the FDF, which, in 1971, a few years after its creation, became the first party of the Brussels electoral districts, with 34.49 percent of the vote) were, on balance, more interested in erecting political and institutional safeguards against "minorisation" than in full federal separation—although there were important elements urging precisely such a "solution." (Renard himself believed in the desirability and inevitability of federalism from approximately 1950 onward.) As already noted, only the *Volksunie* had a full federalist program on the Flemish side, as recently as 1967. In 1968 it rose to third place (behind the Christian Social and Socialist parties) in the northern provinces; and, while its ranking remained unchanged in the 1971 elections, its vote total increased.

What these particularist "minor" parties had in common was that they had not been coopted and did not strive to become "cooptable"; in fact, they based their appeal to their ethnic constituencies largely on their intractable opposition to a regime that owed its success to its ability to incorporate virtually all groups and shades of opinion.[56] In a political system such as Belgium had in the post-World War II period, groups (whether based on interests or on ascriptive relationships) were likely to get favorable outputs through the regime if they became regular participants in the policy-making process. The RW, FDF, and *Volksunie*—the most important particularist forces in Wallonia, Brussels, and Flanders—did not pursue such advantages, since their aims—indeed, the reasons for their existence—were different. Instead of working for access to the policy-making machinery, they sought to dismantle it or, minimally, to alter it drastically. They clearly lacked the power to achieve this aim through their own (unconcerted) actions, but they managed it indirectly through the traditional parties, in less than a decade.

The latter first accommodated their internal structures to regional (i.e., ethnic) pressures by establishing regional wings (or, in the case of the Socialists, co-presidencies), and then moved to implement the regionalist goals through the three stages outlined in the next section. These steps simultaneously confirmed and accelerated the demise of the party subsystem structure that had been one of the hallmarks of the old regime. This, in turn, indicated that massive regime change was imminent.

The traditional parties were built to operate at the level of the whole system. While they had evolved infrastructures that accommodated ethnic distinctions, they could not become effective agents for the particularistic

56. The *Volksunie* considered its programmatic "uncooptability" a major point in its program, and crucial to its continuing and expanding appeal. (Interview with the founder and president of the *Volksunie*, Mr. Frans Van der Elst, 11 January 1964.) It is interesting to note that Mr. Van der Elst attended the funeral of André Renard in 1962, though perhaps the only link between the two was their intractable opposition to the regime. See Huggett, *Modern Belgium*, p. 146.

goals and values of the ethnic groups and the Bruxellois without losing their three major stress-ameliorating capabilities. By way of review, these were: (1) consociational bargaining among the leaders, who were also, of course, the spokesmen for the political arms of the spiritual families; (2) the conversion of politicized issue positions into relatively dispassionately negotiable, technically defined problems; and (3) serving as the cooptive core of the regime—a capability indicated by the success of the three traditional parties in preempting the electoral arena.

There were two direct manifestations of the crumbling of the party subsystem's structure. First, it can be seen in table 11 that the three major parties' share of all votes had declined rapidly and substantially. Second, the regional "wings" of the Christian Social and Liberty and Progress (the former Liberal) parties became, in fact, separate parties which formed (not entirely convincing or effective) coalitions for general elections and sometimes acted in concert in parliament, especially for the purpose of establishing and sustaining a government.

Table 11. The Decline of the Traditional Parties

Election	The Three Traditional Parties' Share (percent)	The Christian Social and Socialist Parties' Share (percent)
1958	95.44	83.61
1965	84.34	62.73
1968	80.59	59.72
1971	73.74	57.28

Source: Adapted from Fraeys, "Analyse des résultats," p. 386, table 2.

To those more accustomed to the French, Italian, or Dutch electoral scene, the drop in the traditional parties' share of the vote from 95 percent to 74 percent or of the combined total of the Christian Social and Socialist parties electoral support from 84 percent to 57 percent may not appear critical. *The cooptive structure in Belgium, however, depended on the traditional parties' monopoly for the legitimation of outputs.* The three parties were the political aspects of the segments into which the society had been organized during the preceding 130 years of the country's existence. If they, claiming to represent all shades of *reasonable* political opinion (the insignificant Communist party and the frequently changing, short-lived Flemish extremist and/or quasi-fascist parties together could not generate more than a handful of votes, and were generally justifiably ascribed to the "fringes"), defined the major issues of the day in common terms—and often agreed on a particular course of action—then the output was relatively easily legitimized.

Many important crises of modern Belgian politics had been confronted and at least partially or temporarily managed in this setting. But now the "nontraditionalist" or antiregime parties' strength cannot be written off as a statistical curiosity without political significance. Their present strength and future prospects put them on more or less even terms with the traditional parties, particularly when the second major source of the party subsystem's devastation—the division of the major parties into regional entities and splinter groups[57]—is taken into account. Given these divisions, the traditional parties have to work hard to bring together coherent *intraparty* coalitions before they can begin the increasingly problematic task of creating viable interparty coalitions.

One consequence of the decline of the traditional parties is that revisions of the constitution and the passage of important legislation requiring special majorities can no longer be undertaken by a two-party coalition, since no two parties possess the necessary two-thirds majority in the Chamber and Senate. Thus the implementation of the regionalization scheme outlined in the constitutional revisions of 1967-70, discussed below, can be achieved only if all three traditional parties—or, more accurately, the five or six parties that were the Christian Social, Socialist, and Liberal parties until a few years ago—act in concert. Since the three parties split because the conflicts entailed in ethnic differences were serious, putting together such a coalition is difficult. And once in existence, its joint course is likely to be rough. It was under these circumstances that the *francophone* co-president of the Socialist party, Edmond Leburton—the first prime minister in decades who is not, himself, bilingual—put together a "tripartite" coalition in the winter of 1972–73, with the expressed aim of implementing the regionalization plan. Whereas a few years ago the notion of a "tripartite" cabinet was synonymous with a government of national union, now it is merely a broader-than-minimal coalition, needing the adhesion of virtually every deputy from every faction of each party to provide the two-thirds majority required for the implementation of constitutional provisions.

The erosion of the party subsystem structure has critical implications for the regime's survival, but it does not jeopardize the system's ability to persist. As I have suggested, the system has moved from a condition of low mobilization and maldistribution in the nineteenth century, when the input-channeling structures were of crucial importance for the institutionalization of cleavages, to become a highly mobilized, group-politics-based welfare state, in which the administration of already achieved balances is the primary concern of the citizens.

The legitimation of outputs now depends more on the rationalized operation of the cooptive policy-making and output implementation processes than on the operation of the party subsystem. Consequently, such

---

57. Thus, when Edmond Leburton's proposed "tripartite" cabinet and the governmental agreement or program on the basis of which it would operate were brought before the memberships of the prospective coalition partners, the Belgian press headlined "five party congresses meet on the government accord." See, for instance, *De Standaard*, 22 January 1973.

questions as "What value referents will be used in decision-making?" or "Who is going to implement decisions, at what level, and with how much sensitivity to the cultural milieux of the client groups?" have replaced questions about "Who will get how much?" or "How will our needs be satisfied, and our position represented?" In the final section, I shall note the major features of the emerging regime, as they bear on these questions—questions that underlie the institutionalization of the politicized ethnic cleavage in Belgium.

The Particularization of Outputs: Toward Regionalization

The development of a cooptive policy-making structure and the growing importance of the output side of the system were adumbrated earlier. Also noted was the devastating effect of the politicization of the ethnic cleavage on the traditional party subsystem—a crucial component of the cooptive structure. During the past decade the slow processes through which a politicized societal division *may* become institutionalized have been converting the politically relevant concerns of Belgians into distinctions between issues that affect them as Belgians and matters to which they turn their attentions as Flemings, Walloons, and—in an inconsistently and incompletely defined sense—as Bruxellois. Beginning with the legal formalization of the historic "linguistic frontier" in late 1962, and culminating in a constitutionally redefined state in which the three partially autonomous regions correspond to the presumed ethnic reality, these processes have sought to provide distinct contexts for the legitimization of outputs.

The politicians who designed and engineered these measures—for the most part leaders of the traditional parties—have been accused of yielding to extremist pressures, of doing the currently popular thing for immediate electoral rewards—in general, of base expediency. While such criticisms are partly valid, the regionalization venture can also be supported on theoretical and practical bases on a higher ground. For the confrontation between the ethnic groups seemed of the zero-sum sort, wherein each considered gains accruing to the others—actually or in their minds' eye—to have come at their own expense.[58] When groups are locked into a zero-sum confrontation, regardless of the "objective reality" (or social-psychologically-induced "reality") of the situation, institutionalized separation may be the best means for reducing stress in the system to manageable levels.[59]

The perspective of Huntington's concept of institutionalization is particularly relevant to the Belgian experiment with regionalization. Recall

58. See the discussion of the zero-sum game syndrome on pp. 43 f.
59. See, for example, Ralf Dahrendorf, *Class and Class Conflict in Industrial Society* (Stanford: Stanford University Press, 1959), passim; and Enloe, *Ethnic Conflict and Political Development*, esp. chaps. 4 and 5.

that, for Huntington, institutionalization occurs when "organizations and procedures acquire value and stability," when they become vehicles for legitimization. People have to accept the organizations on their own terms, through their own values, and in terms of their own expectations and aspirations. In other words, the organizations and procedures that act as means for legitimization have to be legitimate.

When, in an earlier developmental phase, the political parties were the crucial organizations and input processes the vital processes for institutionalizing politically salient conflicts in Belgium, they possessed such legitimacy. Now the output side is important; and the processes and agencies of decision making and implementation have to meet that test.

In increasing numbers and in more and more truculent terms, Belgians have indicated a gross dissatisfaction with and distrust of the traditional unitary processes and organizations. Walloons are particularly afraid that the numerical superiority and economic and political dynamism (and, just possibly, revanchist motivations) of Flemings will lead to a progressively disadvantageous decision-making situation, in which they will not obtain "their fair share" of outputs. Flemings, especially since their political and economic achievements in the postwar period, have bitterly complained about cultural (principally, though not exclusively, linguistic) discrimination and "imperialism" on the part of *francophones*. The formal delineation of spheres of authority and modes of application in ethnic terms— legally erected and sanctioned barriers to cultural interpenetration, in effect—seems a not altogether unwarranted experiment.

Separation: From Linguistic Segregation to Administrative Regionalism

The regionalization process has gone through three phases. The first consisted of a legal and administrative formalization of the de facto "lingustic frontier" that has demarcated the southern limits of the Dutch language and the northern extent of French for nearly fifteen hundred years.[60] The second involved the administrative and budgetary separation of some particularly sensitive public policy sectors, such as education, cultural affairs, regional planning. This process—I shall refer to it by its connotation-rich French name of *dédoublement*—has been very costly, but some measures of success in terms of defusing these areas of sharp conflict

60. On the history of this remarkably stable social and cultural demarcation line, see the short but brilliant standard, Charles Verlinden, *Les origines de la frontière linguistique en Belgique et la colonisation franque* (Bruxelles: La Renaissance du Livre, 1955); and J. Stengers, *La formation de la frontière linguistique en Belgique, ou la légitimité de l'hypothèse historique* (Bruxelles: Latomus, 1959); and Heisler, "Political Community and Its Formation in the Low Countries," pp. 86–90. The late Pieter Geyl, the most outstanding historian of the Low Countries in modern times, largely based an extensive and much controverted theory of the "Greater Netherlandish Nation"—i.e., the organic unity in history of the Flemish and Dutch populations—on the linguistic frontier.

has already been noticeable. The third, most recent, comprehensive and dramatic phase involves the full regionalization of the country. A major revision of the constitution was necessary to build the legal base for this step. That was completed in 1970.[61] The arduous and not at all routine stage of implementing the regionalization scheme is now at hand.

The Formalization of the Linguistic Frontier

The historic boundary—never before an actual political demarcation line—has remained virtually unchanged since the last days of the Roman Empire or, at any rate, the century after its demise. The only visible shifts have occurred of late in the Brussels metropolitan area, where the expanding city has overflowed into the surrounding countryside. The city is slightly to the north of the line dividing the language groups (see figure 1). It is predominantly French-speaking,[62] international, and cosmopolitan. Through suburbanization, it has insinuated its culture into the Flemish religious, traditionalist farm region around it, creating predictable conflicts. These tensions have contributed to the Flemish pressure to restrict the Brussels region outlined in the new constitutional scheme to the core city itself—thereby stifling further expansion.

The population on either side of the line is remarkably homogeneous, *from the point of view of language*. While no reliable census data on language usage or preference exist,[63] an estimated 95 percent of the in-

61. See Robert Senelle, "The Revision of the Constitution: 1967–1970 (August–December 1970)," *Memo from Belgium* 132–133 (January–February 1971).

62. There are no reliable census data on language usage for Brussels (or, for that matter, for the rest of the country, as I suggest in note 63). It is generally estimated that approximately 80 percent of the population is principally or exclusively French-speaking, while approximately 20 percent is mainly or only Flemish-speaking. Two factors should be kept in mind when working with these figures: (1) many apparently *francophone* Bruxellois—especially such members of the petit-bourgeoisie as storekeepers and government clerks—are native speakers of Flemish who find it profitable to use French in their public lives (e.g., they operate a business in an exclusively *francophone* neighborhood); and (2) there is a slow though steady influx of provincials into the city—which has a flourishing economy and the lowest unemployment rate in the country—presently weighted toward the Flemish provinces but liable to shift.

63. Figures were adjusted somewhat from an "unofficial" tabulation given me by a staff member at the Institut National de Statistique (Brussels) in 1963. That handwritten sheet indicated that in five of the nine provinces more than 98 percent of the native, non-German-speaking population spoke either exclusively or primarily Flemish (in Limburg and East Flanders) or French (in Luxembourg province, Namur, and Liège), while between 94 percent and 97 percent spoke the legally designated language in West Flanders and Hainaut. The city of Antwerp was accorded an 18 percent *francophone* minority, while the rest of the province was said to be more than 95 percent Flemish-speaking. These figures are probably close to the actual situation, but the militant Flemish posture of my source makes a cautious use advisable. Verification is not possible, but informal information obtained in more recent visits to provincial centers has confirmed specific entries and led to but slight modification of a few. Of course, some persons use both languages but prefer one. Since 1962, language is stipulated by law, according to place of residence: the number of Flemish and Walloon people in Belgium is indicated for official purposes by the general population figures for the Flemish and French language areas on the linguistic map of Belgium. This is the manner in which the figures presented in table 1 were derived, for instance.

habitants (not including aliens) of each of the four northern and four southern provinces speak their "official language,"[64] with the actual proportion probably exceeding 98 percent in all but the largest cities. Antwerp, in particular, has a substantial French-speaking population. Members of the upper and upper-middle classes, for the most part they have so far appeared able to cope with the problems introduced by the linguistic laws. The central providence of Brabant, which has been divided into three regions— Brussels, formally bilingual (i.e., French and Dutch are both recognized and public agencies must accord full equality to the two languages); a Flemish district in the north; and a somewhat smaller French-language district in the south—is also quite readily divisible in these terms.

Thus, in 1962 a broadly based Christian Social–Socialist coalition created a "linguistic regime" which regulates the administrative, legal, and educational use of language: Dutch is the official language in the northern portion of the country, French is used in the south, and both prevail in Brussels. This measure has facilitated the administration of public policy from the point of view of client-citizen and bureaucrat alike. Private relationships and everyday life have been complicated for some—especially for travelers, in this day of the family car and the high-speed autoroute. Stories recounting discourtesies and discrimination are numerous. There is a lack of freedom—a lack of choice—involved in this arrangement (as well as a tenseness signaled by a complete absence of humor), but to date there has been little public concern expressed.

More troublesome have been problems involving enclaves. Three instances became important because they were rapidly and dramatically politicized: (1) the Fourons (*Voer* in Dutch); (2) Mouscron-Comines; and, most important, (3) the French-language branch of Louvain, the great Catholic university. The Fourons consist of six small agricultural villages with a combined population of 4,500. They are bounded on the west by the

---

There are no census data for language, because in the late 1950s the census itself became politicized. Some Flemish political figures saw the periodic census as a referendum on language preference, and feared that the internationally more significant position of French would woo upward mobile, educated Flemings away from their mother tongue. Some *francophones* sought to defer the census because they suspected it would show a relatively substantial loss in the number of *francophones* (whose birthrate is much lower than that of Flemings), thereby putting the minority into an even more disadvantageous position. For an excellent description and analysis of the politicization of the census, see Paul M. G. Lévy, *La querelle du recensement* (Bruxelles: Institut Belge de Science politique, 1960).

64. The constitution recognizes three "national languages": Dutch, French, and German. Historically, language was determined by the user (or, in the case of children, by parents). Now, the law provides for the exclusive use of the first or the second in designated areas: the Flemish region is associated with Dutch, the Walloon region with French; and both are to have currency in Brussels on a legally equal basis. The 50,000–60,000 German-speaking Belgians in the eastern cantons are apparently denied "equal protection" in terms of language usage in the capital and in most governmental business. The cost of conducting business in two languages is substantial, and the prospect of doing it in three is frightening to Belgian administrators. The very small rural, provincial German minority has not pressed for consistency.

Meuse River, on the north by the Netherlands, on the east by Germany, and on the south by the *francophone* province of Liège. The inhabitants speak a Low German dialect which, while linguistically more closely related to Dutch than to French, is manifestly neither, and have long had economic and cultural links with Liège. They were, nevertheless, relegated to the Dutch side of the linguistic frontier (as a part of the province of Limburg) by a Flemish-controlled parliament. Inasmuch as a large majority of the residents has expressed a strong preference for association with Liège, their case has become a rallying point for *francophones*. Mouscron-Comines involved two larger communities with a total population of approximately 75,-000 French-speaking people, which had been part of the province of West Flanders. In 1963 they were transferred to the French-language side of the line, to the province of Hainaut. The third case, that of Louvain, brought the downfall of the government of Paul Vanden Boeynants in 1968. The university, the larger and more important section of which is French-speaking, is located in the Flemish portion of Brabant Province; and it served as an irritant to Flemish particularists—especially students and faculty at the Flemish branch of the university, Leuven. Riots and a long-lasting system-wide public debate resulted in the decision to move the French-language section south of the linguistic frontier. Construction of the new campus is now underway.

The most important long-term effect of the 1962 language law was that it provided a legal status for the linguistic frontier. North of the line, the use of Flemish in public business and in education became exclusive; in the south, French came to occupy the same position. For Flemings, the exercise of their mother tongue and their culture would never again require an act of psychological assertion—to wit, "We are as good as they are." The law provided a counterweight to the international attraction of French. For Walloons, the possibility that the numerical superiority and increasing political power of Flemings would be converted into cultural—or, for that matter, geographic—imperialism became more remote.

Implementation posed no problems since, as already noted, in practice the Walloon provinces had been administered in French by *francophones*, and French was the language used in education. Virtually the same homogeneity of language usage existed in the north. In fact, the implementation of the law generally facilitated the legitimization of administrative acts. Further, from the point of view of subsequent steps toward regionalization, *this formal distinction of linguistic regions prepared the way for the separation of authority on a regional basis.*

Dédoublement: Toward Cultural Autonomy Through Administrative Separation

The bulk of the power of a modern bureaucracy will be found between the central decision-making subsystem and the public contact level. For, while the public contact administrator is instrumental in effecting outcomes and the decision makers formulate the general guidelines for administration, the functionally organized agencies generate the technical information and budget proposals in terms of which the latter make overall policy and budgetary allocations. It is in the agencies that specific substantive policies, priorities, and modalities of implementation are developed and program evaluations made.

The same pressures for cultural autonomy that led to the language law of 1962 also militated in favor of autonomy for the functional agencies. The Lefèvre-Spaak coalition cabinet, alluded to earlier in connection with the encoding into law of the linguistic frontier, initiated both the *dédoublement* process and the constitutional regionalization of the country.[65] The process began with the largest functional area from a budgetary standpoint: education and culture. Served by the Ministry of National Education and Culture, the sector accounted for approximately 18 percent of the central government's expenditures—the largest item in the budget—in the early 1960s, prior to its division.[66] In addition to being unwieldy because of its size, multiplicity, and complexity of tasks, the Ministry also worked with the ethnically most sensitive subject areas. In practice, the Lefèvre-Spaak government distinguished between the French and Dutch-language communities' affairs in the Ministry, by appointing one cabinet member to the post of Minister of National Education and Culture and charging him with the administration of public school programs and primary responsibility for *francophone* affairs, while naming another to be Minister for Culture, in charge of Dutch-language cultural matters and the state's side of the administration and oversight of nonpublic education (principally consisting of the administration of the parochial school assistance programs that emerged from the *pacte scolaire* in 1958).

This "in-house" arrangement proved temporary. By January 1963—less than two years after the entry into office of the government—the structure of the Ministry was altered by the division of educational and cultural matters into separate agencies, with only a secretariat linking them. For some time the formal lines of responsibility were unclear.[67] In the Harmel cabinet (1965-66), a Minister of National Education and three cabinet-level secretaries of state were appointed. The minister was charged with *franco-*

65. For a summary of Prime Minister Lefèvre's important speech to the Mars et Mercure Club, in December 1963—in which the *dédoublement* and projected constitutional regionalization programs of the coalition were outlined and justified—see Senelle, "Political, Economic, and Social Structures," pp. 71–73.

66. See Daniel Norrenberg, "La gestion du Ministère de l'Education nationale et de la Culture," *Res Publica* 10, no. 3 (1968): 373–81. In addition to this article, my information regarding the unfolding of *dédoublement* in the agencies has come from interviews with administrators on both sides of the linguistic aisle, conducted principally in 1963–64 and in June–September 1971, in Brussels.

67. Norrenberg, "La gestion du Ministère," esp. pp. 373–75.

phone educational matters, while one secretary assumed charge of Dutch-language education and the other two directed Dutch and *francophone* cultural affairs. Inasmuch as some former power of the formerly monolithic ministry continued to adhere to the office, the minister in charge of *francophone* education and not superordinate to his three colleagues sought to assert a "senior" role. The only workable arrangement appeared complete separation; and by 1966 each of the four agencies (i.e., French and Dutch-language departments of education and similarly distinct departments of cultural affairs) prepared and submitted a separate budget, which was debated and voted upon separately in parliament.[68]

Public works, housing, land use and environmental planning, and most aspects of economic planning and development have been similarly distinguished and separated on the administrative plane since then. In sum, *between 40 percent and 50 percent of the central government's expenditures are now appropriated for functional tasks administered in a regionally distinguished manner.*[69] In the incoming Leburton government, thirteen of thirty-six ministers or cabinet-level secretaries of state are charged with a regionally identified responsibility, and the number of agencies in which in-house distinctions have been formalized in the last seven years is substantial.

Dédoublement has paved the way toward formal regionalization, especially since the group actors working through the cooptive processes characterizing Belgian policy making have had time to reorient their thrust toward ethnically identifiable public organisms. As the Swiss federal experience has shown and the patterns found in the European Communities discussed in the next chapter suggest, the group-actor–administrative agency networks that are a distinguishing feature of the European polity type system[70] do not require a unitary state context; and the Belgian structure seems to be retaining its essential problem-solving capabilities vis-à-vis the sectors that have or are experiencing *dédoublement*.

The impact of *dédoublement* on the institutionalization of the ethnic cleavage appears very substantial. While the overall budgetary allocation for ethnically distinct departments will continue to be made at the central level (along with the budgets of other departments), until the regionalization becomes fully operative within a few years, program planning and implementation in the most sensitive areas now take place inside the cultural

68. Ibid., p. 377.

69. These estimates were derived in the following manner: (1) the de facto administrative division of an agency was established through interviews in 1971; then (2) the overall functional area's budget was obtained from Senelle, "Political, Economic, and Social Structures," pp. 164–65; and (3) "on-balance" judgments were made regarding the preponderance of split or nonsplit agencies by functional area. The only major budgetary categories in which no significant effects of *dédoublement* were noted were national debt (18.1 percent in 1970), national defense (7.1 percent), and state insurance (8.6 percent). Several other areas showed important but not overwhelming *dédoublement*, and thus were treated as not (yet) split.

70. See, especially, type characteristics J through N of the European polity model in chap. 2.

community. Political, economic, locality, and other dimensions of disagreement are present in the processes of making and administering policy, of course. The cooptive mechanisms noted will in all likelihood manage these at the regional level at least as effectively as they have until recently for the overall system. The ethnic dimension has been largely removed in the divided sectors, and Flemings and *francophones* can now relate to outputs and output implementation in terms of consistent sets of norms closely linked with the cultural community. In this sense, *dédoublement* has helped to convert politically loaded issues into technically treatable matters.

Regionalization: The Revised Constitution

The language legislation of 1962 that helped to institutionalize ethnic cleavage, and the separation of the administrative subsystem—or, more accurately, of some agencies in it—into Flemish and *francophone* organisms was an important step in the management of the stress induced by the politicization of the differences between the cultural communities. Five important lacunae remained: (1) providing input-side control—i.e., channels for the expression of the political will of each region's populace, (2) the systematic distribution of the powers of the central and regional authorities, (3) creating overall executive coordination at the regional level, (4) the special problems of the bilingual capital region of Brussels, and (5) especially in light of the alien nature of regionalism vis-à-vis Belgian political and constitutional theory and practice, a philosophical justification. The constitutional revisions promulgated in 1970 helped fill the first and second gaps, but they made little progress with the other three. Nevertheless, the implementation of regionalism is about to begin.

Given limitations of space and purpose, I shall not attempt to describe the revised Belgian constitution here. [71] Rather, I shall restrict this very brief review to points germane to the institutionalization of the ethnic cleavage.

A number of new entities are designated by the new constitution, some of which are not particularly important. Thus, while at one point (Article 3b) four linguistic regions are identified (the French, the Dutch, the bilingual Brussels-Capital, and the German), only three are accorded formal legal and administrative powers: the Walloon, Flemish, and Brussels regions (Article 107d). Similarly, while three cultural communities are distinguished—in conformity with the three recognized "national" languages (Article 3c), only two—the Dutch and the French—are accorded legal and institutional autonomy for decision-making purposes.

The Dutch and French cultural communities' legislation will be un-

71. See Robert Senelle, "The Revision of the Constitution 1967–70," *Memo from Belgium* 128–129 (September–October 1970), and "The Revision of the Constitution 1967–1970 (August–December 1970)." See also the quarterly of the Belgian Institute of Political Science, *Res Publica* 13, nos. 3–4 (1971), an issue devoted to symposia on federalization in Belgium.

dertaken by "cultural councils," consisting of the members of the French and Dutch linguistic groups in the Chamber and the Senate of the Belgian parliament (Article 59b). The spheres of legislative authority encompass cultural and educational matters (excluding from the latter "all matters appertaining to student unrest, compulsory education, teaching structures, diplomas, subsidies, salaries and the standards of governing student populations"), and the use of languages in most contexts. The cultural councils' decrees are binding in their respective regions and, to the extent that such institutions can be identified with one or the other cultural community, for institutions in Brussels as well.

The provision establishing the three regions (Article 107d) has attracted most attention from Belgian analysts. It makes possible the establishment of comprehensive regional governments for Brussels, Flanders, and Wallonia. The legislative and executive institutions of these regions remain unspecified; and, while such an arrangement is possible, the cultural councils may not be the general legislative organs of the new regions. The constituent assembly that drafted the revisions envisioned the regional authorities' jurisdiction to be very broad. It noted the following, not comprehensive, areas "by way of guidance: town planning, land development, real estate policy; regional economic expansion and employment; housing; family and demographic policy [particularly crucial at a time when the religious cleavage is rising to the fore again, in connection with policy toward birth control and abortion—a policy area in which the generally secularized French-language population and the more devout Catholic Flemish population are far apart]; fishing, hunting, and forestry; tourism and accommodation policy." [72]

The law-making procedure stipulated for the regions is interesting and important. Laws made by the not-yet-specified legislative bodies for the regions "must [also] be passed with a majority vote within each linguistic group of both Houses [of the Belgian parliament], providing the majority of the members of each group are present and on condition that the total votes in favour in the two linguistic groups attains two thirds of the votes cast" (Article 107d, para. 3). Thus regional self-government is subject to a central governmental check (i.e., the votes in the two houses of parliament), and a modicum of support must come from the other linguistic group in parliament.

A special protection was accorded *francophones* at the overall system level by the provision (Article 86b) that "with the possible exception of the Prime Minister, the Cabinet comprises an equal number of French-speaking and Dutch-speaking ministers." Paralleling this provision, the regional executive of Brussels, the bilingual region, will also have linguistic parity. Given the already noted numerical superiority of *francophones* in the

72. Senelle, "The Revision of the Constitution 1967–1970 (August–December 1970)," p. 29.

capital, this measure must be regarded as special protection for Flemish-speaking citizens in the Brussels region.

The capital region, treated in Article 108c of the new constitution, presents more problems than it resolves. Indeed, the special circumstances of Brussels are probably the most likely to produce difficulties for the entire regionalization undertaking.

Brussels is located in Flemish Brabant; it is predominantly *francophone*. The political balance has shifted from the Liberals and the Christian Social party (French wing) to the militantly federalist FDF during the last few years. Yet it is understandable that not only Flemish-speaking residents of the city but also Flemish-speaking citizens of the country should want to feel at home in their capital. The pressure toward the (Flemish) surrounding areas has resulted in a quarantine by Flemish politicians: they have sought to restrict the capital region to the nineteen communes (boroughs) that have comprised the city proper for many decades. Bruxellois, on the other hand, tend to feel that the city must have the opportunity to expand through "natural" urban-suburban processes. Additionally, most *francophone* residents are extremely uneasy with the prospect of linguistic parity in the region's government. They argue that in addition to being the country's capital—perhaps before it is the country's capital—Brussels is their place of work and home. Given the more than three-to-one majority they enjoy, linguistic parity for the regional executive represents in effect a denial of that degree of cultural autonomy accorded the other regions.

There is no simple solution to the problem of Brussels. The situation promises to remain intractable for the foreseeable future, and it is conceivable that it will seriously and adversely affect the general regionalization venture. It is ironic that these difficulties should come to the surface at a time when the city's international role and economic situation—as well as a modest cultural revival—make it an increasingly interesting and important place in which to live and work.

When a stress-troubled country purposefully undertakes major regime changes, the rationalist hopes that the petty aspects of day-to-day political life will not leave lasting marks on the less time-bound work of shaping the rules and institutions by which the system will operate. Such a wish is generally forlorn, and its wisdom should not be assumed a priori.[73] In any event, some idiosyncratic imprints are already noticeable in the current work of Belgium's politicians-become-regime-builders. The three-party (five-party) Leburton government was formed in such a manner that M. Leburton's inability to work in Flemish was "bargained" against con-

---

73. Students of the American Constitution's drafting are familiar with the story—perhaps apocryphal—that the responsibility of the presidency for the function of commander in chief of the armed forces devolved upon that office because the Founding Fathers expected George Washington to be elected the first president, and everyone thought he made such a fine commander in chief.

cessions to the Flemish Christian Social and Liberal factions in the coalition. The shape of the Brussels region (especially the critical question of whether the region will or will not be restricted to the nineteen urban communes) may be determined by the relative balance between M. Leburton and his Socialist party on the one hand and the powerful Flemish-language Christian Social group (CVP) on the other.

Regionalization: A Summary

Each phase has contributed appreciably to the institutionalization of the ethnic cleavage. By dividing 90 percent of the country's population and 99 percent of its area into either Flemish or *francophone* entities, *the law establishing the linguistic regions in effect decreed that the ethnic cleavage should be regarded as permanent and right.* While clearly not all Belgians have accepted this, it is equally evident that for a large majority of Flemings and *francophones* political decisions and processes of policy implementation appear more acceptable—especially in the subject areas touched by linguistic, cultural, and historical feelings of ethnic identity—and, therefore, they will be more readily institutionalized. *Dédoublement* and constitutional regionalization have, in a sense, rounded out that first legitimation of linguistic particularism.

The old epithet long used by *francophone* as well as Flemish polemicists, "There are no Belgians—only Flemings and Walloons," seems to be changing to "By law, there will be no Belgians." Regionalization began in the early 1960s, almost as soon as the religious and socioeconomic-class cleavages had ceased to be important. The old regime's structure did not institutionalize the ethnic cleavage, but it never had an opportunity to try: regionalization, or at least some form of substantial cultural autonomy, was preordained by the 1962 language law.

Dédoublement generated an arena—albeit a short-lived one—for legitimizing most of the important outputs in daily life. While it was highly effective in removing ethnic considerations from many policy sectors, the input side's elaboration on the regional plane and the constitutional completion of these administrative modes of ameliorating stress was as necessary as it was predictable.

As the constitutional revision has not yet been implemented, it is not possible to judge the effectiveness of its provisions for institutionalizing the cleavage between *francophones* and Flemings. Nevertheless, the number of crucial questions that remain not only unanswered but also inarticulately formulated is substantial: (1) the problems surrounding Brussels-Capital are serious; (2) the nature of the regional executives and legislatures is uncertain; (3) the relationships between the regional and central government will take shape more as a consequence of practice than on the basis of constitutional stipulation. The superordinacy of the central government's parliament is not in question. Depending upon the final provisions made by that body for the regional assemblies, however, we may see a situation in which, for all intents and purposes, the central parliament is simply an assembly of the regional bodies. Put another way, the regional bodies will consist of segments of parliament. How then will the electorates weigh their preferences? Will the regional role of their representative be deemed more or less important than his role as a Belgian legislator? All these questions militate in favor of deferring a judgment on the regionalization venture. But it does seem warranted to say that if the revamping of the regime is accepted as a feasible course of action, then the separation of the populations (in terms of the language regions) and the bifurcation of culturally sensitive areas of administration has led to a degree of institutionalization of the ethnic cleavage on the output side of the political system.

Conclusions

One sign of the feebleness of the old cooptive regime in Belgium is that the current (January 1973) parliamentary opposition consists of three parties (the *Volksunie*, FDF, and RW) which are also opposed to the regime. The Belgian regime structure was effective in mediating profound and pervasive cleavages for over a century. The structure was established by a consociational elite in the period prior to mass mobilization. In this context Belgians became full, meaningful participants in the political and economic systems. The regime structure was adaptable enough to welcome ultraconservative and radical leftist, devout Catholic and militant anticlerical, pacifist and militarist. It permitted the development of the economic and political potentials of the population—and even of its geographic location. The cleavages it institutionalized so successfully were hardly less important than those which brought coups, revolutions, and civil wars to countries such as Austria, France, Spain, and Northern Ireland.

The old structure did not institutionalize the ethnic cleavage, for reasons already elaborated. It managed, however, to prepare for peaceful regime change; and it began the institutionalization of the cleavage even in its last years through its important and adaptable administrative subsystem.

The regime change can, in fact, be analyzed in terms of the developmental notions outlined in chapter 2. In particular, if European polity-like systems manifest a salience of the output side and a decline in the importance of the input side, then it is reasonable to expect that the greatest stabilizing and support generating capabilities will be found on the output side. Hence the decline in the efficacy of the party subsystem-based cooptive structure in the old regime should not have been unexpected, nor should it have been surprising that the basic steps of the new regime would involve administrative accommodations to the ethnic division.

It will be interesting to see whether the preeminence of the Christian Social party (more precisely, of its Flemish wing, the CVP) will be reflected in the regional political subsystem of Flanders. Similarly, the future evolution of the parties in the south and in Brussels should be watched with attention. Will, in the latter two settings, the Socialists, Christian Socials, and Liberals regain their earlier importance in electoral terms as the particularist parties' original platforms are largely realized through the regime change? Or will the FDF and RW in the south, and the *Volksunie* in the north, continue to agitate for full federal separation? If the latter situation prevails, how will the electorate respond to these demands for still greater separation?

Finally, there is reason to anticipate the emergence of a cooptive polity-type structure—though perhaps of a different and more complex variety. The cooptive bargaining habit is, as Lijphart has suggested, hard to break.[74]

---

74. Lijphart, "Consociational Democracy," pp. 216–17.

6

Leon N. Lindberg

The Political System of
the European Community*

Introduction

It is a basic fact of politics that political preferences or "values" and political resources, no less than economic values and resources, are unevenly distributed and relatively scarce. How advantages are distributed is the fundamental concern of the study of politics. In any society conflicts among political preferences are endemic. The fundamental political question is to know how particular preferences come to predominate. From this perspective, the decision-making process is one of the critical facets of politics. Thus, politics is that process whereby values are authoritatively allocated for a given society.

Since the sixteenth century, the basic political unit within which this allocation has typically taken place has been the state. It is one of the unique (and most studied) characteristics of the new "European society" that a substantial range of authoritative policy choices, involving major economic and political stakes, have been and are being made in a new political arena which transcends the individual states.

In establishing the European Community the participating nation-states committed themselves not only to the goal of a customs union and to an eventual economic union and, hence, to refrain from certain kinds of activities that had been traditional expressions of national autonomy (e.g.,

---

* The description and analysis of the European Community political system that follows on pages 225 to 249 are reprinted with only minor changes from chapter 3 of Leon N. Lindberg and Stuart A. Scheingold, *Europe's Would-Be Polity: Patterns of Change in the European Community* © 1970 (reprinted by permission of Prentice-Hall, Inc., Englewood Cliffs, New Jersey). The introduction and conclusion are the responsibility of Leon N. Lindberg alone.

raising tariffs, setting quotas on imports, etc.). They also undertook to set up a series of institutions, to which they assigned a variety of tasks, ranging from a simple secretariat to an ultimate decision maker. They laid the foundations of a distinctly new collective decision-making process, which in the intervening years has grown rapidly in scope and political significance and has progressively enfolded the member governments in a kind of symbiotic decision-making relationship. That is to say, these governments are obliged to take more and more decisions together and in association with so-called supranational institutions, which are intended to represent the presumed common interests of the members and of a nascent "Europe." The power of final decision on most matters of political significance remains with the national governments involved; yet the process by which they decide is very different from autonomous national control. The difference derives from the fact that most decisions must be taken on proposals from the "supranational" institution, and only after bargaining and exchanging concessions among the governments.

As the governing elites of the six founding countries (France, Germany, Italy, Netherlands, Belgium, Luxembourg) have gone about the task of creating a system of rules, a set of transnational institutions, and a unique collective decision-making process, they have confronted problems and invented solutions in a fashion strikingly analogous to that of the segmented, pluralistic national societies considered in this volume. The political system that has evolved, described in the pages that follow, shares many of the type characteristics identified by Arend Lijphart, Val Lorwin, and Martin Heisler. It will be seen that in the European Community polity—or "would-be polity," as we have termed it—the input side is indeed atrophied, structural cooptation is the prime means for generating elite support and broad legitimation, and administrative decision making and technocratic control are dominant.[1] The societal environment for this system is indeed characterized by political cultural heterogeneity, or fragmentation, or segmental pluralism, or separate "pillars"—in this case six (and now nine) nation-states with long histories of separation, if not mutual enmity, and with proud cultural and linguistic traditions.

This essay also points out that the historical process whereby the governing elites of these separate societies created the European Community system has closely followed Heisler's three logical developmental stages:

1. "Elites at the system and group levels seek to cope with the divisive effects of groups that manifest predispositions to assert particularistic or narrowly perceived interests."[2] Governing elites in post-World War II Europe were confronted with a need to search for solutions to the twin tasks of *economic reconstruction*, which seemed to require an unprecedented degree of cooperation between nations, and of *political* reconstruction, so as

1. See Martin O. Heisler, with Robert B. Kvavik, chap. 2 in this volume, pp. 36–37.
2. Ibid., p. 78.

to create situations in which nationalism and competition could not once again plunge Europe into destructive internecine warfare.

2. The institutional solutions to these problems were to create elaborate cooptative mechanisms assuring access to national (sectoral) decision makers and at the same time to establish system-wide leadership and administrative roles. And "once coopted, the group leaders [national elites] begin to formulate their concerns less in terms of distributive zero-sum games and more in terms of technical-problem solving, satisficing, administrative amelioration of problems, and maximizing stabilizing conditions at the system-level."[3] The implicit European Community decision rules or "procedural code," which reflect this process of accommodation, bear a striking resemblance to the seven "rules of the game" described by Lijphart for the consociational Netherlands:[4] a pragmatic and nonexpressive orientation to politics; respect for the fundamental convictions of each party and commitment to rule by "concurrent majority"; the handling of all important matters at "summit meetings"; adherence to proportionality in the distribution of policy outcomes; the use of complicated economic arguments or legal principles to neutralize sensitive issues; and secrecy and executive discretion in decision making as a requirement for flexibility and pragmatic compromise.

3. "The effectiveness of the system—and subsequent feedback induced public response to its operation—is judged largely in terms of the effective delivery of desired values and things."[5] This describes a fundamental tenet of the theory of international functionalism which claims to explain how and why transnational organizations like the European Community may grow in scope and capabilities over time. In *Europe's Would-Be Polity*[6] we argued that:

> . . . under certain circumstances the Community system—its functional scope, supranational structures and decision norms and rules—can stimulate a decision-making process that involves a wider and wider circle of political actors who anticipate some potential benefit flowing from European-level decisions. Each mechanism describes a distinct way in which different groups of actors may be brought to a realization that these benefits are possible or available. We do not assume that actors will be primarily or even at all interested in increasing the scope and capacities of the system per se. Some will be; but by and large most are concerned with achieving concrete economic and welfare goals and will view integration only as a means to those ends. Thus, often on purely instrumental grounds political actors may be brought into a coalition in favor of European-level policies.

3. Ibid.

4. Arend Lijphart, *The Politics of Accommodation: Pluralism and Democracy in the Netherlands* (Berkeley and Los Angeles: University of California Press, 1968), chap. 7.

5. Heisler, with Kvavik.

6. Lindberg and Scheingold, *Europe's Would-Be Polity*, pp. 117–20.

In functional spill-over, actors are brought in because they find that tasks (or policy-making areas) are functionally related to one another. That is, because of the nature of the task or area involved, actors discover that they cannot do A (or cannot do it satisfactorily) without also doing B and perhaps C; or, having done A, they so change the circumstances of B and C that joint action there may become necessary in order to prevent inconvenience or disruption. . . .

Another way . . . is by means of log-rolling and side-payments. These represent ways in which actors are brought into a growth-inducing coalition because of the disparity of their interests and priorities in integration. A growth-inducing outcome results because of the efforts that are made to adjust and balance the interests of the multitude of political actors who may be affected by a proposed European policy. As we have already learned, at its best the Community legislative process has involved on the one hand the acceptance of a spirit of joint problem-solving in which issues are not seen in isolation but as part of a continuous bargaining process that may involve many different policy areas simultaneously; and on the other, a sympathetic understanding of each nation's goals and interests and a willingness to compromise and exchange concessions. Marathon sessions and package deals typify this process. . . .

The autonomy of functional contexts can also be gradually eroded and growth-inducing coalitions encouraged as the immediate participants in the policy-making process, from interest groups to bureaucrats and statesmen, begin to develop new perspectives, loyalties, and identifications as a result of their mutual interactions. This is the actor socialization mechanism that is potential in the integration enterprise. Here it is not so much that new actors are brought into a developing coalition, but rather that the commitments or aspirations of those already engaged are intensified. . . .

In the case of the feedback[7] mechanism, it is the outputs of the Community that have an impact on attitudes and behavior. And it is primarily the perceptions and behaviors of nonparticipants that are involved. The public at large, or categories within it such as farmers or workers, or elites who are as yet not aware of the Community's relevance for them, may be made more attentive or even mobilized to action as a result of decisions the Community takes. The formation of growth-inducing coalitions is enhanced in several ways. Effective performance in already established areas may both increase the willingness of actors (interest groups, for example) to try to use the Community system for the satisfaction of a demand and help establish its authority as a decision-maker deserving attention and perhaps respect generally (i.e., not restricted to political actors). It can also accustom the public to expect that in the Community system governments will deal with each other according to new rules. Deviations from these rules by a national leader might

---

7. Our usage of the term "feedback" is a rather restrictive one. For a full exposition of feedback processes in political systems see David Easton, *A System Analysis of Political Life* (New York: John Wiley & Sons, 1965), chaps. 22–28.

then evoke strong disapproval and perhaps constitute a restraint on those who are tempted to invoke nonconsensual norms and procedures. At a more general level, continued existence and operation of the system may have an impact on economic and social transaction patterns and conduce to the development of feelings of mutual identification based on a growing perception of a common "European" interest. These may in turn make national publics and elites more receptive to proposals designed to increase the scope of European policy-making.

The following analysis of the European Community political system consists of four parts: first, a characterization of the substantive scope of decision making and its consequences for participation and support; second, a description of the Community's institutions, which emphasizes cooptative structures and mechanisms and the interaction between national (sectorial) elites and Community (system) elites in policy making; third, an analysis of the role definitions and accommodative decision rules evolved by different actors in the Community dialogue, including a discussion of how they have been evaded and of what the overall "costs" of these rules and procedures might be; and finally, some speculations about the future of the Community system as it absorbs new members and faces new stresses and demands.

Substantive Scope and Its Consequences

A look at the kinds of functions encompassed by the Community leads us to a number of observations about its implications for the citizens of the member countries, including both elites and the ordinary public. For example, joint decision making tends to take the form of regulation, rather than the direct provision of goods and services for the broad public. As a consequence, the political "constituency" of the Community is restricted, as we shall see.

One way of showing this relative dominance of regulation over the public provision of goods and services is to compare the amount of Community expenditures with the budgetary expenditures of the national governments (although this does weight the case on the side of the governments, since it includes costs of security establishments, police, civil service, etc.). In 1965 the Community spent $783 million, an impressive sum by the standards of international organizations: in 1964, the budget of the entire United Nations system (administration, peace-keeping, economic aid, specialized agencies) was less than $500 million.[8] But this amounted to under one percent of total governmental expenditures in the six-country

8. Philip E. Jacob and Alexine L. Atherton, *The Dynamics of International Organization* (Homewood, Ill.: Dorsey Press, 1965), p. 41.

Table 1. Public Expenditures in EEC Countries, 1965, in Billions of Dollars

Germany	34.2
France	24.6
Italy	15.2
Netherlands	3.97
Belgium	4.4
Luxembourg	.16
Total National	82.53
Community	.78

Source: Karlheinz Neunreither, "L'Organisation financière de la Communauté Européenne: Indice d'une structure préfédérale?" (Paper delivered at the 7th World Congress of the International Political Science Association, Brussels, 18–23 September 1967, Appendix, table 2.

area (including local and regional governments as well as central governments).[9]

Most often Community activity will involve only joint decisions *not to do* certain things (e.g., to raise tariffs or form monopolies), or joint approval of national requests for exclusion from universal rules (e.g., tariff quotas). There is as yet very little activity in social welfare, labor-management relations, education, public safety, and the maintenance of order. Using our expenditure index again, total expenditures for social welfare programs by the European Community in 1965 amounted to only $31.3 million, about three-tenths of one percent of total direct governmental expenditures (which totaled over $10 billions).[10]

When combined with the fact that Community activity seldom involves actual policy implementation and enforcement, it is clear that Community decision making is not often directly relevant for most individual citizens of the member countries. Indeed, the general level of public knowledge or interest in European Community decision making is quite low, even though the general goals of integration are widely supported. Table 2 summarizes some illustrative findings from national surveys carried out in the countries of the Community in 1962. One shouldn't deduce too much from such figures, however; the levels of information about and attention to the activities of national governments are also low among the public at large. The major point we want to make is that while the Com-

9. Mainly because of increases in agricultural expenditures, the budget increased by 1972 to over $5 billion. This is close to 4 percent or 5 percent of all governmental expenditures.

10. Neunreither, "L'Organisation financière," Appendix, table 5.

Table 2. Levels of Interest in and Knowledge About European Integration, in Mass Publics, 1962

	Are Strongly or Moderately in Favor of a United Europe	Think Often or Very Often About European Unity	Can Correctly Answer Questions About the Institutions, Their Work and Accomplishments	Spontaneously List European Problems as Among the Most Important
Netherlands	87%	45%	29%	10%
Germany	81	43	25	6
France	72	33	22	7
Belgium	65	30	14	11
Italy	60	29	4	1

Source: *Sondages* (Revue Française de l'Opinion Publique), no. 1 (1963): 39, 45, 46.

Table 3. Levels of Interest in Politics in General, in Mass Publics, 1962

	Very Interested in Politics	Moderately Interested in Politics	Think Often or Very Often About Europe
Netherlands	11%	43%	45%
Germany	16	31	43
France	10	33	33
Belgium	7	23	30
Italy	7	26	29

Source: *Sondages*, no. 1 (1963): 40.

munity operates in policy areas that are important, its specific activities are not perceived by most people as affecting them in their daily lives. The situation for elites and other population categories is quite different, however, as can be inferred from table 4. But the great majority of the general public will probably continue to be for the most part oriented toward the national political systems in terms of their perceptions of the origins of the authoritative decisions that most concern them. By and large most people perceive neither specific gains or losses from integration.

The major exception to the above generalizations about perceptions of the relevance of the system is to be found in the area of agricultural policy. By the 1970s most basic policy decisions will be taken in the Community system, including the regulation of trade and marketing, the provision of guarantees of agricultural incomes through price maintenance and production controls, preference vis-à-vis outside producers, the disposal of surpluses, export subsidies and structural reform policies. By 1972 Community expenditures as a result of joint decisions in agriculture will reach

Table 4. Levels of Interest in and Knowledge About European Integration, by Socioeconomic Status, Profession, Foreign Travel, and Education

	Professionals, Industrialists, and Upper Classes Who:		Employees and Middle Classes Who:		Those Who've Traveled Who:	Those With Advanced Education Who:
	Think Often About Europe[a]	Can Answer Questions[a]	Think Often About Europe	Can Answer Questions	Think Often About Europe	Can Answer Questions
Netherlands	63	42	52	38	49	54
Germany	50[b]	30[b]	50	36	55	46
France	70	42	46	30	47	37
Belgium	53	30	38	22	34	40
Italy	70	15	65	10	19	28

[a] Figures are estimates based on bar graphs.
[b] Includes also traders and artisans.

Sources: Jacques-René Rabier, "L'information des Européens et l'intégration de l'Europe" (Institute of European Studies, Free University of Brussels, 17–18 February 1965), p. 51. *Sondages*, no. 1 (1963): 30–38.

$3.5 billion a year.[11] We may thus expect that farmers and farm organizations will be more aware of the system and its products than is the public at large.

Thus the major constituency for joint decision making in the Community, that is, those who so far perceive direct advantages and disadvantages, are to be found primarily among the economic, political, and administrative elites of the member countries. Most concerned are industrialists, bankers, and traders, who stand to gain (or lose) most immediately from the freer movement of economic factors and the creation of a larger economic space, and those politicians and governmental officials responsible for the maintenance of economic stability and full employment. By and large, such groups and elites have accepted the Community as a fait accompli and as a relevant arena in which to pursue their economic and political goals. They may or may not be convinced "integrationists." They may or may not favor extending the scope of joint decision making. The point is that the existence of the Community alters their situation, and they must adjust their goals and political activities accordingly. As far as we can tell, there is little overt opposition among such elites to the idea of integration or to the general goal of creating a larger economic space in which economic factors can move unhindered. Indeed, former EEC Commission President Walter Hallstein himself attributed the early and striking success of the EEC largely to the rapidity with which businessmen and traders accepted it and adapted their activities to it.

One indication of such an adaptation on the part of economic elites is the formation of interest groups at the Community level. Faced with the emergence of a new decision-making system, groups have organized across national boundaries so as to maintain contacts, secure information, and seek access to policy makers. Although systematic studies have not been made of this growing "supranational" interest group network to which the Community has given birth, some indicative data are available. Occasional tallies have been made of the groups that have been set up as a response to the creation of the Community.[12] These have shown 10 supranational interest groups in 1957, 222 in 1961, 233 in 1964, and 350 in 1966. With enlargements of the scope of Community decision making have come increases in the number of groups. Such data are, in a sense, behavioral indicators of *elite systemic support*. They give us a rough measure of the extent to which the emerging Community system has been able to stimulate the participation of groups and individuals in its work.

11. For earlier estimates and more details see Neunreither, "L'Organisation financière," Appendix, table 6. For 1972 budget estimates see Commission des Communautés Europėennes *Cinquiême Rapport Général sur l'activité des Communautés*, Brussels, 1971, p. 433.

12. See, e.g., Ernst B. Haas, *The Uniting of Europe* (Stanford: Stanford University Press, 1958), pp. 324–33; Leon N. Lindberg, *The Political Dynamics of European Economic Integration* (Stanford: Stanford University Press, 1963), pp. 97–98; W. Hartley Clark, *The Politics of the Common Market* (Englewood Cliffs, N.J.: Prentice-Hall, 1967), p. 103.

Furthermore, these groups have intensified their activities over time. Their budgets and staff have steadily increased. So have the number of internal meetings among national interest group leaders within the Community level groups. Many groups have evolved relatively cohesive communications networks devoted to defining a common interest and a common strategy for the group that cuts across national boundaries. As such they probably contribute to *identitive support* at an elite level.

Governmental officials and administrators have also been swept up by the work of the Community, perhaps even more extensively than interest groups. Indeed, it is not an exaggeration to characterize the entire Community system as essentially bureaucratic and technocratic. The role they play in the process will be explored more fully later. Suffice it here to note that yet another interaction and communication network has grown up among national bureaucrats, and between them and interest group representatives and officials of the Commission. Again we have only incomplete and unsystematic information on the extent of such contacts, but they show much the same trends as do the interest-group data. For example, in the early 1960s the European Commission more and more frequently met with national officials and representatives of interest groups: it called 733 such meetings in 1960, 856 in 1961, 1,344 in 1962, and 1,539 in 1963.[13] Most of these meetings are held in Brussels at the headquarters of the Commission. As a result there is a steady flow of members of the national economic and administrative elites to the seat of Community decision making. In 1963, for example, 944 meetings were held in Brussels with 11,744 non-Community participants. This represented a substantial increase over an estimate for 1960 of 430 meetings and 8,000 participants.[14]

As we would expect, given the scope of Community action in that field, interest group activity and bureaucratic interactions have been especially extensive in agriculture. Thus, of the 222 Community-level interest groups counted in 1961, 82 were in agriculture, and of the 944 Brussels meetings in 1963, 245 (with 2,974 participants) were convened by the Commission's Directorate for Agriculture.[15]

13. Interviews by Leon N. Lindberg with commission officials. Even more meetings are convened by other Community institutions like the Council of Ministers, the Economic and Social Committee, etc. Hence, these figures give only a partial picture of the extent of the involvement of group leaders and bureaucrats.

14. See Lindberg, *Political Dynamics*, p. 58. The calculations are not entirely comparable, however, and only the trend of the data, not the precise figures, is meaningful.

15. Another indicator of interaction is the number of telex messages received and sent by the General Directorate for Agriculture as part of its information gathering and rule-applying activities as they have evolved over time. In 1962 an average of 230 messages a month were received and 250 a month were sent. By 1967 these had increased to 1,400 and 2,700 a month, respectively. European Communities, Joint Information Service, "Newsletter on the Common Agricultural Policy," no. 14 (October 1967).

The Community Arena vs. the National Arena

Excluded from any joint decision making are a number of functions long considered most fundamental to the character of the sovereign state, for example, maintaining military security and internal order, regulating or providing for political participation, and the like. Economic and welfare functions of the state may have increased greatly in terms of their relative saliency for general publics, but they have still not completely displaced military security, nationalism, and democracy as symbolic focuses of attention and affect. Here the nation-state remains the predominant framework for action. Political actors desirous of affecting the distribution or allocation of advantages and disadvantages at this level, for example, a de Gaulle seeking a place in the sun for France or German politicians seeking primarily to promote national reunification, may thus be either indifferent to the activities of the European Community or will oppose them unless they contribute to the desired end.

This implies that the Community exists in a setting of potential conflict between different sets of elites with a largely indifferent public looking on. One set of elites has for a variety of reasons accepted the European system as a permanent part of the political landscape, and has begun to develop vested interests in its continuation and perhaps in its further expansion. The other set of elites has policy preoccupations, needs, and ambitions which may impel them to view the European system solely in terms of its contribution to other goals which transcend the economic or welfare spheres, or the political effort to unify a long-divided Europe. The general public is by and large favorable to the goal of unifying Europe, but seldom perceives any direct impact of the system on their own lives.

When the latter kind of elite is in control of the government (as in France under de Gaulle), the prospects for integration may well suffer. We need not assume, however, that such elites need necessarily be opposed to integration. They may indeed decide that it is a necessary prerequisite for the achievement of their goals. Ernst B. Haas has described the problem in terms of patterns of interaction between two contrasting types of political aims and styles: the dramatic-political and the incremental-economic.[16] The distinction he has in mind is very close to the one made above, namely between those concerned with economic and welfare benefits, and those concerned primarily with foreign policy, national security, grandeur, and the like. As long as both types in all of the politically relevant countries favor integration, albeit for different reasons, the process can be expected to proceed more or less without interruption. The implications for the

---

16. "The 'Uniting of Europe' and the Uniting of Latin America," *Journal of Common Market Studies* 5 (June 1967): 328–29.

Community of developing patterns of divergence and conflict are much harder to predict.

Thus we see that not only was the Community born of compromise, with many potentially divisive issues merely set aside temporarily, it also in fact serves a quite special constituency. Some are progressively advantaged by its activities; others may be disadvantaged; most have as yet felt little direct impact. The future growth of the Community would seem to depend upon its success in broadening its constituency, upon how well that constituency is served, and upon the ways in which the potential conflicts between that constituency and those who are adversely affected are resolved. In short, it will depend on its capacity for producing collective decisions. Of determining importance here will be the Community's institutional capacities, that is, the kinds of decision-making structures and decision-making norms and rules that it has developed and that it can maintain over time.

Now that we have gained a sense of the functional scope of the decision-making activities of the European Community, and a sense of for whom the system is most revelant, let us turn to the following set of questions: Through what institutional structures and processes are decisions typically taken and how well do they work? What are the basic norms or implicit "rules of the game" governing the behavior of decision makers in the system and with what regularity are they "obeyed"? How can fluctuations in institutional capacity be explained?

Decision-Making Institutions: Appearance and Reality

There are four basic institutions in the Community system: a supranational Commission, a Council of Ministers representing the governments, a European Parliament in which sit members of the national parliaments, and a Court of Justice.[17]

The Commission is the one institution that actively seeks to represent "the Community interest." Its members are appointed for four-year terms by agreement among the member governments, but they are in no way responsible to the governments. They are supposed to act independently as guardians of the treaties, as animators of the integration process and as representatives (or even discoverers) of the collective interests of all the member countries. The Commission and its staff (dubbed "Eurocrats")

17. The Community institutional system is actually much more complex than this if we take into account all of the ancillary bodies that have been set up for special purposes. They are not included here since they are not essential to our purposes. For a partial listing and good, brief discussion see Richard Mayne, *The Institutions of the European Community* (London: Chatham House, Political and Economic Planning, 1968). See also Clark, *The Politics of the Common Market*.

thus constitute a sort of European civil service—a Eurocracy—although, as we will see, it is more politically active than most civil services. As the scope of the Community has expanded, so have the Commission's activities and responsibilities, as evidenced by the steady increases in its staff size and administrative budget. (See table 5.)

Table 5. Eurocracy Staff and Administrative Budget

Year	Staff	Budget (Million $)
1955	550[a]	8.0
1959	2,870	44.0
1962	3,726	53.5
1964	4,127	58.7
1966	4,463	69.5
1968	4,882	86.0

[a] The staff figure for 1955 is Haas's estimate of the High Authority. The High Authority components for 1959 and 1962 are straight line estimates based on the difference between the 1955 estimate and 1964 figure (when precise data are available).

Sources: Budgets of EEC and Euratom as published in *Journal Officiel des Communautés Européennes* and *Financial Reports* of the High Authority of the ECSC.

The Council of Ministers is the institution in which representatives of the national governments meet in order to try to concert their behavior and make collective decisions on matters within the scope of the Community. Ministers of Foreign Affairs or Economic Affairs meet for general and for very important questions, and specialized ministers (e.g., Agriculture, Transport, Finance) come together when more technical matters are involved. Normally, the Council does not itself originate policy proposals; rather it acts on the basis of studies and proposals that come from the Commission and its staff. Proposals are then examined in the light of individual national interests and the process of seeking some balance among these interests is begun. There are complex rules governing voting in the Council, but by and large all important questions are in fact decided by unanimity, even though a number of majority voting procedures also exist. This puts a premium, as we shall see, on the success with which the national representatives develop "efficient" procedures for bargaining.

The European Parliament is made up of delegates appointed by the national parliaments of the member governments. It is supposed to provide for parliamentary control and surveillance of the activities of the Commission and Council.[18] It meets in plenary session an average of seven or eight times a year, and in many ways resembles a national legislature: attendance is good, members are seated by political party and not by national delegations, and debates take place on concrete issues and range over the entire scope of the Community. There is an extensive committee system in which much of the work is actually done—preparation of studies, resolutions, and the like. The more active committees may meet an additional three or four days a month.

The Court of Justice is made up of judges appointed for six-year terms by agreement among the governments. Its primary function is to act as a kind of supreme court for the Community. Appeals may be brought to it by individuals, firms, Community institutions, or member governments. Appeals may be made against acts of the Council, the Commission, or a member government that contravenes the treaty or its obligations. Individuals, firms, Community institutions, and governments are all legally bound by the Court's rulings, for it is the final authority on matters of treaty interpretation.

What are the relationships among these institutions and how do they work in practice? On a first examination of figure 1 the formal relationships on the Community level appear to resemble those of a continental European parliamentary system. There is a "cabinet" (the Council of Ministers) that makes the great bulk of the authoritative decisions. It is assisted by a civil service (the Commission). These decisional activities are restrained in different ways by two other institutions, which round out the system: a parliament, and a court.[19] But this picture is complicated by the fact that this apparent parliamentary system is linked to national parliamentary systems as well.

In formal terms it also appears that the relationships between the national political systems and the Community system are clearly articulated so as to provide for the kinds of democratic controls we associate with parliamentary regimes. National electorates choose parliaments, which in turn have the power to legislate and to control cabinets which are selected from their memberships. The cabinets determine what specific policy positions to take with regard to Community matters, and then the Minister of Foreign Affairs or Economics or Agriculture will negotiate in the Council of Ministers with the other governments. When a final decision is reached the cabinets are responsible to the parliaments for the concessions they may have made in Brussels.

18. For more extensive treatments see Ernst Haas, *The Uniting of Europe*, Kenneth Lindsay, *European Assemblies* (London: Stevens, 1966), Murray Forsyth, *The Parliament of the European Communities* (London: Chatham House, Political and Economic Planning, 1964), and Leon N. Lindberg, "The Role of the European Parliament in an Emerging European Community," in *Lawmakers in a Changing World*, ed. Elke Frank (Englewood Cliffs, N.J.: Prentice-Hall, Inc., 1966).

19. There is also a consultative body representing economic interest groups, the Economic and Social Committee.

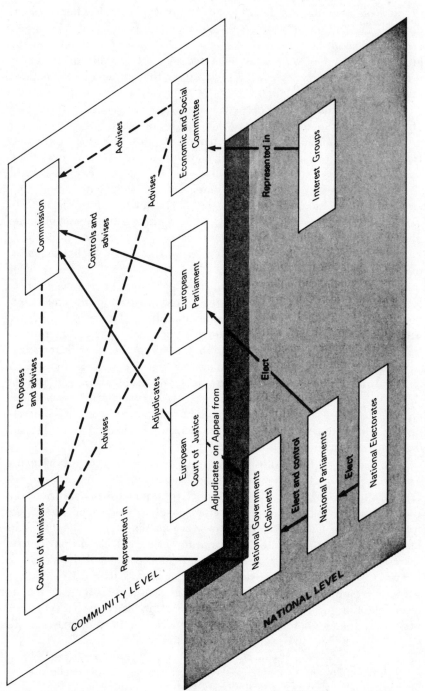

Figure 1. Formal Institutional Relationships in the European Community

But organigrams and descriptions of formal relations seldom suffice to describe the realities of power and influence in any political system, and it is no less so in the European Community. In the next section we discuss in some detail how Community-level decisions are actually made. Let us first say something about relationships between that system and the national political systems.

The post-World War II period has seen a general decline in the vitality of European national parliaments, and this is nowhere more obvious than in European Community decision making. In ratifying the Community treaties the member countries' parliaments in fact created a new policy-making system over which they would have in the future very little control. In the decision-making areas encompassed by the Community, such authoritative decisions as are taken jointly do not require ratification by any national parliaments, no matter how important and fundamental they might be, and the ability of any national parliament to control its cabinet's negotiators effectively is severely limited by the highly technical nature of most of the subject matter and by the fact that final Community decisions are delicately balanced compromises that cannot be undone after the fact, except at the price of calling the whole integration movement into question. Several of the general causes of the secular trends associated with the long-term decline in the rule-making and control functions of European national parliaments, reach a kind of apotheosis with the European Community. Most notable among these are the onset of the welfare state with its politics of technical expertise and problem solving, and the steady increase of administrative and executive power. Thus cabinets and civil services are virtually autonomous of legislatures when it comes to determining national positions on Community problems. Here is bureaucratic decision making par excellence.

To partly fill the resulting "control gap" the treaties established a European Parliament which must be consulted by the Council and the Commission and which has final authority to dismiss the Commission. But the Commission is not the final decision-making body. Such powers are reserved for the Council of Ministers in which the representatives of the national cabinets meet, and the European Parliament has no power over the Council at all. The body that does influence Council decisions and participate intimately in the decision-making process is the Commission, yet another administrative-technocratic body, this time at the Community level. The European Parliament, as the national parliaments, has then been little more than an onlooker when it comes to actual decision making. The system's anomalies can be summed up as follows:

> Structurally, the institutions of the European Economic Community are very nearly as Janus-like as the treaty that gave them birth. There is a legislature (the European Parliament) which doesn't legislate; an ad-

ministrative organ (the Commission) which both initiates legislation and administers it; a cabinet (the Council of Ministers) which is responsible to no one; and a supreme court (the Court of Justice) which is supposed to act as if these glaring weaknesses and strange anomalies didn't exist.[20]

In fact, it is no exaggeration to view the whole policy-making process in the Community as a dialogue between the Council representing the national cabinets, and the Commission, appointed originally by the governments but acting autonomously in terms of its own view of the "interests" of the Community as a whole. Figure 2 depicts the key political relationships within the Community. Inside what we might call the Community political arena (indicated by the double-lined circle) are the essential actors as a result of whose constant and intensive interaction (the Community dialogue) come final Community decisions. Outside the circle are others who seek in various ways and by means of various strategies to have some influence on what goes on inside. Let us turn now to an analysis of the nature of this Community dialogue. We begin by first describing the path that a typical piece of "European legislation" takes through the system, so as to indicate how the various relationships are expressed in action. Then each of the major participants in the dialogue (the Commission and the Council) is discussed in some detail. We describe the methods they use, the resources at their disposal, their successes and their failures.

How European Legislation Is Made[21]

As we have said, the heart of the decision-making process is a complex pattern of formal and informal relationships among cabinet members and civil servants of the participating countries, and between them and the members of the supranational Commission and its staff. This European "legislative process" typically operates as follows:

1. The Commission's staff perceives the need for some sort of action, because the Treaties require it, a government or interest group has sought it, or because the Commission itself desires it.
2. They will consult with academic experts, national civil servants, and perhaps with interest group representatives, European Parliament committees, or members of the Economic and Social Committee, so as to get an initial idea of the prob-

20. Stuart A. Scheingold, "De Gaulle vs. Hallstein: Europe Picks Up the Pieces," *American Scholar* 35 (Summer 1966): 478.
21. For an excellent discussion see Stephen Holt, *The Common Market: The Conflict of Theory and Practice* (London: Hamish Hamilton, 1967), chaps. 4–6. For further details see Lindberg, *Political Dynamics*, chaps. 4, 5, and passim.

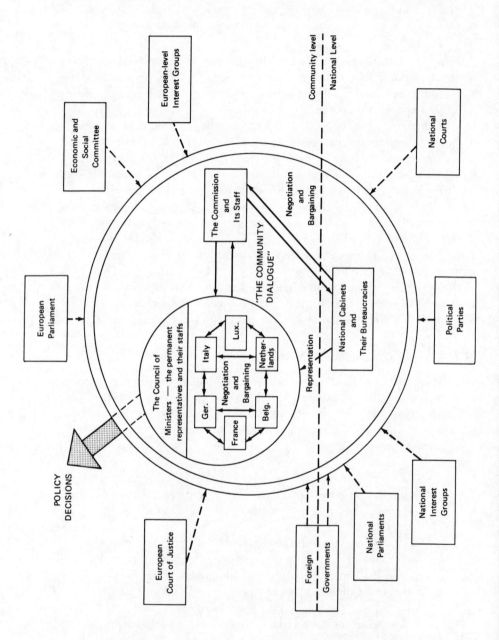

Figure 2. Actors in the Community Legislative Process

lems, pressures, and possibilities in the area under consideration.

3. The Commission and its staff then prepare a formal proposal upon which they will again consult the Economic and Social Committee, interest groups, and probably, committees of the European Parliament.

4. The proposal is then sent to the Council of Ministers which in turn transmits it to one of a number of study groups made up of national civil servants.

5. These study groups examine the proposals in the light of the individual national interests involved. A representative of the Commission usually attends. National interest groups and national parliaments may express themselves at this stage. There is usually substantial conflict at the national level as to what positions shall be taken by any government in the Community negotiations, for the governments are not monoliths. Individual national ministries often see conflicting interests in European legislation—as they do in national-level legislation —and often ministries and their client interest groups seek to forge alliances across national boundaries to promote a particular European policy, as for example when Ministries of Agriculture and agricultural pressure groups unite to oppose the budgetary conservatism of Ministers of Finance. As we shall see, the existence of such disparities of interest within each nation is an important determinant of the Community's bargaining and decision-making style.

6. These national studies typically lead to a list of conflicts of interest among the governments (and often *within* each government) that need to be resolved before a European decision can be taken. Such lists are ordinarily sent to the Committee of Permanent Representatives: high level representatives of each government who meet almost continuously in Brussels and who prepare the Council's agenda. A member of the Commission meets with them and may alter the Commission's proposals in order to facilitate agreement.

7. All conflicts that cannot be ironed out in the Committee of Permanent Representatives are sent on to the Council. Here once again the Commission participates. If national positions can be reconciled with each other and with the Commission's proposals, a final European decision will be made.

Indeed, in some ways it is quite an oversimplification to describe this process as a *dialogue* between Commission and Council, even though that describes its essential nature for our purposes. But there are any number of other interactions going on simultaneously. For example, representatives of national bureaucracies meet constantly with each other in a myriad of committees to examine problems posed by integration and to consider alternative solutions. The Commission's staff will also meet with such technical experts, either singly or collectively. The governments themselves also negotiate and bargain with each other either bilaterally or multilaterally in order to reach agreement on matters before the Council. Figure 3 is a summary flow chart representation of the relationships among the various participants in the legislative process at the several stages of that process. The numbers correspond to those in the text above.

Activity within this inside network is steady and intense and appears to grow in volume each year. For example, in 1964 cabinet ministers of the 6 members met in the Council of Ministers on 36 separate occasions, spending a total of 67 days in high-level Community bargaining. In 1960 they had met 15 times for 29 days. The number of special committees, study groups, etc., set up to bring Community and national bureaucrats together at earlier stages of the decision-making process, increased from 127 in 1960 to 210 in 1964. Thus, as we have already documented in greater detail earlier in this chapter, more and more national officials and civil servants spend more and more time either actually in Brussels or working with Community problems at the national level. And interest groups are forced to pay attention to this new decision-making system by organizing both at the national and at the Community level. Special professions have sprung up for the purpose of keeping track of, reporting on, studying, or defending one's clients in this new system. Even the popular press devotes substantial attention to it. In sum, a whole new political arena is coming into existence, one that centers on European policy making rather than national policy making. As a result, new relationships among individuals and groups may be forged that will cut across national lines and that may one day serve as the basis of a genuine sense of "European" identity.

While control or direct participation in decision making on the part of parliaments is clearly absent from this system, it would be too much to say that it completely lacks responsiveness. Cabinets and the Commission do operate within broad policy constraints as determined by the composition of the parliaments and the positions of the different political parties. Similarly, both cabinets and the Commission must be attentive to interest group demands and preoccupations. This is particularly important for the Commission, which, in order to get its proposals accepted by the Council, must appeal to as many groups in as many countries as it can. The Commission, in fact, maintains close and direct contacts with national and Community-wide interest groups and political parties as one way of promoting its proposals and perhaps overcoming national resistance.

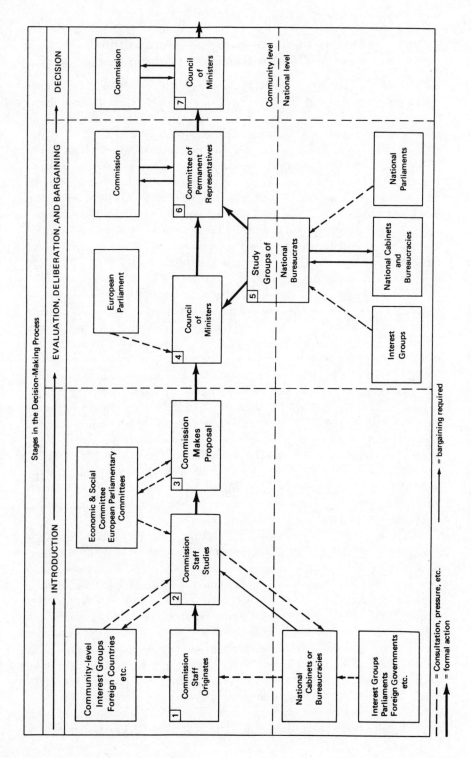

Figure 3. The Legislative Process in the European Community

Stages in the Decision-Making Process

INTRODUCTION → EVALUATION, DELIBERATION, AND BARGAINING → DECISION

Community-level Interest Groups Foreign Countries etc.

Commission Staff Originates — 1

National Cabinets or Bureaucracies

Interest Groups Parliaments Foreign Governments etc.

Economic & Social Committee European Parliamentary Committees

Commission Staff Studies — 2

Commission Makes Proposal — 3

Council of Ministers — 4

European Parliament

Study Groups of National Bureaucrats — 5

Interest Groups

National Cabinets and Bureaucracies

National Parliaments

Committee of Permanent Representatives — 6

Commission

Council of Ministers — 7

Commission

Community level / National level

- - - = Consultation, pressure, etc.

——— = formal action

——→ = bargaining required

Actors in the Dialogue: The Supranational Commission, Its Roles and Capabilities

It is not surprising to find a transnational decision-making system in which representatives of the governments, normally acting by unanimous vote, make the final decisions. What is striking about the European Community is the scope of the things that are discussed and the fact that a supranational body, the Commission (and before 1958 the High Authority of the ECSC) sits in the Council with the governments as a virtual bargaining equal, and that it has consistently been instrumental in shaping the decisions that have emerged. With occasional fluctuations in effectiveness this role has been sustained since 1952. The Commission survived the crisis provoked by de Gaulle's veto of the British application for membership in 1963 and his six-month boycott of the Community institutions in 1965–66 to achieve a major success in the 1966 agricultural negotiations and in the Kennedy Round tariff negotiations concluded in 1967.

If we define power traditionally, that is, in terms of formal authority or the ability to impose sanctions or the possession of a monopoly of legitimate force, then it is clear that the Council is all-powerful and the Commission is powerless. But political scientists have tended to move away from such formal or "negative" definitions of power. In this revised view, power can be defined "positively," that is, as *participation* in decision making, as *objective success* in getting one's preferences or goals accepted by others. By such a standard the Commission has wielded and continues to wield substantial decision-making power in the Community process. Most decisions of the Council must be made on the basis of a proposal from the Commission, which thus has most of the "power" of initiative. The Commission, not the Council, is the body with a European perspective and the command of the technical expertise required for intelligent policy proposals. If the Council wants to amend the proposals it must secure the Commission's agreement unless there is unanimity in the Council on a new text.

Of course, if the Commission wants to see its proposals accepted, it must secure the assent of the governments. To the extent that both the governments and the Commission prefer a decision to a deadlock, both would seen likely to have incentives for bargaining and the exchange of concessions. By and large, integration has moved forward in those areas where a sufficient number of governments were convinced or could be convinced that joint action was necessary or desirable and where it was possible to offer compensatory rewards to those who might see their interests damaged. This has not always been possible. But as our discussion so far has indicated, the system has been working in many areas and joint decisions have been produced that constituted more than a mere lowest common denominator of what the governments might have originally wanted. Such successes need to be explained, for our normal expectations of a joint decision-making system among nations of such disparate histories would have been more nearly a situation of deadlock. One basic ingredient has been the way in which the Commission (or High Authority) has operated in a given situation or issue area. To have said that the Commission *can* move the system and influence decision is not to say that it always does.

If the Commission is to play a role it must make creative use of the resources it has for influencing the behavior of the governments. This means, above all, playing an active rather than a passive role and making proposals that are well designed technically, with both the common goals of all the members and the specific needs or problems of individual nations taken into account. It should not come as a surprise that the Commission and High Authority have not always succeeded in operating optimally. There is a high premium on particular political skills in institutions like these, operating in as fluid a system as the European Community. Such skills are unevenly distributed among commissioners, and since the Commission's internal organization provides for considerable decentralization of policy responsibility the requisite skills may or may not be brought into play, depending on the policy area involved. Also personnel may change. Politically adept commissioners such as Jean Monnet or Walter Hallstein may leave and be replaced by men with less vision and tactical skill.

What kinds of skills are we talking about? Can we draw up a list that would describe the "ideal" Commission? On the basis of the record over the first two decades years of the Community's existence, we would stress the following as necessary if the Commission is to realize its optimal potentialities.[22]

1. *Goal Articulation.* The Commission can articulate long-term goals for the Community that can in turn be ligitimated in terms of some belief in a European common interest. This would include public advocacy of specific proposals by invoking long-term goals as one way to mobilize supporters and neutralize opposition.

2. *Coalition Building.* The Commission can take the initiative in identifying problems to be solved by joint or coordinated action, and in making specific proposals. Proposals are typically developed through intensive consultation and compromise with client groups and with relevant national bureaucracies, so as to assure full information and expertise, and to build a policy consensus and a coalition of supporters at the national level.

22. This discussion is based on Haas, *The Uniting of Europe,* passim, and Lindberg, *Political Dynamics,* passim. See also Haas, *Beyond the Nation State: Functionalism and International Organization* (Stanford: Stanford University Press, 1964), chap. 5.

3. *Recruitment and Organization.* The Commission can recruit its staff so as to maximize prior national contacts and experience, technical expertise, and, at the higher levels, political experience and prestige.

4. *Expand Scope.* The Commission can be alert to the possibilities of convincing governments and present or potential client groups to redefine their goals and purposes in the direction of more joint activity. Calls for new policies, new tasks, new powers for Community institutions can also be justified in terms of their usefulness to the governments and to national goals.

5. *Brokerage and Package Deals.* The Commission can play an active and constructive role in intergovernmental bargaining at all levels and stages of the decision-making process. It can do so only by fully understanding the positions of each government and the possibilities that exist for movement and promise on the part of each. It defends and explains its own proposals, but also makes changes where necessary to accommodate specific national demands. The Commission can also act the role of an "honest broker" by seeking to help construct a final "package deal" that optimizes the joint gains of the member governments.

What should be clear from this list is that the European Commission should not be considered as simply an administrative-technical body. Were it to became one, as is possible since the governments appoint the members and may so choose, it seems likely that the integration movement would lose much of its force. The skills we have listed are political skills par excellence. Another thing that should be clear is that the "power" of the Commission depends primarily on the way in which it is able to interact with national political authorities and with interest group and other elites. Observers have usually described the Community institutional system in terms of conflicts between supranational power and national sovereignty. To do so is to assume that each gain in capability at the European level necessarily implies a loss of capability at the national level. We reject this "zero-sum" interpretation. European integration, although it may involve conflicts, is more accurately seen as a way in which new forms of decision capability are created to cope with new problems and to achieve new goals. Our basic point has been that the relationship between the Commission and the Council, as between the European Community and the national political systems, is more nearly a symbiotic relationship than a competitive one. The Community emerged, in part at least, as a result of the inability of national systems to process certain kinds of economic, social, and welfare demands. Its continued growth will be a function of its ability to provide decision capabilities that national governments acting alone cannot command. National governments, on the other hand, continue to provide a source of support and legitimacy for the Community institutions. They also play a vital role in collecting and transmitting specific demands to the institutions, and in absorbing most of the negative reactions from those groups who are disadvantaged by the dislocations attendant to the Community-engendered processes of economic modernization.

Actors in the Dialogue: The Governments, the Rules and Norms Governing Their Behavior in the Council

In the foregoing discussion of the Commission it was necessary to consider in some detail its relationship to the Council, for its roles and powers largely derive from its interactions with that body. In this section on the Council it will be seen that it too depends on the Commission, but more importantly, it will be our argument that the role the Council plays in the integrative process will depend on the kinds of interactions that develop among the different governments as they try to concert their behavior in response to Commission initiatives. Along with the development of new decision structures and interaction patterns, can we also discern the development of new patterns or norms of behavior in the relations among these countries?

If a collective decision-making system of this scope is to persist or to grow, we would expect participants in it (in this case the governments) to gradually develop stable sets of rules and conventions governing the way in which conflicts are to be resolved, the procedures and tactics that are acceptable or unacceptable, and who is to have primary responsibility for negotiating differences or establishing authority. Failure to do so would mean that decision makers would have to argue each time about how to go about doing things, as well as about the things themselves.[23] Given limited resources of time, energy, and skill, this would almost certainly place serious limits on the capacity of the system to produce collective decisions. Thus, agreement on some set of "rules of the game" constitutes a vital resource for any decision-making system. With regard to the European Community, to what extent can we answer the following sorts of questions in the affirmative? Can we point to the emergence in the Council and among the governments of a style of bargaining based on the mutual predictability of behavior, a perception of common interests, and a spirit of compromise and adaptation to each other's interests and preoccupations? Do the governments really *bargain* with each other, offering significant concessions and exchanges in the interests of joint action? Or do they merely present each

23. Easton, *A Systems Analysis of Political Life*, p. 191.

other with nonnegotiable demands or faits accomplis? Are the power-based and rank-conscious relationships among states that we generally associate with international politics being replaced by more consensual ones?

We cannot, unfortunately, give unequivocal answers to such questions. The dominant experience since 1952 has been one of a gradual emergence of a distinct "procedural code" that came to be called "the Community method."[24] It consists roughly of the following expectations and practices:

1. The governments show frequent and strong commitment to the Community by stressing the expectation that it will persist, that substantial rewards and benefits are to be expected, and that withdrawal or failure are out of the question.
2. The governments accept the Commission as a valid bargaining partner and accord it a degree of legitimacy as spokesman and advocate of the interests of the collectivity. They expect the Commission to play an active role in building a policy consensus in the Council of Ministers.
3. The governments deal with each other in a spirit of problem solving. It is assumed that collective decisions are desirable, and negotiation is about how to achieve them, not whether they should be sought.
4. The governments, as well as the Commission, are attentive and responsive to each others' interests, preoccupations, and goals. They avoid making unacceptable demands or proposals, and divisive issues are usually postponed.
5. The governments and Commission show themselves willing to compromise and make short-term sacrifices in the common interest or in expectation of future long-term gains.
6. All agree that unanimous agreement is the rule and that negotiations should continue until consensus is achieved and all objections have been either overcome or "losses" in one area compensated for by "gains" in another. Issues are not seen as separate and unrelated to each other but in the context of a continuous process of decision. It is thus possible to engage in side-payment and logrolling behavior, whereby trades can be made within an area or across a wide range of policy areas (e.g., agricultural concessions in exchange for approval of a new form of indirect taxation). Bargaining is thus likely to be complex, laborious, and time-consuming, and it is characterized by so-called *marathon negotiations* which result in *package-deal* outcomes. Marathon negotia-

24. Lindberg, *Political Dynamics*, passim, and Haas, *The Uniting of Europe*, passim.

tions refer to the penultimate bargaining sessions of the Council of Ministers when all the unresolved problems in a particular decision area (or in several areas) are put on 'the table simultaneously. They may go on practically around the clock and for a week or more until it has been possible to agree to some combination of heterogeneous items that all can accept as more or less equitable. These package deals are usually constructed by the Commission, which is in the best position to know (or guess) exactly what combinations of concessions and achievements each government can be brought to accept.

But beginning in 1963 this "code" was "violated" dramatically and repeatedly by General de Gaulle whenever it suited his purposes to do so. He threatened French withdrawal from the Community if his demands were not met. He mounted a bitter campaign against an active and independent role for the Commission. French bargaining was punctuated by threats, the making of extreme demands, a general disregard for the interests of her partners, and an unwillingness to make meaningful concessions.[25]

As a consequence, the system was plunged into a succession of crises attended by prolonged periods of stagnation in the decision-making process: in 1963 over de Gaulle's veto of the British membership application; in 1965 over his boycott of the Community institutions; and again in 1967–68 over his refusal to reopen membership negotiations with Britain. The effect of each of these crises has been to further erode the procedural consensus that had emerged. While it has still been possible to take some important decisions in a few areas, notably agriculture and commercial policy, and while no other country has seriously considered withdrawal, the "procedural code" appears to automatically govern fewer and fewer decision situations. It has often seemed as if everyone were trying to keep engagements to the minimum required to keep the system going. Only time can tell if this vital decision-making resource can be replenished. Until it is, marathon negotiations will probably occur and package deals will emerge, but they will be more and more difficult and the probabilities of failing to make needed decisions or to meet deadlines will increase.

Some Costs and Benefits of This Kind of System

Given the decision-making system's complexity and ambiguity, a number of doubts must naturally arise about its overall efficiency, its flexibility, and its equitableness. With what regularity can it be expected to cope effec-

25. For some details see Nina Heathcoate, "The Crisis of European Supranationality," *Journal of Common Market Studies* 5 (June 1967); John Newhouse, *Collision in Brussels: The Common Market Crisis of 30 June 1965* (New York: W. W. Norton, 1967); and Leon N. Lindberg, "Integration as a Source of Stress on the European Community System," *International Organization* 20 (Spring 1966).

tively with the problems brought to it? Will it be able to produce roughly comparable gains and impose commensurate sacrifices on each of the participating nations? The future of the Community would certainly be in doubt if it were to consistently fail to achieve appropriate joint decisions, or if one or two nations were to reap most of the benefits of integration. These are clearly basic problems for the future of the Community but they will be considered only briefly here.[26] First of all, it must be agreed that the system of "marathons" and "package deals" is time-consuming and tedious. But its inefficiency in this regard should be balanced against its efficiency as a promoter of consensus by means of the gradual juxtaposition of national positions leading to the redefinition of individual national interests in terms of some notion of a collective goal or benefit. Of course, even in that perspective, the record is mixed, as we have seen. Besides being time-consuming, the intricate negotiations and carefully balanced bargains that marathons and package deals involve also impose a potentially serious rigidity on the system. Once a decision is taken as part of a package deal it cannot be easily reversed or changed should circumstances warrant, for that might upset the original delicate balance of gains and sacrifices. Thus it is, for example, extremely difficult for the Community to amend its internal legislation in order to offer concessions in international bargaining like the Kennedy Round, or to provide for the difficulties applicants for membership in the Community are likely to encounter. Finally, hardly any decision can be considered as "routine" in a system in which equivalence of benefits is as important as in the European Community. De Gaulle's breaches of the Community operational code had the effect of making the bargaining partners even less willing than before to make sacrifices in the present in anticipation of a future gain. But it will almost certainly become more difficult to avoid doing this in the future, especially if the Community system is forced to tackle problems of general economic stability, full employment, balance of payments, etc. It is also likely to become more difficult (as Stanley Hoffmann has pointed out) to calculate equivalences when you deal with areas of policy that have high political saliency, and where monetary or trade or production values cannot be assigned. The general success the Community has enjoyed to date in providing a rough equality of benefits and sacrifices may be much harder to sustain in the future. Indeed, the necessity to maintain equivalence in the short run may prove a barrier to further integration. Whether or not the Community can move to a system of long-term balancing of gains and losses will depend on the extent to which events continue to push the member countries together and the extent to which political leaders, elites, and mass publics in these countries come to identify with and trust each other.

26. For a fuller analysis, see Lindberg and Scheingold, *Europe's Would-Be Polity*.

The Future of the European Community

One of the things that has emerged clearly from our analyses in this chapter is that both scope and capacity can change. So far, the Community's scope has shown a steady overall increase in both extent and intensity. Governments have come to make more and more decisions through collective or joint procedures and to do so in more and more decision areas. But there have been failures. There is also reason to believe that the Community may now be entering an era of stagnation or nongrowth, perhaps even of decline. The system's capacity to regularly and effectively concert behavior (to make decisions) has already known its ups and downs. Over the Community's history, the potential "power" of supranational institutions has been demonstrated, but so has their fragility, their dependence upon creative personnel and governmental acquiescence. Over the same period we have seen that the governments could move very far in the direction of evolving a distinct and unprecedented consensual procedural code. But this too is a fragile development, as General de Gaulle made clear to all. Alongside notable achievements in the areas of tariff cutting, agricultural and competition policy, and international negotiations like the Kennedy Round, we must array the failure to make progress in transport, energy, and social policy, and most notably the inability to deal satisfactorily with the problems posed by British entry. Such "failures" may well be responsible for the marked return to nationalist themes by national decision makers (not only de Gaulle) after the mid-1960s, and for the general drop off in optimism about the future of European integration on the part of the general public.

In the volume from which the foregoing discussion has been excerpted, we sought to construct a model of the European integration process and to use it to speculate systematically about the future of the Community by projecting forward on the basis of the model and of information available to us in 1970. Our conclusions can be summarized in two parts. We sought first to deal with the question of what would happen if there were a fundamental change in the pragmatic ideological climate for integration, including how likely such a change was and how responsive the Community system could be expected to be. This question is, of course, a fundamental one, since our model assumed a continuation of a "permissive consensus" based on a dampening of political conflict, a political quiescence generated by the satisfaction of material needs, and a general spread of middle-class values. Our findings generally parallel those of Heisler for his "European polity," namely, that this kind of system would encounter severe strains in an ideologically conflictual environment in which stability, incremental decision making, moderation and harmony, and rational discourse are not valued as ends in themselves, and in which expressive, "quality of life," and "power and privilege" demands come again to the fore.[27] Thus, the limits of the Community's constituency, the tenuousness of its operational code, and the constraints within which the European Commission operates, all led us to question the system's likely adaptiveness. We concluded further, however, that if such an ideological transformation was occurring, it was not likely to intervene in a way such as to prohibit *short-term* projections from our basic model.

The intervening two years have seen little to alter these conclusions. Although the issues of the environment, limits to economic growth, and quality of life are beginning to emerge and make themselves felt on the Community scene, it is too early to estimate their impact on the general ideological climate. Commission President Sicco Mansholt made the Club of Rome's famous "limits to growth" thesis[28] his own during the winter and spring of 1971–72, in an apparent effort to respond to such new demands and concerns and to expand the Community's potential constituency.[29] However, his term ended early in 1973 and there has been little indication that the governments—or indeed his Commission colleagues—are prepared to follow his lead. Moreover, his initiatives evoked the hostility of some groups out of which such an expanded constituency might be expected to be forged. For example, one of the main arguments given by the PCF in their opposition to French President Pompidou's Spring 1972 referendum to approve British entry into the Community was that such proposals to limit growth reflected the capitalist bias of the Community, since it would have the consequence of frustrating the workers' just demands for a more equitable future share of the material benefits of industrial civilization!

The second set of conclusions we reached in 1970 was thus based on a simple projection of our model of the determinants of growth, decline, or stability in the Community system. These conclusions were summarized as follows:

> "1. We found that some growth in scope seems quite likely in certain issue areas, namely, monetary and countercyclical policy, balance of payments, research and development, and agriculture.
>
> 2. But we also found that individual sectors or issue areas seem to tend toward equilibrium, and that as integration pro-

---

27. See Heisler, with Kvavik, chap. 2 in this volume, pp. 83–85. For a full exposition of our analysis see *Europe's Would-Be Polity*, chap. 8.

28. See Donella Meadows et al., *The Limits to Growth* (New York: Universe Books, 1972).

29. See Mansholt's letter to then Commission President Malfatti reprinted in *Agence Europe* Documents No. 665, Février 1972. The letter became a minor cause célèbre in Europe and Mansholt appeared at meetings regularly, in television and radio debates, with representatives of the entire political spectrum during the spring and summer of 1972.

ceeds, more and more sectors are likely to follow suit and the whole system may become both more stable and more resistant to growth. Hence our projection of an overall equilibrium or plateau to be reached some time within the next several years.

3. Even if the French government becomes more European, and even if Great Britain gains entry, our long-term projection is still for an overall equilibrium situation.

4. A substantial measure of uncertainty as to the Community's eventual scope and even to the validity of our basic projection is introduced by the possibility of the occurrence of various sorts of crises. No probability statements are possible as to their effects; they could either induce more growth or cause spill-back or collapse.

5. The long-term implications for the system and indeed its ability to survive will in all likelihood vary with its scope (i.e., whether it includes defense, monetary policy, etc.) and its institutional capacities. But that scope and capacity do not seem to us likely to be qualitatively different from what exists today. There will be more or less intensive collective decision making (more coordination than common policies) in more or fewer issue areas. Many matters will remain to be decided at the national level, and almost all Europe-level decisions will be implemented via national or regional authorities. We see very little prospect of a federal or near-federal European political union.

6. It is an oversimplification to attribute the slowdown in integration that became apparent in the 1960s to the malevolence of one political leader, de Gaulle, or even to a "lack of political will" among political actors more generally. That de Gaulle's influence was primarily negative and disruptive, at least after 1962, cannot be denied. Nor can we deny that political leaders in the countries of the Community are still divided as to long-term goals and as to their conception of what Europe is to become. So they were in the 1950s. Similarly, it is true that nationalism is more respectable these days and that there is also a growing preoccupation in all Community countries with domestic problems. Perhaps as important as these factors depressing leadership, however, are the two trends we have stressed in these concluding chapters: the conservative dynamics set in motion by the integration process itself, and the possiblity that the societal and international parameters that sustained and

conditioned the growth of the Community from the 1950s to the mid-1970s are in the process of being transformed."[30]

That the process of polity formation in the European Community is relatively slow and halting should not be surprising in view of the degree of symmetry/asymmetry between the characteristics of this system and those of the general type identified by Heisler for "the European polity," or by Lijphart for "consociational democracy." It seems undeniable that political cultural heterogeneity is more marked, that the operational code is less institutionalized, that environmental inputs provide a greater share of the decision load and hence reduce system autonomy, and that the bulk of implementation takes place within the sectoral systems: All of these can be expected to place limits on the Community system's scope, intensity, legitimacy, and stress-reducing capacity. Indeed, there may be some sort of boundary beyond which the European Community will find it very difficult to move simply because of its geographical and functional scope, its degree of internal diversity, and its international importance. For example, Lijphart hypothesizes that one of the most important conditions favorable to the emergence and continuity of consociational systems is "a relatively low total demand on the system" and that this has generally been associated with small countries which constitute the chief examples of consociational systems. In such systems "the management of subcultural cleavages is already a major burden requiring much of the leaders' energies and skills."[31] If a country is small in size "external threats are more likely to be considered serious and worthy of an unusual international response; nationalism is less likely to be of an extreme variety; and the total load on the system is likely to be lighter, if only because of a small country's limited power on the international scene and its greater chance of avoiding difficult decisions in this realm."[32]

The events of the intervening years tend to support our general forecasts. The agricultural system continues to function haltingly in a way requiring constant adaptation, alteration, and the steady involvement of elites in collective decision-making settings. And the member countries would seem to have little alternative but to eventually adopt some kind of common front in monetary matters, if only in opposition to the United States and Mr. Connally. But progress is very slow indeed! France under President Pompidou has not operated very differently from France under De Gaulle. The hard negotiating line, the ultimatum and fait accompli, and the imperious assumption of superior "European virtue" and of an inherent mission of European leadership continue to characterize France's European

30. *Europe's Would-Be Polity*, pp. 305–6. The elements in the model are stated in chap. 9.
31. Arend Lijphart, "Typologies of Democratic Systems, *Comparative Political Studies* I, no. 1 (April 1968): 30.
32. Ibid.

policy. Nor do the other members show very much more inclination to accept these tactics. Moreover, fundamental policy differences, which persist among the member governments, are not likely to be diminished by further erosions of the Community's operational code.

In addition, there is every reason to expect that the entry of Great Britain and the other new members will increase the difficulty of reaching acceptable compromises, both by increasing the diversity of interests represented and by injecting into the system new actors who have not shared in the creation of the institutions, the existing corpus of rules and laws, or the operational code or decision rules upon which the system is based. At the very least, a breaking-in period of undertermined duration will be required to enable socialization and institutional and rule adjustments to take place. This will be all the more important *within* a country such as Britain, given the general hostility to entry evident in British public opinion, and given the vigorous opposition to entry led by Wilson and the Labour party and their threats to withdraw once back in power unless the terms are completely renegotiated.

All of this is not to say that we expect the system to collapse or substantially regress. The most likely immediate future will be one of slow, incremental problem solving and adjustment of the system at roughly the present scope and capacities, a task likely to occupy fully the skills and energies of national and Community elites. But if the new members can be successfully coopted into the system's institutional consensus and procedures, and if these are able to cope with the existing array of problems with which it is confronted, it will be no mean achievement.

Part III

POLICY MAKING IN EUROPE:
Structures and
Processes

7

B. Guy Peters

The Development of Social Policy in France, Sweden, and The United Kingdom: 1850–1965*

This essay discusses the development of social policy in three European nations: France, Sweden, and the United Kingdom. It also focuses on an important aspect of the political development of these three nations during the period 1850–1965. Unlike most studies of development, however, the definition of development used here is directly related to the performance of the political system, rather than changes in capabilities of the social and political systems.

This difference may be illustrated with reference to a number of the more commonly cited discussions of development, all of which characterize development by changes on the input side of the political system. For example, Lerner discusses development in terms of changes in the communications system of a nation, and its relationship to participatory attitudes among the population.[1] Lipset and Cutright speak of democratization as the primary criterion of development, referring largely to the manner in which elites are selected.[2] Almond and Powell speak of development in terms of changes in political culture and structural characteristics of the

*The author would like to thank the Computer Centers of Emory University and Michigan State University for assistance in this project. He is also indebted to Timothy Hennessey, Paul Abramson, and John Collins of Michigan State University, and Eleanor C. Main of Emory University, for assistance in the development of this project.

1. Daniel Lerner, *The Passing of Traditional Society* (Glencoe, Ill.: Free Press, 1958), pp. 43–75.

2. Seymour Martin Lipset, "Some Social Requisites for Democracy: Economic Development and Political Legitimacy," *American Political Science Review* 53, no. 1 (March 1959): 69–105; Philips Cutright, "National Political Development: Measurement and Analysis," *American Sociological Review* 28, no. 2 (April 1963): 253–64.

social system, with some attention given to increases in governmental capabilities.[3] It is assumed that the changes in capabilities will indeed be related to changes in the impact which government has on the lives of the individuals in the system, but that linkage is never shown directly.

The above definitions, therefore, deal rather obviously with the input side of the system. The concentration of this study, however, is on the output side. Thus, political development is defined as the increasing ability of the political system to ensure the quality of life of its population.[4]

Several things should be noted about this definition. First, it posits a very positive role for the political system in providing as high as possible quality of life for the population. Thus, governments are judged by their impact on the citizens. This is as value laden a definition as any other, but at least it offers a means of judging the performance of the system, as opposed to judging simply its attributes.

The second thing to be noted concerning the definition is the rather ambiguous phrase, "quality of life." This embraces a number of characteristics of human life, and a single essay cannot possibly deal with all of them. Therefore, our attention in this paper is concentrated on services provided by the political system in health, education, and economic security. These are all important contributors to a high quality of life, and they are all areas in which modern government has sought to have an impact. This chapter describes that impact and evaluates the performance of the systems.

Finally, no end point is posited by this definition which represents the attainment of a state called "development." Systems may be more or less developed, but there will never be a fully developed system. This is true not only because of the seeming impossibility of the satiation of human wants, but also because of the virtual impossibility of deciding what level of education or what level of infant mortality represents an adequate job on the part of government. Therefore, this essay discusses relative states of development, and the patterns through which these states of development have been attained.

Our discussion covers three political systems that fall into the general category of more developed. France, Sweden, and the United Kingdom all have relatively high life expectancies and relatively low rates of infant mortality. They all provide free public education at least through a secondary level, with greater and greater extensions into higher education. Finally, all three countries have made a commitment to the provision of at least a minimum level of economic security for their people, both in old

3. Gabriel Almond and G. Bingham Powell, *Comparative Politics: A Developmental Approach* (Boston: Little, Brown, 1966).

4. For similar definitions, see Karl de Schweinitz, "Growth, Development and Political Modernization," *World Politics* 22, no. 4 (July 1970): 518–40. Also, Joyce M. Mitchell and William C. Mitchell, *Political Analysis and Public Policy* (Chicago: Rand McNally, 1969).

age and in times of economic crisis during the normal working years. Despite these basic similarities, these three countries are far from identical in either their present level of benefits or in the path through which they arrived at that state of development. Therefore, in this comparative study we can say a great deal about the political and social systems of the three countries, as well as make some general inferences about patterns of change in public policy.

The first section of this chapter discusses the historical development of social policy in these three nations, with the purpose of providing the reader some background knowledge of the time sequences involved in this development. Following this is an analysis of time-series data relating to the development of governmental impacts on society, in order to explain these impacts as a product of social, economic, and political forces.

Historical Development

Our discussion of the developments of social policies is by policy areas, and an attempt at comparisons between nations is made as we proceed. Also pointed out are some of the differences in the policy areas as they have developed in all three countries.

Education

In all three countries, education was traditionally a private function, the responsibility of the church or the individual.[5] This rather naturally produced elitist systems of education, with little or no possibility for the children of the working classes to advance through education. In all three countries, as in all industrial systems, education has now become a public function. Nevertheless, both the timing of increased government intervention and the apparent reasons for that intervention were different.

In the United Kingdom the first significant intervention was the beginning of grants to local districts for primary education in 1833. Prior to this time, localities had supported education in some boroughs, but this marked the beginning of central government action. It was not until 1879, however, that public education was assured for those who did not have access to private education.[6] Following this, the school-leaving age was consistently increased; it is now sixteen.

---

5. See, for example, S. J. Curtis, *History of Education in Great Britain* (London: University Tutorial Press, 1967); Luc Decaunes, *Projets de réforme de l'enseignement Francais de la revolution à nos jours* (Paris: Institut Pedagogique National, 1962); Rolland G. Paulston, *Educational Change in Sweden* (New York: Teachers College Press, 1968).

6. J. W. Adamson, *English Education 1789–1902* (Cambridge: Cambridge University Press, 1930); G. A. N. Lowndes, *The Silent Social Revolution* (London: Oxford University Press, 1937).

Despite the provision of adequate elementary education relatively early, the involvement of the government in providing secondary and higher education was not significant until after the beginning of the twentieth century. The Education Act of 1902 provided support for local districts wishing to offer secondary education, but it was not until the Education Act of 1944 that secondary education was provided for all who sought it. Public funds were first granted to universities in 1882, but the level of support was minimal until 1920. Since 1920, both public funding of universities and of university students has increased rapidly.

The needs of the society appear to have prompted a good deal of the early educational reform. Personnel to occupy white-collar jobs were in insufficient numbers, and there were problems in acquiring adequately educated officers for the military. Therefore, in order to keep the industrial and commercial systems of the nation operating, and to preserve the image of the officer corps, the system was willing to grant its citizens more and more educational benefits. This, of course, is a bit of an overstatement, but its basic accuracy can be rather well documented.[7]

The large-scale involvement of the French government in education began as early as the Revolution of 1789, although involvement with certain types of technical education had begun during the ancien régime.[8] The major issue in the growing involvement of the French political system for most of the period from 1850 to the present has not been so much the problems of industrialization, but rather the conflict between church and state. At the beginning of the time period under study, the church was relatively firmly in control, due to the passage of the *Loi Falloux* (1850).[9] Viewed as a victory for the clerical educators, the law provided a special place for the church in the university, as well as increased involvement in elementary education. In 1879, however, with the appointment of Jules Ferry as minister of education, the fortunes of the clericals took a final turn for the worse. The culmination of Ferry's anticlerical and democratization campaigns came with the passage of the reforms of 1904–05, and the establishment of education as a virtual monopoly of the state.[10] There was some "scholarly guerrilla warfare" during the 1905–14 period, but the issue was basically decided.[11]

Given this monopoly, the question arose as to what would be done by the political system. Elementary education was provided free and was

7. David V. Glass, "Education," in *Law and Opinion in England in the 20th Century*, ed. Morris Ginsburg (London: Stevens and Sons, 1959), pp. 319–46.

8. Felix Ponteil, *Histoire de l'enseignement en France, 1789–1965* (Paris: Sirey, 1965).

9. Antoine Prost, *L'enseignement en France 1800–1967* (Paris: Armand Colin: 1968), pp. 155–71.

10. Ibid., pp. 198–221.

11. Ibid., p. 210. Also, Jean-Marie Mayeur, *La Séparation de l'Eglise et de l'Etat* (Paris: Julliard, 1966).

compulsory, so the only major adjustments that had to be made concerned the age of school leaving and the curriculum. Furthermore, the secondary and university levels had always been greatly influenced by the government, through the prestigious *lycées* and the *Grands Écoles*. What has followed, therefore, has been an increasing centralization of power in Paris, and significant extensions of the accessibility to secondary and university education. Most significant in this respect were the reforms of 1946.

The major thrust for educational reform in Sweden has been the *folkskola* ("people's school") movement, with the basic point of democratizing the educational system.[12] The first significant movement in this direction was the Act of 1842, which began state involvement in mass education. For some years the government had supported the gymnasiums, whose clientele were largely the children of the upper and middle classes. With the *folkskola* act of 1842, there was free compulsory education for all children until the age of fifteen.[13] After this major reform, the remainder of Swedish educational history in the nineteenth century concerned whether the *folkskola* should be the one and only means of preparation for entrance into higher levels of the educational system. The reformers favored such a policy on the grounds of equality and social mobility, while the conservatives opposed it on grounds of educational inefficiency, as well as on the grounds of its effects on the social structure. The Education Act of 1894, the major result of this debate, required three years of *folkskola* education before admittance to other forms of state-supported education, but with some loopholes to placate the middle classes.[14]

Following the Great School Commission of 1918 and limited reforms in 1927, the next date of importance in the history of Swedish education is 1930. This year saw the passage of the Communes Act. This act transferred greater responsibility for education to the localities, although certain national standards and programs were retained.[15] During the 1930s the Social Democratic party initiated a number of relatively minor reforms which further democratized the educational system.

The next major educational reform arose over the issue of the *enhetsskola* ("comprehensive school") proposals following World War II. This

---

12. See, for example, Stig Jägerskjold, *Från prästskola till enhetskola* (Stockholm: Almqvist & Wiksell, 1959). It is also interesting to note the importance of the conflict between church and state in this instance. See, Wilhelm Sjöstrand, *Pedagogikens historia, från antiken till forsta världskriget* (Malmo: C. W. K. Gleerups Förlag, 1954).

13. Paulston, *Educational Change in Sweden*, pp. 13–34.

14. Torsten Husen, *Problems of Differentiation in Swedish Compulsory Schooling* (Stockholm: Svenska Bökforlaget, 1962); Fridtjuv Berg, *Folkskolan såsom bottenskola: nutidsfrågor på uppfostrans område* (Lund: SAF Pedagogiska Skrifter, 1911).

15. The importance of this act can be shown empirically. See B. Guy Peters, "The Development of Social Policy: A Longitudinal Analysis of Social Expenditures and Their Impacts in the United Kingdom, France and Sweden" (Ph.D. dissertation, Michigan State University, 1970), pp. 193–95.

was a revival of the conflict over the *folkskola* in the nineteenth century. The proposal called for a "unity" school which all would attend and which would thereby foster national unity, and integration, especially between the social classes. This program was passed into law in 1950, by legislation that has become the foundation of the present *grundskola* ("basic school") system of nine years of very similar education for all students, with differentiations made at a later stage.[16]

As for higher educational levels, the state-run gymnasiums and universities continued as relatively elitist institutions until after the Second World War. Minor reforms had taken place throughout the time period, but secondary education and university education remained largely the province of the upper classes. Since 1945, extensive democratization of both levels of education has taken place, and now almost complete educational equality is assured. Further, an extensive system of adult education exists, of which Sweden and other Scandinavian countries are rather justifiably proud. This allows those who may have missed the opportunity for the type of education they desired in youth to receive it at a later date.

In summary, then, the involvement of the political systems in these three countries in the educational process appears to have sprung from a mixture of motives. The discernible major thrust in each is quite different: the United Kingdom for skilled workers, France for anticlerical reasons, and Sweden for ostensibly democratic and egalitarian reasons. Whatever the motives, the results have been approximately the same—extensive governmental involvement at all levels of education, and widespread educational opportunity for all children in the nations.

Economic Security

In the area of economic security, two major movements took place in these three countries, as in virtually all Western systems. The first, dealing with the problem of public assistance, has been movement from a system of poor relief to a system of family allowances. In the latter scheme, all families with certain economic and social characteristics receive payments from the state. This system is designed to remove the stigma of relief and, at the same time, to remove some of the administrative burdens of poor relief. The second movement has been from the care of the needy elderly as a part of the general population of poor people to the anticipation of such need through a system of social security or other form of social insurance. Once again, these insurance schemes provide for the care of the elderly without the stigma of charity or relief.

Speaking specifically of the United Kingdom, these two movements

16. Paulston, *Educational Change in Sweden*, pp. 105–41.

have been especially noticeable. The United Kingdom began the time period under investigation using the famous Poor Laws as the major form of providing for the indigent, both of working age and the aged.[17] In fact, shortly before the beginning of this time period, there was something of a step backward in social policy with the passage of the Poor Law Reform Act of 1834 allowing the use of the workhouses by the Poor Law Districts. A number of minor reforms in this system occurred during the remainder of the nineteenth century, and considerable agitation for better conditions, but the first major reform did not take place until 1908. In this year the Old Age Pensions Act was passed, constituting the first step in the formation of a system of social insurance.[18] This trend was continued in 1920 with the adoption of unemployment insurance. Nevertheless, the Poor Laws were not finally abolished until 1948, with the adoption of a comprehensive social security program, which included family payments.

The French system of economic security followed a similar pattern, although the French adopted the family payments idea more quickly. In fact, France and Belgium were pioneers in this type of social program.[19] At the beginning of our time period, the care of the indigent was provided by a system of public assistance and by the church and charitable organizations. These services were organized on the local level and provided wide ranges of benefits. The services were centralized in 1886 and benefits became uniform throughout France.

At the same time that the public relief system was being standardized, the foundations for the family payments system were being laid. Interestingly, this was initiated by private industry.[20] The salaries of mine workers with three or more children were supplemented by a mine owner, and this system spread to others in the mining and metalworking industries. This trend increased during World War I, and after considerable agitation, the *Loi d'allocations familiales* was passed in 1931. This scheme was extended in 1939 immediately prior to the outbreak of the war, and was finally incorporated as an integral part of the social security system in 1956. As now organized, families with a certain number of children and with incomes below a certain level receive supplements from the state intended largely for the welfare of the children.

In the realm of social insurance, the first major piece of legislation was

17. Samuel Mencher, "Introduction to Poor Law Reports of 1834 and 1909," in *Social Welfare in Transistion*, ed. Roy Lubove (Pittsburgh: University of Pittsburgh Press, 1966), pp. 37–40; Thomas McKay, *A History of the English Poor Law*, Vol. 3, *1834 to the Present Time* (London: P. S. King & Sons, 1899).

18. Karl de Schweinitz, *England's Road to Social Security* (London: Oxford University Press, 1943).

19. Walter A. Friedlander, *Individualism and Social Welfare* (New York: Free Press, 1962), p. 160.

20. Dominique Ceccaldi, *Histoire des prestations familiales en France* (Paris: Union Nationale des Caisses d'Allocations Familiales, 1957).

the Workers and Peasants Pensions Law of 1910, providing pensions for retired people after age sixty-five.[21] This program was greatly extended to cover all forms of social insurance in 1928, but a fully developed social security system was not passed until 1946. The major reform of 1946 included *all* citizens, not merely employees and their families as had been true previously. This social security program was reorganized in 1956, but the 1946 law constitutes the major operating legislation for the system.

Finally, Sweden has adopted virtually the same forms of change as the other two systems. The Poor Relief Act of 1847 was modeled to some extent on that of the United Kingdom and had some of the same flaws. This system was made even more stringent by legislation passed in 1871. There was a liberalization of the Poor Relief system in 1918, but a system of family payments was not adopted until the 1956 Social Help Act.[22]

The development of a system of social insurance began relatively earlier than the family payments. In 1910 a sickness insurance scheme was passed, followed in 1913 by a general pensions act, providing rather comprehensive coverage for the elderly. This system was expanded even further through legislation in 1935 and 1946, and in 1959 pension payments were tied to the cost of living in an attempt to ensure a stable standard of living for the recipients. Finally, all forms of social insurance were consolidated and integrated under the 1962 Pensions Act.

All three countries had rather similar patterns in the development of these programs of economic security. In all three, there was a beginning of a social insurance program around the period 1908–13, although the circumstances surrounding the adoption of this legislation were quite different in each. Also, at a later date, there was a movement toward a system of family payments. This movement was generally regarded as a more significant step for the policy makers of the three countries since, unlike the pensions, they did not require contributions on the part of the recipient. These plans have been adopted and have remained in force for a number of years without serious attempts to revoke them.

Public Health

Finally, in public health services, the general movement in these countries has been from the care of the sick who could not afford private care under the general mechanisms of poor relief to the care of virtually all citizens under a system of national health insurance, similar to other forms of social insurance.

At the beginning of the time period studied most national programs

---

21. Friedlander, *Individualism*, p. 170.
22. See Albert Rosenthal, *The Social Programs of Sweden* (Minneapolis: University of Minnesota Press, 1967); Wilfrid Fleisher, *Sweden the Welfare State* (New York: John Day, 1956).

in public health consisted of sanitation, vaccination, and some relief for the indigent poor through public hospitals. The first significant movement toward a system of medical insurance was the French *Loi nationale d'assistance medicale gratuite*, passed in 1893.[23] This legislation made the first differentiation between those who were indigent for medical purposes and the general body of the poor. Thus, people previously excluded from public medical services because they made too much money but who could not adequately provide their own medical care could receive assistance under this legislation.

The next significant piece of legislation was the National Health Insurance Act of 1911 in the United Kingdom.[24] Far from a comprehensive or adequate program, this was nevertheless a first attempt on the part of a government to take over the financing of medical services through insurance. A similar piece of legislation was adopted in 1928 in France, but it was not until 1956 that Sweden adopted a medical insurance program on a national scale. However, the program adopted by Sweden in 1956 tends to be more comprehensive than that of the other two countries. Of course, these early programs were not the final pieces of legislation in France and the United Kingdom. France adopted a full-scale system of medical insurance in the social security legislation of 1946, and expanded this even further in the reforms of 1956, mainly by providing more services to the elderly. In the United Kingdom the passage of the National Health Service Act of 1948 was the turning point in providing a truly comprehensive system of medical services. This has been modified by the various governments since 1948, but serves as the foundation of Britain's system of socialized medicine.

One factor that will be of importance at a later point in this analysis is the question of the provision of medical personnel by these governments. Sweden began quite early (the middle of the eighteenth century) to provide district medical officers to ensure that all areas of the country would have at least a minimal level of medical personnel available.[25] This system has been greatly expanded throughout the history of the country. France began later (under Napoleon), but the same idea of distributing medical personnel was important.[26] This idea was of little importance in the foundations of the medical care system of the United Kingdom, and has only recently been accepted. Prior to this, the major reliance for distribution was on private charities which would attempt to provide care in all sections of the nation.

23. Friedlander, *Individualism*, pp. 37–40.
24. For a discussion of this legislation, see Richard M. Titmuss, "Health," in Ginsburg, *Law and Opinion*, pp. 299–318.
25. Thorsten Sellin, ed., *Social Welfare in Sweden* (New York: Royal Swedish Commission, 1941), p. 33.
26. René Sand, *L'économie humaine par la médicine sociale* (Paris: Rieder, 1934).

Summary

The general direction of policy in all these areas has been first toward greater benefits, and second toward a more equitable distribution of those benefits. Only relatively recently has the question of removing the stigma of some social services been addressed. The use of insurance schemes is an obvious step in that direction, as is the system of family payments. The problem is far from solved in any of the three countries, however, nor in any advanced country of the world.

Another problem concerns the manner in which the levels of expenditure and benefit are decided by the political system. The past history of these programs has been largely a history of social and political pressure exerted on decision makers. This has resulted in improved benefits, rather obviously, but over a very long time span and with relatively high expenditures of time and influence. The question, then, is whether the social policy systems of these countries can be made more directly responsive to objective needs of the population. The basic questions concerning the commitment to the welfare state have been settled, and now the remaining questions appear to be minor adjustments to emergent conditions. This question, as well as the more general question concerning the importance of variables in explaining the development of programs, is dealt with in the following section on the analysis of our data.

Analysis of Data

Services Provided

To this point, we have been discussing the development of social policy rather generally. We must begin to discuss the particular types of services to be analyzed. As noted, our discussion centers on health, education, and economic security. This allows us to make comparisons not only between countries, but between issue areas as well. The problem is complicated, however, by the number of possible indicators for services in each issue area. We have narrowed the indicators down to one each for education and health, and two for economic security.

First, for education, the indicator used is the percentage of school-age children (ages 5–14) who are actually receiving some sort of education. This is referred to here as the *school rate*. Obviously, several assumptions underlie the selection of this indicator. The most important assumption is that children should receive at least nine years of formal education. This assumption may not have been valid during the early portion of the time period studied, but has become increasingly valid with increases in the technological levels of the three societies. Elementary and secondary education could have been dealt with separately, but this would probably only have confused the results, rather than clarifying them. Furthermore, the indicators chosen are standardized for the number of children who are potentially educable, and are therefore more comparable both across time and across political systems.

Second, for the area of economic security, we have two indicators. The first is related to provisions for economic security for the elderly and infirm. This indicator, called the *pension rate,* is the percentage of the population over sixty-five years of age who receive some sort of pension from the government. In the beginning of the time period, this was largely pensions for retired civil servants and their survivors, but in the latter portions the benefits are almost entirely through social security systems. Once again, this indicator is standardized for the number of potential beneficiaries.

The second indicator for economic security deals with security during the normal working years. In the latter portions of the time period, the availability of unemployment benefits may have been the best indicator of this type of service. This indicator is not applicable for a very large portion of the period, however, and the indicator used instead is the number of people who received either public assistance or family payments, as a percentage of the working-age population. This may be a last line of defense against economic difficulties in some instances, but it still provides good information on the availability of services.

Finally, for health, the indicator of services used is the infant mortality rate. This is the number of deaths during the first year of life per 1,000 live births. This is a standard indicator of the quality of health care in a country, and is more reliable over time than the data on life expectancy at birth. Finally, the infant mortality rate is highly intercorrelated with other possible measures of services, such as life expectancy and gross death rates. Unlike the other indicators used, however, it does not directly measure the delivery of services, but rather the effects of those services. The question of the actual delivery of services arises in the analysis of the health data.

Possible Explanations of Levels of Service

In seeking to offer an explanation for the level of services provided to the populations of these countries, we face a number of problems. First, there are a number of possible explanations, all of which have a certain amount of plausibility. Second, in dealing with time-series data of this type, all the factors tend to move together through time; consequently, one encounters a great deal of difficulty in sorting out the independent effects of each explanation. In the same vein, there is a problem in assuming that the effects are in the same time period; in reality, the effects of social changes may not manifest themselves for a number of years. Despite these problems, this section attempts to explain the development of these policies using statistical analysis. It details the possible explanations, as well as the operational definitions of the concepts that will be used in the analysis.

Economic Development

The first, and probably most common, explanation of these changes is that they are a function of economic development. This explanation has a good deal of empirical support, especially in the explanation of public expenditures.[27] It is assumed that as the ability of the economy to provide goods and services increases, a "slack" develops.[28] This slack is available for extraction and reallocation through the public budget. In other words, as production increases, the marginal utility of that production decreases, and voters and decision makers are more willing to be taxed for social services. Furthermore, the development of the economy provides a general resource base on which to draw in the implementation of public policy. This may be especially important in the area of public health. Expenditures by government for health services are important in improving health conditions, but a number of factors, such as adequate diet, sanitation, and rest are also associated with good health. These factors also tend to be associated with higher levels of economic development. Therefore, the effects of economic development on health are both direct and indirect. The direct effects come through improved living standards, while the indirect effects come through making funds available for public expenditures for health programs. Similar effects may be imagined for education and economic security, especially with respect to the indirect effects, but they are more obvious with health.

As the objective indicator of this concept, the standard measure of per capita gross national product is used. This is unavailable for Sweden over the entire period, and therefore national income per capita is used in that instance. These two indicators are highly related, and both adequately assess the level of economic growth. They are measures of the total economic resources available to the decision makers of the countries, with the previously mentioned assumptions concerning increased ability of reallocation being associated with the development of these resources.

Education

A second possible explanation of the improvements and growth in social programs is the level of education of the population. The paths through which the general educational level may affect social programs are even

27. See, for example, Thomas Dye, *Politics, Economics and the Public* (Chicago: Rand McNally, 1966); Philips Cutright, "Political Structure, Economic Development and National Social Security Programs," *American Journal of Sociology* 70, no. 5 (March 1965): 537–50. For a different view, see B. Guy Peters, "Economic and Political Effects Upon the Development of Social Expenditures in France, Sweden and the United Kingdom" *Midwest Journal of Political Science* 16, no. 2 (May 1972): 225–38.

28. See Albert O. Hirschman, *The Strategy of Economic Development* (New Haven: Yale University Press, 1958); Richard M. Cyert and James G. March, *A Behavioral Theory of the Firm* (Englewood Cliffs, N. J.: Prentice-Hall, 1963).

more complex than those of economic development, but our discussion lists several possible effects.

A rise in general educational level leads to an increase in abilities of the population which result from education. Once again, this factor may be especially important in the policy area of health. Not only does the implementation of a health program require a supply of highly trained professional personnel, but it also requires a population capable of producing and absorbing information about medicine. In addition, specifically for the policy area of education, parents who have been educated usually want at least the same, and usually higher, levels of education for their children.[29] Thus, educational services provided at one point in time produce a demand for education at a future date. Operationally, this concept is realized through a measure of the proportion of the population who received at least a secondary education. The level of measurement in this instance is relatively rough, but the data do show the changes which have occurred with reasonable degrees of accuracy. In tables, this measure is referred to as the *lagged education*.

Governmental Action

A third possible explanation for the improvements in services relates to the development of societal resources such as the economy and education through specific governmental actions. These actions are of two types: expenditures for specific purposes, and the growth of administrative abilities.

Expenditures. Increases in governmental expenditures for a specific service are associated with increases in services actually rendered to the population. One cannot deny that there have been marked increases in expenditures which appear to be related to the services provided. Furthermore, these expenditures are more directly related to the services than the diffuse effects discussed for economic and educational resources. Associated with these distributive outputs of government have been commensurate regulative activities. Thus, having the ability to do so, government appears to have exercised its authority to provide services for the population. Nevertheless, the argument presented here cannot prove the importance of expenditures, a fact we hope to demonstrate.

The operationalization of public expenditures involved the examination of the budget documents of the three countries in question and the isolation of expenditures for the purposes studied. Per capita expenditures are used for education, general welfare, pensions, and health as the measures of public effort through expenditures. The raw data used was converted to constant monetary units so that the data might be more comparable across time.

29. F. M. Martin, "An Inquiry into Parents' Preferences in Secondary Education," in *Social Mobility in Britain*, ed. D. V. Glass (London: Routledge & Kegan Paul, 1954), pp. 160–75.

Administrative Ability. The expenditure of public funds may be a necessary condition for changes in services, but it may not be a sufficient condition. In order for funds to have a significant impact, the programs of government must be administered effectively. Unfortunately, it is virtually impossible to assess the effectiveness of administration over such a long time span. Therefore, we have chosen to deal with quantitative growth rather than attempting the measurement of effectiveness. Therefore, increases in the size of the bureaucracy will indicate some attempt on the part of the political system to implement programs as effectively as possible. This concept is measured operationally as the percentage of the working-age population employed by the government in nondefense programs. It is referred to in the analysis as the *civil service rate.*

Systemic Responsiveness

The last of the possible explanations mentioned is the least probable, but it is at the same time the most intriguing. This explanation is that the political system has begun to respond to social and economic conditions in its environment in making and implementing public policy. It is obvious that this has always been one characteristic of government, but in this case, we are speaking of direct reactions to changes in needs of the population. This is therefore, rather close to the ideas of a cybernetic policy system mentioned by Deutsch.[30] If these models have any validity in the explanation of policy, we would expect it to appear in nations such as the three under study. All are highly developed economically and have relatively highly developed communications systems. Furthermore, all are parliamentary democracies, and may therefore tend to be more responsive than authoritarian, or even presidential, systems.

In seeking to operationalize a method of examining systemic response, an operational measure of need for each of the policy areas seemed required. Ingenuity failed with respect to the area of health, so this portion of the analysis is limited to education and economic security. First, for education, we use changes in the technological level of the society, measured by *per capita energy consumption*, as the indicator of the need for education. In general, as the technological level increases, more and more trained personnel are required by the economic system. This places an obvious burden on the educational system of a nation for the production of such personnel. For example, Frank Bowles has said that

> achievement of a complex industrial society rests upon a technology resting in turn upon an educational system which can develop the technology. This implies a continuous reciprocity of development as between science and technology on the one hand and education on the other.[31]

30. Karl Deutsch, *The Nerves of Government* (New York: Free Press, 1967).
31. Frank Bowles, "Education in the New Europe," in *A New Europe?*, ed. Stephen S. Graubard (Boston: Beacon Press, 1967), p. 441.

Therefore, we hypothesize that political systems which are attempting to respond to relevant needs for expansion of education will increase educational rates in response to technological increases.

Economic security again requires two indicators. First, for the pension rate, we use the ratio of the population employed in the industrial and service sectors of the economy, called *industrialization* in the tables, as an indicator of need. This is used because of the breakdown of traditional means of care for the elderly which is associated with the industrialization process.[32] The extended family no longer provides the support, with many of the young moving to the cities, where they are either unwilling or incapable of caring for older relatives. Furthermore, the traditional charities tended to break down under the strain of the number of people requiring services during periods of industrialization.

For public assistance services, we use the *unemployment rate* as an indicator of need. Obviously, when unemployment increases, the need for services of this variety will tend to increase, even when there are provisions for unemployment relief. The time span for unemployment benefits tends to be limited, and after these benefits expire, the use of public assistance may be the only alternative. Furthermore, with the institutionalization of family payments schemes, the family would probably receive benefits of some variety throughout the period of unemployment. Once again, this is especially important when traditional means of social welfare have been at least partially undermined by the industrialization and urbanization processes.

It should be obvious that the level of measurement of the needs for services is relatively rough. More complex models using interactions between industrialization and other social conditions may be required for a full explanation of the processes. However, this analysis allows us to begin the investigation of a very important question concerning the development of public policies in these issue areas.

The Nature of the Data and Methods of Analysis

The data used in this study were compiled from the official statistical publications of these three countries, where possible.[33] The remaining data were collected from a number of secondary sources. These sources were also used to cross-check the data from the official publications. The collection of data over such a time span and for three countries presents some rather obvious problems of reliability, but the data set used in this analysis is as accurate as possible. One of the major difficulties normally encountered in data collection of this type is that of comparability of categor-

32. See, for example, the work in Bert F. Hoselitz and Wilbert E. Moore, *Industrialization and Society* (The Hague: Mouton, 1966); Bert F. Hoselitz, *Sociological Aspects of Economic Growth* (Glencoe, Ill.: Free Press, 1960).

33. For a complete description of data sources, see Peters, "Development of Social Policy."

ies among the systems. This analysis has a distinct advantage over most in this respect: it is conducted *within* countries with the comparisons then made across systems. Therefore, if the definitions of variables are consistent within countries, as they generally are, and if they are reasonably congruent across systems, as they are, there should be no serious problems in the use of the data.

The data used are not year-by-year compilations, but rather are based on an every-five-year sample. This was done to ease some of the difficulties in collection and to eliminate some problems of serial autocorrelation.[34] Therefore, for the United Kingdom and France there are twenty-four observations, and twenty-one for Sweden, the data for 1850–64 being unavailable for that country.

Although the data are available for the entire time period, our analysis uses smaller periods. Specifically, we discuss the first four alternative explanations in halves of the total period. The first time period for France and the United Kingdom runs from 1850–1905, and the second from 1906–65. For Sweden, these periods are 1865–1910 and 1911–65. This not only splits the data into even portions, but it also breaks it around the 1905–10 time period which was so important in the formation of social policy in these three countries. Therefore, we are operating with the implicit hypothesis that the two time periods are different. Furthermore, we expect the impact of governmental activities to predominate in the second period, while the influences of available resources predominate in the first period.

For the assessment of the effects of the systemic response variables, we use different time periods. For all three countries, the periods are 1900–30 and 1935–65. This provides seven observations in each period. This is a relatively small number, but it allows some tentative analysis. The time periods were chosen because the idea of systemic responsiveness would only appear to fit systems that have first made the decision to commit the resources of the nation and the government to the provision of social services. This decision was made in these countries shortly after the turn of the century, and consequently these two time periods were chosen. The idea of systemic responsiveness may be no more appropriate in 1900 than it was in 1850, but it may have meaning by the end of the total period. Therefore, we are again hypothesizing differences in the two time periods. In the first time period (1900–30) the effects of political variables are expected to predominate. In the second, however, we should see an increased influence of the cybernetic, or need, variables. That is to say, the development of the social policy systems of these countries is hypothesized to go through three stages —from socioeconomic determinism to political determinism and finally to determination by needs.

34. Hubert M. Blalock, *Theory Construction* (Englewood Cliffs, N. J.: Prentice-Hall, 1969), p. 140.

The major statistical technique employed in the analysis of the data is stepwise regression.[35] From a set of potential explanatory variables, such as the ones we have outlined, the computer program first selects the variable explaining the greatest amount of variance in the dependent variable. At the second and successive stages, the program selects the independent variable explaining the greatest amount of *residual* variance from the preceding step. Therefore, although two variables may be both more strongly related to the dependent variable than any of the other potential independent variables, they would not necessarily enter the regression equation in first and second order because of their own intercorrelations. This would indicate that the two variables were actually indicators of the same underlying concept and little is to be gained, either statistically or theoretically, by the use of both to explain the dependent variable. In the results presented, the program is allowed to run to conclusion, i.e., all the variables are entered. This allows the reader to determine more about the relative importance of the whole set of variables.

Two statistics are used in the evaluation of the effects of the potential explanatory variables.[36] The first is the order of entry into the regression equations. This is based on the program mentioned above and the value of R^2, the coefficient of multiple determination. This is a measure of the percentage of variance in the dependent variable explained by the independent variable(s). The values of R^2 reported in the tables are measures of the additive effects of the independent variable included in the equation up to that point.

As well as measuring the variance explained by our independent variables, we are also interested in their relative effects on the dependent variable. The most common measure of effect used is the beta weight, or standardized regression coefficient. This statistic measures the change in the dependent variable, measured in standard deviation units, resulting from a change of one standard deviation unit of the independent variable. Whereas the values of R^2 reported are cumulative, the values of the beta weights are measures of the independent effects of each of the independent variables.

Because of the small number of observations in the period in which we are examining the response of political systems to environmental needs, the use of the multiple regression technique outlined above is not appropriate. Therefore, we rely simply on the relative values of the simple correlation coefficient in the discussion of this data. While not as complex as the above analysis, it allows us to make some preliminary examination of the response.

35. See N. R. Draper and H. Smith, *Applied Regression Analysis* (New York: John Wiley, 1959), pp. 163–95.
36. Mordecai Ezekiel and Karl A. Fox, *Methods of Correlation and Regression Analysis* (New York: John Wiley, 1959), esp. pp. 147–50.

Results of the Analysis

We again have several service areas and several countries to discuss. We use the strategy adopted in the historical section, and present the data by policy areas, and then make the comparisons across countries.

Education

The first policy area to be discussed is education. As noted, the patterns of development in the three countries have been quite different. In general, there has been a greater reliance on the private sector in providing education in the United Kingdom than in the other two systems. This may be contrasted most specifically with the centralization of the French educational system. The Swedish pattern has been more moderate, with some early reliance on the central government, but with significant impacts at the state (*lan*) and communal levels.

Given these historical and administrative patterns, the results presented in tables 1–3 are rather surprising. For both France and the United Kingdom, the influence of government was very strong in the first period. In both cases, the civil service rate entered the equation first, with educational expenditures second. In addition, these two variables had large beta weights. Therefore, it seems that although government appeared to have relatively little interest in education during this period, especially in the United Kingdom, the efforts they did make had rather great effects. The influence appears to have been rather diffuse, i.e., through the general growth of the administrative apparatus, but there was influence nonetheless. Furthermore, the more direct actions taken through expenditures also had significant effects.

Sweden, in contrast, had an educational system that was quite closely

Table 1. Explanation of the School Rate in the United Kingdom

Independent Variable	R^2	Beta Weight
First Period (1850–1905)		
Civil service rate	0.822	–1.182
Educational expenditures per capita	0.825	2.067
GNP per capita	0.917	–1.249
Lagged education	0.930	–0.449
Second Period (1906–65)		
GNP per capita	0.741	1.109
Civil service rate	0.820	–0.532
Lagged education	0.824	–0.116
Educational expenditures per capita	0.826	0.144

Table 2. Explanation of the School Rate in France

Independent Variable	R^2	Beta Weight
First Period (1850–1905)		
Civil service rate	0.925	0.767
Educational expenditures per capita	0.936	0.660
Lagged education	0.952	−0.594
GNP per capita	0.953	0.164
Second Period (1906–65)		
Lagged education	0.483	1.031
Civil service rate	0.498	0.135
GNP per capita	0.502	−0.814
Educational expenditures per capita	0.527	0.392

Table 3. Explanation of the School Rate in Sweden

Independent Variable	R^2	Beta Weight
First Period (1865–1910)		
GNP per capita	0.602	−1.207
Civil service rate	0.657	0.164
Educational expenditures per capita	0.677	−0.002
Lagged education	0.724	4.079
Second Period (1911–65)		
Educational expenditures per capita	0.875	1.058
GNP per capita	0.892	−0.324
Civil service rate	0.896	0.122
Lagged education	0.897	−0.064

tied to changes in available resources during the first time period. The most covariant independent variable was per capita gross national product, while the largest beta weight was with lagged education levels. We may therefore assume that in both instances, the availability of resources, rather than the actions of government, was most important in determining the level of educational services. This may have been expected from the generally lower level of development in Sweden during this time period, but the contrast is still quite obvious.

The contrasts between Sweden and the other two countries become even clearer in the second time period. In France and the United Kingdom, a resource measure is both most covariant and has the largest beta weight with the school rate. In Sweden, however, the direct influence of government through expenditures has the greatest effect on the growth of education. The Swedish system, therefore, has developed exactly opposite to that of the other two systems. While France and the United Kingdom have moved from a system reliant on government to one reliant on resources, Sweden has moved from reliance on resources to a greater reliance on government.

These findings may be given several possible interpretations. If one did not have some knowledge of the large growth of expenditures for education in France and the United Kingdom, or had not seen the lists of reforms enacted, he might assume that these two countries had abandoned education to the general influences of societal development. However, we do know about these actions and that interpretation cannot be easily accepted.

A second explanation is that although the political systems of these two countries have made strong attempts at influencing education, their attempts have been overshadowed by the rather remarkable growth of the economic system. Thus, instead of arguing that the political systems have abandoned education, it appears more reasonable to argue that the political systems have simply been unable to keep pace with changes elsewhere. In Sweden, on the other hand, the great attempts at the democratization of the system have tended to make the changes in the educational system move more closely with changes in governmental support.

The third possible argument is built on the second. If the educational system is, in fact, responding more to the economic system than to the governmental, the dynamic relationship between industrial society and education mentioned previously may be operative.[37] In other words, the educational system has become cybernetic in France and the United Kingdom. We will leave a more complete examination of this possibility to a later point in the discussion, but this would appear to be an interesting alternative explanation.

Social Welfare

We now turn to the question of economic security. We have seen that all three countries have developed extensive systems of benefits both for the elderly and those in need during the working years. The patterns of historical development have been rather similar, and we may therefore expect similarities in the data analysis. However, we may also expect some differences from the other two policy areas examined. In particular, we expect greater political influence in economic security benefits than in the other two types of service. In the first place, these services are more directly tied to governmental action than health and education where there is the possibility for significant private action. Second, the need for economic se-

37. Bowles, "Education in the New Europe."

curity, or "welfare," legislation is less widely accepted than the needs for education and health. There may be some question as to the means of delivery of the latter two services, but the intrinsic values of the two services are rarely if ever questioned. Finally, the benefits of education and health programs would appear to fall in the economist's category of public goods. That is, the benefits accrue equally to all citizens. The benefits of economic security programs, however, benefit one group of the population while disadvantaging others through taxation. This is especially true of public assistance and family payments, but those who are capable of providing for themselves in old age tend to perceive little direct benefit from social security programs. Therefore, we classify education and health as principally distributive governmental activities, while economic security is more directly redistributive. Given this redistributional nature of the programs, we may expect a greater impact of the political system in this area than in the other two areas where general economic change is more likely to "spill over" into increased benefits.

When we examine the results of the data analysis, we find quite good support for this hypothesis. First, for pensions, in all three countries a political variable is the most covariant with the pension rate in both time periods. In most instances, the beta weight for the political variable is also the strongest. We therefore have a very consistent pattern for the development of pension programs in the three countries. The major effects on the extension of pension rights comes from the political system and its decisions on how to allocate resources, rather than being determined by changes in the availability of resources. It is especially interesting that this pattern is stable both across time and across political systems.

When we analyze the data for public assistance and family payments, a

Table 4. Explanation of the Pension Rate in the United Kingdom

Independent Variable	R^2	Beta Weight
First Period (1850–1905)		
Pension expenditures per capita	0.817	.322
Civil service rate	0.868	–.168
GNP per capita	0.872	1.520
Lagged education	0.878	.057
Second Period (1906–65)		
Pension expenditures per capita	0.708	0.429
Lagged education	0.816	0.143
Civil service rate	0.822	0.037
GNP per capita	0.826	0.038

Table 5. Explanation of the Pension Rate in France

Independent Variable	R^2	Beta Weight
First Period (1850-1905)		
Civil service rate	0.953	0.578
Lagged education	0.975	0.629
Pension expenditures per capita	0.981	-0.256
GNP per capita	0.982	0.055
Second Period (1906-65)		
Civil service rate	0.284	0.649
Pension expenditure per capita	0.348	0.374
Lagged education	0.393	-0.629
GNP per capita	0.403	-0.776

Table 6. Explanation of the Pension Rate in Sweden

Independent Variable	R^2	Beta Weight
First Period (1865-1910)		
Civil service rate	0.926	-0.196
Pension expenditures per capita	0.938	-0.632
Lagged education	0.940	-1.977
GNP per capita	0.951	1.140
Second Period (1911-65)		
Pension expenditures per capita	0.759	.314
GNP per capita	0.773	.181
Civil service rate	0.834	-.121
Lagged education	0.874	-.154

similar pattern emerges, with the exception of France. In Sweden and the United Kingdom, the political measures tend to enter the equations first, and to have large, if not the largest, beta weights. In France, however, the educational level of the adult population was most important in explaining the level of assistance granted, in both variance explained and effect. The size of the civil service had some effect during the first time period, but there is a definite pattern of influence of the educational resource measure.

We are now faced with the question of why France should be different from the other two systems. One possible explanation is that France has been less influenced by the "Protestant ethic" than the other two systems,

Table 7. Explanation of the Relief Rate in the United Kingdom

Independent Variable	R^2	Beta Weight
First Period (1850-1905)		
Welfare expenditures per capita	0.641	.351
GNP per capita	0.698	−.339
Civil service rate	0.714	−.573
Lagged education	0.729	.115
Second Period (1906-65)		
Welfare expenditures per capita	0.708	1.71
GNP per capita	0.726	−0.968
Civil service rate	0.735	−0.010
Lagged education	0.743	0.688

Table 8. Explanation of the Relief Rate in France

Independent Variable	R^2	Beta Weight
First Period (1850-1905)		
Lagged education	0.791	1.177
Civil service rate	0.805	0.974
Welfare expenditures per capita	0.822	−0.539
GNP per capita	0.836	−0.672
Second Period (1906-65)		
Lagged education	0.832	0.566
Pension expenditures per capita	0.841	−0.130
Civil service rate	0.848	−0.104
GNP per capita	0.860	0.050

and therefore social programs of this type do not have the same stigma as in the United Kingdom or Sweden before the postwar changes. Some support for this stand is to be gained from the brief historical discussion, and the part which private industry played in the beginning of the family payments system.[38] This explanation, however, appears to run counter to the rather well documented individualism and misanthropy in French political culture.[39] This contradiction may be resolvable if we remember that a very

38. Friedlander, *Individualism*.
39. See the articles by L. Wylie, J. Pitts, and F. Goguel in Stanley Hoffmann et al., *In Search of France* (New York: Harper Torchbooks, 1963).

Table 9. Explanation of the Relief Rate in Sweden

Independent Variable	R^2	Beta Weight
First Period (1865-1910)		
Civil service rate	0.644	1.178
Welfare expenditures per capita	0.679	1.363
GNP per capita	0.701	0.080
Lagged education	0.724	−1.420
Second Period (1911-65)		
Civil service rate	0.787	.281
Welfare expenditures per capita	0.800	−.624
Lagged education	0.809	.361
GNP per capita	0.811	.330

consistent form of reaction to pressure in a political culture such as this is bureaucratic decision making. Thus, the system appears to have reacted to general societal development, indicated by the growth of education, with increased social welfare benefits. This reaction, however, was not in a traditional "political" manner, but rather through the bureaucracy. We see some influence of the bureaucracy directly in the first time period, and we may expect some more direct reactions to the environmental conditions in the second period when that is tested directly. This explanation is far from fully satisfying, but if it can be supported from the data on the response of the system to need, we can be more confident as to its usefulness.

In summary, we have rather good support for the basic assumption concerning the relatively greater politicization of programs of economic security. We may therefore assume that programs of this type do not respond as directly to societal resources as do health and education programs. Rather, they require the direct intervention of the political system to develop. The only variance from this general pattern occured for public assistance in France, but a tentative explanation for this deviation may be supported in the analysis on systemic response to needs.

Health

Finally, we discuss the policy area of public health.[40] The question of the proper role of the political system in providing health services has now been settled in these three countries, as in virtually all developed political

---

40. An earlier version of this section was presented as B. Guy Peters, "An Inquiry into Objective Security: A Longitudinal Analysis of Public Health in France, Sweden and the United Kingdom" (Paper prepared for presentation at the Annual Meeting of the Midwest Political Science Association, Chicago, 30 April–2 May 1970).

systems. This settlement has been in favor of some form of socialized medicine, although the coverages and benefits in the three systems are rather different. Passing over the fine points of these differences, we may say that in general, the public medical system of Sweden tends to be the most well articulated, while that of the United Kingdom is the least well developed, even before the recent changes adopted by the Conservative government.

Discussing public health adds an additional potential explanatory variable to the analysis: the number of physicians per capita. While this makes the analysis even more complex, any explanation offered without the inclusion of this variable would be misleading.

We include the availability of medical personnel as something of an effect of the political system, although this effect may be rather indirect. Doctors do not somehow spring fully trained from the brow of some deity. They must be trained, encouraged, and retained once they are in practice. These activities in the promotion of the number of medical personnel may be regarded as a regulative activity of government. A political system willing to make the regulative efforts necessary for the maintenance of an adequate medical personnel pool will tend to be able to provide better medical care and greater health benefits and greater health care than a country that is less able to provide such personnel.

The regulation of the training and recruitment of medical personnel began relatively early in France and Sweden, but did not occur until after the passage of the National Health Service Act of 1948 in the United Kingdom. Even after the passage of that act, the inducements to enter the medical profession do not appear as strong in the United Kingdom as they do in the other two countries. This is especially true given the relative ease of immigration of the British physicians to the United States or the Commonwealth countries. This inability to provide an adequate number of physicians (the per capita rate in the United Kingdom is approximately half that of the other two countries), would appear to be a severe handicap to the provision of adequate medical services in the United Kingdom. Therefore, we might expect the health programs of France and Sweden to be more effective than that of the United Kingdom. Table 10, presenting the figures for infant mortality, gross death rates, and life expectancy in the three countries tends to confirm that tentative conclusion. In all three categories, the United Kingdom has a level of services inferior to that of the other two countries. This is true despite equal or better economic resources.

Given the relative inability of the United Kingdom to provide adequate numbers of medical personnel, and its generally less-developed system of public medicine, we can expect it to be a deviant case in the regression analysis. In particular, we expect a greater influence from the resource measures on the level of infant mortality than is found in the other two countries. This difference should be especially marked in the second time period, when the public health services of the two other countries are developing rapidly, while that of the United Kingdom tends to lag due to the relative lack of personnel.

Turning to tables 11–13, which present the results for our analysis of the health data, we find that our expectations are borne out in the results. A resource measure is the prime explanatory variable in all three countries in the first time period, although this is true only for the beta weight in France.

Table 10. Values of Health Indicators and Percentage Changes

	Sweden		France	United Kingdom
		1865		
Infant mortality	139.0		191.0	160.0
Death rate	19.4		24.7	23.2
Life expectancy	44.6		39.8	41.2
		1910		
Infant mortality	77.0 (45)		135.0 (135)	105.0 (34)
Death rate	14.0 (28)		19.6 (21)	13.5 (42)
Life expectancy	57.9 (30)		47.0 (18)	53.5 (30)
		1965		
Infant mortality	15.0 (81) from 1910	18.1 (87)		19.6 (81)
	(89) from 1965	(91)		(88)
Death rate	10.1 (28)	11.1 (43)		12.2 (10)
	(48)	(55)		(47)
Life expectancy	73.7 (27)	71.4 (52)		71.3 (33)
	(65)	(79)		(73)

Table 11. Explanation of the Infant Mortality Rate in the United Kingdom

Independent Variables	Infant Mortality		Beta Weights
	R^2	R^2 Increment	
First Half (1850–1905)			
Lagged education	0.366		−2.783
Civil service rate	0.432	0.066	−2.069
Health per capita	0.498	0.066	−1.564
GNP per capita	0.511	0.013	−0.280
Doctors per capita	0.512	0.001	−0.783
Second Half (1906–65)			
Civil service rate	0.810		−0.220
Health per capita	0.900	0.090	−0.331
GNP per capita	0.927	0.027	−0.438
Doctors per capita	0.924	0.015	−0.186
Lagged education	0.951	0.009	−0.202

Table 12. Explanation of the Infant Mortality Rate in France

Independent Variables	Infant Mortality R^2	R^2 Increment	Beta Weights
First Half (1850-1905)			
Doctors per capita	0.351		-0.414
Health expenditures per capita	0.541	0.190	-0.974
Lagged education	0.568	0.027	-1.719
GNP per capita	0.582	0.014	-1.446
Civil service rate	0.647	0.065	-0.251
Second Half (1906-65)			
Doctors per capita	0.810		-2.946
Civil service rate	0.854	0.044	-0.882
Lagged education	0.872	0.018	-0.642
GNP per capita	0.891	0.019	-0.471
Health per capita	0.892	0.892	-0.178

Table 13. Explanation of the Infant Mortality Rate in Sweden

Independent Variables	Infant Mortality R^2	R^2 Increment	Beta Weights
First Period (1865-1910)			
Lagged education	0.971		-1.646
Health per capita	0.985	0.014	-0.061
GNP per capita	0.987	0.002	0.571
Doctors per capita	0.989	0.002	0.140
Civil service rate	0.990	0.001	0.113
Second Period (1911-65)			
Doctors per capita	0.869		-2.228
GNP per capita	0.952	0.083	0.934
Lagged education	0.983	0.031	-0.416
Civil service rate	0.983	0.000	0.023
Health per capita	0.983	0.000	0.038

It is especially interesting to note the importance of the educational levels of the adult population in this analysis. As mentioned previously, we expected this variable to be especially influential in the area of health, and this expectation is strongly confirmed. In the second time period, the influences of government, or more exactly the influences of the availability of medical personnel, become of prime importance in France and Sweden. In the United Kingdom, however, the civil service is the most covariant with changes in the infant mortality rate, and the educational level of the adult population again has the largest beta weight. Therefore, we may say rather conclusively that the United Kingdom is indeed a deviant case in the area of public health, relying as it does on the resources of the population and a rather diffuse influence of the political system through the civil service rate. Furthermore, we can see the importance of medical personnel to a health program. Where the medical personnel have been available, their presence has been of prime importance, and where they have been lacking, the levels of health service have been poorer than might have been expected from other characteristics of the social and economic systems.

The distinctiveness of the health care system of the United Kingdom is even more evident when we compute the partial correlations between the measure of educational resources and the level of infant mortality, partialling out the effects of the activities of government. In all three countries, there was no significant effect of governmental activity during the first time period. In the second time period, however, the partial correlations in France and Sweden were not significantly greater than zero, while those in the United Kingdom remained strong. This only substantiates further the arguments concerning both the distinctiveness of the United Kingdom and the importance of the activities of government in the second time period.

Summary

It is interesting to note that each of the three countries included in this analysis has been the deviant case in one of the three policy areas. In education, it was Sweden. Unlike the other two countries, Sweden has not been changed from an educational system reliant on the activities of government to a system attuned to changes in available resources. This may indicate a reliance on environmental conditions in the determination of educational policies.

In the area of economic security, France was the deviant case. In the other two systems, benefits were highly related to the operations of the political system. This was true in both time periods. From this, we concluded support for our assumption of the greater need for constant political input into a program such as public assistance which is directly redistributive. Programs of this type cannot rely on economic development to produce their benefits, and in fact, the operations of economic development may tend to be redistributive in the opposite direction. France, however, has been changed from a system reliant on the political system to one related on a resource measure—the educational level of its adult population. This led to a preliminary conclusion that this was the result of the proverbial French individualism. However, it is also possible that outputs have become more directly related to needs for services. This may be especially true in France, given the greater acceptance in recent years of technocratic guidance of social and economic policy, and a history of bureaucratic decision making.

Finally, in the area of health, the United Kingdom is shown to be the deviant case. This appears to be due to the lack of qualified medical personnel, as compared to the other two systems. In the other two countries, the burden of explaining the level of health impacts has been transferred from the educational levels of the population to the availability of medical personnel. In the United Kingdom, however, the principal factor associated with the reduction of infant mortality remains the educational level of the adult population. This is argued to be a rather important failure of the regulative process of the United Kingdom in providing the needed personnel.

As well as isolating differences in the three political systems, we find rather important differences among the three issue areas. First, the three areas could be classified according to the terminology used by Lowi in the classification of public policies.[41] Economic security programs are rather directly redistributive, while educational programs tend to be distributive, given that all persons can receive their benefits. Health may appear to be redistributive, and is to a large extent, but we may also think of it as a regulative policy, especially as it concerns the relationship between patient and doctor.

Associated with these types of policy are rather different explanatory variables. First, economic security legislation and benefits require direct and consistent political inputs. Throughout the development of these policies, political variables have been most important in their explanation. Second, education programs can receive a very direct spillover from the economic and social development, which is to be expected because of their distributive benefits. Finally, health programs appear to be affected by the political system largely through regulation, which is one principal factor in their classification as regulative programs. We obviously do not have the extent of information concerning the differences in these programs which would be required for a full analysis using Lowi's scheme, but the classification and findings presented are a useful first step in the more complete analysis of the development of public policy.

The explanation of policy impacts has been shown to be a rather complex task, and no simple reliance on economic or political determinants is likely to be fruitful. We have shown that influences on policy tend to change over time, and that several factors play a role in explanation. In seeking to explain the direction of public policy in these three nations, we now move to a discussion of what has been called the "postindustrial state." It has been argued that this is the direction in which public policy formation is likely to move in Europe and other developed systems, and we want to examine empirically the degree of movement that has already occurred.

The Postindustrial State

One of the most persistent discussions concerning the changes in European politics concerns the "end of ideology," and the movement toward

---

41. Theodore Lowi, "American Business, Public Policy, Case-Studies and Political Theory," *World Politics* 16, no. 4 (July 1964): 677–715.

a bureaucratic or technocratic system of government.[42] The arguments on this point have been largely normative. The normative argument concerns the importance of involvement of citizens in the decision-making process of the political system, even when the decisions are seemingly too complex for public comprehension. This side is taken quite forcefully by Gunnar Myrdal in *Beyond the Welfare State*.[43] He points out the human problems resulting from mass society and the lack of personal involvement in decisions that affect the lives of the individuals. The same point is made, although more dogmatically, by Jacques Ellul in *The Technological Society*.[44] Ellul sees the eventual domination of society by the decisions of computers and technical experts, with a consequent lack of ability for individuals to affect their own destiny or the destiny of their society.

The more positive side of this argument is taken by Amitai Etzioni and, to some extent, Karl Deutsch.[45] Etzioni speaks of the concept of the active society, which in its simplest form, is a self-steering society acting to respond to inputs from the environment through public means. Such a society would be in contact with its environment and seek to make decisions which would maximize certain valued goals. Deutsch speaks of a similar form for the political system in *The Nerves of Government*. He speaks of the importance of the combination of input from the environment and known goals in the societal memory in order to maximize the quality of decisions made by the system.

The normative conflict over the nature of the postindustrial state would therefore appear to center on the question the relative values of the quality of decisions and the manner in which the decisions are taken. Those of the school of Myrdal and Ellul value the process, and make the assumption that decisions taken in a democratic manner will be at least minimally acceptable on empirical grounds. Those of the Etzioni and Deutsch group argue that the quality of decisions may be more important, and decisions taken in a more technocratic manner would be the decisions taken by mass publics if they had sufficient information and abilities. Both arguments have rather significant assumptions which will not be discussed at length here. Instead, we now move on to a more empirical assessment of the movement toward a system either favored or deplored by the authors mentioned.

Our operational conception of the postindustrial state is one in which the political systems makes decisions in relationship to objective conditions in the environment. Thus, in Deutsch's terminology, they are cybernetic

42. See Daniel Bell, *The End of Ideology* (Glencoe, Ill.: Free Press, 1960).

43. Gunnar Myrdal, *Beyond the Welfare State* (New Haven: Yale University Press, 1960), pp. 38–87.

44. Jacques Ellul, *The Technological Society* (New York: Alfred A. Knopf, 1964), pp. 229–378.

45. Amitai Etzioni, *The Active Society* (New York: Free Press, 1968), pp. 1–16, 179–90; Deutsch, *Nerves of Government*.

systems. The systems would be capable of recognizing need, and of making some positive response to the needs. The closest approximation of such a system now is in strategic defense. The major powers have vast networks of radar apparatus and computers to assess the condition of the environment. Of course, the most significant environmental condition in such a situation would be the launching of an attack on the nation. If such a situation is perceived, the system is programmed to begin a sequence of actions which, although the ultimate authority rests in human officials, prepares for a retaliation. This system can presumably make a correct definition of a situation and a correct response in the space of some fifteen minutes.

In the area of social policy, we obviously have nothing to rival the speed and complexity of such a decision-making apparatus. However, in some countries, economic problems are handled in something of the same manner. The central planning of the economy, perhaps best developed in the Netherlands, seeks to respond to a set of economic indicators in order to steer the economic system.[46] Given a set of known relationships with the desired economic goals of full employment and an acceptable balance of payments, the manipulation of governmental monetary and fiscal policy is used to attempt to ensure these goals. Of course, the presence of some un-manipulable parameters, such as the trade policies of other nations, prevents the complete planning of the economy, but this is still the best example of systemic response to the environment in social policy making. Furthermore, the planning process is not so totally devoid of human input as some of the deprecators might have us believe. The values which the plan seeks to maximize are set by a combination of political leaders and economists. In addition, the plan is largely indicative, and does not bind the relevant decision makers.

When dealing with the types of social programs discussed to this point, we are even further removed from the ability to measure trends accurately, and to make acceptable responses to those trends. However, we will now use the cybernetic variables discussed earlier as measures of such societal needs for educational and economic security benefits. The level of measurement is admittedly rather rough as yet, but this analysis should be illustrative of changes in policy making, if they in fact do exist.

The first stage of the analysis was to use the variables in their raw forms. The comparative explanatory ability of the cybernetic variable and the variables which had previously been shown to be most important in explaining outputs during the 1905–65 time period in the original analysis were computed. In all cases, the explanatory values of the original variables were significantly greater than those of the cybernetic variable. If any change could be noted, it was slightly negative, with the effects of the

---

46. Andrew Shonfield, *Modern Capitalism* (New York: Oxford, 1965).

cybernetic variables being slightly greater in the 1900–30 period than in the 1935–65 period. These initial findings obviously give no support for the idea that these nations are moving in the direction of becoming postindustrial states. However, some further analysis might salvage this idea. The analysis undertaken was the use of rates of change for the variables (first differences) as the values of the variables in each time period, rather than the raw figures. The use of this analysis can be justified on several grounds. First, methodologically, first differences are often used with economic data to reduce the level of serial autocorrelation. Although this is not a primary concern in this analysis, it is still useful to have such autocorrelation as does exist reduced. Second, and more substantively, we may be more interested in systemic response to *changes* in an indicator than we are in systemic responses to the actual values of the same indicator. Thus, in terms of policy responses, it may be more important to know that the unemployment rate increased 10 percent during a time period than to know what the absolute values of the index were at any point in time. Furthermore, the use of the first differences should allow us to sort out the effects of individual variables, all of which are moving together through time in a general developmental process.

With these justifications, we proceed with the analysis using the rates of change. To be more specific, the data now used in the analysis is the percentage change in the value of a variable from time t to time $t + 1$. The results of this analysis provided much more positive evidence that these three political systems are moving toward a cybernetic method of policy making. The evidence is not so complete as that for the original analysis, due largely to the relative lack of observations, but it does point to some relatively important changes in the manner of policy making. First, there are definite differences in the two time periods, with the cybernetic variables having relatively larger correlations in the second time period. Second, there were several reversals in the sign of the correlation coefficient from negative to positive for the cybernetic variables. Thus, in the early portion of the twentieth century, the policy systems responded in a negative manner to indicators of need, while in the second period the responses were positive. We now move from these general statements to a discussion of each policy area.

Education

The results of this analysis of education are presented in table 14. For France and Sweden, the results show rather marked changes in the response of the system to the environment. For France, in the first time period, the response to technological change would appear to have been negative, while the response in the second period became positive. It did not, however, surpass the influence of the level of education in the population in predicting changes in educational outputs. For Sweden, although there was no reversal of sign, the same general pattern holds. There were much larger

Table 14. Correlation Coefficients for Changes in Cybernetic Variable and Traditional Explanatory Variables in the United Kingdom

	First Period (1900-34)	Second Period (1935-65)
School Rate		
	r	*r*
Energy consumption	.603	−.008
GNP per capita	.888	.320
Pension Rate		
	r	*r*
Industrialization	−.476	.151
Pension expenditures	−.144	.621
Relief Rate		
	r	*r*
Unemployment	−.277	−.553
Welfare expenditures	.877	.550

influences of energy consumption in the second period than in the first, although once again, the influences of variables related to more traditional forms of policy making remain dominant. Thus, the difference of Sweden from the other two systems in its educational policy cannot be fully explained by this response. Nevertheless, there is some evidence to show that the response is stronger in Sweden than in the other two systems.

The data for the United Kingdom would appear to represent something of a step backward. Although the influence of technology certainly was not great during the first time period, there was almost no relationship during the second period. It would therefore seem that the educational system of the United Kingdom is actually becoming less related to the needs for such services. The more traditional variable used in the analysis is per capita GNP, however, and given the relationship between technology and this variable, this movement cannot be interpreted too strongly.

Economic Security

The findings for economic security are similar to those for education (see tables 15 and 16). There is a general movement toward making policies in relationship to environmental conditions in France and Sweden, particularly the latter, while the movement in the United Kingdom is in the opposite direction. This is especially pronounced in the granting of public assistance and family benefits. In France and Sweden, the effects were negative prior to 1931, but after that date they became relatively strong in the positive direction. At the same time, in the United Kingdom, the relationship changes from weakly positive to strongly negative. Once again, however, this variable does not account entirely for the deviation of a system from the patterns of the other two systems.

Table 15. Correlation Coefficients for Changes in Cybernetic Variable and Traditional Explanatory Variables in France

	First Period (1900-30)	Second Period (1931-65)
	School Rate	
	r	r
Energy consumption	-.136	0.234
Lagged education	.203	0.272
	Pension Rate	
	r	r
Industrialization	0.559	0.159
Pension expenditures	0.117	0.198
	Relief Rate	
	r	r
Unemployment	-.647	0.299
Lagged education	-.177	-.271

Table 16. Correlation Coefficients for Changes in Cybernetic Variable and Traditional Explanatory Variables in Sweden

	First Period (1900-30)	Second Period (1931-65)
	School Rate	
	r	r
Energy consumption	-.444	0.495
Education expenditures	.566	0.616
	Pension Rate	
	r	r
Industrialization	0.143	0.307
Pension expenditures	0.584	0.284
	Relief Rate	
	r	r
Unemployment	-.416	0.430
Civil service rate	.626	-0.465

The relationships for both the cybernetic and the more traditional variables are not as strong for pensions as they are for the granting of public assistance, but there is a similar pattern. In Sweden, the relationship with industrialization has become the stronger relationship, while in France the values of the two correlations are only slightly different. In the United Kingdom, the relationship in the second time period does not become negative, but it becomes small relative to the increased value of the relationship with expenditures for pensions.

Summary

As noted, this discussion of the movement toward the postindustrial or cybernetic state is obviously very tentative. There are insufficient observations to allow the manipulations of the data which might be desirable, especially given the complexity of the operationalization of environmental conditions which may ultimately be required. However, these preliminary results offer some encouragement for the continuation of this analysis by the collection of a more and further refinement of concepts and measurement. This is especially true of the economic security data, where more interactive models may be required. Also, it may be quite fruitful to look at the level of expenditures which are made by these systems as a function of environmental need to determine the extent to which systems seek to respond simply by spending more money.

Summary and Conclusions

In summary, we have discussed the development of important social services in these three countries as a measure of the increased impact of the political system on the lives of the population. We have also attempted to describe the political development of the three systems. The analysis presented shows a definite growth of the impact of government in providing services in education, health, welfare areas. However, a further analysis of the data for the twentieth century reveals something of a movement away from the direct control of service levels by the political system to a more responsive model of service delivery. The responses in question are made to needs in the environment, rather than to political pressure, as is assumed in earlier periods. In performing this analysis, we have isolated three styles of policy making on the macro level which may also be seen as three levels of political development. The first level is characterized by policies determined by the availability of resources. In this situation, given general social and economic development, some of the excess created in that process will "spill over" into improved social services. At this stage, the political system appears to have little or no control on the amount or direction of the spillover.

The second stage of development is characterized by the direct intervention of the political system in the provision of social services, with the level of services being manipulated largely through the level of public expenditures of the specific purpose. Despite the predominant effect of expenditures, however, some effects on services may be seen as coming through the general growth of the public bureaucracy because of increased regulative activities of the political system. In these cases, it would appear that the level of services is decided upon by the political system within the margins or error resulting from a lack of knowledge of all parameters of the policy system.

The third and final stage of the development is characterized by a pattern of nondecision making by the political system once policy is determined. That is, once the government decides upon the response which it desires to make to certain environmental changes, it leaves the decisions on day-to-day responses to relatively low-level officials. Of course, the government does not retire, assuming its work is finished. The policies made at this third stage are made with approximately the same lack of information that characterized the second stage. This ignorance is both about the relationship of possible indicators to real needs, and about the relationships of actions to impacts on the population. Therefore, constant readjustments of the decision rules for the administrators of programs must be made. These modifications may result from improved information, or they may result simply from a trial-and-error process. In either case, the more political branches of the system will tend to consistently readjust the rules under which the administrators act, especially in democratic systems such as the three discussed here. Despite this manipulation, however, the decisions taken will be taken in response to environmental changes within the limits set from above.

An increasing volume of governmental legislation is being phrased more directly in terms of environmental response, such as planning legislation. This has resulted from an increased ability of administrative apparatuses to process social information and to react to it quickly. This is true especially when compared to the cumbersome practices of most legislative bodies. For whatever reasons, we believe this to be the direction that much of present policy making is taking, and that even more future policy making will adopt. In terms of the original definition of development, this style of decision making has the potential for attaining very high levels of development. It will produce reactions when they are necessary, and to the extent to which they are necessary. However, the normative implications of such a decision-making style are rather immense. This is one more example of the constant demand on democratic regimes to control their administrative structures, for in maximizing certain values on the content of decisions, we may lose equally valuable values concerning the manner of decision making.

8

William G. Andrews

The Politics of Regionalization in France

Introduction

From Charlemagne to Charles de Gaulle, the history of France has been a story of centralization. Centralization produced France. For twelve hundred years and more, France was built—bit by bloody bit—through extension of the central power of the state ever more fully into an ever larger territory. Since 1954, the state has made persistent efforts to reverse that process, especially through regionalization. Both the parliamentary Fourth Republic and de Gaulle's Fifth Republic have pursued policies of regionalization. This essay examines those efforts as a case study in governmental decision making.

Adequate understanding of recent regionalization requires a glimpse at its historical context. The millennial centralization process occurred in two overlapping phases. Until 1791 it consisted largely of the acquisition of territory, but since the days of Cardinal Richelieu (1624–42), assimilation also had been a deliberate, articulated policy of state. After 1791, acquisition of contiguous territory ceased.[1] Assimilation continued. In fact, after momentary hesitation, the Constituent Assembly of the Revolution under Jacobin leadership accelerated the process. Indeed, the matter was regarded as so important that, less than a month after the fall of the Bastille, the Assembly abrogated "all the particular privileges of the provinces, principalities, cities, corps, and communities," most of which antedated the rise of the centralized state, and decreed that they be "merged in the common

---

1. Except that Savoy and Nice became French in 1860.

293

law of all the French."[2] Several months later, form followed substance as the thirty-three provinces were replaced by eighty-three "Departments."[3] The basic structure was completed in 1800 when Napoleon established the corps of prefects, officials appointed by the national government and given "sole responsibility for the administration" of their respective Departments.[4] Finally, the Napoleonic Code of 1804 imbedded the structure in the cement of a single, uniform legal system. These institutions—Department, prefectoral corps, Napoleonic Code—remain today the main governmental bonds between the French state and the French people.

From the beginning, however, the rigidity of that system was attenuated somewhat by the existence of special administrative "regions" between the Department and national levels. These have included military, financial, economic, and educational regions.[5] By 1955, some forty-nine different regional systems were used by various French governmental ministries.[6] Furthermore, at least since the middle of the nineteenth century, efforts have been made to create general administrative regions.[7] Still, as late as 1953, a leading student of the subject could write that the "experiments in regional government since 1939 have . . . evoked so much hostility that it is improbable that any further extension of regional administration is now politically feasible."[8] The following year, however, such extension began in earnest and has continued to the present time.

The pages that follow review those efforts in order to gain a better understanding of the processes through which governmental decisions are reached in France. Although most of the attention is directed toward the period since General de Gaulle returned to power in 1958, a glimpse into the preceding regime, the Fourth French Republic, permits a comparison of decision making before de Gaulle, under de Gaulle, and after de Gaulle. The text explores the extent to which parliament has been bypassed, even during the Fourth Republic, on this very important issue. It discusses the importance of "corporatist" political references.[9] Next, it examines closely

2. 11 August 1789. Brian Chapman, *The Prefects and Provincial France* (London: Allen & Unwin, 1955), p. 14.

3. *Départements* in French. Laws of 9 December 1789 and 26 February 1790. Jacques Ellul, *Histoire des institutions* (Paris: Presses Universitaires de France, 1956), 2:608. A. Mirot, *Manuel géographique historique de la France* (Paris: Picard, 1930), contains a map (p. 240) showing how the provinces were divided into Departments.

4. Law of 28 pluviôse, an VIII. Antoine J. Escudier, *Le Conseil général* (Paris: Ed. Berger-Levrault, 1964), p. 15.

5. Mirot, *Manuel géographique historique*, pp. 236–89.

6. Chapman, *Prefects and Provincial France*, p. 170.

7. Philippe Brongniart, *La région en France* (Paris: A. Colin, 1971), pp. 46–48.

8. Brian Chapman, *Introduction to French Local Government* (London: Allen & Unwin, 1953), p. 226. Also see M. Bourjol, *Les Institutions Régionales* (Paris: Berger-Levrault, 1969).

9. Corporatism is a constitutional doctrine according to which popular representation is based on social and economic affiliation rather than residence location. The terms "socio-occupational" and "corporatist" are used interchangeably in this essay.

one of the very few large-scale experiments in "participatory democracy" undertaken in a Western democracy. Finally, it reviews the radical change in style and process that has occurred under President Pompidou. Before launching into the body of this study, however, let us take a brief look at the territorial structure of the French state in order to understand better the issue involved.

Territorial Structure of the French State

A diagram of the territorial structure of the French state forms a tidy pyramid—with one large gap. The base of the pyramid is the commune, heir to the "parish" of the ancien régime and kissing cousin of the New England town. Of the 37,708 communes, about 35,500 are rural, of which nearly half have fewer than 300 inhabitants. Excluding the Paris metropolitan area, communes average 1,132 inhabitants and 5.6 square miles in area. Most rural communes consist of a hamlet or village and some surrounding countryside. Most small towns form single communes. Large towns and cities contain several communes, comparable to wards in American cities.[10] Each commune has an elective, largely advisory Municipal Council.

The second key element in the pyramid is the Department, the most important subnational unit, politically, administratively, and electorally. In 1791, 83 Departments were formed. They number 95 now. They average about 2,250 square miles in area and, excluding the 8 Departments of the Paris basin, they average about 500,000 inhabitants. Thus they compare in size and population to large American counties. The advisory, elective bodies for the Departments are called General Councils.

Between the communes and the Departments are cantons and districts (*arrondissements*), which are principally electoral units, though the districts have some fairly important administrative functions also. Usually 10 to 15 communes form a canton, 10 to 12 cantons form a district, 3 or 4 districts form a Department—and 95 Departments form France. The pyramid, then, rises quite smoothly from base to apex, except that a big gap lies between the Department and the nation. This is the gap that has attracted the attention of the regionalists, who would like to form every four or five Departments into a region and the resultant twenty or so regions into the nation. In order to understand why, we must look briefly at some of their key reasons.

10. Jacques Riboud, "Défense du département," *Revue politique et parlementaire* (February 1970): 17; Club Jean Moulin, *Les citoyens au pouvoir* (Paris: Seuil, 1968), p. 11; Malcolm Anderson, *Government in France* (Oxford: Pergamon, 1970), 1: 135; Francois Perin et al., "L'Aménagement du territoire en France," *Notes et études documentaires*, 9 February 1968, La documentation française, Paris, p. 14; Lowell G. Noonan, *France: The Politics of Continuity in Change* (New York: Holt, 1970), p. 155.

Arguments for Regionalization

Regionalists argue, first of all, that the Departments no longer meet the administrative needs of the state. Their boundaries were laid out in 1790 so that each French resident could reach his Department's capital within a day's ride on horseback.[11] That rationale became outmoded long ago. Modern transportation and communications are said to make regions more practical economic and demographic units.

Also, Departments are alleged to have inadequate financial resources. They cannot finance many projects and operations that their inhabitants require. Such projects could be managed by several Departments pooling their resources as a region. Then, too, economies of scale would result from the use of regions rather than Departments and waste by duplication could be reduced.

Finally, regionalists say that regionalization would facilitate decentralization. Central governmental agencies could delegate authority to a score of regions that a hundred Departments could not manage. This would permit many decisions that now go to Paris to be taken closer to the origin of the matter.

These and other reasons have inspired moves toward regionalization for many decades. The present campaign, however, need lead us no further back than the period immediately after World War II. Both the Gaullists and the Fourth Republic leaders began their efforts then.

Early Gaullism

Charles de Gaulle was born into a family of devout monarchists almost exactly a century after the monarchy had been overthrown in the same Revolution that had replaced provinces by Departments. His uncle and namesake had been a regionalist and Breton poet.[12] Thus, de Gaulle was predisposed by his background to favor regionalism. Because his early career lay in the army, rather than politics, however, he made no public record of his views on that topic until after World War II. Nor did he mention regions in his most important early postwar speech on constitutional doctrine, his Bayeux speech of 16 June 1946.[13]

In 1943, Michel Debré, a young Gaullist in the wartime Resistance, prepared the first Gaullist regionalization proposal. He argued that Departments be enlarged to about twice their existing size and reduced in number from 90 to 47. After the war, de Gaulle commissioned Debré to study

11. Riboud, "Défense du département," p. 25. Perhaps even more importantly, the *gendarmérie* could reach him equally quickly.

12. *Le Monde* (hereinafter cited as *LM*), 4 February 1969.

13. An English translation appears in William G. Andrews, *European Political Institutions* (2nd ed.; New York: Van Nostrand Reinhold, 1966), pp. 35–39.

administrative reform including regionalization, but de Gaulle resigned from the premiership before the project was finished. Nevertheless, Debré published his proposal in 1947.[14] Another young civil servant, Jean-Marcel Jeanneny, whose father had been the last president of the Third Republic, collaborated with Debré on the project. As we shall see, Jeanneny played a key role in de Gaulle's later regionalization efforts. Also, Debré served as one of de Gaulle's *Commissaires de la république,* or regional prefects, in the first Gaullist experiment with regionalization.[15]

Ironically, that experiment was not based on Debré's proposal, but on the system established by de Gaulle's wartime arch-foe, Marshal Pétain, and the collaborationist Vichy regime. Vichy had organized eighteen regions for police and economic administration and had placed a "regional prefect" in charge of each. De Gaulle retained the system intact, changing only the men and their title. After de Gaulle's resignation, parliament forced the government to abandon the system, but that was not the end of regionalization for the men of the Fourth Republic.

The Fourth Republic

Less than two years after the Pétain-de Gaulle system was buried, it was partly resurrected. In April 1948, in the aftermath of the Communist-led insurrectionary strikes of late 1947, Interior Minister Jules Moch persuaded parliament to authorize eight "inspectors general for administration on special mission" (IGAMEs). The IGAMEs had special responsibilities for internal security in the large regions they served. Unlike the Pétain-de Gaulle system, however, they had no responsibilities in the area of economic policy. The IGAME system was set up as an urgent, pragmatic response to an emergency situation, rather than as part of a philosophically based program, but it survived until the 1964 Gaullist reforms discussed below.

The Fourth Republic also restored the other prong of the Pétain-de Gaulle regional system: economic affairs. In fact, its moves in that area set in motion the developments that have continued until the present time. The initiative, however, was not governmental, but private. As early as 1944, businessmen, farmers, trade unions, and others in various parts of France perceived—apparently largely independently and spontaneously— the desirability of forming local organizations of a "civic booster" or chamber of commerce variety to assist them in obtaining their share of the

---

14. *La mort de l'état républicain* (Paris: Gallimard, 1947), esp. pp. 70 ff.

15. Michel Debré, *Refaire une démocratie, un état, un pouvoir* (Paris: Plon, 1958), Foreword; *LM,* 22–23 March 1964; idem, "Un grand mouvement préfectoral: épisode de la Resistance," *Cahiers politiques* (February–March 1946), as cited in Chapman, *Prefects and Provincial France,* pp. 57–61.

economic recovery assistance France was receiving. As French economic planning developed, it found those committees to be useful collaborators and encouraged them. Representatives of various economic sectors— banking, agriculture, labor unions, commerce, etc.—and certain governmental and political officials composed most such committees. As the system caught on, committees were formed above the local level, for Departments and even regions. As early as 1952, the committees had become so widespread that they formed a National Council of Regional Economies and held a national convention.[16]

Finally, on 12 December 1954, the Mendès-France government responded to those developments with a decree designating "Regional Committees of Economic Expansion" to be "associations of public utility" and requiring that they be consulted on "the measures to be used in carrying out local economic development within the framework of the general policy of the Government." Their composition was modeled closely on that of their wholly private predecessors. The decree mentioned expressly representatives of the following sectors as suitable members for such committees: banking; agriculture; commerce; industry; fishing; transportation; artisanry; labor unions; local "collectivities";[17] economic regions; chambers of commerce, trade, and agriculture; employers associations; and regional committees on foreign trade. Interregional committees, composed of the prefects in the regions, certain functionaries, and the chairmen of the regional committees, were to deal with problems extending beyond a single region.[18]

The December 1954 decree was issued under authority of special economic powers delegated to the government by parliament in August 1954. In requesting those powers, the government expressed its intention of introducing a regional development program. Decrees issued under the special powers were subject to retroactive approval by parliament.[19] In fact, however, such approval was given routinely. Thus, the first real step in the development of French regionalism as public policy was taken by executive decree, despite the fact that it occurred in the Fourth Republic, a regime dominated by parliament.

The same method was used more dramatically for the next step in the process. Edgar Faure, who had been Mendès-France's finance minister, had succeeded him as premier and had received from parliament a renewal of the special economic powers. On the last day before expiration of the

16. *LM*, 12 October 1968.
17. A term the French apply to the organized politico-administrative territorial units, e.g., communes and Departments.
18. *LM*, 14 December 1954.
19. *Journal officiel, Débats parlementaires*, 5 August 1954, p. 3881; *Journal officiel, Documents parlementaires Assemblée nationale*, Annexe No. 9034, 1954, pp. 1579–83.

powers, his government issued a set of eleven decrees promoting regional economic development.[20]

The Faure decrees had two main purposes. They established a process for the formulation of programs of regional economic action *and* they provided for various kinds of financial and technical assistance to stimulate the economies of those regions that were lagging economically. Not until late 1956, however, were the regional boundaries drawn (again by executive decree).[21]

The principles on which the Fourth Republic's regionalization program rested have remained the basis of regionalization in France. The predominance of executive, as opposed to parliamentary, action; the almost exclusive orientation toward economic matters, rather than political, social, or legal concerns; the incorporation of corporatist concepts of representation were the leading features of regionalization before 1958. They have remained so during most of the time since.

The Early Fifth Republic

The continuity between the republics was very much evident during the first decade of de Gaulle's republic. Despite the many dramatic changes from the parliamentarist Fourth Republic to the presidentialist Fifth Republic, regionalization continued on, much as before, in process, in form, and in content. Even the contrast between the pragmatic reluctance of the Fourth Republic leaders and the philosophic regionalist commitment of de Gaulle's first premier (Debré) did not change things much during those early years.

De Gaulle's first steps toward regionalization fell squarely in Faure's pattern. Like Faure, de Gaulle received broad economic powers when he became premier.[22] Like Faure, he issued a battery of regionalization decrees in the last few days before the powers lapsed in January 1959. The most important of the decrees required that any administrative regions used by government agencies and ministries be aligned with those used for economic affairs and planning.[23]

Over the next five years, a series of decrees and other types of executive orders built a fairly elaborate regional administrative structure on those foundations. At the regional level itself, the office of regional prefect was revived, but was given authority only in the economic area. Each regional prefect was to combine that job with the position of prefect for the Depart-

---

20. *LM*, 30 June 1955, 3–4 July 1955; *Journal officiel, Lois et décrets*, 2 July 1955.

21. 28 November 1956. Escudier, *Le Conseil général*, p. 105. Corsica was made a separate region on 2 April 1957.

22. The text appears in *L'Année politique 1958*, pp. 542–43.

23. Escudier, *Le Conseil général*, pp. 106–7.

ment in which the regional capital was located. He was given the assistance of a small coordinating staff of civil servants called a Regional Mission and a consultative Regional Administrative Council composed of the other prefects in the region and certain other civil servants from the Departmental level.

Finally, each region was endowed with a Committee for Regional Economic Development (CODER) that took over the official functions of the Regional Committee of Economic Expansion without replacing it in its nonpublic roles. Like the committees, the CODERs were composed in a corporatist manner, though their membership was prescribed more precisely. Each CODER was to include twenty to fifty members. At least one-fourth of the members were to be elected officials, including (1) one or more General Councillors designated by each General Council from among its members, (2) one or more mayors from each Department designated by each General Council from outside its membership, and (3) the mayor of the regional capital. One-half of the members were to be representatives of "the chambers of commerce and industry, of agriculture, and of trade or of the organism that they form at the regional level; and of the professional and labor organizations of employers and wage-earners of industry, agriculture, and commerce, the president of the regional committee of expansion always to be included by right." The remaining members were to be "persons designated by administrative order of the prime minister by virtue of their competence in the economic, social, family, scientific, or cultural domains."[24] The CODERs were to be consultative organs on questions of economic and social planning and development at the regional level.

During the 1960–63 period, special national-level administrative organs to deal with regionalization were created for the first time. Originally, matters of regional development were handled by the Planning Commissariat and the Ministry of Construction, both of which gave their principal attention to other matters. In November 1960 an interministerial committee on regionalization was established and attached to the prime minister's office. Early in 1963 a set of decrees created a much more elaborate national administrative structure for regionalization. The Delegation for Territorial Management and Regional Action was created as a ministry-type agency headed by Olivier Guichard and attached directly to the prime minister's office. It was provided with a staff of about twenty professional-level civil servants and had several interministerial agencies attached to it. Its role was to coordinate the regional activities of the various ministries, to stimulate regional economies through investments of multiplier effect, and to encourage industrial decentralization. It was given a major voice in the

24. Les grandes lignes de la politique d'action régionale en France," *Textes et notes*, 28 November 1967, pp. 17–18; *L'Année politique 1964*, p. 114.

control of various funds that had been established to promote regionalization and of a new fund that was created at the same time.[25]

The National Committee for Territorial Management was set up by decree the same day and was attached to the Planning Commissariat as a consultative body. It consisted of fifty socio-occupational representatives and twenty-seven high civil servants with special responsibilities in the area of regionalization.[26] Its mission was to advise the Planning Commissariat on ways the plan could serve best the objectives of regionalization.

The 1958–64 wave of regionalization reforms carried forward from the Fourth Republic and accentuated the principle that authority over this area of policy lay almost entirely within the executive branch. Unlike the Fourth Republic, the Gaullist system did not even provide for parliamentary review of the executive decrees that established policy. Parliament entered the process only through review of the Fourth and Fifth national economic plans, in which regionalization figured prominently, and of the annual budgets, which provided the funds. Even here, the government could require en bloc approval or rejection of the plan or the budget. Furthermore, parliament played no role whatsoever in the elaboration of the regional structures.

The government not only ignored parliament, also, it deliberately snubbed all elected officials in preparing its policies. The 1964 decrees, for instance, were preceded by about one hundred consultative meetings with administrative, ministry, and legal personnel, from which elected officials were excluded purposely. Also, immediately before the decisions were announced, the prime minister and the appropriate members of the government discussed them with chairmen of Regional Committees of Economic Expansion but not with MPs. Finally, both prime ministers during that period (Debré and Pompidou) and President de Gaulle took part actively in elaborating regionalization policies. For instance, de Gaulle personally required that special ministerial council meetings on regionalization be held every three or four months.[27] These arrangements were changed dramatically for the next phase in the development of regionalization. The decision-making process was dragged out of the bureaucrats' closets, without, however, being placed in conventional parliamentary channels. This was de Gaulle's abortive 1968–69 experiment with "participatory democracy." Before it ended with de Gaulle's resignation in April 1969, it included intensive bureaucratic preparations, systematic and widespread popular consultation, perfunctory consideration in parliament, and a popular referendum.

25. Perin et al., "L'Aménagement du territoire," p. 48; *L'Année politique 1963*, p. 366; Jerome Monod and Philippe de Castelbajac, *L'Aménagement du territotre* (Paris: P.U.F., 1971), pp. 37–39.

26. Perin et al., "L'Aménagement du territoire," p. 48; *L'Année politique 1964*, p. 368.

27. *LM*, 4 September 1963, 13 February 1964, 18 and 22/23 March 1964.

Participatory Democracy

Preliminary Preparations

After four years of inattention, regionalization returned to the forefront of activity in 1968. President de Gaulle kicked off a new regionalization campaign with a speech in Lyons in March 1968. Before that campaign was completed, his administration had conducted a unique, massive consultation program, had brought regionalization before the electorate through popular referendum, and had been buried by its collapse.

De Gaulle's Lyons speech announced that the "multi-centuries effort of centralization, which was needed for so long in order to produce and maintain the unity [of our country] is not necessary any longer. On the contrary, regional activities appear to be the springboards for tomorrow's economic success." He only hinted at "what remains to be done," but everyone assumed that he had chosen the regionalists over the centralists in the continuing quarrel over French economic development.[28]

His speech gave no hint of the methods he intended to use to prepare and implement new policies in this area. In fact, his first steps followed closely the pattern of the 1954–64 phase. His government issued two decrees on 10 May. One strengthened the regional prefects at the expense of the Department prefects. The other broadened the mission of the CODERs and strengthened their structure.[29] Nothing suggested that de Gaulle's approach was about to change dramatically.

Then, the May-June 1968 civil disorders erupted. They precipitated an abrupt and radical change in the decision-making process regarding regionalization. In his first public effort to regain control of the situation, de Gaulle announced on 24 May that he intended to hold a referendum in June on a request for special powers.[30] When the proposed referendum text was published five days later, it included authorization for "the President of the Republic, the government, and parliament" to take by 1 June 1969, "all measures" necessary "to adapt the economic and administrative structures and to promote social progress in conformity with national and international necessities by . . . the organization of economic activity within a regional framework with the increased participation of local elective bodies and of labor unions and professional associations, as well as through administrative decentralization and deconcentration."[31] Also, the bill provided for reforms in the educational system and the introduction of "participation" in the management of commercial, industrial, agricultural, and

28. *LM*, 26 March 1968.
29. *Le Dossier*, p. 57.
30. *L'Année politique 1968*, p. 379.
31. *LM*, 30 May 1968.

public service enterprises, but made no mention of the Senate reforms that were to loom so large in the 1969 referendum.

This first effort to jar regionalization out of conventional decision-making channels aborted when the printers refused to prepare the referendum ballots. De Gaulle then called parliamentary elections instead, apparently at the suggestion of Prime Minister Pompidou. The regionalization issue played no significant role in those elections.[32] De Gaulle had no intention of abandoning regionalization or the referendum approach, however.

In announcing the elections, he announced also that he was only postponing the referendum until a more propitious moment.[33] The second-round balloting in the elections was held 30 June. On 1 July, Pompidou told the Gaullist deputies that work was beginning on the "bill on participation" and, on 3 July, de Gaulle told the Council of Ministers that the bill would include regionalization reforms and would be submitted to referendum.[34] Pompidou's successor, Maurice Couve de Murville, in his inaugural address to the National Assembly on 17 July, announced the big leap toward "participatory democracy" in explaining that the referendum would not be held until Spring 1969, and that "all interested collectivities and organizations" would be involved in the task of drafting the bill. Also, he reported that the bill would introduce "representatives . . . of regional activities" into a chamber of parliament and would "reform the regional organization" so as to become "more representative and responsible."[35] When Couve de Murville formed his government, he transferred Jean-Marcel Jeanneny from minister of social affairs to minister of state in charge of preparing the government's proposals on Senate reform and regionalization.[36]

Governmental Consultations

The process of preparing for the consultations began with a memorandum from President de Gaulle to the appropriate ministers in late July. It instructed them to reform the Senate to include "representatives of local collectivities and regional activities, as well as representatives of great economic and social organisms" and that regional councils should be created, "composed of delegates of local collectivities, General Councils, Municipal Councils, and delegates of economic and social activities in the region." Both institutions "must include university representation."[37] This was the

32. See William G. Andrews, "France 1968: Crisis Election and Long-Term Trends," *South Atlantic Quarterly* 68 (Winter 1969): 1–15.
33. *L'Année politique 1968*, p. 381; *LM*, 9–10 June 1968.
34. *LM*, 3–4 July 1968.
35. *LM*, 19 July 1968.
36. *L'Année politique 1968*, pp. 60, 375–76.
37. *LM*, 30 August 1968.

first clear indication that Senate reform was to be tied to regionalization in this project. In a sense, this was logical. Regionalization could be strengthened by providing for regional representation in the national parliament, and the Senate was an appropriate chamber for such representation. That fit neatly into de Gaulle's constitutional doctrines since the Bayeux speech. If the Senate contained such representation, de Gaulle had long argued, it should not have full legislative powers. Thus, the package of reforms naturally included a reduction in the legislative power of the Senate.

On the other hand, the Senate was the only institution of the Republic that remained in the control of de Gaulle's opponents, not only his opponents in partisan terms, but also opponents in the sense that they were intermediaries par excellence, notables, a political species that was anathema to de Gaulle's constitutional doctrines. What could be more natural for de Gaulle than to use the popular issue of regionalization as a vehicle to destroy the Senate! In any case, whether from a sense of constitutional propriety or for reasons of political vindictiveness, de Gaulle linked the fate of regionalization to that of the Senate.

A governmental "work group" to give effect to de Gaulle's instructions was set up under the direction of a civil servant whose position was similar to that of a Special Assistant to the President in the United States.[38] By the end of the August holidays, the work group had prepared a plan for proceeding. It was reviewed by the four ministers most concerned and, a few days later, by the interministerial regionalization committee under the prime minister's chairmanship and was approved. On 4 September, the proposal was approved by the Council of Ministers.[39] So far, the decision-making process was very conventional.

Popular Consultations

Then a dramatic new step was taken. The prime minister sent to all regional prefects instructions to conduct a series of consultations on the government's regionalization plans. Four thousand questionnaire kits— two hundred per region—accompanied the instructions. Another thousand kits were reproduced by the prefects at the request of prospective respondents. Each kit contained a set of guidelines, a fifteen-page questionnaire, a set of maps of France, and a lengthy reference bibliography on regionalization. The prefects were instructed to ask all organizations represented in the CODERs to complete questionnaires and to have all Department prefects meet in all district capitals with anyone else who wished to complete one.

38. *Conseiller technique en secrétariat général de la présidence de la république, LM,* 30 July 1968.
39. *LM,* 30 August 1968, 5 September 1968.

The MPs representing the Departments of each region were to be kept informed of the consultations. During the last week in October, the CODERs were to meet, synthesize the results, and report on them to Paris through the regional prefects. The guidelines indicated that a final round of consultations would take place on the national level and that the government would be guided by the results of the consultations in preparing a bill to be submitted to parliament.[40]

With its strategy set and the consultation process put in motion, the government directed its energy toward attracting attention to the effort. De Gaulle, of course, was the most effective publicist. In ten years he had held only sixteen press conferences. Now he scheduled another to promote the reform projects. With respect to regionalization, he announced his intention "to create in each region an assembly" with socio-occupational representation and with authority in the economic and social domain, for, in that domain, "the region seems today to be the essential local element. In fact, its ethnic and geographic character, its size, its resources permit it to have a life of its own, and it must have this life in order that our country may develop everything of value in each of its parts and stop emptying itself by drawing all its substance into Paris and its environs." To accomplish this, the government intended (1) to provide the regional prefects with "adequate administrative means" by decentralization, (2) to set up regional councils composed of representatives of "local collectivities and various economic, social, and university activities," (3) to bring before such councils "all projects which concern the equipment and development of the region, especially through Planning," (4) to confer on them "certain financial responsibilities in the use of resources furnished by the State, by special regional taxes, or by borrowing," and (5) to involve them in the election of senators.[41]

Other members of the government joined vigorously in the refrain. The prime minister told a Gaullist party meeting that, although no regionalization bill would be submitted to parliament, "I plan to open the Autumn session [of parliament], through the government's declaration, with a broad debate which will permit opinions—that certainly will be diverse—to be expressed and we will take them into account, if necessary, in drafting the final text." Also, he was interviewed on television concerning regionalization.[42] The ministers most directly concerned with regionalization—especially Guichard, Jeanneny, and Interior Minister Raymond Marcellin—

---

40. This system was modeled on one used successfully on a pilot basis for local planning in a single Department eighteen months earlier. Olivier Guichard, "Déclaration . . . à l'Assemblée nationale, le 11 décembre 1968," *Actualités–Documents* (January 1969): 58; *LM*, 4, 5, 6, and 11 September 1968.

41. *LM*, 11 September 1968. An abbreviated English version was distributed by the French embassy in the United States.

42. *LM*, 13 and 25 September 1968.

made a large number of public speeches and statements on the subject, including provincial tours, during the period of the consultations.[43] Guichard answered questions on regionalization in the National Assembly early in October and in the Senate at the end of the month.[44] He and his ministerial collaborators made an interim report to a Council of Ministers meeting in mid-October.[45] The prime minister conferred on this topic with delegations of two major Gaullist parties.[46] Obviously, de Gaulle had given top priority to publicizing the consultation campaign and his ministers had responded accordingly.

The government's efforts had the desired effect. Political leaders, parties, and all sorts of public organizations entered into a lively public discussion. Through September, October, and November, every issue of the newspapers carried their statements on regionalization. Guichard reported that newspapers throughout France carried a total of at least 4,400 articles on the consultations. Even the militantly anti-Gaullist Unified Socialist Party plunged into the act in a big way by sending its leader, Michel Roccard, on a tour of public meetings in major cities and holding "study conferences" followed by public meetings in all twenty-one regions on 7–8 December. The chairmen of some ninety General Councils and the national associations of mayors and of elected officials held special meetings on the subject and issued public statements.[47] In short, the government's campaign was very successful in stimulating debate on the issue. Furthermore, the views were almost unanimously favorable to the principle of regionalization, although they varied greatly on what were understood to be the details of the government's project. The details of those differences emerge from analysis of the questionnaire responses.

Consultation Results

During the public debate, the official soundings proceeded on schedule. By 1 November the regional prefects had returned to Paris 3,260 completed questionnaires. The Paris region returned the largest number, 272. Alsace, the least populous region, returned the fewest, 57. The other nineteen averaged about 150 each. By type of respondent, the completed questionnaires were distributed as shown in table 1.

Although the sample was large and broad, it was not designed to be "scientific." Of course, not all organizations responded and no effort was made to ensure that the respondents reflected the makeup of French society accurately. Nor were the responses weighted to take into account the

43. *LM*, 17, 24, and 25 September; 2, 6/7, and 13/14 October; 10/11 November; all 1968.
44. *LM*, 13/14 and 31 October 1968.
45. *LM*, 11 October 1968.
46. *LM*, 27 September 1968, 9 November 1968.
47. *LM*,25, 27, and 28 September 1968; 1, 9, and 23 November 1968; 13–14 April 1969.

Table 1. Distribution of Questionnaires

Sector	N	%
Industry and commerce	719	(22)
Political and administrative (overall)	622	(19)
municipal councils	299	(9)
general councils and big-city mayors	154	(5)
political parties and clubs	54	(2)
Social, cultural, university organizations	587[a]	(18)
Labor unions	460	(14)
Agriculture	342	(10)
Liberal professions	293[a]	(9)
Economic organizations	293[a]	(9)
Totals	3.823	(117)[b]

[a] Indicates author's estimates based on percentage figures reported.
[b] Figures add to more than 100% because some questionnaires were counted in more than one category.

enormous variations in size of membership of the responding organizations. Also, most respondents left some questions unanswered. The largest number of responses (88 percent) were received on the questions concerning the boundaries of the regions and on the councils. The more technical questions on territorial management and planning received the fewest responses (as low as 35 percent).[48] Finally, the questions were framed deliberately to elicit information that the government wanted in drafting a final bill. This constrained the responses within the framework already adopted by the government. The survey, then, provides an interesting view of the state of French thinking on the government's regionalization policies, but should not be treated as a wholly reliable and accurate reflection of French public opinion in the way a Gallup poll, for example, seeks to be.

The questionnaires were analyzed by computer. The analysts coded 215 responses and prepared 450 analytical tables from the results. Those results dealt with five major areas: the boundaries of the regions, their financial resources, their authority, the designation of the councils, and the regional executive authority. Fifty thousand copies of a brochure reporting a summary of the results were distributed by Guichard's office.[49] The responsible ministers reported and explained the results to the government in public statements and interviews, to party meetings, and to parliament.

They noted that the level of agreement varied greatly among the questions. For instance, almost all (96 percent[50]) of the respondents favored both types of representation (territorial and socio-occupational) in the regional councils, but only 68 percent agreed that they should have equal weight. Direct election by universal suffrage was favored for the territorial

48. Guichard, "Déclaration," p. 60.
49. *LM*, 24/25 November 1968, 3 December 1968, 13/14 April 1969.
50. These figures are percentages of those who responded to the specific questions, not of those who returned questionnaires.

representatives by 67 percent, but for the socio-occupational representatives by only 31 percent, while 42 percent favored designation of the latter by appropriate associations and 27 percent wanted indirect suffrage through socio-occupational "colleges." Unicameral councils were advocated by 70 percent and a single executive by 85 percent, 81 percent agreeing that the regional prefect, responsible to the national government rather than the regional councils, should be the executive.

Forty percent of the respondents approved of the boundaries in use. Another 48 percent accepted them for the time being but wanted changes later. Ten percent wanted the boundaries changed at once.

With respect to the authority of the councils, 82 percent of the respondents favored transfer of powers exclusively from the national level, rather than at least partly from the local or Department level. Only 47 percent, however, agreed that the socio-occupational representatives should share fully in those powers, while 46 percent believed that their role should be consultative only. On the detailed specification of the areas of activity of the regions, the results were reported to be too fragmented to permit drawing conclusions from them.

As to finances, a long list of possibilities was considered. The most popular, the creation of specific regional taxes, was favored by 55 percent. Others, in descending order of popularity, were: (1) cession by the state to the regions of part or all of some taxes (49 percent), (2) borrowing authority (46 percent), (3) state subsidies (40 percent), (4) automatic allocation to the regions of a portion of the state's receipts (36 percent), and (5) authority to add a mill levy to state taxes (21 percent).[51]

Parliamentary Consultations

While the popular consultation's results still were being evaluated, the government began the next (parliamentary) phase of the process. It began by seeking support for its proposal from the major Gaullist political party, the UDR. The UDR Central Committee adopted a resolution in mid-November that favored (1) retention of the existing regional boundaries; (2) popular election of both territorial and the corporatist members of the regional councils, indirect for the former and direct for the latter category; (3) regional prefects as the regional executives; (4) the regions' areas of authority to include planning, territorial management, and public facilities; and (5) the regions' financial resources to include taxing and lending powers transferred from the national government and subsidies provided by it.[52] A few days later, Jeanneny and Guichard also reported to the Policy Bureau of the UDR parliamentary group.[53]

51. Guichard, "Déclaration," pp. 60–66; *LM*, 23 and 24 October 1968, 3 and 4 December 1968.
52. *LM*, 17/18 November 1968.
53. *LM*, 22 November 1968.

The government itself received a report on the consultations in a Council of Ministers meeting on 20 November and scheduled a debate on regionalization and Senate reform to begin 26 November. This was to be the last of only four major parliamentary debates of the session, but was not to close with a vote as the government regarded it as being for informational purposes only. In fact, the press of other parliamentary business forced its postponement until 11 December.[54]

Interest in the debate was erratic. One-fifth of the deputies (93) signed up to speak in the debate which consumed thirty hours spread over four days, but attendance was spotty. The chamber was well filled to hear Jeanneny and Guichard lead off on Wednesday afternoon. But by the time the prime minister spoke on Friday afternoon only about 80 deputies turned out, and as few as 10 were present at the end of the night sessions. A leading political writer suggested that interest was low because (1) the Assembly sensed that it was being bypassed by the popular consultations and the proposed referendum, (2) it believed that the government had made up its mind already and was not susceptible to influence by parliament, and (3) a decision on the matter might be deferred for a long time.[55] Jeanneny also presented the project to the Senate, but that body was preoccupied with its own fate and gave scant attention to the matter of regionalization.[56]

The ministers' speeches to parliament shed considerable light on its intentions. For the most part, its plans conformed to the preponderant views that emerged in the consultations and the UDR resolution. On the critical matter of the composition of the councils, however, the government differed from both. Both the questionnaire respondents and the UDR had advocated *direct* election of the territorial representatives by universal suffrage, *direct or indirect election* of the socio-occupational representatives, and *parity* of the two categories. The government announced that it intended to provide for *indirect* election of the territorial representatives, *appointment* by representative organizations for the socio-occupational members, and a *60–40 balance* of the two types. Although the questionnaires favored (by a hairline margin) full participation of the latter category, the government intended to require that no measure could pass a council unless it had the support of a majority of the council and of a majority of the territorial members. If it had the support of the latter but not the former, the latter could pass it alone after twenty-four-hours' reflection.[57]

By mentioning the points of disagreement with the consultation results, the government made clear that it listened to the people but would not necessarily be bound by what it heard. By presenting its proposal so concretely, the government suggested that it would not be influenced

54. *LM*, 21 and 22 November 1968.

55. Pierre Viansson-Ponté, *LM*, 15/16 December 1968; *LM*, 11 and 12 December 1968.

56. *LM*, 18 December 1968; the speeches of Couve de Murville, Jeanneny, and Guichard are reproduced *in extenso* in *Actualités–Documents*, January 1969.

57. *LM*, 13 and 14/15 December 1968.

greatly by the parliamentary debate it had arranged. Not surprisingly, then, the government did not take long to undertake its final drive toward the referendum.

Preparing the Referendum Bill

That campaign was launched, in effect, by President de Gaulle's speech at Quimper in Brittany on 2 February 1969. Speaking in the most particularist section of France, where a militant autonomist group had detonated more than two dozen bombs the previous year, he quoted a Breton poem by his uncle and stressed with a heavy hand the regionalist aspect of the referendum. Clearly, he intended Senate reform to be the tail to the regionalization kite. His speech was publicity more than information, however, and he added nothing of substance to what his ministers had told parliament in December.[58]

Meanwhile, the draft bill for the referendum moved ahead. On 18 February, it was approved by two interministerial committees, one chaired by the prime minister, the other by the president. Those meetings resolved several points of detail that were still pending. In response to a vigorous lobbying campaign, the bill was changed to give Corsica the standing of a separate region.[59] Also, the socio-occupational categories, the electoral system for the territorial representatives, and the financial base were agreed upon. The following day, the prime minister made a progress report to the Council of Ministers and announced the schedule for further consideration of the referendum proposal. It would culminate in voting on 27 April. That date was dictated by a constitutional provision permitting the president to submit bills to referendum "at the request of the Government" only while parliament is in session.[60] As the constitution stipulates that the regular spring session begin 2 April, the referendum could have been held earlier only if a special session had been called. The campaign, to intervene between the government's "request" for a referendum and the polling date, moved the latter to the end of April, even though the bill was virtually ready by mid-February. In the meantime, the bill was subject to review by the Council of Ministers at a special 27 February meeting and by the Council of State [61] and to reconsideration by the Council of Ministers in the light of the advice from the Council of State.

Before that process had begun, however, the government's press spokesman discussed the proposed composition of the regional councils (except Paris and Corsica), on the grounds that the decisions of the recent in-

58. *LM*, 4 February 1969.
59. *LM*, 5, 19, and 25 February 1969.
60. Art. 11.
61. A unit of the high civil service that includes among its activities advisement to the government on constitutional matters.

terministerial meetings on that point, "in principle, will not be called into question again." The councils would vary from 50 to 127 members. All National Assembly deputies would be members by right of the councils for their regions. The remaining seats would be divided fairly evenly between territorial and socio-occupational members with the deputies and territorial councillors, combined, always outnumbering the socio-occupational ones.[62] A few days later, a complete text of the draft bill was published by *Le Monde*, though the government denied that it was official.[63]

The Council of Ministers approved the draft and referred it to the Council of State which submitted it to a committee of fourteen experts. On the basis of the committee report, the Council of State concluded on 17 March that the method of proposing the referendum was unconstitutional and that the bill itself was unconstitutional (1) in not providing for revision of Article 72 of the constitution which identified the territorial units of the Republic, and (2) in diminishing the "parliamentary" character of the Senate by providing for appointive rather than elective Senators and by eliminating its "political" quality.[64] The Council of Ministers accepted the Council of State's advice on revising Article 72 but rejected the rest, made some technical changes, and approved the revised bill on 24 March.[65]

The Referendum Bill

The bill contained some ninety-five hundred words in sixty-eight articles and proposed amendment of about one-third of the constitution. The first forty-eight articles dealt with regionalization. They gave the region the same constitutional status as the commune and the Department by calling it "a territorial collectivity" and identified its mission as "to contribute to the economic, social, and cultural development, as well as to the management, of the corresponding part of the national territory." Twenty-two regions, including Corsica, were delineated.

The roles and relationship of the councils and regional prefects were defined in a way that made clear that the state had no intention of foregoing its veto powers over local government, even at the regional level. The heart of the reform lay in its transfer from the state to the regions of authority over a list of twenty-five types of public facilities (sanitary, cultural, educational, sporting, highway, airport, waterway, park, forest, and touristic installations) and its grant to the regions of concurrent authority for housing and urban renewal projects. The regions were authorized to use proceeds from (1) taxes transferred by the state to them, (2) state subsidies, (3) loans,

62. *LM*, 21 February 1969.
63. 26 February 1969.
64. *LM*, 21 and 28 February 1969; *L'Année politique, 1969*, p. 20.
65. See *Journal officiel: Lois et décrets*, 3 April 1969, pp. 3315–24; and *LM*, 26 and 27 March 1969, for the text.

(4) income from the operation of their facilities, and (5) other minor revenue sources.

The composition of the councils was to follow the lines described to parliament in December and by the press spokesman in February. Socio-occupational representatives were to be two-thirds as numerous in each council as the other two categories combined and were to be designated by seven categories of organizations: those for wage earners; farmers; industrial, commercial, maritime, and artisanal enterprises; the "liberal" professions; families; higher education and research; and social and cultural activities. The articles dealing with the Senate concerned regionalization to the extent that the 160 senators (of a 323 total) representing "territorial collectivities" of France proper were to be elected "in the framework of the regions" by electoral colleges that included regional councillors.

According to Guichard, the referendum bill conformed to the preponderant views of the respondents to the questionnaires in every respect, except the manner of composition and designation of the councils.[66] Nevertheless, all evidence indicates that it conformed *in every respect* covered by the questionnaire to the intentions of the government as formed already before the consultation campaign began, except that Corsica became a separate region later. Not the soundings, the party deliberations, the parliamentary debates, or the advice of the Council of State seem to have had any significant influence on the substance of the project. The main issues that arose within the government itself seem to have been matters of detail that had not been objects of discussion in the public debate or the questionnaires. In short, for all the fancy footwork of public consultation, debate, and discussion, the bill was almost entirely the product of nonpolitical deliberation between de Gaulle and high-level technocrats.

Referendum Campaign and Results

Small wonder, then, that when the government "proposed" its bill to President de Gaulle in April, he responded by calling a referendum on it for 27 April, with the official campaign beginning on 14 April. The referendum was designed to require each voter to approve or reject the reform package in toto (regionalization, Senate reform, presidential succession, constitutional amendment procedure, abolition of the Economic and Social Council, etc.) An accompanying presidential declaration urged approval so that "each person . . . may participate actively in his destiny" through regionalization and by introducing corporatist representation into the Senate. He never even hinted that the referendum bill reduced greatly the legislative power of the Senate.[67] The government sent each voter a fourteen-

66. *LM*, 13/14 April 1969.
67. *LM*, 4 April 1969.

page brochure containing the text of de Gaulle's declaration, a map of the regions, and the text of the referendum bill (which covered twelve pages).

The government's package kicked off the campaign. The Gaullists stressed the regionalization aspects of the bill and de Gaulle's threat to resign if the bill were defeated. The opposition expressed little dissatisfaction with the regionalization proposals, but attacked the proposed emasculation of the Senate as portending dangerous concentration of power in de Gaulle's hands.[68]

These strategies were dictated by the state of public opinion at the outset of the campaign. For instance, one survey indicated that 54 percent of the voters favored regionalization and 20 percent were opposed, but only 26 percent favored Senate reform and 33 percent were opposed.[69] The Gaullist campaign was unable to overcome the voters' resistance to Senate reform. Furthermore, de Gaulle's image of "indispensability" had been shattered by his bungling of the May 1968 disorders during which Pompidou had emerged as a viable alternative president. Finally, the local "notables"—who had so much at stake in the Senate—were able to mobilize their neighbors in its behalf. As a result, the referendum bill was rejected, 10,901,753 (47.6 percent) to 12,007,102 (52.4 percent), and de Gaulle resigned and retired the following day.

The fate of the regionalization proposals was ironic. They could have been enacted by parliament, for the disciplined Gaullists had a lopsided Assembly majority, and the Senate favored them as well. Nonetheless, de Gaulle craved Senate reform even more than regionalization, and the Senate was not inclined to confine itself to a legislative wheelchair voluntarily. Therefore, de Gaulle tried to hoist Senate reform as a tail to regionalization's kite. The tail was too heavy and, despite all the huffing and puffing of the Gaullist campaign, it brought the kite crashing down. The "intermediaries" and "notables" on whom de Gaulle had trod for more than ten years rose up and struck him down.

Pompidou

Launched Again

Regionalization policy underwent sweeping transformation from de Gaulle to Pompidou. The Senate reform project was abandoned definitively once Pompidou became president and regionalization was laid aside for a long time. When it revived, it had undergone considerable metamorphosis and was handled very differently. It ceased to be "the great French reform

68. For my account of the campaign, see William G. Andrews, "The Fall of de Gaulle," *Orbis* 13, no. 3 (Fall 1970): 642–56.
69. Sofres in *LM*, 25 and 26 March 1969.

of our century" and became "prudent, but evolutive reform." Also, "participatory democracy" was discarded and regionalization proceeded through conventional parliamentary channels. Yet, in the end, Pompidou's quiet approach may have been more fruitful than de Gaulle's drama. At least his reform bill became law.

Even without its weighty tail of Senate reform, the regionalization kite was a very long time getting airborne. Pompidou made his first public presidential pronouncement on the matter on 29 October 1970—eighteen months after de Gaulle's referendum—in a speech in Lyons, the same mode and city in which de Gaulle had launched his regionalization campaign in March 1968.[70] Nine more months passed before the project came to a Cabinet committee and another seven months elapsed before the Cabinet as a whole dealt with it. The parliamentary phase was even more extended. A year after the Cabinet broached the matter, parliament did, and another five months passed before it cleared the critical hurdle of National Assembly passage—three hours too late for passage on 27 April 1972, the third anniversary of de Gaulle's referendum defeat.[71]

The change from de Gaulle to Pompidou was more than a loss of intensity of urgency. Pompidou also changed the character of the reform considerably. From the outset he made clear that his project was much more modest than his predecessor's. "The region," he said in his Lyons speech, must be "not an administrative level superimposed on those that exist, but, above all, the union of Departments permitting the rational construction and management of major collective facilities." Its structure would consist of a regional prefect, "representing the State"; of "representation . . . of . . . local collectivities"; and "a consultative organism of the social and occupational elements of the region." Whereas de Gaulle's regions would have received authority only from the state, Pompidou's would receive authority from the communes, the Departments, and—at the request of the regions—from the state. The authority delegated might vary considerably from region to region.

Delay and dilution did not, however, dampen debate. Support for the principle of regionalization remained general. In fact, the Gaullists were outflanked by Radical-Socialist party leader, Jean-Jacques Servan-Schreiber, and his plan for "political," as opposed to purely "administrative," regions. His proposal was presented with spectacular publicity, adopted by his party, and precipitated lively debate in the press.[72] The

70. *LM*, 31 October 1970.

71. *LM*, 9 April 1971, 19 November 1971, 29 April 1972. The prime minister had expressed the hope in November 1970 that a regionalization bill would pass parliament during the Fall 1970 session. *LM*, 1/2 November 1970.

72. Jean-Jacques Servan-Schreiber, *Le Pouvoir régionale* (Paris: *Grasset*, 1971); *L'Année politique 1970*, pp. 103–4; *LM*, 6/7 December 1970. The debate was reported fully in *Le Monde*, especially the issues of 6/7, 8, 9, 10, 12, 15, 16, 18, 19, and 20/21 December 1970.

Christian Democratic group, Democratic Center, put forward a less drastic counterproposal.[73] The Gaullist UDR and the Communists took rival positions on the Servan-Schreiber proposition.[74] The topic arose in question period in the Senate and was discussed in newspaper opinion columns frequently.[75]

The New Bill

However spectacular may have been the proposals and the debate, the government's stand became no bolder. In fact, when it finally disclosed its bill in November 1971, it was even less "political" than de Gaulle's version. Consequently, it retreated still further from that implication of the 1968 questionnaires.[76] The councils were to be "deliberative" but bicameral. The Regional Councils were to be composed ex officio of all deputies and senators representing the region in parliament plus at least an equal number of members appointed by the General Councils and municipal councils. The other chambers would be consultative Economic, Social, and Cultural Committees composed in the same way as the CODERs. The role of the regional prefect was not changed. The decline in the political character of the regions from the de Gaulle to the Pompidou bill was underlined by the legal label given them. De Gaulle's regions had been "territorial collectivities," the same term as is applied to communes and Departments. Pompidou's regions were "public establishments," the label used for nationalized enterprises, public universities, etc.[77]

The same process of shrinkage occurred in the list of activities to be assigned to the regions. They would "participate in financing collective [public] facilities of direct interest to the region . . . as a whole," sponsor regional development studies, propose ways to coordinate public investments in the region, and construct public facilities themselves by agreement with "other interested local collectivities, or even with another region, or the State." Finally, the list might be lengthened if local governments "on their own initiative" or the state were to make transfers to the regions.

The reduction in activities implied, quite logically, a reduction in financial resources. The Pompidou bill provided for transfer from the state to the regions of authority to collect automobile drivers' license fees (about $10 million per year) and conferred authority to add a mill levy to three other state taxes. Also, the regions were to be authorized to float loans. The tax receipts were to be limited to 25 francs per inhabitant, that is, between about $4 million and about $22 million a year, depending on the size of the

73. *LM*, 19 December 1970.
74. *LM*, 10 December 1970; *L'Année politique 1970*, p. 109.
75. *LM*, 10 December 1970.
76. *LM*, 19 November 1971.
77. *LM*, 19 November 1971, 16 March 1972.

region, and the potential total was estimated at about $200 million per year, only about 5 percent as much as the aggregate receipts of the communes and Departments and about 10 percent as much as the de Gaulle reform had intended, but about four times as much as the regions had been receiving.[78]

The spirit of the Pompidou bill was expressed well by M. Chaban-Delmas in a statement to Agence France-Presse.[79] He called it "an illustration of the policy, both pragmatic and resolute, which the government has undertaken to place the exercise of responsibilities directly in touch with realities and men." He argued that the modest resources of the regions would not prevent them from exerting substantial influence. "It is well known," he said, "that, in economic matters, the additional infusion, even though its amount is limited, very often is decisive." Even so, this was a far cry from "the new framework for initiative . . . the great reform" of which de Gaulle had spoken at Quimper.

The gap between the de Gaulle and the Pompidou regionalization programs was symbolized by the resignation of M. Jean-Marcel Jeanneny from the UDR in the same month as the presentation of the bill. Jeanneny, the main architect of de Gaulle's regionalism, had been dropped from the government when Chaban-Delmas had become prime minister in July 1969.[80] Roger Frey, who had exhibited a pronounced "centralist" bent in various ministerial assignments, had succeeded him and was responsible for the Pompidou bill. When Jeanneny resigned from the UDR, he criticized Pompidou's regionalization on the grounds that it failed "to transfer to the regions and to the Departments real responsibility for certain facilities and for the operations of certain public services," that it risked "complicating administration further," and that it confused responsibility more than ever.[81] In a later interview he complained that the Pompidou reform "did not go far enough," because the powers and resources of the regions would be inadequate and the regional councils would be consultative rather than genuinely legislative.[82]

To Parliament

Despite such reservations, as well as others expressed by such groups as the National Movement of Local Elected Officials, the regionalization bill finally went to parliament for its Spring 1972 session. The Committee on Laws turned its attention to the bill on 14 March and the floor debate began

78. *LM*, 19 November 1971, 16 March 1972, 27 April 1972.
79. *LM*, 27 January 1972.
80. Olivier Guichard, de Gaulle's other regionalization specialist, had become minister of education at the same time.
81. *LM*, 6 November 1971.
82. *LM*, 27 April 1972.

on 25 April.[83] Two days earlier, the French had approved by referendum British entry into the European Economic Community. Thus, in the same week (1) Pompidou had used an institution (referendum) *introduced to republican France by de Gaulle* to overturn a policy that had been one of the hallmarks of de Gaulle's administration and (2) had used another institution (parliament) *scorned by de Gaulle* to enact a much-diluted version of one of de Gaulle's projects that had been defeated by referendum three years to the day earlier. It seemed as though Pompidou was capitalizing on every available irony to manifest his independence of the man who had invented him politically. In fact, in one critical respect Pompidou's bill was the reverse of de Gaulle's bill for it gave the *notables* control of the regions whereas the whole purpose of de Gaulle's referendum had been to destroy the political power of the notables. If 27 April 1969 had been their revenge, 27 April 1972 was their vindication.

When regionalization finally came before parliament in the form of a bill after some eighteen years—under two republics and eleven prime ministers—of being handled as a preserve of the executive branch, the performance was disappointing. Although the prime minister called the debate "one of the most important, if not the most important, of this [1969–73] parliament," the deputies seemed unconvinced. Debate was desultory. The first day's discussion, for instance, had to be recessed early because too few speakers were present.[84]

The initial debate was highlighted by speeches by the prime minister and by the *rapporteur* of the Assembly's Committee on Laws explaining and defending the government's bill. Immediately thereafter, a Communist deputy moved the "preliminary question" (*question préalable*).[85] That motion was defeated by 377 votes to 94, with 3 abstentions.

Debate on the general lines of the bill consumed the remainder of the first day's sittings. Two principal themes of criticism emerged. First, the reform was "too timid" in failing to confer ample powers on the regions. Second, the overseas possessions and Paris should have been included. Among the other points raised were objections to ex officio membership of senators and deputies on the regional councils and to what was said to be disproportionately low representation of rural communes on the councils. Deputies from government parties were as numerous as opposition-party deputies among the critics in the general debate. Eleven were majority members, seven were opposition members, and two were unaffiliated.

The second day of debate was dominated by speeches by spokesmen

---

83. *LM*, 16 March 1972, 26 April 1972.

84. The debate is reported in *LM*, 27, 28, 29 April 1972.

85. This is a parliamentary device that says, in effect, that the matter raised is not worthy of parliament's attention. If passed, the Assembly moves immediately to the next item on its agenda. It gives an early picture of the Assembly's lineup. This was the device that slew the European Defense Community in 1954.

for the three majority and three opposition parties. Also, M. Roger Frey spoke on behalf of the government. As minister of state charged with administrative reforms, he had been responsible for preparation of the government's bill. A motion by Servan-Schreiber to return the bill to committee was defeated after discussion, 365 to 105, with 1 abstention.

Assembly Adoption

The bill was then discussed and voted on article-by-article, most of this part of the deliberation taking place on the third day of debate. The government resisted successfully all efforts to make substantive amendments or to defeat individual articles. Some decisions were fairly close, however. For instance, an amendment to increase the representation of small communes was defeated, 254 to 202, with 8 abstentions, and another that would have achieved the same end, but less directly, lost by 242 to 210, with 6 abstentions. As with most French parliamentary debates, discussion concluded with "vote explanations" by representatives of the various parliamentary parties.

The bill as a whole was adopted by 343 votes to 105 with 28 abstentions. All 52 Socialists and 34 Communists voted against the bill. They were joined by 10 unaffiliated deputies (including Servan-Schreiber) and 9 members of government parties (4 PDM Christian Democrats, 3 UDR Gaullists, and 2 Independent Republican Gaullists). The bill was passed with the votes of 265 of the 281 UDR, 50 of the 61 Independent Republican, and 19 of the 35 PDM deputies, joined by 9 unaffiliated members. The remaining members of the majority parties and 3 unaffiliated deputies abstained.[86] Thus, the opposition was completely united in the vote and only about 2.4 percent of the government's supporters joined them. The high level of voting discipline was the more impressive in view of the critical stance of many government-party deputies during the debate and their failure to win concessions from the government. When the chips were down, they swallowed their consciences and accepted the fact that they had been put in office to support—sometimes while criticizing—a Gaullist government and not to make policy decisions.

"Navette"

The bill went to the Senate next. As has been typical during the Fifth Republic, it encountered stiffer resistance there than in the Assembly. After a day's general debate, the Communists and Socialists attempted to kill it with the same device, the *question préalable*, that had been tried in the Assembly. It failed again, 80 to 176.[87] Debate turned, then, to nearly 150

---

86. *LM*,30 April/2 May 1972. *Journal officiel* . . . *Assemblée nationale*, April 26, 27, 28, 29, 1972.

87. *Journal Officiel* . . . *Sénat*, 1 June 1972 p. 603.

proposed amendments. About twenty-two were adopted. They fell into three main categories: (1) to provide greater protection for the authority and fiscal resources of the Departments and communes; (2) to restrict the authority of the national government over the regions; and (3) to make technical changes in the bill.

Also, the Senate attempted to increase the financial resources of the regions at the expense of the national government and to prevent regions from imposing certain additional "nuisance" taxes. When that amendment passed, the government found the main financial articles unacceptable and they were defeated, leaving the regions virtually without a fiscal base. Thus emasculated, the bill passed, 131 to 95. Communists, Socialists, and die-hard, true-blue Gaullist regionalists provided most of the opposition.[88]

The bill returned to the Assembly for the second reading under the so-called *navette* procedure. During *navette*, the chambers can consider only the parts of a bill on which they disagreed on first reading. The Assembly accepted twelve of the Senate's amendments and passed the bill again, 356 to 102.[89]

Back to the Senate again. This time, the Senate yielded the point on financial resources and moderated its position somewhat on the autonomy of the regions from the national government. However, it insisted on giving the regional councils broader authority over their proceedings. The bill passed again, 130 to 109.[90] *Navette* had accomplished much of its purpose of producing a compromise bill.

The remaining issues went to a joint conference committee, as provided by the constitution, immediately after passage on second reading by the Senate. The committee reported back a bill essentially like the second version adopted by the Senate, except that the national executive, by decrees, rather than the parliament, by laws, was given the authority to decide on transfers of powers to and from the regions. The Assembly prevailed on the question of finances, the Senate on the internal functioning of the regional councils. The government considered the conference committee version to be acceptable. It passed the Assembly by a show of hands but only squeaked through the Senate, 124 to 120.[91]

This was the meager lot of parliament the only time in eighteen years that it had a real opportunity to influence regionalization policy. Pompidou may have changed from de Gaulle's style and procedures, but the distribution of power between executive and legislature remained the same. Procedurally, Pompidou had found a middle ground between the "bureau-

88. *Journal Officiel . . . Sénat*, 31 May, 1 and 2 June 1972; *LM*, 3 June 1972.
89. *Journal Officiel . . . Assemblée Nationale*, 14 June 1972, pp. 2416–28; *LM*, 15 June 1972.
90. *Journal Officiel . . . Sénat*, 29 June 1972, pp. 1288–1303; *LM*, 30 June 1972.
91. *Journal Officiel . . . Assemblée Nationale*, 30 June 1972, pp. 3008–9; *Sénat*, 30 June 1972, pp. 1380–82; *LM*, 1 July 1972.

cratic" approach to policy making on regionalization that had prevailed from 1954 until 1968 and the "participatory democracy" experiment of 1968–69. Substantively, he reached an accommodation between the pre-1954 centralization syndrome and the political regions of the 1969 proposal.

Pompidou is from Auvergne, the hillbilly country of France. *Auvergnais* have a reputation for cunning pragmatism. Regionalization policy is a prime example of the extent to which Pompidou introduced that quality into the brassy dogmatism of Gaullism.

Close study of the French experience at making policy on regionalization since 1954 discloses several features of interest to students of contemporary government in Europe. One of them is the slow progress made despite almost no public opposition. More than eighteen years after the first hesitant step was taken, the regions remained insignificant politically and minor elements administratively. The task of creating a new level in the structure of the state proved to be agonizingly difficult. Another striking feature of this study has been the small part played by parliament in the decision-making process, perhaps even less under the parliament-dominated Fourth Republic than under the president-dominated Fifth Republic. A third was the disappointing result of de Gaulle's experiment with "participatory democracy." It had very little perceptible effect on the content of the referendum bill and was abandoned when that bill was defeated. It had even less impact on the content of the Pompidou-Frey bill. Indeed, one suspects that, if de Gaulle had chosen a more conventional route for his regionalization reforms, they would have been enacted with little difficulty. Finally, an American observer must be struck by the readiness with which the concept of corporatist representation has been accepted, no matter what the context.

This study has examined one case only. In some ways the case may be atypical, for it deals with a relatively technical, apolitical issue. Yet, it has generated great interest among the "political class" in France and has occupied much of the time and attention of political officials of a succession of governments and regimes. Given the technical character of much of today's governmental business, it may be instructive nevertheless. If so, it suggests that the humdrum routine of legislation by decree and by quiet consultation between government technicians and members of parliament may accomplish more with less effort than the more entertaining flourishes of participatory democracy.

Appendix: The Impact of Regionalization on France

The preceding study concerns decision making in the French government with respect to regionalization. It does not deal with the substance or effects of those policies more than is necessary to explain the process that produced them. Perhaps the story is not complete, however, without at least a short note on their impact.

The chief activity in the regionalization programs has been the provision of governmental financial and technical assistance to economically troubled regions of France. Fairly substantial amounts of money are involved. By 1971, the amount of funds disbursed annually had reached 270 million francs in grants and 330 million francs in loans, a total of about $120 million. The aggregate total awarded for the 1963–71 period was $670 million.[92]

One of the main objectives of the regionalization program has been to promote the creation of jobs, especially industrial employment, in those areas suffering economic lag. To this end, corporations receive special assistance to transfer operations from the Paris region into those areas or to expand their operations there. From 1955 through 1967, that program had assisted in the creation of about 382,000 jobs at 2,200 plants outside the Paris region.[93]

This program has had its most striking success in Brittany. Industrial employment in that region had fallen from 227,000 workers in 1896 to 207,-000 in 1946 and 130,000 in 1962. By 1968, however, that trend had been reversed to the extent that the number of industrial workers had increased to 153,000.[94] From 1946 to 1954, Brittany's population increased at an annual rate of 0.20 percent, but when the regionalization campaign began to take effect in the 1962–68 period, the rate jumped by 150 percent to 0.50 percent. Even more dramatically, the region's emigration rate in 1962-68 fell to one-fifth the 1954–62 level. [95]

The same reversal of trend occurred throughout the western half of France, though less strikingly. The ten western regions lost 400,000 workers, 1954-62, and gained 200,000 workers, 1962–68. The number of their *industrial* workers increased 48,000 in 1954–62 and 155,000 in 1962–68. The change was also reflected in population trends. From 1962 to 1968 they gained 353,000 inhabitants. This was 26.7 percent of the total national population growth during that period, compared to 17.7 percent in 1954–62.[96] Their share of industrial investments increased (in percentages) from 22 in 1954 to 30 in 1960 and 37 in 1969.[97]

The ten eastern regions were also beneficiaries of those trends, although not so uniformly or dramatically. For instance, their share of industrial investments (in percentages) increased from 45 to 52 in 1970 and 53

92. *L'Année politique 1968*, p. 360; *1969*, p. 379; and *1970*, p. 412.

93. *Dossier*, p. 155; J. F. Gravier, *Economie et organisation régionales* (Paris: Masson, 1971), p. 122.

94. Robert Laffont, *La révolution régionaliste* (Paris: Gallimard, 1967), p. 86; Gravier, *Economie et organisation régionales*, p. 123.

95. *Dossier*, p. 155.

96. Monod and Castelbajac, *L'Aménagement du territoire*, pp. 67–8, 113, 115. About 70,000 more new jobs were created in the West in 1969 and 1970. *L'Année politique 1970*, p. 413; *1971*, p. 409.

97. Ibid., p. 68.

in 1969. However, their share of population growth fell from 50.7 percent to 49.8 percent.[98]

On the other hand, the place of Paris in France's economic and demographic life declined after the regionalization programs began to take effect. For instance, the Paris region's share of the country's population growth was 10.4 percent, 1801–51; 59.0 percent, 1851–1901; and 100 percent, 1901–54; but it fell to 31.6 percent, 1954–62; and 23.5 percent, 1962–68.[99] Even that growth was much less at the expense of the provinces. In the 1954–62 period, Paris received 335,000 immigrants from the provinces. In 1962–68, the number fell to 68,000, but 297,000 immigrants came to Paris from outside France. The region's net growth rate fell from 1.7 percent annually in 1954–62 to 1.4 percent in 1962–68.[100] The city of Paris itself actually declined in population by 7 percent in 1962–68 and the region's growth was 408,000 lower than had been forecast officially by the National Institute of Statistics.[101]

The economic picture was much the same. After at least a century of constant growth, industrial employment in the Paris region declined about 5 percent (73,000 jobs) in 1962–68; and 22,920 of those jobs were in the six most dynamic industries. In 1960 more than two-thirds of automobile manufacturing workers were employed in the Paris region. By 1970 the figure had fallen to 50 percent. Paris had 43 percent of French university students in 1953 but only 27 percent in 1971. The region's share of industrial investments fell from 33 percent in 1954 to 18 percent in 1960 and 10 percent in 1969. Before 1955, about 30 percent of the country's industrial construction permits were issued for Paris. This fell to 18 percent in 1960 and between 8 percent and 12 percent each year after 1962. In fact, by the late 1960s more space was removed from industrial use in the Paris region each year than was added.[102]

Of course, any situation of this sort is much too complicated to permit easy conclusions concerning cause and effect. Other national centers of population have shown similar reversals of population trends. Nevertheless, the coincidence in timing between the development of the regionalization policies and the reversals in economic and demographic trends is so dramatic as to suggest that the former must have had something to do with the latter.

98. Ibid., pp. 68, 113.

99. Gravier, *Economie et organisation régionales*, pp. 79–80; Monod and Castelbajac, *L'Aménagement du territoire*, p. 113.

100. Gravier, *Economie et organisation régionales*, pp. 76–77; Monod and Castelbajac, *L'Aménagement du territoire*, p. 114.

101. *LM*, 1/2 September 1968.

102. Monod and Castelbajac, *L'Aménagement du territoire*, pp. 68, 115; *L'Année politique 1970*, p. 415.

9

James H. Wolfe

Corporatism in German Political Life: Functional Representation in the GDR and Bavaria

In postindustrial societies the liberal theory of representative democracy is coming increasingly under attack. How can an individual, be he elector or member of a parliament, possibly cope with the complexity of issues confronting his government? Despite periodic outbursts of political activism, especially on the part of youth, the typical citizen usually withdraws from politics and prefers instead to place his faith, either grudgingly or with confidence, in the technocrats of government. Popular control of government through representatives elected either on the basis of single-member districts or proportional representation seems at best intermittent. To ensure the responsiveness of government in meeting the demands of discrete publics, contemporary political theorists are turning their attention to the European model of representation through corporations, i.e., the socioeconomic groups which comprise a heterogeneous society.

The European Experience

The origins of the corporate idea date from the end of the thirteenth century, when representative assemblies began to play a role in the governance of England, France, and Spain.[1] Both the medieval *Regnum* and *Sacerdotium*, the temporal and spiritual realms, were conceived of as unions of corporations, each with a role to fulfill and with a claim to representation. Typical of the early constitutions predicated on corporatist theory was that of the Republic of Florence during the fourteenth century.

1. John B. Morrall, *Political Thought in Medieval Times* (New York: Harper & Brothers, 1958), p. 64.

Whenever the city had not fallen to a despot, the government was in the hands of the Signoria, a parliament, whose members were elected representatives ("Priors") of the ruling guilds.[2] Similarly, in the sixteenth century the Diet of the Holy Roman Empire was composed of three Estates: electors of the emperor, princes, and townspeople.[3] Representation by social class and economic interest was the guiding principle in this supra-national parliament as in many local assemblies.

The social dislocation resulting from industrialization stimulated a renewed interest in corporatism as a means of securing economic freedom. In Great Britain, G. D. H. Cole, Samuel G. Hobson, George Stirling Taylor, and Sydney and Beatrice Webb advocated the doctrine of guild socialism, by which they intended that interest articulation and aggregation should be functions of governmentally chartered organizations of socioeconomic interests. The House of Commons, they claimed, was not representative because the individual elector had little actual influence over his member of Parliament. To the guild socialists, "all true democratic representation is therefore functional representation."[4]

The corporatist tradition is alive in other European countries, particularly Germany. During the decade 1880–90, Prince Otto von Bismarck, then imperial chancellor, promoted corporatism as a new orientation away from liberalism. But his plan to supplement the lower and popularly elected house of parliament, the Reichstag, with the formation of a National Economic Council representing economic groups failed.[5] Article 165 of the Constitution of the Weimar Republic (1919) incorporated the principle of representation according to economic interests through the creation of a hierarchy of Workers Councils extending from the factory to the national level. In effect, the Republic had two legislatures: one political (the Reichsrat and Reichstag) and the other social (the Economic Council of the Reich), creating a dualistic arrangement similar to that proposed by the Webbs in their draft constitution for a corporate state.[6]

While English social theorists and German constitutional lawyers emphasized the need to make government responsive through corporatism, the idea of restructuring political life along economic and social lines also attracted its more authoritarian adherents. Among these was the Austrian sociologist Othmar Spann, whose theory of the "true state" was one based on an atomized view of society in which guilds (*Stande*) would be coordinated in the formulation of national policy, yet at the same time they would enjoy

2. G. F. Young, *The Medici* (New York: Modern Library, 1933), p. 16.

3. James Bryce, *The Holy Roman Empire* (rev. ed.; New York: Macmillan, 1904), p. 367.

4. George Douglas Howard Cole, *Guild Socialism Re-Stated* (London: Leonard Parsons, 1920), p. 33.

5. Ralph H. Bowen, *German Theories of the Corporative State* (New York: Russell & Russell, 1947), p. 148.

6. Howard Lee McBain and Lindsay Rogers, *The New Constitutions of Europe* (Garden City, N.Y.: Doubleday, 1922), pp. 117–35, 208–9.

the freedom to regulate their internal affairs as they saw fit. Spann was careful to point out that the guilds did not delegate authority to the government, as in a democracy, but received their right of self-determination from a political authority. Every citizen would possess the degree of freedom associated with the rights of his guild as typified by the maxim "equality under one's peers." The state itself would remain the highest level of political organization and the guarantor of social unity.[7]

Traditionally, the corporations had been viewed as the protector of the individual against the overwhelming power of the state, and indeed they often appeared as an implicit negation of the state.[8] Spann turned the conventional theory on its head and made the corporations subordinate to the state instead of its being their agent. The way was open for fascist corporate theories which soon evolved. In 1934, the government of Benito Mussolini created twenty-two corporations as a means of controlling industry, agriculture, and the professions within the framework of a National Council of Corporations.[9] Fascist ideology justified the existence of corporations as the instruments through which to discipline society and to ensure that individual interests remained secondary to the presumed superior moral and material needs of the nation.[10] In a like fashion, the National Socialist regime in Germany controlled the economy through a system of "guilds" extending from the local to the national level where they were dominated, according to their type of economic activity, by the Agricultural Corporation, the Chamber of Culture, the Economic Chamber, or one of the seven central Transportation Groups.[11] The fascist models of corporatism were corruptions of an ideal form of society and far removed from the original purpose of enhancing the responsiveness of the modern bureaucratic state.

Without wishing to emulate the authoritarianism of fascist regimes, some French political theorists also turned to corporatism in the late 1930s. Their goal was to close what they perceived to be a gap between the actualities of the French administrative state and their country's tradition of liberal individualism. Georges Viance theorized that the only institution adaptable enough to control the economy of France's organic and hierarchical society would be a council of corporations.[12] The National Economic

7. Othmar Spann, *Der wahre Staat: Vorlesungen über Abbruch und Neubau der Gesellschaft* (4th ed.; Jena: Verlag von Gustav Fischer, 1938) pp. 163, 192–94.

8. Joseph H. Kaiser, *Die Repräsentation organisierter Interessen* (Berlin: Duncker & Humblot, 1956), pp. 63–64.

9. Arnold J. Zurcher, "The Government and Politics of Italy," in *Governments of Continental Europe*, ed. James T. Shotwell (New York: Macmillan, 1940), pp. 674–701.

10. Gaetano Bagala, *Fascismo e corporativismo: essenza e definizione* (Bologna: Editore Cantelli, 1942), p. 324.

11. L. Hamburger, *How Nazi Germany Has Controlled Business* (Washington, D.C.: Brookings Institution, 1943), pp. 86–88.

12. Georges Viance, *Democratie, dictature, et corporatisme* (Paris: Flammarion, 1938), pp. 189–98.

Council of the Third Republic did indeed encompass an embryonic notion of corporatism. Writing in 1942, Louis Baudin advanced a model of corporatism that would avowedly limit individual liberty, and under which designated functional ministries of the government would not be passive guardians of the public interest in the sense of guild socialism, but would exercise hierarchical authority.[13] Baudin had to admit that his version of corporatism was poorly suited to French political culture—an assumption borne out by the failure of the Vichy government (1940–44) to develop popular support for its corporate plans.[14] Despite this historical experience, the Economic and Social Council of the Fifth French Republic represents a mild form of corporatist theory in practice.

Corporatism has its roots in British guild socialism, in the French administrative state, and the German theory of an organic society. As the Reformation exposed the individual directly to God, so had liberal democracy removed all intermediaries between him and his government. Corporatist structures were needed to protect the individual and achieve social justice to a degree beyond that which either capitalism or communism could accomplish. Samuel G. Hobson articulated the major doubt concerning the theoretical underpinning of the liberal state when he wrote, "Democracy does not build upon single individuals however brilliant. . . ."[15] Hermann Heller, a German political scientist, expressed similar reservations about a theory of government which recognizes individuals as political actors, but ignores their associations, in his epigram:

> "To govern in German parliamentary
> practice means to be represented;"
> it would be better were it to mean
> "to let oneself be represented."[16]

Blockpolitik in the German Democratic Republic

The collapse of the German political system in 1945 created a void which German democrats, both at home and abroad, were determined to fill with a viable constitution based on consensus. In the trauma of defeat, the partisans of a new democratic regime theorized about ideal ways in which to balance the interests of the individual with those of society and concluded that this delicate equation could best be preserved through the systematic representation of socioeconomic groups as well as individual

13. Louis Baudin, *Le Corporatisme: Italie, Portugal, Allemagne, Espagne, France* (Paris: Librairie Générale de Droit et de Jurisprudence, 1942), pp. 161–64, 187.
14. Matthew J. Elbow, *French Corporative Theory, 1789–1948* (New York: Columbia University Press, 1953), pp. 194–95.
15. Samuel George Hobson, *National Guilds and the State* (London: G. Bell, 1920), p. 143.
16. Hermann Heller, "Genie und Funktionär in der Politik," *Politische Wissenschaft*, vol. 10, *Probleme der Demokratie* (Berlin-Grunewald: Walter Rothschild, 1931), p. 60.

electors. The leitmotiv of this political thought was that the institutions of government should ensure a stable, equitable relationship among the major economic subdivisions of society: trade, industry, management, agriculture, and commerce.[17]

In West Germany the Ahlen program (1947) of the Christian Democratic Union rejected both private and state capitalism in favor of a mixed economy in which associations of an economic character would play an important role in the process of determining the goals of the political system.[18] According to its 1952 program, the Social Democratic party demanded the "right of codetermination"—collaborative decision making on the part of spokesmen for both labor and management—as a step toward the establishment of a social order founded on group rights.[19] This trend of thought received constitutional sanction in Article 9 of the West German Basic Law (1949), which guarantees the right to form associations for the purpose of securing social and economic goals through legal means.[20] The extension of constitutional rights to recognized groups was a primary institutional means of safeguarding the new democracy of the Federal Republic, but the movement to institutionalize these rights in the form of a governmental organ with both legislative and executive powers failed—and with it failed the West German experiment with corporatism at the federal level.[21]

In the German Democratic Republic (GDR), however, the corporate model of political life, although first adopted as a tactical expedient by a Communist cadre in 1945, has today achieved a permanent institutional status. The process of adapting a Communist regime to an industrialized polity led to the development of the theory of *Blockpolitik*—the technique of a popular front uniting heterogeneous elements in support of a common political program. As early as 1935, at a conference of the German Communist party in Brussels, Wilhelm Pieck (president of the GDR from 1949 to 1960) called for a joint effort of Marxist and non-Marxist parties against fascism. When Walter Ulbricht returned to Germany in 1945, he revived the popular-front policy as the basis of government in the Soviet Zone of Occupation, later to become the GDR. While all Berlin was still under Soviet control, Marshal Georgi Zhukov issued a general order authorizing the formation of antifascist political parties. In addition to the Communist and Social Democratic parties, which were founded separately and, in 1946, merged into the Socialist Unity party of Germany (SED), two middle-class

17. Josef Wirth et al., *Das demokratische Deutschland: Grundsätze und Richtlinien für den deutschen Wiederaufbau im demokratischen, republikanischen, föderalistischen und genossenschaftlichen Sinne* (Bern and Leipzig: Verlag Paul Haupt, 1945), p. 20.

18. Wilhelm Mommsen, ed., *Parteiprogramme der Bundesrepublik Deutschland* (Berlin: Gebrüder Weiss—Verlag Lebendigen Wissen, 1951), pp. 11–18.

19. Ibid., pp. 76–77.

20. Kaiser, *Repräsentation organisierter Interessen*, pp. 350–51.

21. Gerhard Loewenberg, *Parliament in the German Political System* (Ithaca, N.Y.: Cornell University Press, 1967), pp. 40–46.

parties also came into being in the early summer of 1945—the Christian Democratic Union (CDU) and the Liberal Democratic party of Germany (LDPD). From 1945 until 1949, the period of the consolidation of Communist control in East Germany, the SED worked closely with the CDU and the LDPD to implement such programs as industrial collectivization and land redistribution.

The popular-front tactic was so successful that in 1948 the Communist leadership created two more minor parties as manipulative structures to augment the "bloc of anti-fascist, democratic parties." The Democratic Peasants' party of Germany (DBD) played an important role in persuading farmers to accept agricultural collectivization, which was effected in a period of eight years beginning in 1952. The National Democratic party of Germany (NDPD) provided a political refuge for former Nazis and military officers whose services in either a civilian or a military capacity were required by the government. The NDPD was indeed instrumental in bringing about East German rearmament. Both the DBD and the NDPD limit their membership to specific groups in society. In a somewhat exaggerated interpretation of the theory of guild socialism, the NDPD may be described as the guild of professional soldiers and civil servants.

The constitution of the GDR, adopted in 1949 and amended in 1968, has given formal institutional expression to the theory of *Blockpolitik*. The German People's Congresses of 1947 and 1949, which promulgated the constitution, consisted of delegations not only from the SED and minor parties, but also from the mass organizations, such as the Federation of Free German Trade Unions (FDGB), the Union of Democratic Women of Germany (DFD), The Free German Youth (FDJ), and the German Cultural Association (DKB). The founding of the National Front of Democratic Germany in 1949 provided a single structure within which the work of the SED could be coordinated with the coalition parties and the mass organizations.[22] As the highest *Gremium*—level of political activity—in the GDR, the National Front institutionalizes the corporate idea by having as members organizations representing social and economic classes and interests within society. According to the theory of East German people's democracy, the SED, for example, is the spokesman for the industrial working class; the CDU for the Christian community; the LDPD for professional men and small shopkeepers; the DBD for farmers; and the NDPD for civil servants and the older military elite. Supporting this arrangement are the four mass organizations whose constituencies are trade unions, women, youth, and artists. The system permits the several roles of each citizen to find expression in the National Front.

An important task of the National Front is to draw up the unity list of candidates who are elected every four years to the Volkskammer—the People's Chamber or parliament. Once again, the principle of representation on the basis of class, religion, social background, age, occupation, and sex is observed. The Volkskammer elected on 14 November 1971 has 500 members whose seats are apportioned as follows: the SED has 127, each of the minor parties, 52; the FDGB, 68; the DFD, 35; the FDJ, 40; and the DKB, 22.

The president of the Volkskammer elected in 1971 is also chairman of the CDU, and similar symbolic roles are customarily assigned to other non-Communists in order to enhance the chamber's legitimizing function. The allocation of the political goods of society rests with other organs.[23] Of these the Council of State, the highest executive organ of the government, is most important. Nominally elected by the Volkskammer, the Council's membership included (at the end of 1971) Ulbricht as chairman and Erich Honecker, the first secretary of the Central Committee of the SED. Nine of the twenty-four members of the Council are officially spokesmen of the SED, and eight of its coalition parties. The remaining seven are listed as a trade unionist, an agronomist, a local government official, a physicist, a collective farm chairman, the president of the National Front, and the mayor of Potsdam.[24] Functional representation is clearly the guideline for recruitment into the collective leadership of the GDR.

To oversee the administration of the government and to provide technical expertise, the Council of State appoints, with the concurrence of the Volkskammer, a Council of Ministers, whose thirty-seven members now sit under the chairmanship of Willi Stoph. As in its parent body, the principle of corporate representation guides the selection of ministers. The officially designated members of the SED are in a minority compared with their ministerial colleagues from the minor parties and the mass organizations as well as those without any formal party ties. Significantly, one-third of the ministers are identified only as being affiliated with a particular economic interest, such as the Ministry for the Glass and Ceramic Industry.[25] The GDR is close to having the government by guilds as envisioned by Othmar Spann.

The preceding institutional discussion should not obscure the political reality of the "dictatorship of the proletariat" as practiced by the SED.[26] Political life in the GDR typifies the "reconciliation system" described by David E. Apter.[27] The system is representative, but not democratic, in that

23. Arnold J. Heidenheimer, *The Governments of Germany* (3rd ed. rev.; New York: Thomas Y. Crowell, 1971.), p. 278.

24. *Neues Deutschland,* 27 November 1971.

25. Ibid., 1 December 1971.

26. Eckart Förtsch, *Die SED* (Stuttgart: W. Kohlhammer Verlag, 1969), pp. 137–38.

27. David E. Apter, "Notes on a Theory of Nondemocratic Representation," in *Representation,* ed. James Roland Pennock and John W. Chapman (New York: Atherton Press, 1968), pp. 291, 310.

the choice of goals is dependent upon the outcome of a continuing struggle between private and functional interests. The personalized leadership of the GDR, as exemplified initially by Ulbricht and now Honecker, relies upon a carefully assembled alliance of minor parties and mass organizations for the purpose of mobilizing major socioeconomic groups and of coping with demands which would otherwise prove dysfunctional. An analyst of East German public opinion has concluded:

> Were there in the GDR a pluralistic party system similar to that of the Western democracies, it might be possible even for a fundamentally socialist electorate, according to prevailing circumstances, to create a considerable majority against the government.[28]

To the disaffected the minor parties and mass organizations offer an opportunity for political activity which varies from genuine demand articulation to mere symbolic participation. The practice of corporate representation, albeit in a manipulative form, is indispensable for the preservation of political stability in the GDR.

The Constitution of Bavaria: A Modern Adaptation of Corporatism

In contemporary Western European parliamentary practice the theory of corporatism has achieved its most promising institutional realization in the parliament of the Free State of Bavaria, the second largest province or *Land* of the Federal Republic. The Bavarian parliament is bicameral. The Landtag, the lower chamber, is elected every four years through a system of direct election which combines voting both on the basis of a plurality and of proportional representation. The Landtag elects the minister-president, the chief executive of the government, and confirms the members of his Cabinet. As is customary in parliamentary governments, whenever the Landtag withdraws its support from the minister-president, he is compelled to resign. In the field of legislation the Landtag cannot act unilaterally, yet it can override opposition in the Senate, the upper chamber, by a simple majority, except in the instance of a constitutional amendment.[29]

Despite its strong position, the Landtag must nevertheless share its legislative authority with the Senate, whose composition and competence are unique among European parliaments. For the Senate is constituted in a corporate fashion so that the various functional interests of Bavarian so-

---

28. Hans Apel, *DDR: 1962–1964–1966* (Berlin: Voltaire Verlag, 1967), p. 381.

29. *Verfassung des Freistaates Bayern* (Munich: Bayerische Landeszentrale für politische Bildungsarbeit, 1970), Arts. 34–42. For the constitutional description of the Senate, the author is particularly indebted to Paul Wilhelm, *Der Bayerische Senat* (2d ed.; Munich: Suddeutscher Verlag, 1970).

ciety—the social, economic, cultural, and religious communities—all receive representation. The constitution specifies that the 60 members of the Senate be apportioned as follows:

11 from forestry and agriculture
5 from industry and commerce
5 from handicrafts
11 from trade unions
4 from professional associations
5 from cooperatives
5 from the religious communities
5 from charitable organizations
3 from universities
6 from local government organizations

Each senator is elected by his organization as a spokesman for its interests. His term of office is six years, and he may be reelected. Biennially one-third of the Senate is elected, providing for the regular introduction of new members while at the same time preserving a high level of continuity in the chamber's membership.

The method of electing senators raises the question of the nature of representative democracy. Since the number of senators is fixed for each group, can the principles of a competitive and freely elected parliamentary body be said to apply? The answer is affirmative to the extent that within each group democratic procedures prevail in the election of its spokesmen. The "Law of the Senate," dated 1947 and amended in 1949, details the method of election in each constituency.[30] For example, the Bavarian Farmers Association alone elects the eleven representatives of agriculture and forestry. By contrast, the five senators from industry and trade are elected by the executive committees of the several organizations of that sector of the economy. Indirect election is also the technique used by the various associations of handworkers and artisans. In this instance, each of the craft industries selects electors who then elect their senators by secret ballot.

The eleven senators allotted to trade unions are divided proportionally according to membership statistics among the Federation of German Trade Unions (DGB), the Union of German Employees, and the Bavarian Civil Servants League. The Bavarian government, acting through the Ministry of the Interior, distributes the senatorial seats among the three unions according to their relative size. The DGB has the largest share, but the electoral law ensures the representation of the other two organizations as well.

30. Klaus Tremel, ed., *Verwaltungsgesetze des Freistaates Bayern* (Munich: C. H. Beck'sche Verlagsbuchhandlung, 1970), sec. 715.

Following the apportionment, the governing bodies of the three unions, themselves chosen by the members, elect the senators.

The "free professions" also indirectly elect a total of four senators through an electoral college of sixty members chosen in accordance with a formula allowing for proportional representation of the professional groups concerned. A typical distribution of seats among the electors gives, among others, twelve places to doctors, six to lawyers, five to dentists, four to pharmacists, three to journalists, and one to an artist. As in the case of the trade unions, the Ministry of the Interior identifies the professional organizations eligible to select electors and apportions the electoral votes to each according to its size. The outcome of the election is, to a degree, predetermined because the associations of doctors, lawyers, journalists, and artists are assured of at least one senator. Further, these groups normally elect as senators their leading members.

The five senators of the cooperatives receive their mandate from an electoral assembly recruited from consumers' organizations. These senators are usually the directors of their respective cooperatives. A similar process is followed in electing the five senators of Bavaria's charities. The boards of directors convene and carry out the election, which customarily assures a senator to each major charitable organization. A system which, for all practical purposes, guarantees a senatorial seat to the principal officers of the major interest groups within each socioeconomic constituency may not appear to qualify as "democratic" in the classical sense of the word; yet the arrangement does ensure a greater divergency of viewpoints in the Bavarian parliament than would be possible if all its members were to be selected on a one-man, one-vote basis. The benefits of assured representation of a wide range of groups are apparent in the recruitment of the five senators from religious communities. Article 36 of the Bavarian Constitution stipulates the selection of these senators by appointment rather than election. By law the Catholic and Protestant churches each designate two senators, and the Jewish community appoints one who, unlike his counterparts, is invariably a layman.

The election of the three senators who represent the universities and academies of Bavarian higher education, like that of most other delegations, is conducted by a specially convened electoral college. The "Law of the Senate" specifies that the faculty senates of the universities each choose five electors, the governing body of the Bavarian Academy of Science two, and the comparable organs of other institutes and schools, so recognized by the Ministry of the Interior, one each. The election of the academic senators differs from that of their colleagues in that there is no guaranteed seat for the largest and best known of the Bavarian universities, that of Munich. By contrast, leading member organizations of other senatorial constituencies are certain to be represented.

Finally, six senators representing local government are elected as follows: two from the Bavarian Municipal League, two from the Bavarian Township Assembly, and two from the Bavarian Association of County Governments. The executive committees of the respective organizations select their senators.

From the standpoint of contemporary Anglo-American theories of representation the apportionment of seats in the Senate and the actual election of senators may appear to be of dubious democratic quality. Nevertheless, it is clear that the framers of the Bavarian Constitution have made every effort to ensure the recruitment of senators from a broad spectrum of groups so that all elements of society are represented irrespective of their numerical strength. One may argue the case that trade unions should have more (or fewer) than eleven senators. The allotment of seats was, to a degree, arbitrary. It is for precisely this reason that the actual size of the delegations is not as important as the reality of a forum encompassing far-ranging perspectives on questions of public policy. James Madison viewed pluralism based on the representation of competing groups as the fundament of constitutional government.[31] The Bavarian Senate institutionalizes this precept. Through its diffuse composition the Senate achieves a balance of group interests, in an informal rather than a formal sense. For example, although the majority of Bavarians are Catholic, the number of Catholic and Protestant senators is the same, i.e., two. The two churches are officially on a level of parity, yet the discrepancy in the size of the denominations is informally redressed by assuring that two of the five senators from charitable organizations are recruited from the Catholic charity Caritas.

It is also notable that the "Law of the Senate" requires that women be elected senators in proportion to their numbers in the groups represented. Although this requirement has yet to be fulfilled, the need to overcome discrimination in public life on the basis of sex has been recognized in law. That the Senate is the institution of government called upon to ensure a role for women in the legislative process is typical of the expectations placed upon it.

Whenever doubt exists as to the eligibility of an organization, e.g., trade union, cooperative, or institution of higher learning, to participate in the election of senators, the question is resolved by the Ministry of the Interior, which may seek the assistance of another ministry, such as that of Culture. If the group involved regards the administrative ruling as unfair, the way is open for an appeal to the Constitutional Court of Bavaria. The executive does not, therefore, have final authority in identifying the specific

31. James Madison, "The Federalist No. 10," *The Federalist*, ed. Jacob E. Cooke (Middletown, Conn.: Wesleyan University Press, 1961), pp. 56–65.

organizations that comprise the constituencies represented in the Senate. The flexible nature of this arrangement merits the respect of constitutional lawyers because it permits the Bavarian government to extend representation by an administrative decision to organizations whose existence was not foreseen when the "Law of the Senate" was passed in 1947 to implement the constitutional provisions (Articles 34–42) establishing an upper chamber of the parliament.

Although the Senate has some judicial and executive functions, notably in the budgetary process, the chamber's most important activities are legislative in nature. The Senate's rights in the legislative process are those of initiation, consultation, review, and investigation through the conduct of hearings. Although Article 39 of the Bavarian Constitution guarantees to the Senate the power to initiate legislation, the authority to do so has fallen into disuse. Josef Singer, the first president of the Senate, defined "initiation" in 1948 to mean simultaneous discussion of proposed laws with the government rather than their unilateral presentation without prior consultation.[32] Critics of the Senate point out that despite its prestige as an assembly of experts, it has failed to initiate legislation in such fields as ecology and higher education. The presence of representatives of trade unions and universities in the Senate has not caused that chamber to introduce legislation providing for social welfare or for educational reform.

The failure to initiate legislation is offset by the Senate's vigorous utilization of its prerogative under Article 40 of the constitution: the right to be consulted and to render an opinion on legislative proposals originating from the government. Constitutionally, the Senate's advice is formally required only on important matters, such as the budget, constitutional amendments, or laws providing for referenda. The question of whether or not a particular bill is indeed important enough to merit the Senate's consideration is technically a matter for the government to decide. Yet precedent decrees that the government respond to the prestigious nature of the Senate by submitting to it all bills that are not routine. Indeed, the value of the Senate as an upper chamber may suffer if its agenda becomes more saturated than it already is. The legislative process would benefit if the Senate were able to devote its time to a smaller and more select number of bills than is presently the case.

The Constitution of Bavaria does not specifically grant to the Senate the right of vetoing an item of proposed legislation, and an official pamphlet describing the Senate asserts that under no circumstances can that chamber veto a measure approved by an ordinary majority in the Landtag.[33] Nevertheless, opinion varies regarding the Senate's power to

32. Bavaria, Senate, *Bayerischer Senat: Stenographischer Bericht*, 13th Sess., 2 July 1948, pp. 302–3.

33. *Der Bayerische Landtag und der Bayerische Senat* (Munich: Bayerische Landeszentrale für politische Bildungsarbeit, 1969), p. 72.

block a bill. Since Article 40 requires the Senate's review and analysis of the budget, what would occur if the Senate exercised a "pocket veto" and declined to formulate a recommendation? The minister-president, the head of government, could not dissolve the Senate and call for new elections. He might seek to reduce the Senate's budgetary power by amending the constitution or to appeal directly to the electorate in a referendum. Both actions would require the concurrence of the Senate (Article 40). Historically such an impasse has never developed, but the theoretical possibility that it might ensures that the government will collaborate with the Senate in the formative stages of the budgetary process. In 1948 the president of the Senate administered a sharp rebuke to the government for not consulting the Senate before transmitting the budget to the Landtag. Since then the government has been at pains to provide the Senate with an opportunity to comment at length on the budget before that document is debated in the Landtag. In the instance of public finance, as in many others, the narrow constitutional powers of the Senate are deceptive in that they disguise this chamber's powerful, yet often informal, role in the legislative process.

As a bill becomes law, the duty of the Senate is to offer expert advice in the form of recommendations for the perfecting of the legislation. The function of the Landtag is to enact the bill into law. Once the Landtag has completed its deliberations and voted in favor of a particular bill, Article 41 of the constitution provides that the Senate shall have a second opportunity to review the legislation and to propose amendments. The process of review must be completed within a month unless the Landtag holds the legislation to be urgent, in which case the Senate must act within a week. Unlike the British House of Lords, which can delay passage of most bills by as much as a year, the Senate lacks the formal authority to impose a cooling-off period in the face of a majority vote by the members of the popularly elected Landtag.

In the process of reviewing legislation approved by the Landtag, the Senate is under significant pressure not to impede its final enactment. Presumably, the time for an extended discussion of the problem has passed, yet the Senate is constitutionally required to conduct a second formal debate which may, at first glance, appear redundant. The meaning of this review becomes clear in reference to a paradigm developed by Robert A. Dahl for the successful resolution of political conflict. Dahl emphasizes the need for institutions that permit involved groups to negotiate in the formative stages of making policy and also provide a legitimate means through which political leaders can terminate these negotiations for the purpose of arriving at a decision.[34] The relationship between the Landtag as the lawmaking body and the Senate as the adviser to the government realizes the ideal of

34. Robert A. Dahl, *Pluralist Democracy in the United States: Conflict and Consent* (Chicago: Rand McNally, 1967), p. 281.

consensual decision making which Dahl regards as fundamental to pluralist democracy.

The sixty senators represent collectively an impressive array of expertise and possess individually considerable prestige as the leaders in their own organizations. As spokesmen for their professions rather than political parties, the senators have a different perspective on legislation than do members of the Landtag. The "Law of the Senate" stipulates that a senator is responsible to his own conscience and is free of obligations to a political party. By contrast, the deputies in the Landtag are organized into *Fraktionen* (caucuses) based on their membership in the Christian Social Union (CSU), the Social Democratic party of Germany (SPD), or the Free Democratic party (FDP). Despite a constitutional proscription against a Landtag deputy's responding to dictates other than those of his own conscience, the political dynamics of the lower chamber are such that party discipline exercised through the *Fraktion* is normally the first consideration in deciding how to cast one's vote. As in most parliamentary regimes, the deputy is either for or against the government. Few opportunities for an uninstructed vote occur. In this setting, the Senate exists to offset the influence of parliamentary parties and their whips. Accordingly, the legislative system is so designed that no act of the Landtag can become law until it has undergone a searching debate in the Senate. It is notable that in two out of every three instances in which the Senate has raised questions about a bill approved by the Landtag, the latter has acquiesced and amended the legislation to meet, at least in part, the upper chamber's demands.[35]

Historically, the Senate's role in the process of formulating public policy is less a matter of constitutional authority than of the collective influence of its members. The typical deputy in the Landtag is a young man who is building his career. His fellow legislator in the Senate owes his mandate not to the promise of success, but to a position of leadership in his professional organization. Viewed from this perspective the constitutional prerogative of the Senate, in conjunction with the government, to undertake parliamentary investigations and to require the testimony of state officials guarantees the input of socioeconomic corporations, as well as political parties, in the formative stages of making public policy.[36] Within the theoretical framework of the constitution of Bavaria, the Senate serves as an adviser to the government and assists it in the perfecting of legislation through special studies and investigations. The role of the Landtag is quite different. The Landtag elects the minister-president who governs only as long as he retains the confidence of that body. Whenever the Landtag conducts an investigation, it may do so with the intention of bringing about the

35. Wilhelm, *Bayerische Senat*, p. 57.
36. Wilhelm Hoegner, *Lehrbuch des Bayerischen Verfassungsrechts* (Munich: Bayerischer Schulbuchverlag, 1949), pp. 74–81; and Tremel, *Verwaltungsgesetze*, sec. 715 (Art. 26).

formation of a new Cabinet. In the lower chamber the government must always face a potential threat to its existence in the form of a motion to censure—a contingency which can be guarded against by gaining the support of public opinion leaders, such as the senators representing the trade-union movement. Article 34 of the constitution expresses the essence of the matter: "The Senate is the representative organ of the social, economic, cultural and communal corporations of the state."[37] The value of the legitimization of a legislative program by such a parliamentary chamber can hardly be overestimated.

Although the principal tasks of the Senate are in its legislative role, Article 34 is sufficiently elastic to permit an interpretation of corporate representation which extends to both the executive and judicial processes of government. Typical of the implied powers of the Senate is the right to hear petitions. The constitution of Bavaria (Article 115) guarantees to every citizen the right to present a petition either to the Landtag or to the government. No mention is made of the Senate. However, the Federal Republic's constitution, the Basic Law, stipulates:

> Everyone has the right individually or jointly with the others to address written requests or complaints to the competent authorities and to the representative assemblies.[38]

Although the language of this fundamental right clearly subsumes the Senate, this body has chosen to limit the hearing of petitions to those matters affecting the interests of a definable group of citizens as opposed to those concerned solely with the redress of individual grievances. The latter fall within the purview of the Landtag, which is charged with overseeing the operations of the executive. Should a citizen address a complaint of a private nature to a senator, it will be forwarded to the Landtag's standing Committee for Petitions and Complaints. On the other hand, a petition concerning deficit financing would receive attention in the Senate. For the issue is of a general nature, and the constitutional requirement for senatorial advisory participation in the budgetary process makes this chamber a "competent authority" in the meaning of the Basic Law.

The hearing of petitions by the Senate is associated with its right to launch investigations of a broad character into the social, cultural, and economic relationships of Bavarian society. The function of universities as institutional means for increasing social mobility would be an appropriate subject for a searching inquiry by the Senate. Yet this and similar topics have been left untouched. Indeed, the Senate has never really utilized its investigative authority. At this stage special funding approved by both the

---

37. *Verfassung des Freistaates Bayern*, Art. 34, p. 17.
38. *The Basic Law of the Federal Republic of Germany* (New York: German Information Center, 1969), Art. 17.

Landtag and the government would be necessary were the Senate to institute and staff investigative committees concerned with broad social issues. The lack of funds and of interest in providing them makes it difficult for the Senate to fulfill its constitutional role as the explicator of fundamental questions facing the whole of society, such as educational reform and protection of the environment.

The judicial competence of the Senate is also worthy of notice. The Constitutional Court of Bavaria has the authority to declare unconstitutional a law that contravenes a basic right, such as the freedom of speech. Nevertheless, before such a decision can be rendered, both the Landtag and the Senate must be afforded the opportunity to offer an interpretation of the matter. Since the question invariably involves a law passed by the Landtag, that chamber is a party to the case before the court and hardly in a position to comment impartially. The Senate's advisory role makes it more detached, and consequently its opinion is of greater value.

Annually, the Landtag reviews the expenditures of the government to ensure that these are in accordance with the law. The Senate participates in this review by sending to the Landtag an analysis of governmental spending. In this instance, the Senate advises the lower chamber rather than, as is usually the case, the government. The Senate is well qualified to carry out the task of fiscal review since its counsel was required in drafting the budget.

Finally, it is interesting to note that the Senate exercises certain executive functions. For the advisory committee of the Academy of Political Education, a government-supported organization, invariably includes one senator. And three senators are on the governing board of the Bavarian radio and television network. To this limited extent, the administration of selected educational and public service enterprises is of a corporate nature.

The Bavarian Senate is an effort to adapt a mode of representation originating in another historical era to the needs of a modern, heterogeneous society. The extent to which this attempt has been successful is disputed.[39] Critics emphasize that the Senate has limited its role to that of being a commentator on the government's legislative program by failing to exercise its right to initiate legislation. Despite some pleas to the contrary by individual senators, the chamber has shown little disposition to introduce legislation dealing with ecological or other long-range problems. The popular stereotype of an indurated parliamentary organ persists. To enhance the Senate's image, it is necessary to draw increased public attention to the chamber's work. The introduction of a "question hour" permitting a direct exchange between members of the government and individual senators would be a step in this direction.

Aside from allegations of inactivity, senators also receive criticism con-

39. Kaiser, *Repräsentation organisierter Interessen*, pp. 352–54.

cerning their dual role as leaders in their own organizations as well as legislators. Those senators representing especially the trade unions, local governments, and agrarian organizations are all heavily engaged in their professions and often cannot devote adequate time to meeting their parliamentary obligations. The growing tendency of the Senate's constituencies to elect organization officials exacerbates the problem of divided responsibility. Moreover, in the "free professions" election to the Senate means a loss not only of time but also of income. Only those professionals who have attained a recognized position of leadership in their fields are politically eligible for the post of senator, yet these are older men and women who are acutely aware that their services in this capacity are not rewarded with a pension. The natural result of this economic disadvantage is that many qualified candidates do not offer themselves for election.

Finally, the people of Bavaria themselves stress the Landtag over the Senate. Opinion leaders in industry and commerce seem to care little for the senior statesmen of the Senate. Youth also has little understanding for the chamber and its contributions to representative government. Radical elements of both the Left and the Right dislike the Senate as being too moderate. Before its defeat in the election of 1970, the National Democratic party of Germany (NDP) had a *Fraktion* in the Landtag and attempted unsuccessfully through these deputies to introduce a resolution calling for the abolition of the Senate. The outcome of this move was a temporary alliance between the SPD and CSU caucuses in the Landtag to defend the Senate.

Despite the criticisms leveled at it, the Senate survives as a unique and socially relevant form of representation. Although democratic theorists recognize the difficulties in designing a constitution on the corporate model, especially that of apportioning legislative seats among the various corporations, the idea of granting a representational role to spokesmen of socioeconomic groups as well as political parties retains support.[40] And in the field of labor relations corporatism is gaining new adherents. As early as 1952, the West German government enacted a statute requiring the election in industrial enterprises of a works council which would participate in the formulation of policy for the factory or business concerned. The pattern of worker-management collaboration in industrial decision making—co-determination—has its roots in the tradition of German corporate thought.[41] Contemporary Social Democrats advocate co-determination because they regard it as a means of democratizing the economic system; Christian Democrats view corporatism in this form as a step toward realizing the ideal

40. Austin Ranney and Willmoore Kendall, *Democracy and the American Party System* (New York: Harcourt Brace, 1956), pp. 68–71.

41. Herbert J. Spiro, *The Politics of German Codetermination* (Cambridge, Mass.: Harvard University Press, 1958), pp. 53–58, 84.

of an economy controlled by functional interests guided by the doctrine of social responsibility advanced in *Quadragesimo Anno* (1931).[42]

Corporatism whether institutionalized in a parliamentary chamber or a works council provides a means of political mobilization supportive of democratic political life in a pluralistic society. Like the upper chamber of the Irish parliament, which is also corporate in nature, the Bavarian Senate exists as an overt recognition of the need to institutionalize the participation of social and economic groups on the political process. The Senate's importance rests not in the fact that it presents some unusual problems for constitutional theorists, but that it offers an example of the increasing role of functional representation in the postindustrial parliamentary systems of Western Europe. In 1951 Josef Singer wrote:

> The Senate represents the people, not in their political form as in the Landtag, but in their natural and unpolitical social organization. The Senate is not really meant to be a constitutional counterweight to the Landtag. The composition of the Senate is supposed instead to guarantee that politically oriented decisions of the people's partisan representatives can be evaluated in light of impartial and informed standards.[43]

The abstractness of this formulation suggests the uncertainty and yet the promise of the corporate style of democracy in German political life.

42. *Seven Great Encyclicals* (Glen Rock, N.J.: Paulist Press, 1963), pp. 125–68.
43. Josef Singer, "Die Bedeutung und die Aufgaben des Bayerischen Senats," in *Ratgeber von Parlament und Regierung*, ed. Josef Singer et al. (Frankfurt: Institut zur Förderung öffentlicher Angelegenheiten, 1951), p. 12.

10
Richard L. Merritt

The Tangled Tie: West Germany and the Berlin Problem*

Political leaders of a country are usually able to separate foreign policy problems from those of domestic policy. This is not to say that such issues are mutually exclusive, for they are not. Nor does the establishment of separate Cabinet offices or ministries for domestic and foreign affairs mean that neat organizational tables and rules prescribe how any particular issue will be handled. Rather, the state can generally define for itself what it considers to be a domestic matter and, instead of having to consult with other states to deal with it, is far more likely to call upon long-standing tradition and canons of international law to warn other states from intervening in this "domestic" matter.

A highly significant example where the line dividing domestic from foreign policy has been blurred virtually beyond recognition is West Germany's treatment of the Berlin problem. In 1945 the victorious Allies of World War II split up Germany into several parts. The territories east of the Oder and Neisse rivers went to Poland and the Soviet Union for a "temporary" administration that has proved to be quite permanent. They divided the remainder into four zones of occupation *and* a separate area comprising Greater Berlin (in its 1920 boundaries), which in turn was broken up into four occupation sectors. The Allies initially intended to govern occupied Germany in a decentralized fashion, but with the Allied Control Council

*Financial assistance for this project stemmed from the Social Science Research Council, Carnegie Corporation, Fulbright Commission, Stimson Fund of Yale University, and, at the University of Illinois, the Institute of Communications Research and Center for International Comparative Studies. Kempton B. Jenkins of the United States Information Agency made several helpful suggestions.

providing joint coordination of policy. In Berlin the Four-Power *Komman-datura* sought to ensure a measure of uniformity in policy.

Interallied unity soon broke down. By 1946 only Britain and the United States were actively seeking greater economic and political integration for their zones of occupation. By the end of 1947, after the collapse of the London Conference of foreign ministers, France had agreed to move toward trizonal fusion; and the gap between Soviet occupation policy and that of the West grew into a chasm that seemed unbridgeable. Mid-1948 ushered in currency reforms that sealed the economic division of Germany in east and west, the beginnings of a constitutional convention to formalize the political amalgamation of the three western zones, and the Soviet-imposed blockade of Berlin. The blockade was lifted in May 1949. By this time, however, plans were well underway to proclaim in September 1949 the Federal Republic of Germany (FRG) in the west and in October 1949 the German Democratic Republic (GDR) in the Soviet zone of occupation.

The political battles of 1945–49 among the giants left the status of Berlin anomalous at best. Ostensibly unified under Four-Power control, the city was effectively divided between east and west. Upon occasion Soviet and GDR spokesmen claimed the right to *all* of Berlin. Similarly, West Germans developed the doctrine that their government was the sole legitimate successor to previous German governments; and that the western sectors of Berlin should be part of the FRG, until such time as the Soviet Union should "return" to the FRG the rest of Berlin, East Germany, and the territories east of the Oder-Neisse boundary. But, clearly, any attempt to regulate the status of "domestic" West Berlin would force the FRG to work closely with the Western Allies, and would rest upon changing levels of tension in the cold war. This chapter focuses upon how the West German government has responded to this set of challenges: the social integration into the FRG of West Berlin; the legal responsibility for West Berlin; and the costs, economic and political, of this tangled tie between West Germany and West Berlin.

The Integration of West Berlin into the Social Fabric of West German Life

The muddled, embattled years of 1945–49 left West Berlin peripheral to the Federal Republic. What made this situation difficult for West Berliners to bear, aside from the ever-present possibility of new Soviet or GDR pressures, was the fact that prewar Berlin had been at the very center of German life as a whole. It was the seat of government. Its playwrights and artists were known the world over. Its fashion designers set standards of elegance for the entire country and at times enjoyed international status. Its newspapers circulated in every part of Germany. More generally, the city was the heart of the nation's financial, commercial, and communication networks. World War II and its consequences changed all that. Aerial bombardments and intense street fighting destroyed the city's central business district; dismantling removed much of the commercial stocks and industrial equipment that remained; an Allied policy of decentralization, together with growing East-West hostility, prevented firms from reestablishing headquarters in the former capital; and the physical isolation of the city, located as it was over a hundred miles inside the Soviet zone, made communication difficult at best. These developments posed the danger that West Berliners would become a separate subculture, isolated spiritually as well as physically from West Germany. A central task of German policy makers, then, was to prevent changed political circumstances from decaying the ties of social integration that still existed.

Social Organization

Among the first normal aspects of life to reemerge from the rubble of postwar Germany were social structures. From the beginning, for instance, occupation authorities excepted churches from the general prohibition of public meetings (although not exempting some of their leaders from denazification proceedings!). Protestant churchmen from all four zones of occupation and Berlin met in August 1945 at Treysa to agree upon a temporary working relationship that resulted three years later in the establishment of the Evangelical Church in Germany (EKD). An integral part of the EKD was the *Landeskirche* (Provincial Church) of Berlin-Brandenburg (LBB) which, for historical reasons, encompassed not only the city of Berlin but also the entire province of Brandenburg. With 1,916 individual church communities, the LBB was the second largest of Germany's 27 provincial churches.[1] Even more significant was the fact that LBB leaders, and particularly Bishop Otto Dibelius, led the EKD as a whole.

The division of Germany in 1948–49 had profound but delayed consequences for the EKD, with member churches in both parts of the country. The ensuing years saw the emergence in each Germany of policies—partly conscious, but also partly unconscious—serving to integrate church organizations into their respective ideological frameworks. The pressures were more noticeable in the GDR. It continued with varying degrees of severity until church leaders in the East accepted the fact that their new Caesar was the Communist government of the GDR. Some churchmen in the West, meanwhile, were outspoken in equating communism with "Godless atheism," and the GDR government with the Nazi regime as yet another totalitarian system which the church must resist. When the FRG rearmed in the mid-1950s, EKD leaders in West Germany were quick to conclude a

1. Heinz Brunotte, *Die Evangelische Kirche in Deutschland: Geschichte, Organisation und Gestalt der EKD* (Gütersloh: Gütersloher Verlagshaus Gerd Mohn, 1964).

contract permitting their pastors to tend to the military flock. Those seeking to maintain church unity, meanwhile, resisted any temptation to align themselves with the policies of their own governments. Indeed, their critics charged that the "neutralists" leaned over backward to lament the mote in their own government's eye while ignoring the beam in that of the other.

Nowhere were these cross-pressures more severely felt than in the Provincial Church of Berlin-Brandenburg.[2] It not only predated by many generations the east-west split of the late 1940s, but even the administrative boundaries characterizing prewar Germany. Hence its domain included a good part of the GDR along with both East and West Berlin. Individual churches drew their members from both sides of the boundary. Ties of religious community remained tight enough as long as there was free access to and from West Berlin. In August 1961, however, the East German government built a wall of concrete and steel around West Berlin, and effectively stopped communication between the two sides. Churches on the border atrophied; the Provincial Church (as well as the EKD) had to hold its synods separately in East and West Berlin; and the tendency toward different concerns and life styles gained momentum. When the formal split of the national and provincial organizations came in 1970, it merely sealed what had been the case organizationally—although not in doctrine—for close to a decade. This sequence of events also brought the Protestants of West Berlin closer to West Germany, and now the split of the LBB ended its claim to special treatment as an organizational bridge between East and West.

The story of the Protestant Church, despite its unique aspects, is exemplary of other areas of social life as well. A distinct pattern of integration is discernible in the postwar years. The first phase saw the emergence of various types of organizations—football leagues, charitable societies, fraternal organizations—in the different *Länder* (states) of the area that later became the Federal Republic. These were necessarily decentralized because of Allied occupation policy, but also because funds were not available for extensive travel and coordination. The second phase was one of partial amalgamation. Social organizations found the Western Allies gradually weakening the barriers they had imposed to higher levels of coordination. Later, economic recovery made this development still more feasible. Discontinuities nonetheless deepened between Soviet-zone and western-zone bodies; and those in Berlin, due to the city's extraordinary political circumstances, maintained an uneasy position between East and West. The third phase came after cold-war lines were drawn through Germany. In it West Berlin organizations formalized their ties to those in West Germany. By this time, however, the latter had had substantial lead time to structure the organizations and their policies; besides, the new

2. Richard L. Merritt, with Susanne Schulthes, "The Church and Political Community in Divided Berlin," publication forthcoming.

political situation made it inevitable that their major activity would center on West Germany rather than West Berlin. In consequence, although they increasingly enjoyed structural unity with their West German counterparts, organizations in West Berlin moved gradually but surely toward the periphery of the FRG's social life.

Political Organizations

As was true of prewar Germany's social life, its politics also focused on Berlin. Among other things, the city was the seat of the major party organizations—although, to be sure, some parties such as the National Socialists drew their main strength from elsewhere. The Berlin population itself generally voted on the left side of the political spectrum. Even in the last pre-Nazi elections the Social Democratic party (SPD) and Communist party (KPD) together garnered well over half the vote. Observers anticipated that these same parties would also dominate postwar municipal politics. But, as it turned out, the KPD was strong only in areas controlled by the Red Army. It was doubtless this realization that led the Soviets and German Communists returned from wartime exile in Moscow to take firm action. In April 1946 they forced the SPD into a merged party—the Socialist Unity party (SED)—which the Communists would ultimately dominate. Social Democrats in Western-occupied areas refused to accept such a merger and hence, where the Red Army did not hold sway, the SPD and KPD remained separate. In the Four-Power city of Berlin, both the SED and SPD functioned in token form in all sectors (the latter in East Berlin only until 1961, when the party's central office in West Berlin dissolved it rather than see it succumb to Communist pressures).[3]

The struggle over the SPD–KPD merger played a prominent role in reducing the centrality of the Berlin SPD in the national party. The notion of working-class unity had always appealed to some Social Democrats. The experience of the 1920s and 1930s, however, had led even these people to be of two minds about a formal merger with the KPD—particularly after the nature of the postwar Soviet occupation became apparent to them. Party organizations in the western zones of occupation were not inclined to pay heed to the SPD Central Committee, re-created in Berlin but with occupation policies formally limiting its influence to the city. This was particularly the case after leading Central Committee members submitted to Soviet pressure and accepted the KPD's bid for merger. The western-zone organizations followed instead the tough, embittered veteran of Nazi concentration camps, Kurt Schumacher, who had located himself in Hannover in the British zone.

From November 1945 to April 1946 the rank and file of Berlin's SPD

---

3. Richard L. Merritt and Ronald A. Francisco, "The SPD of East Berlin, 1945–1961," *Comparative Politics* 5, no. 1 (October 1972): 1–28.

fought their own Central Committee as well as Soviet occupation authorities in a fruitless effort to prevent their party's cooptation in the new unity party.[4] The SPD in Berlin finally split over this issue. The split in turn led to rival claims to represent the party's legitimate interests. Those who joined the SED petitioned the *Kommandatura* to recognize it as the SPD's successor (which would imply the dissolution of the SPD in its older form). Those who balked at the Soviet maneuver wanted the SED disallowed in Berlin. The quadripartite *Kommandatura* eventually struck a compromise that permitted the SPD and the SED to coexist in the city—a solution that Soviet authorities refused to accept in their zone of occupation, where the cowed SPD formally dissolved itself by joining with the Communists in the Socialist Unity party. Social Democrats in West Berlin had won the battle, but it had been a costly one. Reduced in strength, weary from the tough infighting of the previous six months, and limited in practice if not in principle to the three western sectors of occupied Berlin, the city's SPD had little choice but to become an integral part of Schumacher's party in West Germany.

In contrast to other organizations, however, the Berlin SPD did not slip to the periphery of the national party. Until Schumacher died in 1952, he ruled the West German SPD with a firm hand.[5] But increasingly Berlin Social Democrats swung the ideological pendulum. They had already fought the Communists—both in the merger struggle of 1945–46, and up to the end of the blockade in May 1949—and they lived in a city that was in a variety of ways constantly harassed by the Communist government of East Germany. They were simply unwilling to follow meekly a party line espousing unreconstructed Marxism, a naive vision of working-class unity, and neutralism in foreign policy. Aligning with others who were more interested in electoral success than ideological purity, Berlin Social Democrats steadily pushed the party toward the center.[6] This goal was finally attained in the Godesberg Program of 1959. Meanwhile, Berlin's new leaders—most notably Ernst Reuter and, later, Willy Brandt—had become increasingly prominent in policy-making roles. In fact, Lord Mayor Brandt was the party's nominee for the chancellorship in 1961 and 1965 before finally attaining the post in 1969. Whether or not Berlin's centrality in the SPD will endure is an open question. It seems more likely that it was merely the happy conjunction of some magnetic personalities, issues that startled the world and put Berlin Social Democrats in the headlines, and West German

4. Albrecht Kaden, *Einheit oder Freiheit: Die Wiedergründung der SPD 1945–46* (Hannover: Verlag J. H. W. Dietz Nachf. GmbH, 1964); and Klaus-Peter Schulz, *Auftakt zum Kalten Krieg; Der Freiheitskampf der SPD in Berlin 1945–46* (Berlin: Colloquium Verlag, 1965).

5. Lewis J. Edinger, *Kurt Schumacher: A Study in Personality and Political Behavior* (Stanford, Calif.: Stanford University Press, 1965).

6. Abraham Ashkenasi, *Reformpartei und Aussenpolitik: Die Aussenpolitik der SPD Berlin-Bonn* (Köln and Opladen: Westdeutscher Verlag, 1968).

resentment and hostility toward Soviet occupation policies, and that, after Brandt, Berlin's star will fall again. At this point there seem to be few "men of the hour" on the Berlin SPD's horizon.

Roughly the same set of circumstances produced a different outcome in one of Germany's most powerful interest groups, the labor unions.[7] Always close to the SPD, Berlin's unionists suffered a battle similar to that fought by Social Democrats in the first postwar year. In this case, however, the Communist-run Free German Labor Union Federation (FDGB) was established throughout Berlin before effective resistance could develop. When opposition did organize into the Independent Labor Union Organization (UGO), it encountered difficulty securing recognition, first from the *Kommandatura,* and after 1949 from the German Labor Union Federation (DGB) in the Federal Republic. The DGB in particular was disinclined to adopt UGO's anticommunism and, focusing as it did upon domestic rather than foreign matters, still professed a policy of cooperation with the East German FDGB aimed at the ultimate goal of working-class unity.

Even after the Berlin unions were accepted into the DGB there were serious conflicts of interest. Berlin unionists were by and large interested in security from East German communism, and were willing to forgo union militancy and cooperate with the government to attain it. The fact that the SPD governed West Berlin also gave Berlin unionists a greater voice in official policy. They became part of the West Berlin "establishment," and were less anxious than before to rock the boat. West German unions, by contrast, were left out in the cold during two decades of rule by Chancellor Konrad Adenauer's Christian Democratic Union (CDU), very much attuned to business interests. They were by and large opposed to the government's policies of rearmament, firm alliance with the West, and implacable anticommunism, not only because they weakened the chances for working-class solidarity, but also because such policies increased the pressures for domestic conformity to present a solid front abroad. The gradual accession to power in West Germany of the SPD—first as junior partner in the grand coalition of 1966–69 and then, after 1969, in Brandt's minicoalition of Social Democrats and Free Democrats (FDP)—brought DGB leaders more into the policy-making elite. One effect is that the "cold-war gap" between West Berlin and West German unionists has diminished. But it is still the latter who are calling the tune for the FRG's union movement.

Economic Patterns

Prewar Berlin was one of Germany's major industrial cities. The combination of wartime bombing, postwar dismantling (estimated at 67 percent of prewar West Berlin's industrial capacity) by Soviet troops, and the long

7. Ronald A. Francisco, "Postwar West German and West Berlin Unionism: Unity or Divergence?" publication forthcoming.

period of uncertainty about the city's position and future, together with Allied policies encouraging the famed "economic miracle" in West Germany, left the latter in a much stronger position vis-a-vis the West Berlin that emerged from the blockade. As early as 1950 the Federal Republic attained a production level commensurate with that of 1936. West Berlin did not reach this level until 1956. Unemployment (other than structural and seasonal) continued in West Berlin for close to a decade after its end in the FRG. The city's economy eventually caught up, due in large part to economic assistance from the federal government, but even today its standard of living lags somewhat behind that of West Germany.

Political circumstances thus made German industry a bit wary of reliance on West Berlin. There was no guarantee that a new blockade would not be set up and cut off its firms from those in the west. Even without a blockade any trade between West Berlin and West Germany had to cross more than a hundred miles of GDR territory, which meant costs in fees and delays as well as an inevitable degree of uncertainty. To be sure, the federal government insured these shipments, reimbursed costs imposed by the GDR, and gave tax breaks to firms with offices in Berlin or which dealt with Berlin firms. But the inconveniences and uncertainty remained (not to be reduced contractually until early 1972). Moreover, the center of industrial, commercial, and financial activity grew strong in West Germany. This is not to say that West Berlin businesses atrophied, or that national firms withdrew their offices from the city in large numbers. Rather, West Berlin became more and more a provincial city from the perspective of West German businessmen—a nice place to visit or even live, but nowhere to be transferred if one wanted to be in the swim of things in the growing West German industrial world. Apparent threats to Berlin, such as Khrushchev's deadline crisis of 1958–59, merely enhanced the feeling that a firm's over-commitment to the city might not be economically sound.

West Berlin and West Germany share a common distribution and marketing system. The citizen of the Federal Republic who visits Berlin finds that he can purchase all the items and name brands available in any large West German city, and at the same cost (or even, in some cases such a liquor, more cheaply because of slightly different tax bases). Moreover, consumer desires and behavior are roughly comparable for West Berliners and other West German urbanites, controlled for income, age, and other variables.

Behavioral Patterns

Indeed, in their other forms of behavior West Berliners are similar to West Germans. Again controlling for intervening variables, they have common outlooks on life, preferences, recollections of history, behavioral traits such as church attendance, and even attitudes toward domestic political events and personalities. They read the same magazines, watch the same television programs and movies, and share the same culture. Contacts between the two populations by mail, telephone, and travel are strong.

Where they differ most markedly is in their attitudes on foreign policy. By and large, the West Berlin population continues to be far more mistrustful of the GDR and Soviet Union than are West Germans, and far more insistent on close ties with the West, particularly the United States.[8] As suggested earlier, this difference is doubtless due to the bitter experiences of West Berliners in trying to deal with communism—the weeks of Soviet occupation in May and June 1945, the perceived chicanery of Soviet occupation authorities and KPD/SED leaders in the ensuing months, the blockade of 1948–49, the low-level harassment of the 1950s, the Berlin wall in 1961, and, subsequently, the refusal to let West Berliners visit East Berlin, the shooting of refugees trying to cross the boundary, and partial blockages or delays of traffic on the access routes between West Berlin and the Federal Republic. It is worth noting, however, that the younger generation, comprising persons who were raised in and accepted as "normal" a divided Germany and Berlin, is less likely than its elders to respond with cold-war attitudes to all issues. In the 1971 municipal elections, for instance, over one in ten men between the ages of 18 and 25 voted for the Communist SEW (the West Berlin version of East Germany's SED).[9] A stabilization of the status quo and the simple passage of time may therefore produce even greater uniformity of political attitudes among West Berliners and West Germans.

West Berliners and West Germans

Despite some variation and changes over time, then, modern West Berlin is well integrated into the social fabric of the Federal Republic. This finely woven web of social patterns displays several distinct characteristics, not the least of which is the dramatic change in the role that the city plays for Germany. Berlin is no longer the dynamo driving Germany, as it did under the Hohenzollerns, the Weimar Republicans, and the Nazis of the Third Reich. It has neither the physical resources nor talent for that. This

8. Richard L. Merritt, "West Berlin—Center or Periphery?" in *Comparing Nations: The Use of Quantitative Data in Cross-National Research,* ed. Richard L. Merritt and Stein Rokkan (New Haven and London: Yale University Press, 1966), pp. 321–36. West Berliners are particularly conscious of the fact that the GDR that surrounds them has been "occupied" or "defended" by 300,000–500,000 Soviet troops throughout the postwar years. Those who lived in Berlin when the Red Army stormed and occupied it in spring 1945, when it enforced the blockade of 1948–49, and when it put down the East Berlin "workers' uprising" of June 1953 (entailing perhaps 5 percent of the GDR's work force) simply had different life experiences than did the Western Allies or even West Germans, most of whom had never felt the direct impact of the Red Army. One might expect, for example, that West Berliners would have been more inclined than others to take seriously the implied threats of Khrushchev's deadline crisis of 1958–59.

9. *Berliner Statistik* 25, no. 7 (July 1971): 203; the SEW received 2.3 percent of the total vote in 1971, as opposed to 2.0 percent in 1967 and 1.4 percent in 1963.

has forced the city, if it would thrive, to search for new functions. One was as the Jiminy Cricket of the cold war. Whenever the Federal Republic or any of its social organizations, such as trade unions, or even the United States, got slack in its defenses against communism or initiated conciliatory gestures, there was always a Berliner around to point his finger at the perils of softness. The very presence of the Berlin problem was a constant reminder of East-West tension—a reminder that in turn reinforced that tension. Another role was propagandistic. On the passive end of the continuum, the West built up West Berlin as a symbol of what a free enterprise system could accomplish. In its day West Berlin also played a more active role in the cold war. Not only did the West build powerful radio and television stations that could beam its message to millions of Germans in the GDR, in addition easy access before 1961 to the "enemy" world across the Brandenburg Gate made the city a natural playground for espionage activities. Such functions cut both ways, of course, and the East could use them as well as the West. None of them, however, could disguise the cardinal fact that the western sectors of Berlin, not to speak of the city as a whole, had moved to the periphery of German life.

A second characteristic is that a distinct subculture has not emerged in the island-city. This is not to deny the existence of regional differences. Berliners have long been known in Germany for what a Brooklyn baseball fan might call their "lip." There may also be some residual resentment among West Berliners about their fate or concern about their future. And they tend to be more wary of association with communism than are their brethren in the Federal Republic. But, by and large, West Berliners have moved closer to social integration with West Germany throughout the years since 1945, albeit at some cost (to be discussed later). West Berlin and its inhabitants are now as much a part of West German life as is Hamburg or Frankfurt.

Third, the relationship between West Berlin and West Germany has had its symbiotic aspects. The city played a significant role, for instance, in the worldwide rehabilitation of Germany. The steadfastness of West Berliners during the bitter months of the blockade turned them into front-line heroes in the struggle against what the West saw as the new expansionist totalitarianism directed from the Kremlin. The intense hostility toward Germany because of its Nazi past softened into a sometimes grudging acceptance of a revitalized West Germany that could share the burden of defending the West. The events of the late 1940s also turned the spotlight of world attention upon West Berlin and its political leaders. This in turn enabled them to exert influence upon political policy out of proportion to their formal positions in the FRG's organization table or political hierarchy.

No one was more aware of this than the Federal Republic's first chancellor, Konrad Adenauer. He watched from the sidelines in Bonn when Lord Mayor Ernst Reuter visited the United States to receive the tumultuous ovations of Americans; and, in 1959, six years after Reuter's death, when an American postage stamp honored him as a "champion of liberty." Then, too, the construction of the Berlin wall in August 1961, in the midst of a torpid electoral campaign, focused world attention again upon the city and its Lord Mayor, Willy Brandt, who was also Adenauer's opponent for the federal chancellorship. At one point CDU spokesmen even hinted darkly that the Soviet Union, in cahoots with the Social Democrats, had built the wall deliberately to assist Brandt in his electoral campaign.

The very prominence of the Berlin problem, no less than the significance given it in the political rhetoric of the Federal Republic, lent weight to the activities of its representatives to political, social, and political organizations in the FRG. But moral force was in the long run insufficient. As the years rolled by, and the division of Germany and Berlin became more permanent, West Berlin was increasingly in the role of supplicant rather than master builder. The city's resource base did not grow as rapidly as that in the FRG, nor did its physical isolation permit it to play an effective coordinative role. Moreover, the vulnerability of West Berlin left its representatives in political and other structures open to pressure from their West German colleagues. The decline in importance of the Berlin problem was all that was needed to reduce even the moral suasion that West Berliners could bring to bear upon the organized social life of the Federal Republic. In curtailing West Berlin's privileged status, the FRG's social processes were merely catching up with the legacy of Germany's lost war and the ensuing East-West struggle.

The high degree of social integration thus both kept West Berliners and West Germans together in a single political community, and ultimately obviated the island-city's claim to a special position for exercising influence. But what such patterns cover up is the fact that decision makers from other countries—most notably the United States, but also Great Britain and France, and even in part the Soviet Union—share in decisions about social and political life in West Berlin, its ties with the FRG, and its future. West Berlin's legal status is without question unique in the modern world.

The Legal Separation of West Berlin and the Federal Republic

The Four-Power City

Berlin's anomalous status stems from Allied agreements concluded long before the Nazi regime collapsed. At their Tehran conference in late 1943, Churchill, Roosevelt, and Stalin agreed to create a tripartite European Advisory Commission (EAC) to work out details for the occupation of Germany.[10] On 12 September 1944 the EAC representatives signed a pro-

---

10. Unless otherwise specified, the documents referred to in this section are to be found in Wolfgang Heidelmeyer and Guenter Hindrichs, *Documents on Berlin, 1943–1963* (München:

tocol providing that Germany "will, for the purposes of occupation, be divided into three zones, one of which will be allotted to each of the three Powers, and a special Berlin area, which will be under joint occupation by the three Powers." The agreement went on to specify the zonal boundaries for Germany and the sectoral boundaries of Greater Berlin. Each of the occupation zones was to be governed by "a Commander-in-Chief designated by the Government of the country whose forces occupy that zone." Further, "An Inter-Allied Governing Authority (Komendatura) consisting of three Commandants, appointed by their respective Commanders-in-Chief, will be established to direct jointly the administration of the 'Greater Berlin' Area." A subsequent EAC protocol of 14 November 1944 noted that the *Kommandatura*, which would be responsible to the Allied Control Council set up to coordinate the governance of Germany as a whole, would have a technical staff "consisting of the personnel of each of the three Powers." Its purpose was to be "supervising and controlling the activities of the local organs of 'Greater Berlin' which are responsible for its municipal services." (An agreement of 1 May 1945, formalized on 26 July, provided for the accession of France to previous agreements on the occupation of Germany, and specified the zone in Germany and sector in Berlin that the French would occupy.) These principles were repeated in Four-Power statements of 5 June 1945 accompanying the Allied "Declaration Regarding the Defeat of Germany and the Assumption of Supreme Authority with Respect to Germany." And, by the time Attlee, Stalin, and Truman met in late July at Potsdam, the *Kommandatura* was already working out ways to implement them.

The story of the breakdown of Four-Power unity in the Allied Control Council and the Berlin *Kommandatura* is well known and need not be recounted here.[11] Suffice it to say that issue after issue emerged that found the Soviet Union and the Western Allies in basic opposition: war crimes trials, local government and appointed officials, educational policy, reparations agreements. What they all boiled down to was a pair of contradictory notions about how the new, "democratic" Germany should look. By 1947 at the latest the lines were drawn, with the Soviet Union pushing for the type of "people's republic" springing up throughout Eastern Europe, and the Western Powers opting for a modified restoration of the parliamentary democracy of the Weimar Republic.

R. Oldenbourg Verlag, 1963); on the question of boundaries, see particularly Philip E. Mosely, "The Occupation of Germany: New Light on How the Zones Were Drawn," *Foreign Affairs* 28, no. 4 (July 1950): 580–604; and William M. Franklin, "Zonal Boundaries and Access to Berlin," *World Politics* 16, no. 1 (October 1963): 1–31.

11. For an American perspective, see W. Phillips Davison, *The Berlin Blockade: A Study in Cold War Politics* (Princeton, N.J.: Princeton University Press, 1958); for a perspective from the GDR, Gerhard Keiderling and Percy Stulz, *Berlin 1945–1968: Zur Geschichte der Hauptstadt der DDR und der selbständigen politischen Einheit Westberlin* ([East] Berlin: Dietz Verlag, 1970).

The showdown came at the London Conference of Foreign Ministers in December 1947. The realization that further East-West cooperation was not likely to be fruitful led the West to initiate a series of conferences aimed at forming a provisional government for their three zones of occupation. The Soviet Union protested this step, terming it a violation of the Four-Power principles implicit in the "Declaration of Defeat" of June 1945 and the Potsdam agreement of August 1945. When this proved to be of no avail, the Soviet representative, Marshal Vassily Sokolovsky, walked out of the Allied Control Council on 20 March 1948. The remaining three Allies nonetheless continued to plan for a reunified West Germany. One of their first tasks was to restore confidence in its currency system, debased through Soviet practices of printing occupation currency for which there was no backing. Only firm action to end the barter economy that had developed, the Western Allies felt, would get the German economy moving again.

The flash point of tension came in mid-1948 when, on 18 June, the Allies announced a currency reform, effective on 20 June, for the three western zones, excluding West Berlin. The Soviet Union responded by forbidding the circulation of the new currency in its "zone of occupation and in the area of Greater Berlin which comes within the Soviet zone of occupation and is economically part of the Soviet zone." On 22 June Marshal Sokolovsky revealed the Soviet decision "to introduce a currency reform in the Soviet zone and in the Greater Berlin area." This latter currency reform was announced generally on 23 June, to take effect on the following day. On 23 June, however, the commandants of the western sectors of Berlin declared the Soviet move null and void for their own sectors, and extended the western currency reform of 20 June to West Berlin.

On that same night and into the morning of 24 June the Soviet Union closed all road, rail, and canal traffic between the western zones of occupation and West Berlin. It was a clear attempt to give force to the new Soviet interpretation of the city's status:

> Berlin lies in the Soviet zone of occupation of Germany. Economically it forms part of it. Now that the military authorities of the United States, England and France have violated the Agreement on Control Machinery in Germany, that is to say, now that they have robbed themselves of the right to participate in the joint administration of Berlin, the Soviet Military Administration is the only legitimate occupation authority. Therefore its orders have the force of law for the whole of Berlin.[12]

And, a week later, the Soviet representative officially withdrew from the Berlin *Kommandatura*, never to return.

12. Excerpt from an article in the *Tägliche Rundschau*, the official daily newspaper of the Soviet Military Administration, reprinted in Heidelmeyer and Hindrichs, *Documents on Berlin*, p. 67. An irony is that in July 1945 the Soviet commander in Berlin, Marshal Georgi

The West denied the Soviet interpretation of Berlin's status—both in words, by protesting Soviet actions and views, and in deed, by instituting an airlift to provision the 2.25 million West Berliners. The success of the airlift led to an apparent change in Soviet tactics. Evidently realizing that they could not bring the whole of Berlin into their realm, Soviet leaders opted for stabilizing their unencumbered control over the Soviet sector. Greater Berlin's government split effectively in early September 1948 and formally on 30 November with the promulgation of a provisional municipal government for East Berlin. Thereafter sphere after sphere of municipal life divided sharply along East-West lines. And, when the Soviet Union lifted the blockade on 12 May 1949, Berliners faced a new reality: a divided city, with separate currencies and governments. The Western Allies continued to assert the principle of quadripartite authority over the whole of Berlin. In practice, however, their effective control was limited to the three western sectors; and they were unwilling to brook any Soviet interference in their decisions. Similarly, the Soviet Union alone controlled East Berlin. Berlin, albeit divided, remained an occupied city.

Three-Power Authority in West Berlin

During the blockade months, plans for a provisional government in West Germany were proceeding apace. July 1948 saw conferences between the three military governors on the one hand and, on the other, the premiers of the individual *Lander*, as well as meetings among the premiers themselves. They reached agreement to call for elections to a Parliamentary Council, which would meet on 1 September to begin drafting a constitution. The latter produced by February 1949 a draft document—designated "Basic Law" rather than constitution, to stress its provisional nature. Review by the Western Allies and reconsideration by the Parliamentary Council and a conference of *Land* premiers yielded a final draft by May. The stage was set for national elections in August and, on 21 September 1949, the launching of the Federal Republic of Germany, with its provisional capital in Bonn.

The role that West Berlin would play in the Federal Republic was a subject of dispute. At every point in the proceedings of the Parliamentary Council the city was designated a *Land* with the same status as the other states in the federal system. The draft Basic Law approved by the Council in February 1949 simply listed it as one of the twelve *Länder*. The military

---

Zhukov, insisted that the Americans, British, and French supply the western sectors of Berlin, since the Soviet zone would have nothing to spare; had the Soviet Union assumed the burden then, the Western position in Berlin three years later would have been far less tenable than it actually was. See Herbert Feis, *Between War and Peace: The Potsdam Conference* (Princeton, N.J.: Princeton University Press, 1960), p. 248n.

governors, however, objected. Their review of the draft on 2 March noted their appreciation of

> the solicitude which the Parliamentary Council has shown for Berlin. However, in view of the existing situation, that portion of Article 22 which refers to Berlin must be suspended. Nevertheless, there would be no objection to the responsible authorities in Berlin designating a small number of representatives to attend the meetings of the Parliament.[13]

Article 23 of the final document nonetheless retained West Berlin's designation as a *Land*. To this the military governors responded on 12 May, the day on which the blockade ended:

> A third reservation concerns the participation of Greater Berlin in the Federation. We interpret the effect of Articles 23 and 144(2) of the Basic Law as constituting acceptance of our previous request that while Berlin may not be accorded voting membership in the Bundestag or Bundesrat nor be governed by the Federation she may, nevertheless, designate a small number of representatives to attend the meetings of those legislative bodies.[14]

The electoral law of 10 May in fact embodied this interpretation by requesting West Berlin's City Assembly to send representatives to the future parliament rather than calling for the election of Berlin's delegates.

On 12 May the military governors also approved a "Statement of Principles Governing the Relationship between the Allied Kommandatura and Greater Berlin," issued two days later. It specified the fields over which the *Kommandatura* would continue to make decisions, and reserved for the occupation authorities "the right to resume in whole or in part the exercise of full authority if they consider that to do so is essential to security or to preserve democratic government, or in pursuance of the international obligations of their Governments."[15] Subsequent modifications made it clear that the *Kommandatura* comprised American, British, and French officials only, and gradually widened the decision-making latitude of West Berlin's government. All such modifications nonetheless reasserted the basic principle of Allied responsibility for Berlin.

Underlying the principle of Allied responsibility were several practical

---

13. Elmer Plischke, with the assistance of Elisabeth Erdmann, *Berlin: Development of Its Government and Administration* (Bad Godesberg-Mehlem: Office of the U.S. High Commissioner for Germany, Historical Division, Office of the Executive Secretary, 1952), p. 113. On the Parliamentary Council, see John Ford Golay, *The Founding of the Federal Republic of Germany* (Chicago: University of Chicago Press, 1957); and Peter H. Merkl, *The Origin of the West German Republic* (New York: Oxford University Press, 1963).

14. Heidelmeyer and Hindrichs, *Documents on Berlin*, pp. 107–8.

15. Ibid., pp. 108–11.

considerations. For one thing, despite the development of the cold war the Western Allies of World War II were not anxious to relinquish full control over their former enemy. The Occupation Statute of 1949 removed certain areas of decision making from the FRG, most notably defense and security. Ultimately, of course, revisions in 1954 and 1968 would remove even these last vestiges of occupation in the Federal Republic (although not West Berlin).[16] Second was the fear that any tampering with the quadripartite agreements without explicit Soviet approval might give an aura of legitimacy to any unilateral changes made subsequently by the Soviet Union. The West was not anxious to give the USSR the slightest pretext for interfering with access routes to and from the island-city, or halting the limited communication that existed between East and West Berlin. Third was the issue of defense. Should the West give up its right to occupy West Berlin, by what authority could they retain their forces there? Was a contractual agreement with the FRG, given its limited sovereignty, sufficient? If the West were to withdraw its forces, how could a disarmed FRG protect West Berlin from any direct or indirect encroachments? Moreover, the perceived threat posed by the Soviet Union to all of Western Europe made it highly desirable—for deterring any aggressive Soviet behavior, for ensuring Western Europe of continued American support, for mustering popular American support for NATO policies—that Western and particularly American contingents and status be committed in West Berlin.

This is not to say that the occupying powers were entirely happy with the arrangement. All three, but especially Britain and France, were anxious to be relieved of any responsibility for taking care of the West Berliners. They recognized that the FRG would ultimately have to bear this economic burden, and sought ways to make this possible without jeopardizing the city's putative Four-Power status. They also wanted the West Berlin government to assume as much of the day-to-day decision making as was possible without hampering the Allies in what they perceived to be their essential tasks. The maneuverings and pressures among the Western Allies, the government of West Berlin, and that of the FRG—not to speak of the Soviet Union and GDR—to regulate this delicate relationship comprise a crucial part of the political history of Germany since 1949.

Development of a New Status Quo

Those most eager to ensure a firm tie between West Berlin and the Federal Republic were, as may be expected, the West Berliners. During the meetings of the Parliamentary Council, Lord Mayor Ernst Reuter, himself a delegate, solicited support from the British and French for the inclusion of

---

16. "Recent Emergency Legislation in West Germany," *Harvard Law Review* 82, no. 8 (June 1969): 1704–37.

West Berlin as a *Land*. When the military governors turned this down in March 1949, the City Assembly unanimously adopted a resolution protesting the decision, and asking for at least some sort of representation in the future federal parliament. The Parliamentary Council and military governors, as noted earlier, accepted this position. The City Assembly in turn instructed its representatives on 19 May to accept the Basic Law. A month later it nonetheless adopted unanimously a resolution renewing its demand that the Allies cancel their suspension of Article 23 of the Basic Law, and recognize Berlin as the FRG's twelfth *Land*—a demand that the *Kommandatura* turned down on 30 June. What the city fathers could not get in the federal constitution they sought in their own. On 4 August 1950 they submitted to the *Kommandatura* an extensive revision of their 1948 constitution. Article 1(2) stated: "Berlin is a *Land* of the Federal Republic of Germany." Again, however, the Allies stepped in to suspend this paragraph and retain the constitutional separation of West Berlin and West Germany.

On the more practical issue of legislative unity the Allies were more flexible. To be sure, they suspended Article 1(3) of Berlin's 1950 constitution, which asserted that "The Basic Law and the laws of the Federal Republic of Germany are binding on Berlin." They nonetheless gave a friendly interpretation to Article 87(2), which provided that, until Berlin became a full member of the FRG, "The City Council can establish by law that any specific law of the Federal Republic of Germany is applicable in Berlin also without change." In its memorandum of 29 August 1950 the *Kommandatura* interpreted this statement to mean that "the provisions of any Federal law shall apply to Berlin only after they have been voted upon by the House of Representatives and passed as a Berlin law." The Allies thus retained for themselves the right of review for twenty-one days, after which legislation passed by Berlin would become effective. A revision in March 1951 of the statement of principles permitted such legislation to go into effect immediately, "subject to repeal or annulment" by the *Kommandatura*.[17]

The early post-blockade years, then, were ones of parallel legislation. The federal government enacted laws pertaining to the whole of West Germany—and presumably, since West Berlin representatives were (non-voting) participants in both houses of the federal parliament, these laws were by and large acceptable to the city—and subsequently the City Assembly would have to enact them again, possibly even changing them somewhat to suit Berlin conditions. Only then, and provided that the *Kommandatura* did not object, were they applicable in West Berlin. The process was both time-consuming and redundant. It also meant that West Berlin failed to adopt some laws of conceivable importance to federal officials,

17. Heidelmeyer and Hindrichs, *Documents on Berlin*, pp. 121–28.

which could have led to a loss of confidence. It nonetheless worked. In fact, the Berliners were able to enact parallel legislation that even more firmly anchored the city to the FRG, most notably that of January 1951 integrating the *Land* courts of Berlin into the federal superior court and appellate system, but also that establishing the *Federal Reporter (Bundesanzeiger)* as an official organ for Berlin as well.

The drawbacks of the parallel procedure led to the search for more efficient means to accomplish the same goal, but which would also obligate Berlin to accept *all* federal legislation (except that, of course, disallowed by the *Kommandatura*). The *Kommandatura* for its part announced in October 1951 that it would permit "cover laws" that quasi-automatically adapted federal laws and incorporated them into West Berlin's statute books. (In February 1952 this principle was extended from individual to groups of laws already enacted, but without giving the federal parliament a blank check for future legislation.) The federal government, meanwhile, expanded the notion of the "Berlin clause." At the outset, in December 1950, this meant attaching to specific items of legislation a clause noting that it became applicable in West Berlin as soon as the city adopted it. But some laws continued to slip by without such a clause.

The "Third Transfer Law" of January 1952 resolved this anomalous situation once and for all.[18] The law itself regulated financial relations between the federal government and the *Lander,* and effectively brought West Berlin into the FRG's economic structure. This would prove to be significant enough for Berlin's future. But the law also enabled the retroactive transfer to Berlin of much previous legislation enacted by the federal government, permitted the latter to extend to Berlin other laws not contrary to *Kommandatura* stipulations, and required that all future legislation designed to be implemented in West Berlin contain an explicit Berlin clause. The City Assembly would then have a month in which to accept and publish its acceptance of such legislation. A law in May 1966 made this procedure even simpler, but the principle remains the same: except in matters which the *Kommandatura* has reserved for itself, federal laws are virtually automatically a part of West Berlin law.

The Allies also gradually permitted the Federal Republic to represent West Berlin internationally. In March 1951 they indirectly sanctioned West Berlin efforts to secure this representation. And in May 1952 they issued a formal declaration on the "Inclusion of Berlin in International Treaties and Undertakings of the Federal Government." In it they indicated that they would have no objection to such measures, provided that their implementation in Berlin be left to the city's government (under Allied super-

---

18. Plischke, *Berlin*, p. 131n.; see, more generally, Peter H. Merkl, "The Financial Constitution (*Finanzverfassung*) of Western Germany," *American Journal of Comparative Law* 6, no. 2–3 (Spring–Summer 1957): 327–40.

vision) and that the *Kommandatura* be informed, preferably in advance. The *Kommandatura* explicitly reserved the right to exclude Berlin from the purview of such treaties. In practice, the FRG must merely note in any international agreement that its provisions apply to West Berlin or, in the case of economic arrangements, the currency area of the Deutschmark. If the *Kommandatura* raises no objections, the West Berlin government then accepts the agreement and publishes its announcement of acceptance. It should be added that the treaty between the Allies and the FRG ending West Germany's occupation status expressly reasserted the Allies' continued occupation rights in Berlin.

By the early 1950s, then, a new status quo had emerged in West Berlin. The myth of quadripartite control remained, but practice and contractual arrangements made it clear that Soviet interference would not be tolerated. The *Kommandatura* turned over bit by bit to the municipal government control over the daily lives of West Berliners, retaining for itself the principle of complete authority and the right to intervene whenever the security of the city or the occupation rights were threatened. Similarly, the Allies had gradually permitted the de facto integration of West Berlin into the legal, judicial, and financial structure of the Federal Republic. The city still did not have voting rights in parliament—which, of course, affected the distribution of power in the FRG and the type of legislation that would get passed—but for all practical purposes the West Berliner was as much a citizen of the FRG as was the resident of Hamburg or Frankfurt.

Attempted Encroachments on the New Status Quo

The next two decades saw both subtle and open attempts to erode the complicated principles underlying West Berlin's relationships with West Germany and the Allies. The most spectacular of these came from the East.[19] In November 1958 the Soviet leader, Nikita Khrushchev, dusted off the claim—enunciated in mid-1948 but left virtually untouched since then—that all of Berlin lay on Soviet-occupied soil, now under the sovereignty of the German Democratic Republic. The Soviet sector of Berlin, Communist legal experts pointed out, had become the capital of the GDR—an argument that neatly covered up Soviet practice, which effectively precluded the juridical integration of East Berlin into the GDR much as the Western Allies had kept West Berlin separate from the FRG. It was time, the argument continued, to clear up the anomalous status of the western sectors. In a lengthy note addressed to the Allies, Khrushchev charged them with systematic violations of the Potsdam agreement, rearming West Germany in the framework of a military alliance aimed at the Soviet Union,

19. See Hans Speier, *Divided Berlin: The Anatomy of Soviet Political Blackmail* (New York: Frederick A. Praeger, 1961); and Jack M. Schick, *The Berlin Crisis, 1958–1962* (Philadelphia: University of Pennsylvania Press, 1971).

and using West Berlin "as a springboard for intensive espionage, sabotage, and other subversive activities against Socialist countries." From the Soviet perspective, therefore, this behavior rendered "null and void" the protocol of 12 September 1944 and related documents regulating the occupation of Berlin.

Khrushchev proposed that West Berlin become a "free city." Western obstinacy, he asserted, prevented more preferable solutions, such as the reunification of a "democratic" Germany or "for the western part of Berlin, now actually detached from the GDR, to be reunited with its eastern part and for Berlin to become a unified city within the state in whose territory it is situated." Such a free city would "be demilitarized," have "its own government and run its own economic, administrative, and other affairs," and enjoy a neutral status guaranteed by the Four Powers as well as, possibly, the United Nations. The free city of West Berlin could then work out transit agreements with the GDR. Khrushchev added that, should six months not suffice for the wartime Allies to begin working out details, the Soviet Union would be forced to make its own agreement with the GDR regarding the latter's sovereignty over its own territory, and terminate procedural arrangements with the Western Powers.

Needless to say, the West rejected what it saw as an ultimatum. At best it would merely have extended Soviet control to the western sectors, besides delivering up all of West Berlin to the not-so-tender mercies of the GDR. An extensive exchange of notes ensued, Khrushchev postponed his six-month deadline, and in mid-1959 the foreign ministers of the four countries took up the Berlin question at a conference in Geneva. But no substantial change in the status quo took place. Khrushchev's note nonetheless ushered in more than a decade of East German propaganda stressing the viewpoint that West Berlin was on GDR soil and calling for a demilitarized free city.

The West's response also made clear that it was prepared to defend its occupation rights in *West* Berlin only. This was to become even clearer in mid-1961. Khrushchev's renewal of his demands to the new American president, John F. Kennedy, elicited a very strong American promise to protect the West's "three essentials": (1) continued Allied presence in West Berlin, (2) unrestricted use of access routes to and from the island-city, and (3) freedom for West Berliners to choose their own form of government. The Soviet Union took great pains when it authorized the construction in August 1961 of the Berlin Wall to stress the fact that it did not threaten the three essentials. The West, in turn, took no action to tear down the wall or otherwise encroach upon the USSR's sphere of influence. The entire crisis, then, beginning with Khrushchev's note in November 1958 and ending roughly four years later, served to cement the tacit understanding that West Berlin was under the control of the tripartite *Kommandatura*, that East

Berlin was under Soviet control, and that both sides would abstain from actions directly affecting the other.

More subtle attempts to change the status quo of the early 1950s came from West Berliners and West Germans. The former repeatedly sought to legitimate their city-state's standing as a state (*Land*) in the FRG, particularly by seeking the right to vote in federal elections. The latter repeatedly asserted the FRG's responsibility for West Berlin through verbal statements, by moving federal offices to West Berlin, and by holding Bundestag sessions and other official meetings in the city. The East protested such actions as violations of West Berlin's special status under the occupation statutes. Upon occasion it used them as pretexts for harassing West Berliners—slowdowns on the access routes, refusals to permit FRG officials to drive their automobiles to Berlin, even buzzing downtown West Berlin with Soviet MIG jet fighters. The West protested such counterdemonstrations. It also evidently began to recognize the virtual inevitability that harassment would follow upon highly visible manifestations of the FRG's presence in West Berlin, and began to tone down their more overt aspects as well as frequency. But this did not halt the steady pressure from both West Berlin and West Germany that was bringing the two areas even closer together juridically, without, however, removing the principle of Allied occupation in West Berlin.

The Price of Integration

Economic Costs

From the perspective of the Federal Republic, the policy of seeking the closer integration of West Berlin has entailed definite costs. Perhaps the least of these are economic. At the outset, of course, there was the task of reconstructing the city. An estimated 43 percent of Berlin's dwelling units were completely destroyed and another 31 percent partially destroyed in the bombing and street fighting of World War II. The transportation system lay in shambles. And, as noted, much of the industrial capacity that survived the war fell victim to Soviet dismantling teams. Even after reconstruction there remained the task of keeping West Germany's largest city alive. This has meant, among other things, coping with unemployment problems that continued throughout the 1950s; an increasingly overaged population; and an infrastructure of roads, public transportation and utilities, and communication networks that are expensive to maintain. Then, too, there were political considerations: Building up a city that would serve as a "showcase of democracy" could not be done without heavy financial outlays.

Cooperation between the United States and West Germany to rebuild and sustain the city characterized the early post-blockade years. From mid-1949 to mid-1955, through the Economic Cooperation Administration as well as Government and Relief in Occupied Areas (GARIOA) funds, the United States pumped $470 million into West Berlin's economy for such diverse purposes as industrial investment, emergency work programs, and credits to the municipal government.[20] Increasingly, however, the federal government took over the economic burden. One form comprised direct subsidies to the municipal government. This sum increased both in absolute amount (about $736 million in 1970) and in the percentage of the total Berlin budget (from over one-third in the 1950s to an average of more than 40 percent throughout the 1960s). In addition the federal government makes other contributions to West Berlin's budget for compensation payments, the federal road program, scholarships, and other public programs ($145 million in 1970), besides indirect subsidies by way of excess social security payments, unemployment insurance, occupation costs, and similar expenditures ($500 million in 1970). Finally, individual Berliners receive tax write-offs not available to West Germans; and, as noted earlier, business firms with offices in Berlin or which deal with Berlin companies also receive tax rebates. Berlin thus cost the federal government in 1970 at least $2 billion, or about $34 per West German.

The financial cost of maintaining the island-city has upon occasion been a political issue in the Federal Republic. This was most noticeable during the business recession of 1966–67. Although by and large West German citizens and politicians are willing to pay such costs, the recession found a significant minority asking why they had to suffer merely to enable 2.1 million West Berliners to enjoy a high standard of living. Proposed federal budget cuts, however, were quashed. On still other occasions, particularly when Bonn politicians felt that West Berlin spokesmen were being recalcitrant on some important political issue, threatened reductions in federal assistance to Berlin were used as a bargaining instrument. West Berliners, meanwhile, are of two minds regarding their heavy financial dependence on the FRG: some would prefer making the city more self-sufficient, while others want to keep the subsidies as a constant reminder—to West Germans, the Allies, Warsaw Pact states, and perhaps even themselves—of the FRG's ultimate responsibility for the well-being of West Berlin.

Political Costs

The existence and unresolved status of West Berlin affected more generally the character of West German politics. For one thing, some Social

20. Data from Walter Krumholz, *Berlin-ABC* (Berlin: Presse- und Informationsamtes des Landes Berlin, 1968); pp. 86–90; and various issues of the annual *Berlin im Spiegel seiner öffentlichen Finanzplanung* (Berlin: Der Senator für Finanzen).

Democrats, particularly in Berlin but also in West Germany, felt that the conservative CDU government under Adenauer did not try sufficiently to integrate the city into the FRG's political system. Adenauer's personal antipathy to the city was well known. Perhaps because of his own treatment in Berlin by representatives of pre-1945 German governments, the city's persistently "red" leanings, or its position as a stronghold of Protestantism, the Catholic Adenauer was loathe to visit the city or even to find good things to say about it. During the city's greatest crisis while he was chancellor, in August 1961 when the wall went up, Adenauer virtually ignored its plight. Indeed, in campaign speeches of subsequent days he was at his most vicious in attacking his Social Democratic opponent, Lord Mayor Willy Brandt of West Berlin. It all seemed to add up to a pattern. If Berlin were in fact an integral part of the FRG, the strong SPD majority in the city could well swing the balance in West German politics. Adenauer, his opponents charged, was simply interested more in controlling the western portion of what had once been Germany than in uniting all of Germany or even that portion not under Soviet control.

West Berlin's bitter experience with the Communists and its continued exposed position helped to push the whole of the FRG in an anti-Communist direction. This was discussed earlier with respect to the Social Democratic party, but it was true in other ways as well. For example, Berlin was the border opening through which well over half of the 2.6 million refugees from the GDR fled in 1949–61. From reception centers in Berlin they were sent to West Germany where, after some period of relocation, they were integrated into the West German economy. The refugee problem, then, was manifold: the issue itself emphasized cold-war tensions; the refugees caused some economic dislocation, particularly in the early years but not so much after the West German economy got rolling; and they tended to support conservative movements and parties. Similarly, any time opposition politicians spoke against rearmament, West German membership in NATO, or American policies in some area of the world, conservatives could point with alarm at the continuing Soviet "threat" to West Berlin. It is probably true that West Germany would have followed the West in the cold war regardless of whether or not the Berlin problem existed. But it cannot be denied that the issue, as a highly visible reminder of an open wound, served to lend strength to those pursuing anticommunist and conservative policies.

International Costs

Internationally, Berlin as a cold-war issue had a double edge. On the one hand, it helped several states to muster domestic and foreign support for their policies—although clearly its significance was more symbolic than anything else, since the real points of international contention were far broader. During and after the blockade the West saw the city as the "beacon light of freedom in a red sea" and, as noted earlier, sought to turn it into a "showcase of democracy." Just as West German government spokesmen used the Berlin issue to rally its population to policies aligning the FRG with the West, so too it was a prominent symbol in the government's dealing with the Allies. Affirmations of support for beleaguered West Berliners became ritualistic and almost mandatory. When Kennedy failed to respond quickly and dramatically enough to the construction in August 1961 of the Berlin wall, Brandt effectively maneuvered him into a public commitment and course of action that ultimately proved to be dangerous when it led to confrontations at Checkpoint Charlie between Soviet and American tanks.[21] Kennedy's "Ich bin ein Berliner" speech in 1963 at the city hall was yet another attempt to clear away the wreckage left after his initial display of apparent indifference to the fate of the divided city. The wall was also a monument, by the way, to the ability of East Germany's leader at the time, Walter Ulbricht, to persuade Khrushchev to support GDR policies against the opposition of other Warsaw Pact states.

On the other hand, however, what was valuable for firming up alliances was also detrimental to attempts to reduce cold-war hostilities. Berlin was until 1962 the most serious and enduring hotbed of crisis in postwar Europe. But the actual issues at stake were far less important than their symbolic value. If the major antagonists of the cold war wanted to focus their attention upon other problems facing them, or if they wanted to institute an era of peaceful coexistence, then it was necessary to reduce the salience of the Berlin issue. The Soviet Union and the United States, not to speak of their non-German allies, were anxious to do just that. From the Soviet perspective, Khrushchev and his successors evidently wanted to devote more resources to the domestic economy, and the possibility of conflict with China was looming as a major issue of the future. Meanwhile, the United States was looking inward at questions of civil rights, poverty, and the cities, besides getting more deeply involved in its Southeast Asian adventure. And both were having trouble keeping their partner states in line. Given these circumstances, Germans on either side of the border who were too militant in rekindling old cold-war fires ran the risk of getting burned themselves.

Even a measure of detente proved difficult to achieve. If Khrushchev and his associates actually believed that the "free city" notion of 1958 was the way to achieve it, then they sadly misjudged the West's commitment to West Berlin. And yet, in a curious way, the eventual outcome of the 1958–62 crisis was a move toward defusing the Berlin powderkeg. To be sure, the wall and its aftermath—the confrontation of Soviet and American tanks,

21. Richard L. Merritt, "A Transformed Crisis: The Berlin Wall," in *Modern European Governments: Cases in Comparative Policy Making*, ed. Roy C. Macridis (Englewood Cliffs, N.J.: Prentice-Hall, 1968), pp. 140–73.

refugees shot and killed or left to bleed to death in the no-man's land alongside the wall, and the vituperative propaganda on both sides—served only to put Berlin in the world's spotlight once again. But other events, such as the Cuban missile crisis and the Vietnam war, eventually intervened to capture this spotlight; and, more significantly, the city's postwall situation began to be seen as "normal," if not wholly acceptable. The wall stopped the flow of refugees to West Berlin. The East German economy, which had been hit hard by the previous losses of trained personnel as well as bureaucratic inefficiency, began to move forward. West Berlin moved more to the periphery of West German life. And, beginning in late 1966, new leaders with new concepts of foreign policy stood at the helm of the West German government—leaders who saw some advantages to the FRG of detente in Central Europe. The situation was ripe for a clarification of the Berlin question.

The End of the Berlin Problem?

When Willy Brandt became chancellor after the federal election of September 1969, he initiated a far-reaching detente policy that, among other things, earned him a Nobel Peace Prize. Even as foreign minister in the grand coalition of 1966–69 he had tried to push toward relaxation of tension in Central Europe. One of his first moves in early 1967 was to take up diplomatic relations with Rumania, and a year later the FRG had resumed its interrupted ties with Yugoslavia. His push came to an abrupt halt, however. The grand coalition's senior partner, the CDU, continued to favor a policy of strength vis-a-vis the East. Ulbricht, fearing the GDR's isolation by the Federal Republic's demarche, soon began rounding up bilateral pacts with other Warsaw Pact states by which they agreed not to enter into diplomatic relations with the FRG until the latter should recognize de jure the German Democratic Republic. The final blow came in August 1968, when the Red Army moved into Czechoslovakia to snuff out the short-lived "Prague spring" of liberalization. Even so, Foreign Minister Brandt had made a significant start at a new West German foreign policy.

As chancellor, Brandt sought to balance four delicate aspects of foreign policy. He negotiated separately but simultaneously with the Soviet Union, Poland, and the GDR, meanwhile encouraging the Four Powers to negotiate on the status of Berlin. By early 1970 he had initiated the first direct contacts on a formal level that the Federal Republic had ever had with the GDR. Later in the year he signed treaties in Moscow and Warsaw that in effect recognized the territorial status quo resulting from World War II. But he also made clear that further progress toward detente, including ratification of the two treaties, would rest upon steps toward a satisfactory resolution of the Berlin problem. Four-Power talks on Berlin, however, begun in March 1970, continued to drag on.

A year and a half of the periodic meetings finally produced on 3 September 1971 a quadripartite agreement on Berlin.[22] The document sought essentially to stabilize the status quo. Its preamble stressed that the protocol did not affect the wartime and postwar agreements and decisions of the Four Powers, nor did it prejudice the legal positions that had taken; and in Part I the four governments agreed that they "will mutually respect their individual and joint rights and responsibilities, which remain unchanged." Part II and its related annexes contained the heart of the mutual adjustments. The Soviet Union agreed to the principle of unimpeded access to and from West Berlin, and specified adjustments to be worked out in detail by "the competent German authorities." It also promised ways to ease West Berliners' access to East Berlin and the GDR for periodic visits. Except in cases of serious illness or death, West Berliners had not been permitted to enter East Berlin since 1966, and East Germany since 1961 when the wall went up.

The Western Powers for their part made quite clear what the relationship between West Berlin and FRG was to be. First, they were retaining their own occupation rights in West Berlin. The city was not to be a constituent part of the Federal Republic. Those portions of the Basic Law or federal statutes that contradicted this principle would continue to be suspended, but otherwise the ties between the two areas would be maintained. Second, officers or state bodies of the Federal Republic, such as the chancellor or Bundestag committees, "will not perform in the Western Sectors of Berlin constitutional or official acts" which contradict the principle of constitutional separation. This did not preclude them from making an appearance in the city. Third, a permanent liaison agency would represent the FRG in West Berlin. Finally, and again in accordance with the principle of occupation, the Federal Republic would continue to represent West Berlin internationally.

Brandt's government accepted the agreement as "a solid basis for a satisfactory Berlin settlement." For purely practical reasons, however, it did not express overwhelming enthusiasm. The conservative opposition was already angry enough that Brandt's eastern treaties had relegated to the dustbin of history Bonn's maximum demands of the previous twenty years (and perhaps a bit envious of Brandt's successes and the honors accorded him!). Some, including West Germany's largest newspaper chain, owned by Axel Caesar Springer, mounted an active campaign against the accords and their subsequent implementation jointly by the FRG and GDR. The agreement's implicit recognition of the continued division of Germany and the legitimacy of the German Democratic Republic was intolerable to them. West German acceptance of its conditions, according to this ar-

22. Press and Information Office of the Government of the Federal Republic of Germany, *Bulletin* 19, no. 30 (4 September 1971): 225–32.

gument, would be at best unwise, if not unconstitutional and downright treasonable. The Four Powers had not resolved the territorial and other issues left over from World War II, the critics said, but had merely agreed not to disagree about them any longer. Fragmentary evidence suggests that GDR officials were not overjoyed either. The protocol had failed to make good the long-standing claim that West Berlin was on GDR soil, it failed to turn the western sectors into a "free city," and it even imposed limitations on East Germany's sovereignty by specifying what the conditions of travel through GDR territory and access to East Berlin would be. When spokesmen of the Chinese People's Republic accused the USSR of having betrayed East Germany's vital interests, it found a favorable echo in East Berlin.

Both Germanies nonetheless sat down to work out details. Even this, of course, sanctioned as it was by the quadripartite agreement, gave force to the FRG's claim to be responsible for the fate of West Berlin. On 17 December 1971 State Secretary Egon Bahr, one of the architects of Brandt's eastern policy, and GDR State Secretary Michael Kohl signed an intra-German agreement on "Transit Traffic of Civilian Persons and Goods between the Federal Republic of Germany and Berlin (West)." Less than a week later, representatives of East and West Berlin signed an agreement regulating visits to the East and making some minor border adjustments. But the serious work of implementing such arrangements had to await the West German ratification of the Moscow and Warsaw treaties.

The battle to secure the ratification of the eastern treaties proved unexpectedly bitter. Brandt's opposition in the Bundestag mounted a strenuous campaign against them that at one point threatened to topple the government. But the firmness of the Brandt government in pursuing ratification, the generally favorable climate of opinion in the Federal Republic toward the treaties, subtle pressure exerted by the Western Allies, and some timely verbal concessions by the Soviet Union and shows of good faith by the GDR (such as permitting West Berliners to visit East Berlin during the Easter and Whitsuntide holidays despite the absence of formally recognized agreements, and agreeing on 12 May to a treaty with the FRG on traffic questions) won the day. The opposition finally agreed to abstain from voting on the treaties rather than cast votes that might have returned Europe to the darkness and uncertainty of the cold war. On 17 May 1972 the Bundestag ratified the Moscow and Warsaw treaties, and, six days later, President Gustav Heinemann signed them. The way was clear for the foreign ministers of France, Great Britain, the Soviet Union, and the United States to sign, on 3 June 1972, the Berlin accords of the previous September.

Even more progress toward intra-German détente was made in late 1972. On 8 November, the FRG and GDR initialed a basic treaty defining their future relationships. The treaty itself does not mention Berlin. Both parties issued identical statements, however, extending to West Berlin any FRG–GDR cooperation in traffic, science, technology, health, culture, environmental protection, and other fields. The statements add: "The Permanent Mission of the Federal Republic of Germany in the German Democratic Republic shall, in conformity with the Quadripartite Agreement of 3 September 1971, represent the interests of Berlin (West)." In elections less than two weeks later, West Germans gave a solid majority to the coalition which, under Chancellor Willy Brandt, had broken the east-west impasse in Germany. Correctly or not, the new Brandt government has interpreted the electoral victory as a vote of confidence in its policy of détente and a mandate to work more toward easing intra-German tensions.[23]

The Berlin accords of 1971–72 contain a promise of ending the danger to international peace posed by the Berlin problem. But another dimension of the problem continues to exist: the tangled tie between the Federal Republic and West Berlin. West Berliners are still not FRG citizens and cannot vote. And yet the federal parliament will continue to enact legislation directly affecting their lives. The procedures for making federal law applicable in West Berlin will still be indirect and subject to Allied veto. The Federal Republic will still have to coordinate its overall Berlin policy with the tripartite *Kommandatura*. This gives the United States in particular a continued degree of leverage over West Germany that the latter may increasingly resent, especially should the two countries begin to differ more seriously on monetary issues, trade, and American priorities as indicated by a continued American involvement in Southeast Asia. West Berlin will still be a financial drain on the Federal Republic's resources. All these aspects will continue to limit West Germany's freedom of action both at home and abroad, and may well turn the Berlin problem into the country's major domestic political issue of the 1970s.

23. Press and Information Office of the Government of the Federal Republic of Germany, *Bulletin* 20, no. 38 (14 November 1972): 293–304.

11

Guy de Carmoy

The Politics of European Energy Policy

Western Europe is dependent on outside supply for her energy consumption. And because Western Europe is politically divided into a number of sovereign states, there is a collection of national policies rather than a single European energy policy.

The major decisions of the European states in the field of energy are both technical and political. They result from a continuous process of consultation and negotiation between the political authorities responsible for the economic policy of the state and the managers of the large private and/or nationalized corporations engaged in imports, production, and sales of the various forms of energy.

In order to explore such a complex situation, this chapter first presents and analyzes the basic facts and figures, i.e., the global and national energy balance sheets. The latter task consists of an assessment of the industrial structure of the various branches—coal, oil, natural gas, classic and nuclear electricity generation—in terms of size, capital ownership, and control. After this has been done, it is possible to define the policy goals of the major industrial countries and such shifts in these goals as may be occasioned by technological and geopolitical considerations. In order to illustrate these shifts, the case of the French energy policy is studied in greater detail. Lastly, this essay provides a brief description of past failures and an assessment of today's prospects for a European global energy policy.

Facts and Figures

Consumption

The energy picture of Western Europe has changed drastically over the last decade. Energy consumption has increased annually at a rate of 5.5 percent, i.e., faster than the rates of growth of industrial production (4.6 percent) and of the gross domestic product (4.7 percent). This increase in consumption was met by a considerable increase in oil imports, while coal production was reduced because of price competition between these two main sources of energy. Natural gas played a greater, though limited, role through the exploitation of new fields and also imports. Hydroelectricity has barely retained its share of the energy market; the most profitable sites were already exploited. As for nuclear electricity, its share is still negligible, in spite of considerable investments in research and development.

According to the latest Organization for Economic Cooperation and Development (OECD) forecasts, energy consumption will increase annually at the rate of 5.1 percent in the 1970s. This will mean more imports of oil and natural gas. Even when the nuclear investments come to bear fruit, they will not offset the decline in coal production.

Table 1 shows the tremendous shift in the consumption patterns. Hard and brown coal covered 61.5 percent of Europe's needs in 1960 and only 29.0 percent in 1970. The figures for oil are almost the reverse: 32.4 percent in 1960 and 59.2 percent in 1970. The trend will continue during the next decade, with coal expected to fall to a mere 13.0 percent and oil jumping to 63.5 percent.

Table 1. Western Europe's Consumption of Primary Sources of Energy
(In million tons of oil equivalent and in percent)

Type of Energy	1960		1970		1980[a] (projected)	
	Quantity	%	Quantity	%	Quantity	%
Solid fuels	372	61.5	303	29.0	224	13.1
Oil	197	32.4	619	59.2	1134	66.4
Natural gas	11	1.8	75	7.1	198	11.5
Hydro power	25	4.1	36	3.5	51	2.9
Nuclear power	1	0.2	11	1.2	104	6.1
Total consumption	606	100.0	1044	100.0	1711	100.0
Net imports	199.7		634		993	
Dependence on imports		32.9		60.7		58.0

[a] Estimates for 1980 from French Sixth Plan (Energy).

Source: OECD Statistics on Energy.

Production

The production of coal in Western Europe was reduced by one-fifth between 1960 and 1970. It will be further reduced by one-fourth between 1970 and 1980. Oil production was negligible (37 million tons in 1970) but is expected to rise to around 300 million tons in 1980 due to the offshore drilling in the North Sea. Natural gas production, 70 million tep (tons equivalent crude oil) in 1970, is expected to reach around 300 million tep in 1980, in part reflecting the same exploitation of North Sea reserves.

Imports

The explosion of energy consumption is linked to industrial growth and to improvements in living standards. In Western Europe demand could be met only by imports. As shown in table 2, coal and natural gas account for but a small fraction of imports. Coal is imported mostly from the United States, in the form of coking coal. Natural gas is imported from Algeria and Libya, notwithstanding intra-European trade. But the bulk of imports consists of oil from the Middle East and from North Africa (where Algeria and Libya are the major exporters).

In global terms, Europe's dependence on supplies from abroad increased from 32.9 percent in 1960 to 60.7 percent in 1970. Oil from the Middle East and North Africa accounted in 1970 for 79.2 percent of total energy imports and 50 percent of total energy consumption. These figures stress the importance of the demand-supply relationship between Western Europe on the one side and the oil-producing countries of the Middle East

Table 2. Western Europe's Imports of Primary Sources of Energy by Area (In million tons of oil equivalent and in percent)

Area of Import	1960		1970	
	Quantity	%	Quantity	%
Crude Oil				
Middle East	142.0	79.1	307.9	51.8
Algeria-Libya }	9.7	5.4	193.7	32.5
Rest of Africa }			42.7	7.0
Western Hemisphere	20.5	10.5	22.4	3.8
Eastern Europe	6.5	3.7	22.4	3.8
Other countries	2.1	1.3	7.9	1.3
Total crude oil	180.8	100.0	597.0	100.2
Natural gas	0.03		5.0	
Solid fuel	18.8		32.0	
Grand total	199.7		634.0	

Source: Statistics on Energy. Oil statistics 1970. OECD.

Table 3. Dependence on Imports
of Primary Sources of Energy (In percent)

Countries	1960	1969
Germany	8.8	42.4
Belgium	32.9	74.8
France	43.5	64.9
Italy	42.7	82.3
The Netherlands	53.4	55.4
United Kingdom	23.1	41.3
Sweden	79.3	85.0
Switzerland	71.5	78.8
OECD Europe	32.9	57.5
United States	7.0	6.0
Japan	42.0	76.0
USSR	surplus 7.0	surplus 10.0

Source: OECD, Statistics of Energy. UNO, EEC statistics.

and the Mediterranean on the other, a relationship that is bound to continue over the next decade.

What will be the proportion of energy imports in 1980? The figure will depend of course on new discoveries and especially on the resources of oil and natural gas in the North Sea. A reasonable estimate is that Europe's dependence on imports will approximate 65 percent.

In Western Europe, the two largest industrial countries—Britain and Germany—whose development was based on coal up until World War II, still retain a relatively high level (about 40 percent) of self-sufficiency. The Netherlands is already benefiting from the natural gas field in Groningen. The other industrial countries depend on imports for from three-fourths to four-fifths of their total consumption of the primary sources of energy.

The two major industrial giants are in a much more favorable position. In 1969 the Soviet Union had a surplus of supply over demand of 10 percent, and considerable reserves. In the same year the United States had a 6 percent deficit, but can tap the reserves of Canada and Alaska. The only industrial country that is more heavily dependent than Europe on external sources for its energy supply is Japan, which imports 76 percent of its consumption.

The cost of Western European imports of primary sources of energy amounted to $9 billion in 1969, i.e., 18 percent of the value of total imports (with intra-European trade excluded).

Industrial Structure

Coal

The coal industry was nationalized in France and Britain in the wave of nationalization that prevailed after World War II, which generated industrial concentration on a national basis. Charbonnages de France is a production monopoly, while the National Coal Board in Britain disposes of a monopoly both in production and in distribution. In the Netherlands the State Mines (Staatsmijnen) own half the productive capacity. Belgian and West German industries are still in private hands with a multiplicity of companies. But the coal crisis that started in Europe in 1958 has led to the closing of a large number of pits and to a drastic reduction in production. Structural reforms were necessary to implement these measures. In Belgium a Directorate of the Coal Industry was set up in 1961 entrusted with some management responsibilities at the national level. In West Germany a large consortium, Ruhrkohle AG, was created in 1968; a private company from a legal standpoint, it is charged with phasing out the federal government from production and from providing subsidies.

In short, part of the Western European coal industry has been nationalized for political reasons and the remainder has been put under state control as a consequence of crisis conditions that obtain in the industry.

Natural Gas

The natural gas industry is linked to oil insofar as exploration and production are concerned. But natural gas is distributed through the system used for the distribution of manufactured gas, which is generally treated as a public utility. Natural gas in Europe was first discovered in the Po Valley of Italy, where the bulk of the gas fields is exploited by Ente Nazionale Idrocarburi (ENI), a powerful state trust that has also expanded into oil and chemicals. The field of Lacq in France was discovered and is exploited by the Société Nationale des Pétroles d'Aquitaine, a public corporation (in the American sense of the word) and a subsidiary of the state-owned oil company, Elf-Erap. Gaz de France is the state monopoly used for the distribution of manufactured and natural gas and for imports.

In Germany the geographical dispersal of small fields has led to the dispersal of both production and distribution on a local or regional basis. The largest natural gas field on the Continent was discovered in Groningen (Netherlands) in 1960 by Nederlandsche Aardolie Maatschappij (NAM), a joint venture between the state coal mines and two oil Majors, Shell and Esso. (For a discussion of the "Seven Majors," see p. 376 of this essay.) The same partners, together with the state itself, comprise a distribution company, Nederlandsche Gasunie, which sells gas on the domestic market and to the neighboring countries of West Germany, Belgium, and France. Britain is the last country to benefit from natural gas which was discovered in the British section of the North Sea continental shelf. Concessions were granted to a number of oil companies; transportation and distribution are carried out by the Gas Council, a state monopoly.

In short, the natural gas industry is nationalized in Britain, France, and Italy, and state capital has a 50 percent share in the Netherlands. Private capital has the larger share in West Germany. But with intra-European sales of Dutch gas and imports from the Soviet Union and the Mediterranean, the industry is acquiring a more international outlook.

Classical Electricity

The wave of nationalization that hit coal and gas in Britain and in France around 1946 also encompassed electricity generation, transportation, and distribution. State monopolies were set up: the Central Electricity Generating Board (CEGB) in Britain and Electricité de France (EDF). Italy followed the French pattern in 1962 with the creation of Ente Nazionale per l'Energia Elettrica (ENEL). In the Netherlands, the greater part of electricity is produced by the coal mines and is therefore under state control. In Belgium production is free and distribution is handled by the local authorities. A conventional system was installed in 1955 with a management committee in charge of the major policy decisions under government supervision. In West Germany electricity production and distribution are carried out on a regional or a local basis. The Laender and the municipalities are either the sole or the majority owners of the capital of the corporations. The largest company, Rheinisch-Westfälische Elektrizitätswerke (RWE) produces more than one-third of the total electricity in the country.

In other words, full industrial concentration under state control has been realized in Britain, France, and Italy. The industry is dispersed in Belgium and West Germany where regional and local authorities play important parts.

Nuclear Electricity

Fission was used for armaments before it was used for power plants. This explains why nuclear industries were created on a purely national basis and why governments in almost every country played an important role in research and development from the start. For the same reason, governments were instrumental in a number of initial technical decisions, such as the choice of the type of reactor developed.

Britain was the first European country to start producing nuclear electricity. The Atomic Energy Authority, created in 1945, was in charge of military and civilian research and technical assistance for the building of reactors. Since 1969, the greater part of its nuclear research know-how has been transferred, against a share in their capital stock, to two industrial groups, British Nuclear Design and Construction Ltd. and The Nuclear Power Group Ltd. Thus a measure of concentration was realized in the reactor-construction industry. The commercial power plants are owned and operated by the Electricity Generating Boards. The nine plants operating in 1970 are of the natural uranium graphite gas type. In 1963 the decision was made not to develop this type of reactor in the future, since it was considered too expensive. New reactors will be of the AGR type (Advanced Gas Cooled Reactors), using enriched uranium.

France created, also in 1945, an agency in charge of military and civilian research and of the development of nuclear reactors up to the prototype stage, the Commissariat à l'Energie Atomique (CEA). Electricité de France operates the commercial power plants, which are of the natural uranium graphite gas type. The French government gave up this type for the same reasons as the British, but at a later date, in 1969. The new plants will be using enriched uranium. Industrial groups have been set up for the construction of reactors. Framatome (under the aegis of Schneider and using the PWR Westinghouse patents) is presently the industry leader.

Germany had no nuclear ambitions in the military field. Its efficient mechanical and electrical industry started working on the civilian use of atomic energy after 1955, when the United States decided to lift the ban on nuclear technology. Siemens became the licensee of Westinghouse and AEG the licensee of General Electric, respectively, for PWR and BWR reactors. Both companies improved the original American patents and joined forces in setting up Kraftwerkunion, a commercial company that sells both versions of enriched uranium reactors abroad. The federal and Laender governments participated in the drafting of the program and contributed to research and development.

The other European industrial countries ordered various types of reactors, but most of them were of the enriched uranium type. Their industries work in cooperation with the industrial groups in the larger countries.

On the whole, European nuclear industry has developed on a national basis, working on a diversity of techniques and types, with too many manufacturers (ten groups are producing turbines as against two in the United States). This has resulted in the predominance of American technology. And as the natural uranium type reactor was abandoned, Europe became more and more dependent on the supply of enriched uranium from the United States. At this juncture the European countries have not agreed on the building of an isotopic separation plant, nor on the technology for such a plant. As long as the reactor industry is not concentrated at the European level, it will not be able to compete with the American—except perhaps for the German industry which has proved its efficiency.

Two encouraging developments occurred in 1971. First, France, Italy, and Germany—through their producers of electricity: EDF, ENEL, and RWE (Rheinish-Westfälische Elektrizitätswerke)—agreed jointly to build fast breeder reactors in order to try both major techniques. A reactor of the Phoenix type is to be built in France around 1974–75, and one of the SNR type in Germany around 1978–79. The plants, with a capacity of 1,000 MW (megawatts), will be operated by two companies, and the three producers of electricity will be the shareholders. Electricity is to be sold in the three countries. It is most likely that the British CEGB will eventually participate in the venture.

Second, France, Germany, and Britain created a joint company for reprocessing the radioactive fuels of nuclear power plants. The company's goal is to adapt the capacity for reprocessing to the needs of the market. Plans are underway for a plant to be built in Germany once the existing plants in France and Britain are working to capacity.

Oil

The oil industry is in essence international because it operates on oilfields and in consumer markets that span many countries. The industry was first established in the United States and in Britain where, for historical reasons, the headquarters and decision centers of the larger companies are located. Of the latter (called the "Seven Majors"), five companies are American: Standard Oil of New Jersey, Standard Oil of California, Mobil, Texaco, and Gulf Oil. One company is a joint British-Dutch venture, Shell Royal Dutch, while the seventh firm is British Petroleum.

The capital stock of the Shell Royal Dutch group is in private hands, as is that of the five American firms. The British government owns 49 percent of the capital of British Petroleum. The French government owns 35 percent of Compagnie Française des Pétroles and is sole owner of a state company launched in 1966, Elf-Erap. As mentioned above, ENI is the Italian government's trust for oil and natural gas. By contrast, the Belgian Petrofina company is in private hands. There is no sizable West German oil group.

The strength of the Majors lies in their position in the Middle East where 70 percent of the proven reserves are concentrated. The five American Majors account for 56 percent of the Middle East production and BP and Shell together account for 33 percent.

This situation is reflected in the refining capacity in Europe. Obviously BP and Shell are in a very strong position in Britain, but they also account for 25 percent of the refining capacity of the European Economic Community. The share of the American Majors in the same area is 30 percent and that of the American independents 5 percent. This leaves 40 percent for the European national companies.

The French companies were leading in Algeria, but a 51 percent nationalization in 1971 has deprived them of the greater part of their reserves. ENI has not been very successful in its exploration. Petrofina and Hydro Norske struck it rich in the North Sea, as did several Majors. But the proven reserves to date are a trickle compared to those of the Middle East.

In terms of the production of crude oil and in terms of total sales, the European national companies are more readily compared with the

American independents than with the Seven Majors. The financial structure of the Majors is much stronger than that of the European national companies, which do not have substantial access to the rich Middle East reserves and are not of a size that would allow for the maximum economies of scale. The profitability of the European national companies is therefore lower and they cannot meet the bulk of their investment needs from self-financing.

General Appraisal

The energy industries in Western European countries are oligopolistic, largely state-owned, and suffering from major economic and political weaknesses.

Oligopoly in energy is not a distinctively European feature. It derives from two main factors. On the one hand, the operation of coal mines, of oil and gas prospection, production, transportation, refining, and distribution requires very large capital outlays. Without adequate financial resources, these industries would not achieve economies of scale and would be unable to meet the demand for cheap energy. They are, therefore, of a highly capital-intensive character. On the other hand, nationalization has reduced the number of competitors. Several coal, gas, and electricity companies are in a monopoly position in their own branch of their domestic market and compete only with other branches inside this market. In the oil business, competition often exists between one or two national companies and two or more Majors on each individual market. Because of differences in taxation and varieties of subsidy programs, there is no such thing as a European market for energy, even within EEC.

About three-fourths of the assets of the energy industries are state-owned in three out of four of the larger Western countries (Britain, France, Italy). This has some impact on policy making: state agencies often debate between themselves. And it also influences policy goals: energy being nationalized, energy policy tends to become nationalistic.

But the major policy considerations derive from the intrinsic weaknesses of the European energy industries. The weakness in coal reflects geological factors which limit the mechanization of the mines and raises the costs. The decline of coal seems irreversible; the cost of increasing output is greater than the reasonable cost of an insurance premium. The weakness in nuclear energy is caused by a technological gap and a fragmented structure. American technology has prevailed in reactor construction because Europe had too many types of reactors and too many constructors working on small markets. Enriched uranium must be purchased from the United States because the European states have not pooled their resources to manufacture it.

The weaknesses in oil can be traced to both geographic and financial reasons. The bulk of the proven reserves are in the Middle East and they are controlled by the Majors, five of which are American. Oil concessions are very vulnerable. The producer countries have been very successful in having their demands in terms of taxes, prices, and ownership met by the companies. In 1971 the members of OPEC (Organization of the Petroleum Exporting Countries) wrung substantial royalty increases from the oil companies, so that the oil revenues of the Middle Eastern and North African states will more than double between 1970 and 1975. The companies have passed on the increase in their costs in the producer countries to the users in the consumer countries, who are now paying higher fuel prices. Furthermore, in 1972, the Majors agreed to the takeover by the states concerned of 20 percent of the capital stock of their operating companies in the producer countries. Thus, Western Europe is dependent for half of the energy it consumes on sources over which it has only a limited financial control (insofar as five of the seven Majors are American) and no political control.

National Energy Policies

Energy Policy Goals

National energy policies depend on the structural features of the various energy sectors and on the relationship between needs and reserves. From a theoretical angle, energy policy consists of directing the investments of the various sectors according to the long-range prospects of the resources, the substitution possibilities, and the development costs. The economic optimum corresponds to the equalization of marginal costs of competing forms of energy.

But economic considerations of lower costs may conflict with the social optimum because of changes in plant location and job distribution. Further, economic and social considerations cannot be isolated from the political goal of ensuring the security of energy supplies in the long-range perspective. It is in light of these general goals that this brief survey of the policies of several European industrial countries is presented.

Britain

For a variety of reasons, Britain is the country with the most favorable energy balance sheet in Western Europe. Increase in oil consumption was not as rapid in Britain as in Germany because the growth of British industrial production was slower. The discoveries of natural gas and, to a lesser extent, oil in the North Sea are increasing the domestic share of fuel in total energy consumption. Considerable investments have been made in nuclear electricity, the share of which in power generation is greater than in any other industrial country. In spite of the reduction in production, coal still accounted for 51 percent of primary energy consumption in 1969. In short, Britain's is becoming a four-fuel economy.

The protection of coal consists of incentives for the use of coal in power plants and by government departments and agencies; the banning of coal imports; and the taxation of oil burned by power plants, industries, and private consumers. About two-thirds of the output of electricity is coal-fired. But a shortage of coal in 1971 led to the maximizing of the consumption of oil in power plants.

The two major oil companies pursue a policy of diversification. This was traditional for Shell, and the successive Middle East crises have induced BP to follow the same line. BP successfully penetrated the profitable American consumer market and found large oil reserves in Alaska.

The first nuclear power program was completed in 1969 with natural uranium stations. The new AGR-type stations of the second program are under construction.

White Papers on fuel policy set the guidelines for several years at a time. The most recent of these was published in 1967, and another is presently in development. While the Cabinet and Parliament are, formally, the ultimate arbiters in this—as in all other—policy sector, the minister of trade and industry has policy-making authority in this area, having succeeded the minister for power in this function.

The nationalized industries submit important investment proposals to the government, and the government sets the financial targets of the nationalized industries. When the government set rates at a level below that expected by the industry the price of the public enterprise's output fell, which stimulated demand. This led the industries to fall short of the hoped-for targets.

In the oil industry the companies choose their own financial targets, but they must consult with the government on such domestic investments as the location of refineries and oil pipelines, and also on such matters as storage capacity.

West Germany

Like the British, the German economy was based on coal in the 1950s. This pattern changed drastically in the 1960s, when coal ran second to oil (38 percent as against 53 percent by 1970).

For a long time the fuel policy of Germany consisted in protecting coal from oil by a variety of devices: subsidies to the mines, taxation on imported coal, discriminatory taxation on oil, subsidies to public transport, etc. A more direct intervention took place in 1968 when the federal government induced the owners of the Ruhr coal mines, many of them private companies linked with the steel industry, to create a single coal consortium, Ruhrkohle AG. This consortium has the power to reduce and streamline production and to make the best possible use of the federal subsidies Since its inception, Ruhrkohle AG has been encountering great difficulties: successive rises in salaries have increased costs; the price of coal is less and less competitive with that of oil; the banks are more and more reluctant to grant credits; the shareholders will have to give up dividends and the government to increase subsidies. The consortium seems to be evolving from the status of a private to that of a nationalized corporation.

West Germany is the only large European country with no state share in a national oil company. Only recently the government decided to encourage several private companies with diversified interests in energy to pool their resources with a view toward developing exploration and production of oil and natural gas overseas.

The government was instrumental in bolstering a contract with the Soviet Union for massive purchases of natural gas, to be paid for through the supply of pipes by the Ruhr steel industry. The launching of the German *Ostpolitik* was certainly a precondition to such a deal.

In the nuclear field, the policy of the two major mechanical and electrical companies, Siemens and AEG, was to adopt and improve American technology. This decision by the industry was profitable to the manufacturer and saved a lot of money for the taxpayer, who did not have to foot the bill for the natural uranium types of reactors that had proved unsuccessful in Britain and in France. The government has discussed five-year atomic development programs with the companies concerned and has allocated funds to private research centers especially for research on breeder reactors.

In summary, after a period of laissez faire consonant with the well-known *Freimarktwirtschaft* philosophy, Germany is engaged in an active energy policy. Thanks to its strong mechanical industry, it is already the leader in nuclear electricity in Europe. In spite of this, its energy balance sheet will remain dependent upon considerable imports of oil and natural gas.

Italy

Italy has no coal, some hydroelectricity, and medium-size fields of natural gas. Its imports amount to 82 percent of Italian consumption of primary sources of energy.

Enrico Mattei, the first manager of ENI, the state trust for natural gas and oil, was quick to realize that Italy's main need was to import cheaply. He bought cheap oil where he found it, in the Soviet Union or in the Middle East. But ENI was not as successful in exploration as in trade. In the domestic field, ENI and the Majors each own about one-half of the refining capacity of the country and export to Southern European countries about one-quarter of the petroleum products they process.

Italy also imports natural gas. The production of the Po Valley fields has reached its ceiling and cannot meet demands. Contracts have been concluded or are under discussion with Libya, the Netherlands, the Soviet Union, and Algeria.

ENI, Montedison, and Fiat are active in the nuclear power industry. However, their policy is based on cooperation with American or European constructors of reactors, and Italian self-sufficiency is not contemplated.

In summary, Italy has deliberately opted for a cheap energy policy, when one considers that the security of supplies is a problem that goes beyond the national level. The ENI group is very influencial on government decisions concerning all branches of energy. The electricity trust ENEL is partly dependent on ENI for its oil-fired power plants, and the Majors have to negotiate with ENI for their share in the refinery cake. It follows that ENI is in a position of quasi monopoly, in contrast to the oligopoly situation prevailing in Britain and in France.

Decision Making and Policy Issues in France

The Decision-Making Process

Directly or indirectly, the government is able to control the whole energy sector. State-owned corporations exert a monopoly on the production and distribution of electricity (EDF) and natural gas (GDF), and on the production of coal (Charbonnages de France). A government agency is in charge of research and development of civilian and military uses of the atom (CEA). Two national oil companies (CFP and Elf-Erap) cover one-half of the French market. The state holds the monopoly for oil imports under legislation dating from 1928. The operation of the monopoly is delegated in the form of quotas to French and foreign oil companies under close government supervision.

The management of each large nationalized semiprivate or private corporation has its own conception of what should be the corporate goals within the framework of the French energy policy. The government, represented by the minister of industry and the minister of economy and finance, sets national goals taking into consideration the physical and social environment in a regional setting and the political environment in a geostrategical setting. In practice, there are three levels of decision making at which negotiations take place between corporate management and government officials: rates, yearly investments, and long-range planning.

The rates of the various sources of energy are approved by government authority. In the case of electricity, this means selling current at marginal development cost. Obviously this principle cannot apply to coal, the relative cost of which is continuously rising. The price of petroleum is subject to government approval.

Charbonnages de France runs a heavy deficit, which is covered by a subsidy from the national budget. EDF and GDF rates are fixed in such a way that these companies cannot meet more than 30 percent of their investment needs through self-financing. The oil companies have more leeway and, with the exception of Elf-Erap, finance 50 to 55 percent of their investments by their profits.

The investment programs of the nationalized industries are discussed each year at the board of the Fonds de Développement Economique et Social, a development fund financed by the budget. The board decides the amount of low-interest loans to be allocated to each corporation. The surplus of needs is financed by floating bonds on the financial market at the current interest rate. CEA expenditure is entirely covered by appropriations from the budget. As for Elf-Erap, its overseas investments are partly financed by a special tax on petroleum products.

Following an inquiry into the management of nationalized industries, the government is now changing its traditional relationship with its industrial partners. The shift is from "tutelage" to contract. Under the new arrangement, the corporation is committed to certain targets in given economic conditions. In return, the state grants to the corporation stable taxes and rates and a minimum of investment finance per year and gives up any form of "a priori" control. The corporation is free to use the supplementary profit its management is able to generate. The first contract of this type was concluded in 1971 with EDF.

The long-range goals of the energy policy are discussed in the Energy Committee of the Plan de Modernisation et d'Equipement, the name for the five-year development plan. The Sixth Plan is now in operation, covering the period 1971–75. Technical and political developments sometimes lead government authorities to make basic policy changes during the life of a plan. Such was the case with the two most important goals of the French energy policy: the nuclear power reactor and Algerian oil.

Nuclear Reactors

In 1958 no final choice had been made as to the type of reactors to be used on a commercial basis by EDF. The scientists in CEA favored the natural uranium graphite gas type. They were backed by those political circles who wanted to dispense with the American-imported enriched uranium. This school of thought easily found its way to the "Elysées Palace."

As early as 1964, some technicians at EDF believed that the French type of reactor could never compete with the American. The cost per kilowatt hour was 15 percent higher. A special committee was appointed to report on nuclear electricity production. In 1967 the committee advised against the natural uranium type. The matter was discussed at a Cabinet meeting, and the ministers directly involved were prepared to follow the advice of the committee. The president of the Republic himself decided otherwise, however; and production of the French type of reactor was set in motion.

The decision of principle was taken in conjunction with the launching of tenders for a 900-MW nuclear power station at Fessenheim near the Rhine. The tenders confirmed the forecasts of the report, and the building of the plant was postponed because of the financial constraints. In October 1969, with another incumbent at the Elysées, the original decision was reversed. EDF was authorized to launch tenders on the basis of the two American techniques, PWR and BWR.

Increases in the price of oil in 1970 and actions taken by the oil-producing countries in 1971 induced the government to increase from 4,000 to 8,000 MW the power of the nuclear reactors to be built during the life of the Sixth Plan.

Algerian Oil

The decision to explore the Sahara south of Algeria proved to be a good bet: oil and gas were found in the late 1950s, although not in as large quantity or as cheap as in Libya. Production developed during and after the Algerian war. But the 1962 Evian Accords—separating Algeria from France—included the Sahara and its oilfields in the boundaries of the new Algerian state, although existing concessions granted to French and foreign oil companies were retained.

In 1965 a special agreement granted Algeria substantial advantages in matters of taxes, exploration, production, and outlets for Algerian oil and natural gas. Prices higher than those of the market had to be paid by the refineries operating in France, whether they belonged to French or to foreign companies. All companies were obliged to import large amounts of Algerian crude. Gaz de France was likewise obliged to buy Algerian natural gas at a very high price. The 1965 agreement was a political one. France considered Algeria a key state for its policy of cooperation with developing countries; energy policy was subordinated to the policy of cooperation. Elf-Erap, under the chairmanship of Pierre Guillaumat (since 1958 the main adviser to the president of the Republic on all energy matters), was a major instrument of that policy and had to invest heavily in Algeria.

In 1970 Algeria decided unilaterally to increase the price of oil and let it be known that it intended to nationalize French oil companies operating in Algeria. The French government opposed both requests in protracted negotiations. In March 1971 the Algerian government went ahead and nationalized 51 percent of the assets of the oil companies. The French government broke off negotiations between the two states, emphasizing that the "privileged cooperation" between France and Algeria had come to an end. It was left to the French oil companies, CFP and Elf-Erap, to work out arrangements as best they could with the Algerian oil trust, Sonatrach. The French companies lost the greater part of their reserves of crude oil in deals which were concluded, respectively, in the summer (by CFP) and in the fall (by Elf-Erap) of 1971.

What of a European Energy Policy?

The European Communities

Each of the three European institutions has within its sphere of competence a segment of the energy sector. The European Coal and Steel Community (ECSC) is responsible for coal; Euratom for nuclear electricity; and the European Economic Community (EEC) deals with classical electricity, oil, and natural gas. The Treaty of Rome provides for dealing with or developing a global energy policy for Europe.

The 1959 coal crisis was a test for ECSC. Corrective measures were taken, particularly in the case of Belgium, on a national and not on a community level.

Euratom hoped to develop a strong nuclear industry in Europe. But national research and development programs prevailed over the declining resources allotted to the institution. The larger states used different technologies for their nuclear power stations, at very high cost in the cases of Britain and France. The advanced nuclear reactor project, Orgel, developed by Euratom, was not adopted by any member state. Furthermore, each state earmarked all public contracts for its national industry, thus preventing specialization and concentration in the field of reactors.

Concerning oil, EEC was unable to induce the member states to adopt the same rules for the import of crude oil and for harmonizing internal taxes on petroleum products. Supply prices also differed from country to country. In point of fact, there was *no* common market for oil.

EEC made several stabs at defining a global approach to energy policy. The last one consisted of a report issued in 1968, entitled "First Orientation for a Common Energy Policy." This document was a list for data collection and a series of recommendations for joint action—it is unimplemented to date.

Nineteen years after the signing of the Treaty of Paris, and fifteen after that of Rome, there is still no free circulation of energy sources and of some of the connected equipment. No common energy policy has been agreed upon for the simple reason that the European states consider energy policy as one of their fundamental preserves and responsibilities. The question remains whether this responsibility can best be met singlehandedly. The 1971 Middle East oil crisis provides a discouraging answer.

OPEC and the Majors

Western Europe and the producer countries of the Middle East and North Africa are linked by a close supply-and-demand relationship. Western Europe depends on supplies from these areas for 85 percent of its oil imports (and 50 percent of its total primary energy consumption). It is also by far the largest purchaser of oil from these areas (around 70 percent).

The Middle East and North Africa are contested zones of influence between the two superpowers. American influence is receding and Soviet influence is growing. Thus Western Europe's supplies of a basic commodity come from a group of countries on which its direct influence is marginal. Furthermore, half the oil exported by these countries is produced and shipped by the five American Majors, and only one-third by the European Majors, BP and Shell. The oil companies are linked to the various producer countries by concession contracts.

The respective goals of the producer and transit countries are to increase their oil income through taxes and export prices, and sooner or later to nationalize the foreign oil companies. One means used to reach the latter goal was the establishment and support of national companies which in turn gained experience in the technical and trade aspects of the oil industry. Another means was to use the Organization of Petroleum Exporting Countries (OPEC) to conduct collective negotiations with the companies and especially with the Majors. The latter revived the oil cartel of the interwar period, so that the negotiations which took place in January 1971 were not between producer and consumer countries but between OPEC and the Majors.

The leader among the companies was BP at its London headquarters. Oilmen kept in touch with the main consumer governments: the United States, Britain, the Netherlands, France, etc. The companies were prepared to accept a rise in taxes and prices, provided the concession system would be assured for some time. A five-year agreement was concluded. As noted, it amounted to the doubling of the oil revenues over that period for the producer states concerned.

A new wave of claims was launched in September 1971. The producer states asked for and were promptly granted a compensation for the dollar devaluation which was then taking place. They also asked for the takeover of 20 percent of the assets of all foreign oil companies that benefited from concessions on their territory. The major oil companies agreed to this regarding the Persian Gulf states in March 1972, subject to a discussion of the basis for compensation.

Meanwhile, a number of similar incidents took place. Libya decided to nationalize completely British Petroleum's assets, on the ground that Britain had encouraged Iran's takeover of some islands in the Persian Gulf.

Iraq threatened to withdraw part of its concession to the Iraq Petroleum Company if the production of crude oil was not increased in 1972 to the level of the previous year. Saudi Arabia expressed dissatisfaction with a 20 percent takeover and requested a 51 percent participation in the capital stock of Aramco.

With all these setbacks, it is obvious that the Western European countries do not have a collective organization to match OPEC and have not used the European Economic Community to this effect, and that a considerable transfer of wealth is taking place from Western Europe to the Middle East and North Africa.

Politics and Policy

The negotiation between OPEC and the Majors is only the tip of the iceberg. The geostrategic oil game involves four actors: (1) the United States, (2) the Soviet Union, (3) the producer countries of the Middle East and North Africa, and (4) the consumer states of Western Europe.

The United States' influence rests on two pillars: the Sixth Fleet in the Mediterranean, and the concessions of the Majors in the producer countries. The Soviet Union is also showing its naval strength in the Mediterranean. It is intervening in the oil and gas markets by direct purchases and by authorizing purchases through the Eastern European states. Furthermore, the Soviet Union is now selling—and will be selling more—oil and natural gas to several Western European countries. Its geographical extension from Iran to the Elbe (for all practical purposes) allows it to have such a diversified strategy, with many possibilities for intervention on Western Europe's energy supplies.

The strategy of the producer countries has already been described. The producers adopted a common stand in a seller's market. Short of a world economic crisis, the consumption of oil and gas is bound to increase in Western Europe over the next decade. The position of the producer countries will therefore remain strong. Western Europe, being on the demand side, will, by contrast, remain in a weak position as long as it does not carry the weight of a bulk purchaser.

Why was Western Europe unable to evolve a strategy of its own? One explanation for the present vacuum is that the European countries have been relying on American military and economic protection. Another is that EEC was not the proper forum for mapping a strategy, because the centers of decision of the Majors were in New York and in London and because France was playing its own game in Algeria. With Britain in EEC and with France in the same position as her partners, the Community will have more authority.

It is up to Western Europe to assume the responsibility of its political and economic relations with its main suppliers of energy. This involves also the development of a common view on economic relations with the United States and with the Soviet Union. Because of the repercussion of the price of energy on costs and on the balance of current accounts, energy supply is becoming a major foreign policy issue. It is to be hoped that the Europeans will build the decision-making instruments such a policy requires.

Stephen Blank

Afterword: The Future of European Studies*

After years of relative neglect, interest in Western Europe among American social scientists began a slow revival in the middle 1960s. A number of new programs designed to encourage a greater interest in contemporary Western European society and politics were established, largely with support from the Ford Foundation. A Western European division was set up in the Foreign Area Fellowship Program in 1964 to support dissertation research. Western European studies programs were begun at several major American universities and, in 1970, a coordinating organization—the Council for European Studies—was formed.[1]

This revival has been quite limited, however, and its wider effects are just beginning to be felt. No sense of national purpose, such as that which motivated the post-Sputnik surge of support for training in the natural sciences or the early National Defense Education Act programs, has been associated with efforts to improve our understanding of contemporary Western European society and politics. Instead, these efforts come precisely at a time when general interest in Europe seems to be declining.

Funds are in short supply for all programs in higher education, and programs in international education are among the most vulnerable of all. Of these, programs concerned with Western Europe are the most recent and weakest. The U.S. Office of Education and the Ford Foundation have

*Earlier drafts of this essay were discussed with a number of individuals who helped develop these ideas. Raymond Grew, Leon Lindberg, Joseph LaPalombara, and Nicholas Wahl tried to keep me on the right track, although the responsibility for the essay, of course, is mine.

1. The Ford Foundation also supported a number of programs in Europe, the most important of which—the European Consortium for Political Research—was formed in the spring of 1970.

recently announced new programs that will provide support for research and training activities that involve Western Europe, and the new German Marshall Fund will provide additional external support for European studies. But the overall amount of external support for European studies remains small, and is likely to make no permanent impact unless a substantially greater amount of support can be generated within our universities, an extremely difficult task in the present situation.

Before looking at this revival of interest in Europe in more detail, and at its strengths and weaknesses, we ought to ask the more basic question of why we should attempt to promote a greater interest in Western Europe at all. Several reasons seem particularly important:

1. *Reasons of international politics.* The reemergence of Western Europe as a world power demands that there be a large pool of scholars in this country expert in the various aspects of Western European society and politics. No area of the world is so vital in the long run to American interests as Europe, and no part of the world has experienced such rapid and extensive change since the end of World War II. Yet we know little about the impact this growing power is likely to have on American and world politics in the next decade. A generally low level of interest in Europe's postwar development, together with a relatively large community of European social scientists who came to this country after the war and maintained a European presence here, were factors that helped support the view that the existing level of expertise on Europe in the United States was sufficient to meet all demands. The fact is, however, that efforts during the last twenty years to ensure the replacement of the older Europeans by younger American scholars and to sharpen our intellectual resources for dealing with Europe have hardly corresponded to national needs.

2. *Europe offers the most important long-term case study of economic and political modernization and development.* Many central issues examined by American social scientists in the past decade have dealt with national development. Social scientists began to study the non-Western world in an effort to move beyond the descriptive approach that had characterized earlier comparative work on Western Europe. They sought to apply more rigorous scientific standards to their work and to develop a general theory of comparative politics. Increasingly, however, intellectual difficulties involved in the development of general theory and the practical problems of inadequate data to support a more rigorous approach to comparative politics have encouraged a notable "return to Europe." The theoretical and methodological achievements associated with the earlier movement away from Western Europe can, in fact, be most effectively tested and evaluated within the European context.[2] Thus, the need to study

2. L. W. Pye and K. K. Ryland, "Activities of the Committee on Comparative Politics, 1954–70," in *Committee on Comparative Politics, A Report of the Activities of the Committee, 1954–70* (New York: Social Science Research Council, March 1971).

the European experience of national development is rapidly becoming critical in the broad, interdisciplinary field of political modernization and development.

3. *Europe provides the best laboratory for studying problems associated with the future development of advanced industrialized societies.* To an ever greater extent, the advanced industrial nations of Europe and North America are coming to share certain structural similarities as a consequence of economic, social, political, and technological development. Numerous problems of national public policy—economic management, welfare systems, the environment—are common to all. It is vital that past experiences be systematically compared and evaluated, and that future options be explored and tested in a context of the widest array of relevant national settings. Furthermore, many policy dilemmas of worldwide impact— from population to pollution—demand collaborative study and problem solving among the countries of Western Europe and North America, which are in many cases the only ones in a position to propose and implement solutions.

The growing interest in the study of the impact of public policy involves a newly awakened interest in contemporary European society and politics. Increasingly, scholars look at Europe while studying problems and policies which are common to *all* highly industrialized societies rather than as a separate and esoteric field of study. Increasingly, that is, we are drawn to study the European experience as we seek to learn more about the problems that face our own society.

4. *The development of the European scholarly community.* The European scholarly community is expanding rapidly and becoming far more international in its interests—both within Europe and in Europe's dealings with other parts of the world—and far more methodologically sophisticated. The scholarly communities of Europe and North America are the main centers of social science today. American scholars are able, and will continue to be able, to offer much to their colleagues in Europe, particularly in terms of modern social science methodology. Europeans have much to teach Americans, too, especially as Europeans develop their own techniques and style of modern social science research. We cannot assume that Europeans will continue to be relatively passive followers and imitators of American techniques, or that communication between Americans and Europeans will continue to take place on American terms. There is a vital need to ensure the constant cross-fertilization of the two intellectual communities and enormous rewards to be gained in this dialogue, but it will require a far more conscious effort than has been made in the past to maintain an equal and balanced relationship between the two.

The Council for European Studies, in cooperation with the Institute of International Studies of the U.S. Office of Education, is conducting a survey of European studies in the United States. We are still gathering data, but the outline of the situation is beginning to emerge clearly. Our data confirm that remarkably little attention has been directed to the study of contemporary Western European society and politics and that, though interest in Europe seems now to be increasing, the available intellectual resources bearing upon the study of contemporary Europe are still quite thin.

One component of the survey involves an analysis of dissertations completed in recent years in the social sciences. In political science, for example, the number of dissertations completed (as reported by the American Political Science Association) rose from 329 in 1966 to 810 in 1971. Much of this increase was concentrated in a few subfields of the discipline, particularly in American state and local politics and in foreign and comparative politics. In 1965 and 1966 dissertations in foreign and comparative politics accounted for about 26 percent of the total dissertations completed. In 1967 the figure rose sharply to almost 36 percent, and has remained in the lower 30s. This reflects the bulge of non-Western area dissertations coming through the pipeline after 1966, when the effects of the National Defense Education Act began to be felt. In several world areas, especially East Asia and the Middle East, dissertation completions increased at an extraordinary pace during this period. Dissertations dealing with Western Europe also increased, but at a considerably slower rate. In 1966 dissertations completed on the "underdeveloped" nations (Africa, Asia, the Middle East) accounted for 8.7 percent of the total and dissertations on Western Europe for about 6 percent. In 1972 dissertations on Western Europe had declined to a bit more than 5 percent, while those on Africa, Asia, and the Middle East rose to 13 percent.

The number of dissertations on Western Europe rose from 20 in 1966 to 42 in 1971, but the countries studied remained extremely limited. A heavy

Table 1. Political Science Dissertations Completed by World Area[a]

World Area	1966 N (% of Total)	1971 N (% of Total)
Africa	8 (2.4)	27 (3.3)
East Asia	6 (1.8)	30 (3.7)
Eastern Europe	6 (1.8)	23 (2.8)
Latin America	16 (4.8)	50 (6.2)
Middle East	3 (0.9)	16 (2.0)
South Asia	5 (1.5)	16 (2.0)
Southeast Asia	7 (2.1)	16 (2.0)
Western Europe	20 (6.1)	42 (5.2)

[a]These figures show dissertations listed under the "Foreign and Comparative" heading only. A substantial number of dissertations listed under the "International Politics and Organizations" heading also have an area focus, but it is often difficult to place them in a single world area. Our final report, which will be available in the spring of 1973, will cover this.

majority of Western European dissertations focus on France, Germany, Italy, or the United Kingdom.

Finally, until very recently, dissertations on Western Europe have been heavily concentrated at a few universities. Between 1966 and 1971, only eight universities produced five or more dissertations on Western Europe. These eight accounted for some 44 percent of the total number of dissertations completed on Western Europe and two of them—Harvard and Columbia—themselves produced more than 20 percent of the total. Signs of change are more evident here, however. The number of universities that produced dissertations on Western Europe is rising significantly. In 1966 eleven universities recorded a completed dissertation on Western Europe, while in 1971, 27 universities produced a completed dissertation.

The situation in history is similar. Although modern European history is the second largest subfield of the discipline (about 45 percent of dissertations completed, recorded by the American Historical Association, deal with American history, and about 30 percent deal with Europe from the close of the medieval period), a remarkably small percentage—about 7 percent—deal with Western Europe since 1914. As in political science, the coverage by country is extremely concentrated, with almost all completed dissertations dealing with France, Germany, Italy, and the United Kingdom.

In other social science fields being studied in the survey—economics, sociology, anthropology, and geography—the situation is bleaker. It is possible to identify certain limited subfields in which there has been a traditional interest in Western Europe, and we see new lines of interest now emerging, but, so far as we can learn from the completion of dissertations, interest in Western Europe remains very thin in these areas of the social sciences.

I do not want to put too much weight on these individual statistics. The data collected by the various professional associations are admittedly not complete, and our own classification systems are not infallable. But the outline is clear. In the fields of political science and history, where by far the greatest interest in contemporary Western Europe lies, we find that only about 6 percent of the dissertations completed between 1966 and 1971 deal with Western Europe in the twentieth century. The actual figures, all errors considered, might be somewhat greater—say 7 percent or even 7.5 percent (assuming we missed as much as 20 percent in our count, which seems unlikely). But the conclusion is the same. Far less attention has been paid to Western Europe than most of us had thought. As far as we can tell, for example, only about twenty dissertations in history and political science have been completed since 1966 on Italy in the twentieth century—covering First World War, Fascism, Second World War, Political Parties, Postwar Recovery. Perhaps ten have been completed on Sweden, and less than five on Spain.

Table 2. Country Coverage of Western European Dissertations

Country	1966	1967	1968	1969	1970	1971
European Community	1	2	4	2	3	1
France	3	2	5	7	8	6
Germany	4	6	6	3	10	14
Italy	3	2	0	4	5	3
United Kingdom	5	5	7	4	7	9
Other	4	12	8	9	7	9
Total	20	29	30	29	40	42

Table 3. Dissertations Completed in History, 1965-70

	1965	1966	1967	1968	1969	1970
General	0	7	14	18	12	18
Historiography	8	4	5	7	2	7
Ancient	5	0	0	2	5	5
Medieval	33	17	10	15	14	17
Modern Europe						
Early (to 1715)	31	13	14	16	31	44
1715–1814	29	13	20	10	8	25
1815–1914	86	37	45	37	25	66
1914–present						
Austria	0	0	0	0	0	0
Belgium	1	0	0	0	0	1
Denmark	0	0	0	0	0	0
Finland	0	0	0	0	0	0
France	6	4	6	1	2	8
Germany (East and West)	15	6	13	4	8	16
Greece	0	1	0	0	0	0
Iceland	0	0	0	0	0	0
Ireland	0	0	0	0	0	0
Italy	2	0	0	0	1	0
Luxembourg	0	0	0	0	0	0
Netherlands	0	0	0	0	0	0
Norway	0	0	0	0	1	0
Portugal	0	0	0	0	0	0
Spain	1	0	0	0	0	1
Sweden	0	0	0	1	0	0
Switzerland	0	0	0	0	0	0
United Kingdom	5	6	1	2	2	9
Eastern Europe	9	1	5	0	0	11
Other (unlisted)	0	0	0	0	0	0
Nonspecific	7	5	5	11	10	11
Near East	1	3	3	6	2	7
Africa	15	5	7	18	13	21
Asia	42	9	17	22	23	33
Latin America	23	20	16	16	15	24
United States (all categories)	248	176	144	194	129	270
Others	18	9	0	1	0	4
Total	539	335	324	381	303	598

Interest in Western Europe has been inhibited by two factors. In the first place, the field has been dominated by traditional descriptive social science methodology. Attempts to break out of this approach led to the growth of interest in the non-Western world. It is clear now, however, that Europe offers a fertile area for utilizing many of the new techniques and methodologies developed in the past ten or fifteen years in the non-Western world, as well as those which have been limited thus far to the American context.[3]

The second factor inhibiting scholarly activity in Western Europe has been the scarcity of resources. Scholars at all stages in their careers have found it difficult to support research and training efforts in Western Europe. Obviously, however, the problem is not a lack of total resources. At first glance, it is difficult to believe that there could be any shortage of scholars, students, or other resources that support interests in Europe, or that American scholars do not have at their disposal sufficient resources to support every training and research effort necessary to ensure a constant supply of specialists on Europe and a steady flow of information about Europe. Our universities possess an enormous and expensive infrastructure of courses, departments, and programs concerned in one way or another with Western Europe. This has certainly been the view of most donor agencies in the United States, and is the major reason why Western Europe was excluded from almost all support under the NDEA program.

But for all of this infrastructure, the output of trained scholars and of accumulated knowledge about contemporary Western Europe has been very small. We have not provided the foundation for a community of scholars here and in Europe who can bring the intellectual resources at their command to focus upon the problems that confront our societies today.

As executive director of the Council for European Studies, I have had the opportunity to visit many universities and to observe the resources that support various European-oriented activities. I often feel as though I were wandering through a huge, ancient factory. Such an enormous capital investment! And yet, what does it produce? The case of European studies is like that of an old business or of our universities themselves. We are worth a great deal on paper, but our capital is tied up in old commitments and activities, and little is left to meet new needs and opportunities.

The problem is not that which was faced by the non-Western area studies programs—of developing entirely new resources for dealing with previously unstudied parts of the world. Our problem instead is to find new ways of using more effectively and efficiently many resources that already exist. It is to break loose existing resources from old structures, and ensure that they can be used more flexibly than in the past. In many ways, this is a more challenging problem. Several examples come quickly to mind.

3. The growing interest of the Inter-university Consortium for Political Research in Western Europe strongly supports this conclusion.

1. *Language training.* Another dimension of the CES/OE survey deals with language training. We are studying the ways in which social scientists who have recently completed work (mainly dissertations) in Western Europe acquired language skills. Our hypothesis is that they are less likely to have developed language skills through the regular language programs at their home universities than in less conventional ways. The hypothesis rests upon the views of many senior scholars in Western Europe and the United States concerning the inadequate language preparation of graduate students in the social sciences and history. CES has invested a substantial proportion of its resources during the past two years in its Pre-Dissertation Training Program, one of the main functions of which is to provide language training for graduate students intending to do dissertation research in Europe during the next year. Modern European language departments at most of our universities have not been especially interested in providing research-oriented language training for students and scholars whose primary interests lie elsewhere. They might maintain cram courses, which can help a graduate student get through a departmental reading examination, but language departments have their own professional interests—literary criticism, some technical linguistic concerns, etc.—and often refuse to discuss courses and programs to develop research skills for scholars in other fields.

2. *Library resources.* To a very great extent, our holdings of contemporary European materials in this country represent an enormously expensive multiplication of a single mediocre collection. Each major library collects the same things as the others; none collects certain important materials. We are not keeping up, for example, with nonnational European newspapers—the regional, city, and functional press—or in documenting materials from political parties and interest groups, or records of the new, semipublic institutions, such as those involved in economic planning like the NEDC in England or the Commissariat du Plan in France. Individual scholars have collected these materials themselves—often at great expense (and more likely than not, at public expense, in the sense that a piece of the very limited pie that supports all of our work went to support this instead of something else)—but no infrastructure exists for providing bibliographic information and exchange. Few major libraries in this country have trained staff with particular responsibilities for recent Western European materials, especially those outside the usual formats, and scholars interested in contemporary Europe have not taken the initiative to demand improvements. We are far behind other world areas in maintaining bibliographic aids and in encouraging an ongoing dialogue between scholars and librarians with responsibilities for maintaining European collections.

3. *Visiting European scholars.* More scholars come from Europe to the United States than from any other area. Usually they go to a single university for a term or a year and rarely travel much in the country. Often this is fine. It is what they and their host prefer. But funds are increasingly

short for visiting professors and often it would be very useful to visit several universities. We have found that with assistance from CES, European scholars are able to spend a week or ten days at each of several universities, accomplish a great deal at each, and be away from their home base for no more than a month or six weeks. For each participating university the cost is remarkably low. But this requires a rather unheard-of degree of cooperation and forward planning.

4. *There are other equally critical nonmaterial resources that must be used more flexibly in the future.* Information about what's going on in Europe, who's doing it, and where, is a good example. It is unfortunate but true that many scholars working in Europe have no contact with any other scholars, American or European, who are working in a similar field. This is, of course, a particularly severe problem for many graduate students. Those who have access to a center where personal information accumulates, such as Harvard, have an enormous advantage over other scholars in the field. There has been no way (until the formation of CES) of institutionalizing this information and ensuring some equality of access to it.

In the past two years, the Council for European Studies has tried to deal with these problems. What guidelines for the future does the council's experience provide?

First, there is a strong need for a clearer and wider conception of European studies. The European study programs established at a number of universities in the late 1960s were originally developed in much the same fashion as the older non-Western area centers. They were usually organized around a well-known European specialist and provided a base for scholars (mainly political scientists with a light sprinkling of historians) with primary research interests in Western Europe. There were always basic differences, however, between these programs and the non-Western area centers. The Western European programs had a much smaller financial base and were involved in a narrower field of activities. They had little influence on curriculum and did not attempt (except in a single case I know of) to develop degree or certificate programs. Few paid even a part of a faculty salary or were concerned with recruitment. None, I believe, was involved with the language departments on its campus or had much to do with library development. I am quite sure that a considerably higher proportion of available financial resources was used to support faculty and graduate student research, and that much less went to the support of training and teaching programs. For these reasons, the generally low level of support and the less certain constituency (because of the indistinct boundary that defined it), these programs were much less institutionalized than the others.[4] They were more ad hoc and less formalized, less integrated into

---

4. Professor Richard Lambert's forthcoming report on Language and Area Studies, jointly sponsored by the Institute of International Studies of the U.S. Office of Education and the

the university teaching and departmental structures, and have tended to be less permanent.

Area speciality is inappropriate as an organizing principle for European studies. Many social scientists with interests in contemporary Europe are unwilling to identify themselves as area specialists. Even scholars with intensive research interests in the area usually prefer to define their interests in disciplinary and functional rather than area terms. It is clear that a strategy to increase interest in Europe that builds upon an area-center approach is unlikely to succeed. Almost no funds are available, inside or outside our universities, to support old-fashioned area centers and, more importantly, an area-center approach is not likely to attract the continuing commitment of the wider community of scholars with interests in Europe but who do not see themselves as area specialists. Indeed, it is possible that in the long run this approach may hurt rather than help—by developing a sharp line between European area specialists (who control resources) and nonspecialists (who remain on the outside).

The activities of the CES have been directed to this wider community of scholars who share interests in themes and problems relevant to contemporary Western Europe (and to North America) as well as to the more traditional European specialists. Our focus has become more problem-oriented, and more concerned with interregional comparison. Europe is seen as a potential dimension in many fields within our universities rather than as a discrete field in itself, bounded by the walls of area specialization. Rather than area centers, we are trying to encourage the formation of more flexible campus programs that build upon existing research interests and can cooperate in a variety of ways with scholars and programs in other universities with similar interests.

As a second guideline for the future, it must be possible for scholars at different stages in their careers to acquire the skills and knowledge that provide the context for research—and to acquire these skills without greatly upsetting their existing commitments and responsibilities. We must develop those resources that will enable a graduate student (or a senior scholar) whose primary interest, for example, is in urban problems or social welfare policies, to move beyond an American data base and do serious work in Western Europe.

This means that we must create more ready and flexible access to the traditional methodologies and interests that focus on Europe, that grow out of the philosophical and literary traditions of inquiry which have dominated most work on Europe in the past, and to the newer methodological excitement and innovation of the last decade that has been developed mainly in research focusing on the United States and the non-Western world. Our

---

Social Science Research Council, discusses the non-Western area centers in great detail, and develops the criteria for the concept of "institutionalization."

aim must be to build bridges between these approaches and resources and, thus, to break down some of the disciplinary and departmental autonomy characteristic of past research and training efforts.

One key problem is to find ways in which social scientists can better utilize the resources of the humanities to develop the linguistic and contextual skills and knowledge that will improve their work as social scientists. We must also reach out into the professional schools—law, business, social work—and even into the natural sciences to those scientists concerned, for example, with the quality of the environment—to establish linkages that will provide the core structure of future program development.

The basic problem is not one of numbers, nor is it mainly a question of discovering new resources. It is instead a problem of concentration and coordination, of developing a more systematic approach to European studies through which more of the various resources already existing can be more effectively utilized.

To achieve these objectives, certain programs must be created.

1. *Programs that are multidisciplinary.* A clear distinction can be made between *inter*disciplinary and *multi*disciplinary approaches. An interdisciplinary approach is not a necessary goal, either for training or research. A graduate student who intends to work with European data must have access to skill development and information that will enable him to do better work within his own discipline. This means that we must develop, for example, much more efficient ways of utilizing existing language training resources, or more courses in history departments that parallel emerging research interest in other fields, such as graduate level courses on the development of the European urban community. And it means that these must be made available in ways that scholars and students in other disciplines can use without drastically interrupting their own disciplinary responsibilities and commitments. It is necessary not to encourage *inter*disciplinary research, but to make it possible for a researcher from one discipline to benefit from exposure to different perspectives, particularly as we move into a more problem-oriented research environment. The historian and economist interested in the same broad area or theme will do their work differently after having questioned one another; there is *multi*disciplinary illumination.

2. *Programs that are multiinstitutional.* The Council for European Studies has attempted to encourage a wider interest in contemporary Europe throughout our universities rather than to attempt to develop a series of Western European area studies centers. Individual universities can more fully mobilize and utilize existing campus resources than they have in the past, without finding it necessary to establish a highly institutionalized center. But if we are serious about a multidisciplinary and more problem-oriented approach to European studies, programs must be developed that link resources at a number of universities. Single institutions can only rarely

support efforts to identify potential researchers, provide necessary training, develop research designs, plan for the collection of data, and maintain contact with scholars in the United States and in Europe who share interests in the same field. A "critical mass" of scholars, students, and other resources is not likely to be found at any single institution at one time.

We must identify the strongest resources in particular fields, and then make it possible for those who share interests in these fields to have access to these resources. The administrative implications of this are considerable, but a more cooperative, multiinstitutional approach is the only way that sufficient resources can ever be mobilized to support the kind of research and training activities that will permit us to explore the most important and exciting questions involving contemporary Western European society and politics.

3. *Programs that provide support for the scholar over a longer time period.* Financial support must be provided through the various stages of the scholar's career. In recent years, dissertations on Western Europe have been supported by traditional sources and by the FAFP Western European Program, but little support has been available for predissertation training (Harvard and Michigan have run limited programs and CES has offered its Pre-Dissertation Training Grants for the past two years) and almost none for postdoctoral work. Various "early identification" programs must be encouraged. Such programs would ensure that a student interested in Europe receives the linguistic and methodological training that will support his research at an earlier stage than is now common. These programs should also include greater opportunities for predissertation field experience in Europe, both for purposes of skill development and for identifying possible research interests. At the same time, we must attempt to develop much broader sources of support for postdoctoral research and training for social scientists.

4. *Programs that better relate training and research.* We should try to ensure that, wherever possible, research programs involving senior scholars have a training component, and that graduate students have a greater opportunity to participate in the research being carried on at the frontier of knowledge about European society and politics. Organizers of conferences and research seminars can be encouraged to invite younger graduate students whose future research interests might be substantially influenced by this exposure. Proposals for funds to support research can be written to support the joint research and training efforts of a senior scholar and several graduate students. We should also begin to develop techniques for more cooperative and team research institutions that replicate laboratory conditions, in which senior and junior scholars, as well as graduate students, can work together on particular problems.

We, as a community of scholars, can also begin to exercise some judgment regarding what kind of research problems should have the highest priority, and to encourage dissertation research to be carried on within the context of existing communities of scholarship grouped around these areas.

5. *Programs that create a better balance in international exchange between American and European scholars.* It must be possible for more European scholars, and particularly younger Europeans, to spend time in the United States for training purposes, for teaching, and for doing their own research. Better provisions must be made for European scholars to carry on their own research interests in the United States and not to be forced to appear as European area specialists. Bilateral exchanges of faculty (and graduate students as well) must be encouraged as well as exchanges between groups of American and European universities. We should think increasingly of international communities of scholars who share interests in particular problems or aspects of contemporary European and American life, and provide the resources to support the scholarly activities of the communities as a whole.

Index

Abramson, Paul R., *39n., 73n., 80, 81*
Access. *See* Structured access
Adams, Gordon, *117n.*
Adamson, J. W., *259n.*
Adenauer, Konrad, *347, 350–51, 363*
Administration
  compartmentalization through, in Belgium, 211ff.
  defined as output implementation, 36
  growth of, and regime change in Belgium, 199ff.
  increased capabilities of, as possible explanation of political development, 269–70, 275ff., 291–92
  participation in as form of cooptation, in Norway, 93–116 passim
  politicization of, 22, 36, 62–71, 76, 236
Adversarial pattern, as regime style, *52–53*
Africa, *7–10, 32, 36n., 186, 391. See also* North Africa
Aiken, Michael, *21n.*
Ake, Claude, *46n.*
Albinski, Henry S., *63n.*
Alford, Robert R., *18n, 28n.*
Algeria, *7n., 371, 376, 381–83, 386*
Alker, Hayward R., Jr., *16, 76n.*
Allardt, Erik, *39n., 174n.*
Almond, Gabriel A., *10–13, 30n., 35n.,*
36n., 52n., 88, 118n., 135n., 139n., 150, 154, 257, 258n.
Anderson, Malcolm, *295n.*
Andrews, William G., *xi, 25, 296n., 303n., 313n.*
Anton, Thomas J., *60, 61n., 65n., 66, 70*
Apel, Hans, *330n.*
Apter, David E., *4n., 149n., 329*
Arian, Alan, *70–71*
Aristotle, *3*
Ashkenasi, Abraham, *346n.*
Asia, *8–9, 36n., 186, 391. See also* Indochina; Southeast Asia; specific countries
Atherton, Alexine L., *225n.*
Attlee, Clement, *352*
Australia, *5, 52n.*
Austria, *117–77*
  "Great Coalition" between two Lager parties (1945–66), 120–77 passim
  instability in First Republic, 44n., 118–19, 219
  mass concerns in focus on bread-and-butter issues, 132ff., 143
  as member of European polity type-cell, 24, 46–47, 55, 59n., 83, 86, 179
  recent neutrality of, 75n.
  reinforcing cleavages in, 66, 118ff.
  vertical structuring of political society, 45, 118ff. See also Lager

401

Brussels, *86, 180–220 passim, 230. See also* Belgium; Bruxellois

Bruxellois, residents of central Belgian region, *181–220. See also* Belgium

Bryce, James, *324n.*

Buchanan, James M., *61n.*

Buchanan, William, *97n.*

Campbell, Angus, *157n.*

Canada, *5, 37n., 52n., 372*

Carey, George W., *9n.*

Carmoy, Guy de, *xii, 25*

Cartel of elites, *40n., 43–48, 65–66, 83*
    characteristic of policy-making struc-
        ture, in Norway, 116
    differential role-sets in a consocia-
        tional system (Austria), 155ff.
    in Belgium, 184–87

Carter, Gwendolen M., *5n.*

Castelbajac, Philippe de, *301n., 321n., 322n.*

Ceccaldi, Dominique, *263n.*

Center-periphery cleavages, *68–69, 179–80n. See also* Cleavages

Central economic planning, *67–69, 74*

Chaban-Delmas, Jacques, *316*

Chalmers, Douglas, *117n.*

Chapman, Brian, *294n., 297n.*

Charlemagne, *293*

Chlepner, B.-S., *188n., 196*

Christensen, Bent, *104n.*

Churchill, Winston S., *351*

Claes, Lode, *68, 198, 201*

Clark, W. Hartley, *229n., 232n.*

Cleavages
    in France, 219
    institutionalization of in cooptive
        structure, in Belgium, 178–220
    political or politicized, as source of
        stress, 44–47, 53, 61ff., 78, 178–79
    see also *Center-periphery cleavages;*
        Lager; Segmented pluralism;
        Stress; Vertical structuring

Clough, Shepard B., *194n.*

Club Jean Moulin, *295n.*

Cole, G. D. H., *324*

Cole, R. Taylor, *11n.*

Coleman, James S., *10n., 11n., 35n.*

Colombia, consociational characteristics of, *127*

Committee on Comparative Politics (of the Social Science Research Council), *10, 389n.*

Common Market. *See* European Community

Comparative political analysis, *3–37*
    analytic control in, vii, 16–17, 19, 29–32
    "behavioral revolution" phase, 10–18, 25, 30
    country-studies as a level of analysis, 4ff., 28–30
    and European studies, 3–26
    functional emphases in, 10–13
    functional equivalence, 16
    inferential fallacies and, 16–17
    input-side, emphases of, in, 12–14, 17–18, 35–36, 88, 93ff.
        decreasing importance of activities in, 36, 38–42, 62–63, 70ff.
        in Belgium, 186ff.
        in the European Community system, 222, 252
        in political development literature, 257–58
    mid-range theory in, 27, 30, 34, 37
    "most similar systems designs" in, 18–23, 28–34
    "postbehavioral phase" in, 20ff.
    segments of systems as a level of analysis, 27–29
    structural emphases in, viii, 21–25, 32, 34–36, 72, 88–89
    traditional orientation described, 4–6; its rejection, 6–10
    typology construction in, 28, 30ff.
    "withinputs" as concept in
        distinguished from environmental inputs, 13–14, 110
        heightened importance in advanced industrial systems, 71–73, 80, 258–92 passim
        need to accord analytic equality to, 20, 35–36
    whole systems as a level of analysis, 28, 45

Compartmentalization of segments, *66–67, 208ff.*

Configuration of European polity traits, *38, 71–78*

Connolly, William E., *61n.*